Praise for Robert H. Jackson's *That Man*

"*That Man* is a great find—the last memoir of Franklin D. Roosevelt by someone who worked with him and knew him well. Next to Oliver Wendell Holmes, Robert H. Jackson was the best writer on the Supreme Court in the 20th century, and his portrait of 'that man in the White House' is filled with astute insights and warm recollections. It is a book no fan of FDR can do without."

—**Arthur M. Schlesinger, Jr.**

"A diary keeper, Jackson was as observant and analytical in social settings as he was in the courtroom....FDR fans will relish being a fly on the wall with him, eavesdropping on some of history's greatest actors."

—**Professor Susan Dunn,** *The New Leader*

"[Editor John Q.] Barrett has done an admirable and even heroic job....There is now a genuine book, one that contains some illuminating discussion of historical events. Most important, the book offers a fresh occasion for considering the personality and career of the greatest leader of the twentieth century, memorably described by Isaiah Berlin as the only statesman in the world upon whom 'no cloud rested.'"

—**Professor Cass Sunstein,** *The New Republic*

"A very vivid, affectionate, but surprisingly realistic view of Roosevelt. This is the kind of history that is first-hand and observed, that comes in real time. It jumps off the page as valid."

—**Bob Woodward**

"Painstakingly, insightfully—even lovingly—assembled from notes and fragments found in a dusty closet belonging to Robert H. Jackson's recently deceased son, this remarkable and eminently readable volume—a newly available first-hand account of FDR as politician, lawyer, administrator, and commander in chief, written by an astute participant and brilliant observer who also happened to be the most piercingly eloquent writer ever to serve on the U.S. Supreme Court—will intrigue and inform anyone interested in the history of America's involvement in World War II or in the American presidency and the West Wing under FDR in an era a half century old that turns out to bear a surprising resemblance to our own."

—**Laurence H. Tribe,**
Ralph S. Tyler, Jr. Professor of Constitutional Law,
Harvard Law School

"A long lost gem has been unearthed after a half century. Supreme Court Justice Robert Jackson's first hand portrait of Franklin Delano Roosevelt is as close as we are likely to get to deciphering the enigma that was FDR. Jackson, associate and friend, confidante and poker-playing pal of the President, was perceptive enough to recognize the genius and honest enough to admit the flaws beneath his subject's seductive geniality. We are further indebted to the book's editor, John Q. Barrett, for rescuing this priceless memoir from an obscurity that would have left us poorer in our understanding of America's towering 20th-century statesman."

—**Joseph E. Persico, author of** *Roosevelt's Secret War*

"Well worth reading.... Maybe the closest friend of the president to have written about him."

—**Geoffrey Wheatcroft,** *The Spectator* **(London)**

"The freshness of his prose continually enchants.... Little wonder that Roosevelt so enjoyed Jackson's company. This was a true friendship. They talked high policy, plotted political strategy, and played poker together. They sailed together, literally on the ship of state."

—**Professor Roger K. Newman,** *Findlaw.com*

"A fascinating historical document, not only for what it reveals about Roosevelt, but also for what it reveals about Robert Jackson.... With any luck, the publication of this book will be the beginning of a renaissance in interest in Jackson, one of the more influential and important, but least known, public figures of the 20th century."

—**Alexander Wohl,** *Legal Times*

"Franklin D. Roosevelt was the dominant political figure of the last century. Robert H. Jackson, Supreme Court Justice, was one of the essential figures in his life. Professor John Q. Barrett, a highly qualified authority on the subject, has now brought this relationship fully to light. I urge this volume for all who would know more of what could be the greatest days of Washington. I use the term cautiously: an indispensable book."

—**John Kenneth Galbraith**

THAT MAN

An Insider's Portrait of Franklin D. Roosevelt

ROBERT H. JACKSON

Edited and Introduced by John Q. Barrett

with a Foreword by
William E. Leuchtenburg

OXFORD
UNIVERSITY PRESS

OXFORD
UNIVERSITY PRESS

Oxford   New York
Auckland   Bangkok   Buenos Aires   Cape Town   Chennai
Dar es Salaam   Delhi   Hong Kong   Istanbul   Karachi   Kolkata
Kuala Lumpur   Madrid   Melbourne   Mexico City   Mumbai   Nairobi
São Paulo   Shanghai   Taipei   Tokyo   Toronto

First published by Oxford University Press, Inc., 2003
198 Madison Avenue, New York, New York, 10016
www.oup.com

First issued as an Oxford University Press paperback, 2004
ISBN 0-19-517757-6

Oxford is a registered trademark of Oxford University Press

The Library of Congress has cataloged the cloth edition as follows:
Jackson, Robert Houghwout, 1892–1954.
That man : an insider's portrait of Franklin D. Roosevelt / Robert H.
Jackson ; edited and introduced by John Q. Barrett ; with a foreword by
William E. Leuchtenburg.
p. cm.
Includes bibliographical references and index.
ISBN 0-19-516826-7
1. Roosevelt, Franklin D. (Franklin Delano), 1882–1945.
2. United States—Politics and government—1933–1945.
3. Presidents—United States—Biography.
I. Barrett, John Q., 1961– . II. Title.
E807 .J36 2003   973.917'092—dc21   2003009275

Book design and composition by Mark McGarry, Texas Type & Book Works
Set in Dante

9 8 7 6 5 4 3 2 1

Printed in the United States of America
on acid-free paper

CONTENTS

Not diary - not history not
biography - not auto biog
Recollection

That man -

30 years

As President
    Work
    Relation - Cabinet

    Politician -
        Hague - Kelly - Pendergast Etc

        Love people - Ford

        Speech writing
            Misbehaved

    Lawyer
        Opinion Harvard

    Economist
        Formulae for tax
    Sportsman

Breaking Third Term Tradition

Neutrality   Canada

100 days - Aid to allies

Communism - Fascism - Americans?

War Criminals ?

FOREWORD

WILLIAM E. LEUCHTENBURG

Robert Houghwout Jackson is the most important public figure of the twentieth century no one has ever heard of. That is hyperbole, of course, for historians of the New Deal, of the Supreme Court, and of the war crimes trials at Nuremberg devote considerable attention to him. Still, one could conceivably question ten thousand Americans at random today and not find one who recognized his name. Even in his own day he was hardly a household word. When he was nominated for the American Law Institute, a committee member inquired, *"Who is Jackson?"* And when Franklin Roosevelt contemplated grooming Jackson for the Democratic presidential nomination in 1940, the party chairman, Jim Farley, told FDR, "You could start him at the Battery and walk him to Riverdale, up Broadway all the way, 20 miles, and if ten people know him, I'll buy a hat for you."

Yet the barest outline of the posts Jackson held—Solicitor General, Attorney General, U.S. Supreme Court Justice, United States Chief Prosecutor of the Nazi war criminals—indicates why he deserves, even commands, our attention. Widely spoken of as the next Chief Justice, he was, for a time, frequently mentioned for even higher office. As early as the summer of 1937, when he was only an Assistant Attorney General, there was talk of him as the next President of the United States, and in 1938 a Cabinet officer noted in his diary that one of FDR's closest advisers, Tommy Corcoran, "regards Jackson as possible Presidential timber in 1940," when, it was presumed, Roosevelt would not seek a third term.

Few attorneys ever came close to matching Jackson's skill in expounding an argument. Even commentators who loathed Franklin Roosevelt's scheme to pack the Supreme Court in 1937 expressed admiration for the cogency of Jackson's testimony before the Senate Judiciary Committee on behalf of the plan. Two years later, *Time* commented: "Lawyers like to say that the brilliance of John Marshall as Chief Justice reflected in no small part the brilliance of Lawyer Daniel Webster, who argued often before him. By such token, the Supreme Court term was the term of Solicitor General Robert Houghwout Jackson." His performance on the nation's highest bench in later years enhanced that reputation. "No other Justice, surely," observed the legal scholar Charles Fairman, "has ever been his equal in the ability to catch in one clinching sentence the weakness of a controverted proposition."

When Jackson took leave from the Court to serve as United States Chief Prosecutor at the war crimes trials, he earned acclaim both at home and abroad. A man with no sympathy at all for Jackson's liberal outlook, John W. Davis, called "the leader of the U.S. bar," said of Jackson, "He is undoubtedly a great advocate. I thought his speech at Nuremberg was one of the finest examples of advocacy I have ever read." The London *Times* reported that Jackson's opening address of more than four hours was "generally acclaimed as a magnificent exposition," and the St. Louis *Post-Dispatch* likened it to Richard Brinsley Sheridan's oration against Warren Hastings, which Edmund Burke characterized as "the most astonishing effort of eloquence of which there is any record or tradition."

Jackson's felicitous style won him even greater plaudits than his proficiency in oral argument. "If there were no other justification for holding Jackson in high esteem as a jurist," Henry Abraham has written, "his magnificent prose—second in beauty and clarity perhaps only to that of Cardozo—has earned him a high regard. Who could ever forget the haunting beauty of his phrases?" A prominent British jurist wrote, "Here was a man who had read Blackstone and was obviously a man of law; but here also was a man who had read and loved King James's Bible, and was also obviously a man of letters." In like manner, the distinguished constitutional historian Paul Freund remarked: "He had a style to delight, grace and power of expression to captivate. His was an Elizabethan gusto for the swordplay of words. If his style was like pearls, they were occasionally—as was said of the style of a Scottish judge, surely a forebear—pearls dissolved in vinegar." Jackson himself said that he wrote with "impish candor."

An obscure country lawyer when Franklin Delano Roosevelt enticed him to Washington in 1934 to become General Counsel of the Bureau of Internal Revenue, Jackson quickly established himself as a rising star in the New Deal firmament. FDR's closest adviser in the Cabinet, Harold Ickes, who had enormous clout in his twin posts of Secretary of the Interior and Public Works Administrator, regarded Jackson as "one of the real men of character and ability on the Washington stage" and "one of the finest and most upright men . . . I have ever known." As early as 1937, Ickes commented, "My own feeling is that he is the kind of man we need in our public life if we are to escape disaster." After a visit Jackson paid to Hitler's Germany on official business, the U.S. ambassador in Berlin, William Dodd, entered in his diary, "October 25. Friday. Robert H. Jackson, a very able young lawyer from the Treasury Department in Washington, was one of my callers this morning. . . . Mr. Jackson seems to me to be the ablest and wisest man who has come here from the United States in a long time."

In 1937 Roosevelt took Jackson into his most intimate circle of cronies, the men with whom he relaxed and talked shop, though Jackson was only in the second echelon of officialdom. That year, the President invited him to cruise the Dry Tortugas, fishing rods at the ready, in a small party that included Ickes, Relief Administrator Harry Hopkins, and FDR's son Jimmy. On three occasions in 1939 Jackson played poker with Roosevelt. One of the stag parties, on September 2, went on past midnight, though the President was fatigued from being wakened by bulletins from the European war zone. In October, Jackson was a heavy loser at poker with Roosevelt, not surprisingly, since bluffing was not his forte. When in April 1941 Jackson was invited on a fishing cruise in the Bahamas, he was put in the cabin next to the President's. Meantime, Bob Jackson and his wife had become fixtures in the New Deal social whirl. Ickes wrote of a cocktail party given by the Biddles for Ben Cohen: "The Jacksons were there and the MacLeishes and Tom Corcoran—the usual crowd."

Jackson secured his position in the Roosevelt coterie by the zeal with which he promoted a third term for the President, even when FDR maintained, or feigned, that he had no interest. After rejoicing in the outcome of a California primary, Jackson said, "Some months ago I thought that no one could stop Roosevelt except Roosevelt. Now I don't think even Roosevelt can stop Roosevelt for he will have to submit to the conscription." In an address to an American Business Clubs convention, Jackson asserted that FDR's first term had been erased by the courts, which had struck down his most important initiatives; hence, he intimated, there need be no concern if the President chose to ignore the third term taboo, for he had been permitted only a single term. Though Roosevelt continued to play coy, Jackson was one of a small group who met with the President over dinner at the White House in May 1940 to plot strategy at the forthcoming Democratic convention, and in the course of the evening Jackson's name came up as a possible keynoter. At the national convention in Chicago that summer, Jackson was one of a cabal of four—the others were Ickes, Hopkins, and the veteran

South Carolina senator Jimmy Byrnes—conspiring to draft the President for a third-term nomination.

Roosevelt returned the affection. When Jackson testified on behalf of a New Deal tax measure in 1935, the President sent a handwritten note to "Dear Bob": "My congratulations and thanks to you for that wholly excellent presentation before the Senate Committee. It was a grand performance." Over the next several years, he named Jackson to three of the highest posts a member of the American bar can hope to attain and put Jackson's name forward (we cannot be sure how seriously) as his successor. Even after that effort fizzled, he persisted. Early in 1939, Farley concluded that Jackson was second on FDR's list to take his place (preceded only by Hopkins), and whenever Roosevelt encouraged Secretary of State Cordell Hull to entertain the notion of making a bid for the White House in 1940, he mentioned Jackson for the vice presidential slot on a Hull ticket.

This mutual admiration may imply that Jackson's account of FDR, *That Man,* is a sycophantic book, but any such assumption about Jackson's mindset would be erroneous, in part because the relationship between the two men did not always run smoothly. In 1939 Roosevelt stated that Jackson lacked "it," and fans of Clara Bow, "the *it* girl," had no trouble discerning what he meant—that Jackson did not have the political sex appeal a candidate needed. A year later, he confided that, though Jackson was a marvelous speaker, he was too much of a gentleman: he lacked the brawler instinct that a liberal scrapping with the vested interests required.

Jackson, in turn, had personal grievances with FDR. By May 1939 he had become "restive," it was said, at not being named Attorney General. Roosevelt promised that the nomination would come through soon, but month after month went by with no action. By October Jackson was reported to be "quite upset," and in early November 1939 Ickes wrote in his diary: "I felt very bad about Bob Jackson. Clearly he was very unhappy . . . deeply disappointed." Once, Jackson became so peeved that he informed Tommy Corcoran that he was going to let Roosevelt know that he no longer was interested in becoming Attorney General, and Corcoran had a tough time persuading Jackson not to go to the White House and tell the President to chuck it. In mid-November 1939, Ickes decided to talk turkey to FDR. Jackson, he told him, was "little short of being heartbroken." Not until early the next year was the announcement made. Worse still, Roosevelt assured Jackson that he would be chosen Chief Justice of the United States, but, when the vacancy developed, the President picked someone else. So Jackson had a lot to be miffed about.

Furthermore, Jackson was nobody's toady. In 1937, when he was Assistant Attorney General, Jackson was invited to spend a weekend on the President's yacht. It was the kind of invitation that everyone in Washington hungered for, but Jackson declined. His son, he explained, was graduating from prep school that morning, and he had to give priority to that. When she heard him say this, Jackson's secretary shouted at him, "You can't do that! You can't do that! It isn't done! An invitation from the President is a command!" Even after FDR delayed his departure until after the commencement exercises were over so that the young attorney could join him, Jackson maintained his independence. On the homeward voyage, Roosevelt asked him to head an investigation of tax dodging, but Jackson turned him down.

When Roosevelt finally did elevate him to the attorney generalship, Jackson still marched to his own drummer. On more than one occasion, as when the President wanted a princess who was regarded as a Nazi agent deported, he refused to oblige him because he thought the request could not be carried out properly. The shrewd Federal Loan Administrator, Jesse Jones, said of Attorney General Jackson: "When he was not in full agreement with the President it was interesting to observe the finesse and polished courtesy in his discussions. He was usually able to avoid doing what he thought should not be done." *That Man*, then, is a commentary by a subaltern who thought well of FDR, but who also wrote without fear or favor.

That Man has a special niche in the Roosevelt literature. In the period following Roosevelt's death on April 12, 1945, every week seemed to bring another "me and FDR" memoir, but no new volume has appeared for many a long year. We have good reason to be grateful to John Barrett not only for his discovery of this manuscript, but even more for the craftsmanship with which he has reconstructed it and other fragments of Jackson's recollections. He faced no easy task, and he has carried it off very well. By giving us new insights into two of the movers and shakers of the past century—Franklin Delano Roosevelt and Robert H. Jackson—he has made a significant contribution to our understanding of modern America.

INTRODUCTION

JOHN Q. BARRETT

Franklin D. Roosevelt needs no introduction and, at one time, neither did Robert H. Jackson. The passage of time since his premature death in 1954 and the absence of recent Jackson biographies, however, mean that Jackson today is less well remembered—if not among lawyers, historians, and members of the aptly named "greatest generation," then at least among the younger general public—than his fascinating, classically "American" life and monumental accomplishments deserve. One of the pleasures of this previously unknown and never published text, which Jackson wrote in the early 1950s about his hero, friend, and leader FDR, is that while it conveys Jackson's intimate memories and candid assessments of Roosevelt, it also contributes to Jackson's ongoing, well-deserved return to significant public attention.

This introduction presents the author of this book, Robert Jackson, and traces his relationship with Franklin Roosevelt. It reconstructs, almost fifty years after the fact, Jackson's writing of this book and the developments that kept it, until now, from being published. It concludes by describing the recent discovery of Jackson's manuscript, the steps I took to assemble draft chapters as he had planned, and how I augmented and edited his *That Man* manuscript using other FDR-related pieces of Jackson's unpublished writings.

I. Robert Houghwout Jackson

Robert H. Jackson embodied the success story of the self-made American of the early twentieth century. A descendant of early settlers, Jackson was born in 1892 on a farm in northwestern Pennsylvania. He grew up nearby in the small town of Frewsburg, New York, which is south of the city of Jamestown in the western part of New York State. Blessed with a voracious natural intellect, Jackson was an outstanding student through graduation from Frewsburg High School and during a postgraduate year at Jamestown High School, but he never attended college. Instead, influenced by two devoted Jamestown teachers and mentors—high school principal Milton Fletcher, who taught American history, and his teaching colleague Miss Mary Willard, who taught English literature and history and also read Shakespeare with Jackson after school hours—Jackson was exposed to great ideas and became, philosophically, both an individualist and a liberal humanist.

As young Jackson developed, he also was drawn, over family opposition, to the logic, power, and language of the law. After beginning an apprentice-ship with Jamestown lawyers Frank Mott and Benjamin Dean, who also became additional, powerful role models and intellectual mentors, Jackson enrolled in 1911 at Albany Law School, where he completed a two-year course in half that time. He returned to Jamestown in 1912, resumed his legal apprenticeship, joined the New York bar as soon as he was old enough to take the bar examination (age twenty-one), and, over the next twenty years, became Jamestown's leading lawyer and a major force in the bar of western New York.

As Jackson was developing as a young lawyer, he also was drawn to poli-tics—politics of the Democratic Party variety, despite his upbringing in a strongly Republican region. As a law student in Albany, Jackson took breaks from his studies to watch the capital's courts and state legislature in ses-sion. During one Albany foray to the capitol, Frank Mott introduced Jack-son to Franklin Roosevelt, the freshman state senator who was representing his native Dutchess County.

During the next three decades, as Roosevelt's talents and good fortune brought him to the Wilson administration in Washington (1913), to the Democratic Party's vice presidential nomination (1920), to New York's gov-ernor's mansion (1929), and ultimately to the White House (1933), Jackson kept up this early contact and developed what became an increasingly sub-stantive relationship with the rising politician. As President, FDR called Jackson to Washington and quickly moved him up into a series of increas-ingly significant and highly visible government posts. He became one of Roosevelt's key assistants and personal favorites. Through close work with the President, Jackson had numerous opportunities to observe FDR exten-sively and came to know him intimately. Especially during FDR's second presidential term (1937–1941), they developed a personal relationship that transcended their obviously differing official statuses and the specifics of the projects on which they had contact.

Jackson's full-time work for President Roosevelt began in 1934, when he appointed Jackson to be the General Counsel in the Department of the Treasury's Bureau of Revenue (today's Internal Revenue Service). In that position, Jackson quickly garnered extensive press nationwide when he prosecuted the government's civil case against Andrew W. Mellon for fraudulent underpayment of taxes. Mellon was the former Secretary of the Treasury and Ambassador to Great Britain under Republican Presidents Harding, Coolidge, and Hoover—the last being the candidate for reelection whom FDR had defeated in 1932. Jackson's successful presentation of the evidence, including the admissions he elicited during his effective cross-examination of Mellon, made Jackson one of the most famous lawyers in the country and refuted the Republican charge that the prosecution was "political."

Following the *Mellon* case, Roosevelt moved Jackson from Treasury to, briefly, the Securities and Exchange Commission and then, in 1936, to the Department of Justice to head the Tax Division. During that period, FDR made extensive use of Jackson's skills during the President's reelection campaign—for example, Jackson was part of preparing the message and sat nearby as FDR gave his famous "I Hate War" speech at Chautauqua Institution in August 1936—and also planned to draft Jackson as the Democratic candidate when it briefly appeared that New York Governor Herbert Lehman would not seek reelection.

During the next two years, Jackson's political star rose even higher. In 1937, the President moved Jackson from the Tax Division to run the Antitrust Division in Justice. Jackson began to speak widely, often on national radio broadcasts and always with Roosevelt's support, against corporate monopolists, the Supreme Court, and other perceived opponents of the New Deal. In March 1937, Jackson gave brilliant testimony to the Senate Judiciary Committee in defense of Roosevelt's Court-packing plan. Jackson also gave widely noted public speeches in late 1937 that excoriated businessmen whom he described as seeking to thwart the New Deal and the national economic recovery by using their monopoly powers to charge excessive prices and earn unjustifiable profits.

In the second half of his second term in the White House, FDR decided that he wanted Jackson, a true New Dealer, to succeed him at the helm of the Democratic Party and in the White House. FDR shared and planned this project with other trusted aides. Their goal, as one of them put it in a private document, was "[c]onverting one Robert Jackson into the Sweetheart of the Nation."[1] As the first step toward the goal, Roosevelt endeavored to feature Jackson in public remarks and to travel, very visibly to the press, with Jackson at his side. The President also maneuvered to promote a Jackson candidacy for the governorship of New York State in 1938 because, from that office, Jackson would have been well positioned to seek the Presidency itself in 1940 upon Roosevelt's planned retirement to Hyde Park after two terms in office. But as Roosevelt and his assistants pursued their Jackson agenda, they ran into strong opposition from New York's Democratic machine politicians. FDR proved unable to start a genuine Jackson groundswell or to impose his candidate on the state party. As a consequence, Jackson never really made a run for Governor of New York in 1938 (Governor Lehman, a fellow Democrat, ultimately sought and won reelection to a fourth term in office) or, during his remaining life, for any elective office.

In the late 1930s and early 1940s, Roosevelt advanced Jackson to higher offices and greater responsibilities within the executive branch. After Jackson had headed the Antitrust Division for one year, Roosevelt appointed him to be Solicitor General of the United States. In this office, Jackson continued to be one of the President's key assistants while also representing his Administration and defending New Deal legislation before the Supreme Court. Jackson's Supreme Court advocacy was so dazzling that Justice Louis Brandeis once concluded his description of a masterful Jackson oral argument by saying that he "should be Solicitor General for life."[2]

In 1940, Roosevelt elevated Jackson to the Cabinet by appointing him Attorney General of the United States. As Attorney General, Jackson ran a Department of Justice that was soon, like much of the government at that time, focused on the impending war. Although Jackson himself was mentioned prominently in early 1940 as among the leading prospects—and as the one who was (still) Roosevelt's personal choice—to succeed the President in the event he chose not to seek a third term, the idea of a Jackson presidential candidacy was, by that date, more a newspaperman's notion than reality. Jackson was among the FDR assistants who worked behind the scenes in the spring of 1940 to persuade the President to run again, and Jackson was part of the core planning group at the Democratic convention in Chicago that July that helped orchestrate the convention "draft" that resulted in Roosevelt's renomination.

In early 1941, when Jackson wrote the President offering to resign in the event that he wished to start his third term with a new Attorney General,

Roosevelt's handwritten reply to Jackson, who had been ill, summarized well the closeness of their relationship:

> Dear Bob
>   I do hope you're feeling
> better—Don't try to attend
> anything Monday [Inauguration Day] unless the
> M.D. *really* says yes.
>   Thank you for your note. It
> can only have one answer:
> *Stay put*
>   Affec.
>   FDR[3]

In 1941, Roosevelt nominated Jackson to serve as an Associate Justice of the Supreme Court of the United States. Jackson's appointment was swiftly confirmed, and, as a "Roosevelt Court" took shape in the early 1940s, Jackson established his reputation as a brilliant yet independent and hard-to-categorize judge. In one of his famous early opinions for the Court, he authored its ringing invalidation of a public school's compulsory flag salute because it violated the First Amendment rights of schoolchildren who were Jehovah's Witnesses.[4] Jackson also drew particular attention by dissenting from the Court's decision to uphold the military order following Pearl Harbor that excluded all persons of Japanese ancestry from West Coast areas.[5] But during this same period, Jackson and his colleague Justice Felix Frankfurter came generally to disagree with what they saw as the "political" approaches to judging taken by their fellow Roosevelt appointees, Justices Hugo L. Black, William O. Douglas, and Frank Murphy. As these Justices came to be regarded generally as the Court "liberals," Jackson and Frankfurter were criticized by some and praised by others for their alleged growing "conservatism." Jackson's written opinions also drew general acclaim during this period for their personal style and literary flair. He was described regularly in press reports as the Associate Justice who was likely to become the next Chief Justice of the United States. And he remained FDR's friend and informal adviser throughout the duration of World War II.

As the war in Europe ran down in early 1945, Jackson began to play the role that has defined his predominant place in general public memory around the world. Jackson was among those whose arguments persuaded President Roosevelt that captured Nazi leaders should be tried and, if found guilty of crimes, punished through orderly and lawful trial process rather than simply shot as our British and Soviet allies, along with many senior American officials, were urging.

After Roosevelt's death in April 1945 and the German surrender days later, President Truman appointed Jackson himself to make an international trial of Nazi war criminals happen. Jackson, negotiating with British, Soviet, and French officials in London during the summer of 1945, hammered out the four-nation agreement that an international tribunal would adjudicate the guilt of senior German military officers and government officials.[6] Jackson then took a leave of absence from the Supreme Court during its October Term 1945. He went to Nuremberg, Germany, and served as the senior American prosecutor at the International Military Tribunal composed of the four Allied powers.

Under Jackson's leadership at Nuremberg, the allies prosecuted twenty-two German individuals representing each facet of the Third Reich, including Gestapo founder Hermann Goering (Hitler's second), Deputy Fuhrer Rudolf Hess, and Albert Speer (Hitler's Minister of War Production). Jackson and colleagues built their case, which demonstrated to the world what we now know as the history of Hitler's Germany and of the Holocaust, on captured Nazi documents and other irrefutable evidence. Jackson also gave, as his opening and closing speeches to the Tribunal, two of the most powerful and famous courtroom addresses in history. On September 30, 1946, the Tribunal convicted eighteen of the defendants on charges of conspiracy to commit aggressive war, crimes of aggression, war crimes, and crimes against humanity and acquitted three other defendants.

After Nuremberg, Jackson—by then a figure of enormous international reputation—returned to the Supreme Court. Although President Truman had passed over Jackson when he filled the Chief Justiceship vacancy that occurred while Jackson was at Nuremberg in 1946, he served with distinction as an Associate Justice for eight more years. He wrote, during this period, numerous judicial opinions that are classics in American history, constitutional law, and legal literature. They include

- *Everson v. Board of Education* (1947), where Jackson, who had sent his own children to parochial schools, dissented from the Court's approval of a New Jersey town policy that used public tax monies to reimburse transportation costs of parents who sent their children to parochial schools.[7]
- *Terminiello v. Chicago* (1949), where Jackson dissented with ringing words—"if the Court does not temper its doctrinaire logic with a lit-

tle practical wisdom, it will convert the constitutional Bill of Rights into a suicide pact"—from the majority's decision to reverse the breaching-the-peace criminal conviction of a priest whose incendiary, racist speech in a Chicago auditorium had stirred the large crowd, inside and outside the hall, to violence. [8]

* *American Communications Association v. Douds* (1950), where Jackson joined a Court majority that upheld a federal statute that required labor union officers to foreswear membership in the Communist Party but, as regards the realm of personal belief that Jackson saw as quite separate from actions, dissented from the Court's failure to invalidate another provision that required union officers to disclose anti-American beliefs that had *not* led them to engage in any anti-government activity.[9]

* *Shephard v. Florida* (1951), where Jackson was part of the Court majority that summarily reversed a black man's criminal conviction for (allegedly) participating in the gang rape of a white teenaged girl in Lake County, Florida, because blacks had been excluded from the indicting grand jury, but then wrote separately to state explicitly the separate, and greater, unconstitutionality of the racist publicity that surrounded the case: "I do not see, as a practical matter, how any Negro on the jury would have dared to cause a disagreement or acquittal. The only chance these Negroes had of acquittal would have been in the courage and decency of some sturdy and forthright white person of sufficient standing to face and live down the odium among his white neighbors that such a vote, if required, would have brought."[10]

On March 30, 1954, Jackson, who was only sixty-two years old, suffered a serious heart attack and was hospitalized. Less than two months later, on May 17, he went directly from Doctors Hospital in Washington to the Supreme Court to be present on the bench for Chief Justice Earl Warren's announcement of the Court's unanimous decision in *Brown v. Board of Education*, which held school segregation to be unconstitutional.[11]

Jackson spent the summer of 1954 convalescing and traveling. He was present on the bench when the Court began its October Term 1954. Five days later, on Saturday, October 9, 1954, Jackson succumbed to a final heart attack. Following a funeral in Washington's National Cathedral, the eight surviving Justices of the Supreme Court traveled with other Jackson friends and family on the train that carried his body back to Jamestown. After a church service there, his body was buried in Frewsburg, in the small cemetery that borders a wooded hillside near Jackson's boyhood home.

II. Jackson's Writing of That Man

Although Jackson fully immersed himself in the work of the Supreme Court when he returned from Nuremberg, he also turned his efforts to history. Beginning in 1948, Jackson cooperated with a New York lawyer, Eugene Gerhart, who interviewed Jackson at least ten times over the next seven years, reviewed many of Jackson's personal files, submitted draft biography chapters that Jackson read and commented upon, and ultimately published a Jackson biography after his death.[12] During the early 1950s, Jackson also provided extensive interviews to Dr. Harlan Buddington Phillips of the Columbia University Oral History project. Phillips produced transcripts of these reminiscences and sent them to Jackson, who read them closely and completed editing them just before he died.[13]

During his final years, Justice Jackson also began to write this book, his memoir of Franklin D. Roosevelt. Although the exact genesis of this project is not documented, it is clear that Jackson was, by the late 1940s, thinking and talking privately about writing about FDR. Many of his New Deal contemporaries were publishing their own such accounts,[14] and Jackson was reading and discussing their efforts. In 1948, Jackson's son, William E. Jackson, who was a lawyer in private practice in New York City, sent his dad a *New Yorker* essay in which noted humorist Frank Sullivan spoofed the self-absorbed nature of some of these accounts.[15] In a cover note, Bill Jackson wrote that "[w]ith reference to our chat about the 'I knew FDR' memoirs, the enclosed may prove amusing. In fact, you might want to use parts of it when you do your own job."[16] Jackson promptly sent back a note of "[t]hanks for the *New Yorker* take off on Ickes et al. It is a gem but perhaps too subtle to penetrate where it ought to. Anyway I shall file it for reference when I come to do anything of the sort."[17] But Jackson did not commence the project immediately. During the next year, he was still only talking, including with his Supreme Court law clerk, about getting this project started.[18]

In August 1949, during what had become his annual trip to spend two weeks during the Supreme Court's summer recess at the Bohemian Grove encampment in the woods of northern California, Jackson began to make a "rough outline" of this book.[19] He was, at the time, reading the autobiography of a noted British philosopher and lawyer, and its style and organization convinced Jackson that his "Roosevelt era story . . . should be topical and not chronological in arrangement."[20] But Jackson also knew that his energy and time to pursue this project would "fall off" when he got back to "the heat and dither" of Washington (which he derided privately as "the crony capital"), and that seems to have been the situation after he returned for the start of the Court's October Term 1949.[21]

A year later, as the prospect of the Korean War loomed, Jackson was still only thinking about his FDR project. In a letter to his son, Jackson described his hope to be writing the book during the summer of 1951:

> I look for a turbulent [1950 Supreme Court] term as well as a busy one. Hope, before it begins[,] to get my papers on F.D.R. administration assorted and arranged and then next summer to do the writing. Sometimes I think it isn't worth while for it's a hell of a job as you know unless it were to be a slap stick performance like some others. Anyway, if we move into another war it may be of no importance, or of greater importance—who can tell.[22]

The spur that finally got Jackson writing was the momentous *Steel Seizure* cases[23] that came to the Supreme Court in spring 1952. That litigation began when President Truman acted in April 1952 to avert a nationwide strike by the United Steelworkers of America, who had been working without a contract since the end of December 1951. A steelworkers' strike at that time would have shut the nation's steel mills as American troops were using steel-based weaponry to fight for the United Nations in Korea, and as the United States government also was using steel industry output to increase vastly the national arsenal of atomic weapons. Consequently, to avert a steel shutdown, President Truman ordered his Secretary of Commerce, Charles Sawyer, on April 8, 1952, to seize and run the mills. Sawyer did so immediately, which temporarily averted the strike. But the steel companies then went to federal court and obtained a sweeping declaration that Secretary Sawyer's seizure directive was unlawful.[24] Within hours of this legal "unseizing," the steelworkers went out on strike, the mill owners cut off the fuel that powered their enormous furnaces, and the parties to the court cases persuaded the Supreme Court to review them on an expedited basis.[25]

The *Steel Seizure* cases showed Justice Jackson very concretely that the passage of time had dimmed memories—even among senior officials in the capital—of Roosevelt's presidency. President Truman's Solicitor General and Acting Attorney General at the time, Philip B. Perlman, asserted both in the government's written briefs defending the President's constitutional authority to seize the steel mills and again in his lengthy oral argument before the Supreme Court that Truman's action was no different from Roosevelt's seizure of California's North American Aviation plant in 1941, on the eve of World War II. Indeed, Acting Attorney General Perlman cited then-Attorney

General *Jackson's* written justification for Roosevelt's seizure of North American Aviation as "constitutional precedent" for the Truman seizure.[26]

Jackson did not see the parallel that Perlman claimed. During the oral argument, Jackson answered Perlman's assertion directly by explaining factual aspects of the North American Aviation situation that the Solicitor General seemed not to know.[27] But after the argument concluded the next day, Jackson was still brooding about the matter—he wrote to his son that Perlman had been "struggling and confused," described the Court as "weary," and acknowledged that defining the scope of a President's constitutional powers was a subject that he had "struggled with in several capacities."[28] When the Justices met in their private conference later that week to decide the cases, Jackson heard Chief Justice Fred Vinson compare President Truman's actions "to F.D.R. at length."[29] As Jackson describes in his Introduction that follows, this aspect of the *Steel Seizure* cases made him realize that he was, by May 1952, the only participant in some of the key Roosevelt moments and decisions who was still living and thus able to recount those events accurately.

Confronted by this mortality, and perhaps beginning to think about his own, Justice Jackson finally began to write during the summer of 1952 about FDR and his era. As an initial project in this vein, Jackson wrote and published a short article in the *Harvard Law Review* that revealed FDR's constitutional objection to a portion of the Lend-Lease law that he had signed, after extensive consultations with then-Attorney General Jackson, in 1941.[30]

In 1953, Jackson finally began to write the manuscript that became this book. By summer, he was discussing the project with his friend Alfred Knopf, whose company had published Jackson's previous books on the Supreme Court and on aspects of his work at Nuremberg.[31] Knopf encouraged Jackson to proceed,[32] and, within weeks, Jackson sent him the recently published *Harvard Law Review* article as a preview of the book. Jackson told Knopf that this article, "which has just come off the press, will give you an idea of the sort of thing I am thinking of—a topical treatment of interesting incidents rather than a history or diary."[33] Knopf thanked Jackson for his "very interesting" law review article and then gently cautioned him to write something with a general audience in mind:

> I get the idea and I think the result will be extremely interesting, but of course for us you'll be writing for the general reader and not for the lawyer, in consequence of which I assume that the paper that appeared in the *Harvard Law Review* would be somewhat expanded and perhaps given a rather more personal flavor.[34]

Jackson, taking this advice to heart, worked actively on this book throughout the summer of 1953.[35]

For his book title, Jackson selected *That Man*. The exact etymology of
this phrase and its variants, even as applied negatively to presidents, is hard
to document. One early coinage, which occurred while FDR was still Governor of New York, was NAACP executive director Walter White's calling
President Herbert Hoover "the man in the lily-White House." White later
wrote that his "phrase gained considerable currency, particularly in the
Negro world."[36] With regard to FDR, his first such description (itself perhaps a pun on White's blast at Hoover) was, in the title of an influential
positive biography that journalist Earle Looker published during the 1932
presidential campaign, *This Man Roosevelt*.[37]

Jackson obviously recalled "That Man" from Roosevelt's time in the
White House. This nickname was, particularly during the New Deal years
of FDR's first two presidential terms (1933–1941), the moniker that FDR-
haters used to express their loathing. According to Roosevelt biographer
Geoffrey Ward, the President

> made bitter enemies of the wealthy Protestants among whom he had lived
> most of his life. He had raised their taxes, regulated their business prac-
> tices, threatened their dominance; he was, they said, a hypocrite, untrust-
> worthy, demagogic, a "traitor to his class," and many of them, hating his
> name too much even to utter it, simply called him "That Man in the White
> House."[38]

During Roosevelt's second term, a writer had offered this description of
the phenomenon:

> In the cabañas at Miami Beach the sun-tanned winter visitors said their
> business would be doing pretty well if it weren't for THAT MAN. In the
> country-club locker room the golfers talked about the slow pace of the
> stock market as they took off their golf shoes; and when, out of a clear sky,
> one man said, "Well, let's hope somebody shoots him," the burst of agree-
> ment made it clear that everybody knew who was meant."[39]

In early 1944—in other words, three FDR victories later—another
author smugly turned the epithet around. He used *That Man* as the title of
his book advocating a fourth Roosevelt term,[40] and, indeed, the successful,
and final, FDR reelection campaign soon followed. Jackson's title choice
indicates his similar view that FDR's political opponents had, in the early

1950s as they had in the 1930s and 1940s, lost the argument about "That Man's" merit.

After choosing his title, Jackson mapped out eight chapters that he planned to write, each considering "That Man" FDR in a particular role—in the White House, as a politician, as a lawyer, as commander-in-chief, as an administrator, as an economist, as a companion and sportsman, and as a leader of the masses.

Jackson then set to writing. He wrote some passages in longhand and dictated others for typing by his secretary, Elsie L. Douglas.[41] (Unlike some of Jackson's other extra-judicial writings, his work on this project was not known to either of his law clerks during the Court's October 1952 Term, Donald Cronson or now-Chief Justice William H. Rehnquist.) Because Jackson worked on this project while he also was editing the transcripts of his oral history interviews with Dr. Phillips, a number of passages in the Roosevelt book manuscript not surprisingly mirror Jackson's statements in the Phillips interviews. The dates on various drafts suggest that Jackson worked on his Roosevelt book for the last time during the Court's summer 1953 recess, before he returned to full-time Court work when its new Term began that fall and then, in March 1954, suffered a serious heart attack.

Following Jackson's sudden death in October 1954, his *That Man* manuscript, which was and is contained in a folder labeled "Roosevelt Book," remained for a time in the custody of Elsie Douglas.[42] Although she ultimately provided the manuscript to Jackson's son, she never forgot it or, apparently, its importance to Jackson. Almost a quarter century later, on the occasion of the 1982 centennial of FDR's birth, the *Washington Post* published an op/ed article entitled "Getting Roosevelt Right." Mrs. Douglas, who was retired at the time and still living in Washington, D.C., tore the essay from the newspaper and preserved it for the rest of her life in her inscribed copy of Jackson's 1941 book, *The Struggle for Judicial Supremacy*—suggesting that she recalled clearly his own effort, as he drafted this book, to "get Roosevelt right."[43]

In the late 1950s, Bill Jackson reviewed his father's manuscript and considered preparing it for publication. Bill wrote to publisher Blanche Knopf, Alfred's wife and business partner, that he had some of Justice Jackson's "unpublished manuscripts on FDR and allied topics which, although unfinished, perhaps could be worked up into an interesting small volume if I ever can get the time to go over them."[44] Bill Jackson was more than fully occupied with his demanding and successful law practice and a large family, however, so he never undertook the project. But he did hold onto the manuscript. When he and his sister, Mary Jackson Loftus Craighill, donated

many of their father's official and personal papers and artifacts to the Library of Congress in the early 1980s, this manuscript was not included.

Following Bill Jackson's death in December 1999, his family located a folder labeled "Roosevelt Book" in a closet in his Manhattan apartment. It held a jumble of handwritten and typed pages by Justice Jackson containing detailed, intimate recollections of FDR. The Jackson family immediately recognized this file's importance and, knowing that I was writing about Jackson's life and career, called the file to my attention. Since that time, the Jackson family has been extremely helpful and generous in supporting this project and making this text available for publication.

III. Assembling That Man for Publication

Although this book is Justice Jackson's memoir of Roosevelt—the text is all Jackson's, as are the book title, the chapter titles, and the topical structure of each chapter—it is much more than the incomplete manuscript he left in his files when he died.

To construct this book as you hold it, I started with Jackson's "Roosevelt Book" file, which had become a very disorganized collection of papers since he last worked with it in 1953. I then organized the chapters as he had intended and, after finding multiple versions of particular chapters and passages, identified and used his "latest" version of each portion. In one instance, I also moved some text from the draft chapter where Jackson had it ("That Man as Lawyer") to a less-finished chapter ("That Man as Economist") where it seemed to fit better. I then assembled the pieces to create Jackson's draft "book." Some parts are quite complete and obviously were polished by Jackson's customary process of close editing and thorough rewriting. Other parts contain much less than Jackson evidently planned to write about FDR in the particular contexts that those chapters address. Jackson's drafts do not, regrettably, include discussions of some important topics that he jotted in rough notes—"Chautauqua 'I hate war'"; "100 days—Aid to Allies"; "Communism—Facism—Americanism"—when he started this project and probably intended to write up fully in the book. Each part of the book, and especially some later chapters that appear to be dictated drafts, also is less eloquent than the final text that Jackson, who is widely regarded as one of the finest writers (if not *the* finest writer) ever to serve on the Supreme Court, would have produced.

To complete the book, I turned to Jackson's other writings and documents regarding FDR. I drew primarily on two lengthy and extraordinary texts: (1) an unpublished autobiography that Jackson drafted in 1944, perhaps for publication in the event he decided to leave the Supreme Court and run for political office; and (2) "Bud" Phillips's text based on his interviews of Jackson. I located in these texts Jackson's accounts that correspond to, and in many cases expand upon, his treatments of particular topics in his Roosevelt book manuscript. In these instances, I then merged the respective accounts to create a unified Jackson text.[45] In addition, in instances where other Jackson writings complement but do not directly overlap topics in the Roosevelt manuscript, I augmented the latter by inserting the former at appropriate spots throughout the book.[46]

The most extensive of these "inserts" is Jackson's unpublished essay about FDR's "Destroyer Deal." During the summer of 1940, the President decided to send American destroyers to Great Britain in exchange for rights to lease American military bases on what were then Britain's Atlantic Ocean territories. Jackson's extensive account of this extraordinary, controversial initiative, which FDR undertook as the European continent was falling to Hitler, Britain was under fierce air and sea attack and (barely) standing alone in the war against Nazism, and Roosevelt was campaigning in an isolationist America for an unprecedented third term, is now part of Chapter 4 ("That Man as Commander-in-Chief").

I also added, as an Epilogue, two accounts that Jackson wrote about FDR in April 1945 in the days immediately following his death plus Jackson's remarks one year later at a ceremony commemorating FDR.

Except for making minor changes in grammar, phrasing, word sequence, and punctuation and occasionally adding a few words to explain an event or identify a person, I left each resulting chapter in the words that Justice Jackson wrote or spoke about fifty years ago. I did so because even unperfected Jackson language is almost always of very high quality.[47] I also decided that "pure Jackson" is, for its authenticity of authorship, the correct thing to contribute in Jackson's name to FDR historiography. (In making this decision, I was influenced by Jackson's famous and eloquent blast at the practice of "ghostwriting."[48])

I have written, finally, both notes and an appendix of "Biographical Sketches" to provide background information on people, events, and topics that would have been known more generally when Jackson wrote in the early 1950s than they are today.

The resulting book is, in its text, all Jackson.

This book is a unique perspective on FDR. It is explicitly anecdotal. Jackson wrote detailed accounts of his dealings with FDR, but his writing was based on recollection, not systematic research. Jackson's writing also is evaluative, and although his overall opinion of FDR could not have been higher, his particular assessments are not always adulatory. Jackson simply but eloquently describes the real Roosevelt whom he knew, observed, and pondered.

This book also is the work of a modest author. Because Jackson's special relationship with Roosevelt shaped the course of the younger man's life, some of what follows is necessarily autobiographical. But Jackson's account generally resists the tendency of some FDR memoirists to write more about themselves than the President.[49] Jackson also does not over-claim his place in FDR's life and work, which was significant but not FDR-defining—Jackson was not Sara Roosevelt, Eleanor Roosevelt, Louis Howe, Missy Le Hand, or Harry Hopkins, and nothing in this book suggests that Jackson thought otherwise. He also is commendably candid about some-times just happening to be in the room or on the boat for a notable FDR moment or event.

For all of its modesty, however, this is very much an "insider's" book. As Jackson demonstrates by the moments he recounts, he was one of FDR's closest working colleagues in some of the smallest, least public, rooms of his White House and moments of his Presidency. Jackson also was one of FDR's companions on fishing boats and in other private places of relax-ation. In his work for Roosevelt, Jackson was involved in such key matters as FDR's Court-packing plan, his efforts to reform the tax system, his bat-tles with corporate America, his decision to seek a third term, and his efforts to prepare the nation for, and then to lead it during, an unsought second world war. As such, Jackson was a significant participant in and wit-ness to much of the Presidency and personality of FDR, particularly during the six years (1936–1941) from the end of his first term to the momentous first year of his third term.

This book is also, finally, sadly timely and thus extremely compelling. During the summer of 1950, as Jackson contemplated writing about FDR and the prospect of United States military involvement in Korea, he asked himself whether this book in that context would have great importance or no importance.[50] From today's vantage point, it is not clear how significant this book would have been if Jackson had lived to finish and publish it dur-ing the 1950s, when FDR was still a dominant, personal memory every-where. In the world of 2003, however, to read this book and learn of its FDR is, I believe, to be struck by his direct relevance to the majority of us who never knew "That Man." Our world of complexity, danger, economic turmoil, and wars—some of types that we are facing for the first time—needs greatness, in its people, and especially in our leadership. And that is

Jackson's FDR: far-sighted but nimble in attacking the problems at hand; principled but also flexible in defining his positions; charismatic and popular but unafraid to pick fights, take stands, make enemies. In each of these respects, to learn from Jackson about Roosevelt in their time is to see, and to hope to meet, the needs of our very different, yet strongly similar, moment.

In his "Roosevelt Book" file, Bob Jackson thus left something of true value. This is the book that he scrawled with his very skilled pen, dictated in his powerfully eloquent voice, and expressed with the power of his memory and the conviction of his heart. It is truly a special account of the personality, conduct, greatness of character, and authentic humanity of "That Man" Franklin Delano Roosevelt.

In a time that could use both Roosevelt and Jackson, it is an honor to deliver a book that gives us what we can have: their examples, and some of their lessons.

May 2003

THAT MAN

Introduction.

The conceit of writing ~~these~~ recollections may be
forgiven only if ~~one the author~~ has accomplished something
memorable himself or has witnessed episodes ~~especially~~
of enduring
importance. ~~to this history.~~ I invoke the latter excuse.
At some critical moments during the administration
of President Franklin D. Roosevelt I occupied
posts that afforded opportunity to observe, if not to
                                                those by
influence, events and the words and deeds of ~~many~~ whom
                            as they well may, about
they were enacted. ~~Men~~ Men differ ~~whether~~ these ~~events~~ measures
                for
were ~~for the~~ better or ~~the~~ worse in shaping our
nation's destiny. But no one can deny ~~that the~~
that the decisions of his administration were and are crucial in our history,
~~are important~~ and hence that the future will want
to learn all it can about them. ~~That is why I feel~~
~~justified in~~
~~order to writing at all.~~

Not long ago I was sharply reminded that
                    what I saw?
if I ~~was~~ ever ~~to~~ tell the story of those times ~~at~~
~~all it~~, I must be about it. In defending ~~the~~
President Truman's
seizure of the steel plants (before the Supreme Court,) the
Solicitor General cited President Roosevelt's seizure
of the North American Aviation plant and my ~~part~~
~~reform~~ justification
~~explanation~~ of it as Attorney-General. Turning to the
                              is alive
record it was a shock to ~~find~~ that, of those who
participated in the conference at which that decision was
                                     That hinted
made I am the only survivor. ~~It hints~~ to me
                                    convenience.
that time does not wait upon our ~~convenience~~ ~~and~~
~~this is why I write now~~

I do not, ~~at least not~~ consciously, write as an
advocate to establish or defend Roosevelt's place in
            the under prevailing
history. For ~~modern the~~ standards of historical

INTRODUCTION

THE CONCEIT OF WRITING recollections may be forgiven only if the author has accomplished something memorable himself or has witnessed episodes of enduring importance. I invoke the latter excuse. At some critical moments during the administration of President Franklin D. Roosevelt, I occupied posts that afforded opportunities to observe, if not to influence, events and the words and deeds of those by whom they were enacted. Men differ, as they well may, about whether these measures were for better or worse in shaping our nation's destiny. But no one can deny that the decisions of his administration were and are crucial in our history and, hence, that the future will want to learn all it can about them.

Not long ago I was sharply reminded that if I am ever to tell what I saw of the story of these times, I must be about it. In defending, before the Supreme Court, President Truman's seizure of the steel plants, the Solicitor General cited President Roosevelt's 1941 seizure of the North American Aviation plant in California and my justification of it as Attorney General.[1] Turning to the record, it was a shock to realize that of those who participated in the conference at which that decision was made, I am the only survivor. That hinted to me that time does not wait upon our convenience.

I do not consciously write as an advocate to establish or defend Roosevelt's place in history, for the prevailing standards of historical judgment would apply to his works the philosophy of judgment by results. If, in the long test of time, it is found that Roosevelt's policies turned out well, he will be commended. If they turn out ill, he will be condemned. Hence, judgment of his public service must await some indefinite test period and is no task for contemporaries or collaborators.

This utilitarian standard of historical judgment—that time and results

are the test of greatness—seems to have been best expounded by Machiavelli.[2] Indeed, as Lord Acton pointed out, "three centuries have borne
enduring witness to his political veracity."[3] Acton proves his point by quoting, among many, such better known authorities as Mr. Leslie Stephen,
who "lays down the philosophy of history according to Carlyle, 'that only
succeeds which is based on divine truth, and permanent success therefore
proves the right. . . .'"[4] More recent schools of politics seem even more
devoted to the ideas that, in public affairs, success makes political policies
right, that morality is irrelevant to political policy, and that there is no standard independent of results by which to pronounce judgment upon the
acts of a public man.

While I do not belittle the advantage of perspective, and while I grant
that results may be the best or only test of the wisdom or expediency of a
policy, I must disagree that the moral worthiness of a policy or the mental
intent of a politician is wholly irrelevant in judging the rightness or wrong-
ness of a political course of action. The focus on results is merely a retro-
spective, or *ex post facto*, application of the fond doctrine that the end
justifies the means. This focus on outcome is a false standard of value for
the makers of history. Preoccupation with outcome also may distract their
attention from whether it is right and ought to succeed. And, in my view,
the history-makers' prognostications of a policy's ultimate results are even
less reliable than are their simpler judgments of right and wrong.

We must await many years before the test of long-term results can be
applied to Franklin Roosevelt. I do not profess to know whether, in the
century-run, the policies of Franklin D. Roosevelt will make for the good
or ill of the United States. But if only those who come later can judge him
by results, only those who were present with him can bear witness to what
he did, why he did it, and what manner of man he was.

My attempted answer does not take the form of a diary following the
succession of the calendar, nor a history of the times, nor a biography. Nor
is it an autobiography, although its purpose calls for a good sprinkling
of the first person singular pronoun. It is primarily to be viewed as
testimony—testimony of an interested witness, but testimony by one who
believes that now, after the power Roosevelt bequeathed has slipped
through the fingers of his beneficiaries and his adversaries are busy making
and defending policies of their own, he may cease to be the subject of
undiscriminating idolatry or of unreasoning hate.

For almost a score of years before Franklin Delano Roosevelt came to
the Presidency, I had some acquaintance, but not intimacy, with him. It
grew out of dealings with him on affairs of politics. These are unimportant

here, except to indicate my opportunities for appraising him and the impressions that he made upon me. As an almost even ten years separated our ages and the relationship commenced at the outset of his political career,[5] it is apparent that my earlier observations, while lasting, were not those of a mature or seasoned observer.

In 1910, the Democrats, profiting from division in Republican ranks, won control of the New York State legislature, which put them in position to name a Democratic United States Senator.[6] Led, or more accurately dominated, by Tammany Hall,[7] the legislature prepared to elect lawyer and former Assembly Speaker William F. Sheehan of Buffalo. Strong opposition developed from the independent wing of the party. Then it was that the Democrats discovered that they too had a Roosevelt on their hands.[8]

Franklin Delano Roosevelt, from Dutchess County, had just been elected State Senator. He defied the regular Democratic Party organization and refused to support Sheehan.[9] The anti-machine Democrats of the state began to rally about this new and attractive figure.

I was a son of a Democrat, who was son of a Democrat, who was son of a pioneer who local history described as a "stiff" Democrat.[10] I had entered upon study of law in 1910 with a kinsman, Frank H. Mott, who was recognized as a leader among Democrats of western New York, although the followers were hopelessly few. I was interested in the struggle in my party and, like most Democrats of our section, was anti-Tammany.

I went to Albany,[11] met Roosevelt through my friend Mott and, from the sidelines, watched young Roosevelt in action. I was a little surprised that nothing in his appearance or manner suggested kinship to the Republican Roosevelt. The newcomer to politics was long-faced, tall, slender, and erect. He was immaculate in the rather formal dress that was conventional in those days. His cultured accents were unfamiliar in the New York Senate. He looked and acted the aristocrat. He gave a countryman like me an impression of wholesomeness, earnestness, and naïveté. Politically, he was all amateur, surrounded by cynical and experienced upstate Republicans and downstate Democrats who had more in common with each other than either had with him. He was like a hothouse plant just set out among weathered and hardy rivals. Yet he was leading a popular rebellion against a man who powerful interests of both parties preferred, if they must have a Democrat, and he was so successful that he was able to stop the election of Sheehan and force a compromise on New York Supreme Court Justice James A. O'Gorman.[12] In spite of Roosevelt's victory, and it was largely his personal triumph, my recollection is of charm more than of strength, of urbanity more than of force, and of idealism rather than of practicality.

Then came the nationwide Wilson victory of 1912. Franklin Roosevelt was appointed Assistant Secretary of the Navy.[13] Just at this time, circumstances required Mott and me to look eagerly to Washington for some political help.

I was elected to represent my district on the Democratic State Committee in 1913, as soon as I turned twenty-one. Every city, village, and hamlet had a postmaster, an office that was, by immemorial usage, patronage for the party in power. There were a few other posts of local importance to be filled. There were some obstacles to getting those appointments for those who belonged to our independent wing within the party.

Normal channels of communication with the administration in Washington were all closed to us. A usual medium is the congressman, but ours, Charles Hamilton, was a Republican. So was our state's senior senator, Elihu Root. The Democratic junior senator, James O'Gorman, promptly engaged in a battle against the Wilson Administration over Panama Canal tolls. O'Gorman's knowledge of upstate conditions was limited, and he was inclined to leave our patronage matters to the state organization. The state organization was Tammany-controlled, and we were not in favor with the state organization. Unless we could break through these barriers, no one from the independent wing of the Democratic Party would be appointed.

The obvious thing was an appeal to Roosevelt. He gave Frank Mott and me an appointment, and we appeared in Washington and put our problem to him. Neither of us was a candidate for anything for ourselves. Roosevelt was, as we anticipated, sympathetic to our desire to use these places to strengthen the anti-Tammany wing of the party. He made arrangements for our interviews at the Post Office department and with others from time to time who might control appointments in our territory. Roosevelt always invited us, as troubles or delays developed, to come back to him.

There followed a period of repeated visits and pleas for political help during 1913 and early 1914, and always we got it. Usually our case was laid before Roosevelt himself, and he then arranged appointments for us. Sometimes he actively took up our cause with others in the Administration. Daniel C. Roper was then the First Assistant Postmaster General and the man who named most of the small officeholders. He was friendly to Roosevelt but did not want to get in too wrong with Senator O'Gorman. We had many sessions. We would put our case in Roosevelt's hands and he would fight it out with Roper for us. Sometimes our affairs were handled by Roosevelt's secretary, the dwarfish, gnome-like Louis Howe. Roosevelt's complete confidence in him and the aide's complete devotion were enough to confirm the theory of attraction by opposites.

If Roosevelt had not been in the "Little Cabinet" at that time, we would have had very tough going. We had no access, of course, to President Wilson—almost nobody did. Wilson was very aloof from the people who were working with him. We had no access to anybody in Washington except through Roosevelt. I did meet Josephus Daniels, the Secretary of the Navy. Roosevelt introduced me once to him when he came into the office on some matter. I met the old gentleman, then later came to know him quite well. So I came to Washington in the years 1913 and early 1914 with frequency. Through Roosevelt we succeeded in getting our postmasters appointed in every place where there was a vacancy, including Jamestown, which was the largest and most important of the offices in my district.

As a result of this party squabble for offices, I had some acquaintance in the early days with Roosevelt and also gained some political experience. The fact that Roosevelt was ready to aid us, who had no apparent way of ever being of help to him, displeased the regular party organization. But these meetings further confirmed my impression of a highly amiable man of aristocratic tradition and bearing who was on friendly terms with all of Washington, who liked plain people like Mott and me, and who felt secure enough to risk constantly antagonizing his own state party organization. I doubt if it occurred to any of us who dealt with him then, despite our liking and admiration for him, to think of him as presidential material—and probably he was not.[14]

By the latter half of the first Wilson Administration, my visits to Roosevelt diminished in frequency. The places that we had to fill were filled. The 1913 impeachment of Governor William Sulzer had left the Democratic Party in the State of New York demoralized and discredited. When the end of my term as state committeeman arrived, I said that I never again would hold a party position, and I never did. Because my hereditary party was a hopeless minority in my section of the state and at odds with the predominant state organization, it seemed the height of folly to continue to spend my time doing political chores. I also was getting into fights over these little post office jobs that did not have any importance to anything that I was interested in, in a larger way. So I retired entirely from the organization side of politics, which had filled my law office with people asking political favors and waging political fights. I could see that if I was going to be a lawyer, I did not have time for the organization work. My law practice was growing. When I had to be down in Washington on some political matter and I had a case pending, I had to get it adjourned. It was too distracting. I wanted to be a lawyer.[15]

As a matter of hereditary stubbornness, I would remain a Democrat, retain my interest in my party's affairs, attend its conventions as a delegate, and make political speeches in every campaign—an activity that, in those days, in the rural sections, had many attractions for one who rather liked public speaking. Strangely enough, I may say parenthetically that I never found being a Democrat injurious to my law practice or prejudicial before the courts or juries. We were so few that we were regarded as simply harmless and eccentric.

In 1920, Mr. Roosevelt accepted the nomination for Vice President. His campaign brought him to our community, where he had a small turn-out.[16] But it did seem sportsmanlike, if a little quixotic, to battle so vigorously for an obviously lost cause. Yet in later years, he more than once told me that if he had not made that hopeless campaign for Vice President, he would not have been nominated for President in 1932. He created a sense of indebtedness on the part of the Democrats and made personal friends who remembered him later when his campaign manager, James Farley, went out looking for delegates. Roosevelt's sense of security was such that he did not fear defeat.

Then came disabling sickness. It was not until the 1924 Democratic National Convention, that nightmare convention,[17] that I saw him again. I was not a delegate, but Homer Preston, a well-to-do client and old friend of my family who like ourselves had a long Democratic tradition, persuaded me to go with him to the convention.[18] There was something inspiring in seeing Franklin Roosevelt overcoming his handicap, cheerfully active, trying to win the presidential nomination for New York Governor Alfred E. Smith. It was not possible in that state of the national mind. The effort to nominate Smith at that time was set down as another idealistic but impractical move of an amateur in politics.[19]

I was a delegate to the Democratic State Convention of 1928 at Rochester, at which Roosevelt was nominated for Governor. When we learned that he had yielded to Governor Smith's urging to accept the nomination, Frank Mott immediately wired Roosevelt at Warm Springs suggesting that I, from the west end of the state, be nominated for New York Attorney General. Roosevelt replied promptly that this would be agreeable to him if the balance of the ticket could be preserved.[20] In the dialect of the Democratic Party, that of course meant that because he, a Protestant upstate resident, was to head the state ticket, there must be representation also for Catholics, Jews, New York City men, and others. Mott found quickly that the party leaders had the places allocated among their own regions and constituents, and the matter was dropped.[21]

I spoke in the campaign, and it was easy to see that there was a resist-ance to Smith's candidacy for President that was not felt as to Roosevelt's candidacy for Governor.

Some time after his election, Governor Roosevelt called me on the tele-phone and asked me to accept appointment as a member of the Public Ser-vice Commission. I told him it would be impossible because I had no one with whom to leave my law practice, and because I was representing many public utilities in my community. He replied that he knew that, but gave reasons for his offer that were pleasing for me to hear but have no impor-tance in this narrative. I declined the offer. My friend and client John Wright happened to be in my office. He knew what the conversation was about. He said, "By God, I want you for my lawyer, but I would never want you for my judge."[22]

I had some matters with Governor Roosevelt pertaining to legislation and actively assisted in 1930, his second gubernatorial campaign. While in office, he visited Chautauqua County and spoke at our famous Chau-tauqua Institution. Frank Mott was his host. I assisted in his entertainment at Mott's summer home on Chautauqua Lake and drove with them around the lake to the Institution meeting. Roosevelt was alert, amiable, and full of curiosity about every detail of life and government in our part of the state. His speeches were pleasant but not inspiring, less concrete and informa-tional than those we had learned to expect from Governor Smith.[23]

Roosevelt had the misfortune, in one sense, to follow Alfred E. Smith as Governor of New York. Smith had devoted long study to the state and knew it and its government thoroughly. He effected a comprehensive reor-ganization of the state government. He modernized its administrative sys-tem, its penal institutions, and its hospital facilities. He extended its parks and highways. It had been a most constructive period in the state's history. Following it, there was no such opportunity presented to Roosevelt. His administration might not have been particularly constructive—except for the Depression.

The Depression gave Governor Roosevelt an opportunity to advance a program of his own. His outstanding achievement was to obtain a large appropriation for relief and to make public aid a matter of right.[24] From my point of view at that time, that was a very doubtful thing to do. I had been brought up with a highly individualistic philosophy that made a virtue of both private and public thrift. It seemed to me that the Governor was perhaps too eager to invite people to come to the state for help and relief. But he chose a careful commission to administer it, on which he placed my intimate friend, Philip Wickser of Buffalo. He and Jesse Isidore Straus employed an experienced social worker named Harry Hopkins, who thereby met and impressed Roosevelt. I first met Hopkins at lunch with Wickser and Straus, little suspecting the part he was to play in later affairs.

During his second term as Governor, almost as his preconvention campaign for President was taking shape, I had my first and only really unpleasant disagreement with Roosevelt. In 1931, the Legislature created a commission to investigate the administration of justice in the state and present recommendations for its improvement. It consisted of six legislative members, four nominated by the New York State Bar Association, of whom I was one, and six appointed by the Governor, among whom was Raymond Moley.[25]

Its first meeting, to organize, was held in the Governor's office, and he let it be known that he would like Mr. Moley to be elected Chairman of its Executive Committee and the real executive head of the commission. Moley was not a lawyer, and the cause for creation of the commission largely concerned civil litigation. We of the Bar Association, who included Martin Conboy, the Governor's close friend and later his adviser in the Mayor Jimmy Walker removal proceedings,[26] all favored former state court judge Daniel J. Kenefick. The Governor quite actively intervened to aid Moley and finally sent for me and asked why I was opposing his choice. I could not give very substantial reasons for being against Moley— indeed, Roosevelt laughed at the reasons I advanced. But I could and did give my reasons for being for Judge Kenefick. I stuck by my guns and Roosevelt left no doubt that he was much displeased that I did not fall in line with his suggestions. Finally a compromise was reached by which Kenefick became Chairman of the Executive Committee and Moley the Director of Research. But Moley moved on to other service to Roosevelt in about a year.

Years later—November 1940 to be exact—we were fishing out of a small boat near the mouth of the Potomac River[27] when President Roosevelt began to chuckle for no reason at all that I could see. Then he said, "Do you remember the day in Albany you would not support Moley and the argument we had?" It was my turn to chuckle and I said, "I certainly do, and I well remember that you didn't like it." "Well, I know more about him now," he laughed—and I never knew what brought it to his mind at the moment.[28]

I did not go to the 1932 Democratic Convention in Chicago, but our district was strong in support of Roosevelt. I helped in his campaign in my own county and spent a couple of weeks at the headquarters in New York City, assisting with various phases of the work, particularly within New

York State under the direction of Chairman Farley and Vincent Dailey. But nothing that I did was significant or worthy of political reward, nor was it done with that in mind. I saw Roosevelt when he returned to New York from his western trip, but not to have any significant conversation with him. In a few months, he was President of the United States.

Such is the background against which I view his failings and achievements in that trying eminence.

I <u>The Man</u> in the White House.

It was In February of 1934 that I went with the Administration as Counsel to the Bureau of Internal Revenue and shortly thereafter that began to ~~little~~ attend occasional ~~occasions for personal~~ meetings with the President in reference to a new tax program and other tax problems. These early meetings left a deep impression because, in contrast with what I had ~~having~~ known him before his election ~~and not thinking him particularly cast for the part of President~~ I was somewhat ~~a bit~~ surprised at his ease and aptitude for the role of Chief Executive of a nation in distress.

He had realized his ambition and fulfilled his idea of his own destiny and took over his high office as if born for the part. ~~He seemed to have matured with the responsibility.~~ He never appeared self-conscious about his position, or ~~He did not seem~~ surprised to find himself in it. ~~but took it as matter of course.~~ He never tried to impress one with the magnitude or the difficulty of his job — he simply went ahead and did it. He made no self depreciating remarks about his adequacy for its tasks. ~~He was immersed in work which he enjoyed with the joy of mastery.~~

He was so self assured ~~manifestly born to govern~~ that I never heard him assert his right to command ~~boss~~ or remind any one that, it was he who ~~he was~~ President, ~~after the manner of lesser men.~~ Perhaps there was one jovial exception. On Memorial Day of 1940 the President assembled his newly appointed Defense Advisory Commission with General Marshall, Admiral Stark

THAT MAN IN THE WHITE HOUSE

IN FEBRUARY OF 1934, I went with the Administration as counsel to the Bureau of Internal Revenue and shortly thereafter began to attend occasional meetings with the President in reference to a new tax program and other tax problems. These early meetings left a deep impression because, in contrast with what I had known of him before his election, I was somewhat surprised at his ease and aptitude for the role of Chief Executive of a nation in distress.

He had realized his ambition and fulfilled his idea of his own destiny. He took over his high office as if born for the part. He never appeared self-conscious about his position or surprised to find himself in it. He never tried to impress one with the magnitude or the difficulty of his job—he simply went ahead and did it. He made no self-deprecating remarks about his adequacy for its tasks. He was so self-assured that I never heard him assert his right to command or remind anyone that it was he who was President.

Perhaps there was one jovial exception: On Memorial Day of 1940, the President assembled his newly appointed Defense Advisory Commission[1] with General Marshall, Admiral Stark, and a few of his Cabinet.[2] The purpose was to explain their functions and responsibilities to Edward Stettinius, who was to deal with industrial material, William Knudsen with production, Sidney Hillman with labor and employment, Chester Davis with farm production, Ralph Budd with transportation, Leon Henderson with prices, and Miss Harriet Elliott with consumer interests. These overlapping fields were left vague in the order creating the body, and the President's oral explanation did not much clarify them. It was plain that everyone was pretty much at sea about what to do, and the President suggested that perhaps they would like to ask some questions. An interval of impressive silence was broken by the heavy Danish accent of the practical Knudsen, who said, "Mr. President, there is only one thing I want to know—who is my boss?" The President, amid laughter, said, "Well, I guess I am."

I think much of the President's self-assurance came from his mastery of his illness. Of course his physical impairment was never more than partially overcome. But the psychological shock of his disability was. Although the limitation was always present and visible, he had adjusted his habits of thought and action to it so perfectly that it seemed forgotten. It was not a forbidden subject to be avoided. Nor was it one to be dwelt upon. It caused him no embarrassment or feeling of inferiority to ask that things (sometimes very personal things) be done for him. It was not an invitation to sympathy. That his lower limbs were hopelessly paralyzed, he accepted as a fact, like the fact of his Presidency. He went about his work, not ignoring the realities but seeing them in their true proportion.

Following a meeting with President Truman at the White House shortly after FDR's death, Jackson made a diary entry that includes this additional reflection on FDR's inability to walk:

I never before realized how completely FDR had set in my mind the pattern of the presidential office. As we were waiting to keep our appointment, the President [Truman] himself walked into the outer office and greeted everybody present, opening the door for everyone to come into his private office. Never having seen a President walk into the outer office, I was somewhat startled and he walked out again with us as we left.[3]

If Roosevelt's self-confidence and belief in himself inspired his friends, it also irritated his critics, who thought it mere conceit. It was not the superficial conceit that is sure it always is right, nor was it mere shallow belief in luck. But it was a confidence that his considered decision as to his course was better than a drift with the tide, and he made big decisions with an apparent nonchalance that sometimes took away the breath of his advisers. At other times, he would wait until the tide had shown its direction and speed before he would act. He had great faith in his sense of timing, and who can say it was misplaced?

The President brought with him to Washington a large accumulation of intellectual capital. That is fortunate, because the pace of life there is such that one rarely meets a high official who can honestly say that since taking office he has read a book through. Roosevelt was widely informed in history, and it was not confined to that of his own country. Naval history held a particular fascination for him. A striking characteristic was his detailed knowledge of geography and social and economic conditions of people at home and abroad. When the exchange of over-age destroyers for Atlantic and Caribbean air bases was being negotiated with England in 1940, he had first-hand knowledge of nearly every area involved, and where travel had not informed him, reading had. On one occasion at a Cabinet meeting, he quickly drew from memory a map of the China coast and asked the Secretary of the Navy to locate on it the incident he was reporting. The Secretary had to send for his own maps to refresh his recollection, and they showed the surprising accuracy of the details of the Roosevelt sketch.

He explained the secret of his store of such knowledge to a few of us who accompanied him on a three- or four-day fishing trip down the Potomac after the 1940 election.[4] It was a rainy afternoon and the President was asleep in his cabin when a dispatch came telling of British air raids on the Italian naval base of Taranto.[5] Postmaster General Walker, Harry Hopkins, Stephen Early, General Watson, and I confessed that we had not the slightest idea where it was or what was its importance. When the President came out, we showed him the dispatch. He recognized the port at once, gave its distances from Gibraltar and Malta, and explained its strategic significance.[6]

I asked him then how he acquired his ready knowledge of what often seemed rather unnoticed parts of the world. He told us that while he was confined to his bed with polio, he devoted much time to his stamp collection, which was still his hobby. When he became interested in a stamp, it led to interest in the issuing country. He would have the encyclopedia brought to his bed and would read, or have read to him, all of the information it gave about that country. From its bibliography, he sometimes selected books for further reading on special subjects. I had never taken an interest in stamp collecting and remarked then that this was the only real justification for that hobby I had ever heard, but that it did not improve the minds of all of its devotees in the same way—for instance, Ickes. But Harold, who was there [sic], changed the subject and said he had some stamps he would like to trade for some of the President's. They got out their stamp collections and the two went to bargaining over their stamps like a couple of farmers making a horse trade.[7]

The President always impressed me by his intense application to the work of his office. But it was not labor; it seemed to be his delight. He often worked at his breakfast in bed, frequently seeing Cabinet members or other aides at that time. He was immersed in work nights, holidays, on weekend cruises, and on vacations.

Sometimes the energy with which he applied himself to his office was somewhat embarrassing to me. One of the powers of the President is to extend executive clemency. Petitions for pardon or commutation of sentence reach him through the Department of Justice along with the recommendations of the Attorney General. These petitions and supporting papers are processed and the Attorney General's proposed recommendation is drafted by the Pardon Attorney, who was Daniel Lyons during my time as Attorney General. I had complete confidence in his integrity and respect for his judgment and was confident that his recommendation, after he had studied the papers, was better than my snap judgment, which was all that there was time to give them. I rarely did more than to glance at the recommendations before signing.

Then they would go to the White House. Back they would come with action noted in the President's own hand. Some he would sign without comment, but many would bear lengthy penned notations asking about additional information, or for the opinions of other persons connected with the case, or suggesting that the matter be held another year and then brought to his attention, or other items which showed that he had given more personal attention to these matters than I had done. There were great numbers of them at that time, for many persons had been convicted for violating the Prohibition laws that had since been repealed.

After the war broke out in Europe, the President's intensive application to his work continued to all hours of the night, when he would receive telephone messages or dispatches, prepare answers, or hold conferences. It told upon his appearance and worried those about him. Many times we urged him to delegate more detail. He dined at Sumner Welles's beautiful Oxon Hill home one evening, weary after a sleepless night spent on the transatlantic telephone. After the ladies had retired, leaving the men in possession of the table, the British Ambassador, Lord Lothian, joined us all in giving the President a scolding. The Ambassador, as Philip Kerr, had been secretary to Prime Minister David Lloyd George during the First World War. He told the President how when Lloyd George became Prime Minister, he declared that he was running the war; the war would not run him. He laid down and rigidly observed a program that protected his sleeping hours, including a brief afternoon nap, from any interruption whatever, and he was not only more efficient but lived to a ripe old age. Roosevelt promised to heed Lothian's warning but never did. His diligence never ceased. He was wholly dedicated to his task, from which his affliction allowed him few escapes by way of relaxation.

President Roosevelt combined informality with dignity. He called people easily and naturally by their first names or by nicknames, but those about him called him Mr. President, even when fishing or playing poker. No person of taste or discernment would take liberties with him, and the few who attempted it were easily put in their places. His dignity was native and needed no artificial aids. Roosevelt was a gregarious person and liked light social occasions in company where he could relax. But he knew lightweights when he saw them and used them for light occasions. He was full of anecdotes and told a story very well. But his stories were never vulgar, blasphemous, or profane, and those who got off such stories in his presence won no favor by it.

It was characteristic of the man that he liked to have about him in his moments of relaxation those with whom he worked. And the atmosphere of his service was that you were working with him, not for him. "Missy" Le Hand, Grace Tully, General Watson, and Steve Early were frequently on his trips and at his dinners, though he saw them hourly every day. This was not merely because he liked their company. There was no snobbery about him, and his guest list at official dinners, while it included the most eminent guests, also included many plain workers in his vineyard. Neither was he guilty of that inverted snobbery often seen in public men which condescends and puts on the air of being a "plain person." Roosevelt was always himself the least inhibited of men.

From time to time it was said that Roosevelt was under the influence of this or that person in his official entourage or among his friends. It is undeniable that any high official is influenced by those who are near him, and a President's associations or those of a Cabinet officer are matters of public concern. Merely to be about when problems are under consideration makes one a potential influence on decisions. The timely suggestion of a name for a post, of a person who ought to be consulted, of an additional source of information coming from any source may change the course of events. There were many who, by proximity, had this sort of influence.

Roosevelt liked novel ideas, bold courses, and dramatic actions, and he liked the sort of men who could come up with such suggestions. Some associates had influence in the sense that many of their suggestions bore fruit. But I knew of none who did not have many of his suggestions rejected also.

The man who influenced Roosevelt most, as is the case with most of us, was the one who would marshal him the way that he was going, would provide reasons and arguments for doing what he wanted to do. I never knew any man to dominate him—there was no one to whom he would surrender his own judgment. No one could overbear him and he never abdicated.

Such, in my view, was "That Man" whose position required him to be many men.

Roosevelt was a President toward whom no one was indifferent or neutral. After he had been in office a brief period, the lines began to separate between those in whom he inspired an all-out devotion and those in whom he aroused an implacable hatred.

By 1940, every home regarded him as a household idol or its demon. He was well aware of this. Earlier, I think he found the torrential hate of the upper classes and businessmen baffling, for he looked upon himself as one who was trying to save the system by which they prospered. But he grew to accept their animosity, which proved so impotent at the polls, as something of a tribute and a source of amusement. With great glee, he used to tell of a report by a Pullman car porter during a campaign: "All the passengers in the parlor cars are against you, all the passengers in the day coaches are for you—and our train has two parlor cars and nine day coaches."

2

THAT MAN AS POLITICIAN

THE CHIEF MAGISTRATE does not succeed merely by being magisterial. He will fail as President if he fails as politician. He is not merely the head of state. He is the head of the prevailing political party. The cohesive power of its loyalties and organization is an instrument of government. His office is a political office under the necessity of policymaking, which calls for leadership. He occupies the office that represents the whole nation, not one state or district. If the President does not bring to it the elusive and variable qualities that add up to leadership, he loses much of the influence, if not the legal power, of his office. And in our system, influence on public opinion is the very substance of power.

Roosevelt's aptitude for political leadership had little chance to develop during his governorship, where he inherited a smoothly running and well-organized state government. His capacity as a purely political leader also was obscured in the war period of his presidential administrations because the normal tendency to oppose and resist leadership falters in wartime. Hence the real political leader showed himself only between his accession to the Presidency and the outbreak of the war. But this was a longer period than most Presidents enjoy.

Roosevelt's attitude toward his own party was that of a faithful, strong (or bitter) partisan. His party had long been out of power in the nation, and he recognized that it must win by the votes of those who had not before supported it if it was to remain in power. He knew he must build for it a new constituency consisting of the young and those whose loyalty to the other party was not too strong. He had no hope of converting the hard core of the opposition, of course, but he was quite ready to take into his first Cabinet such Republicans as Harold Ickes and Henry Wallace, and into his Administration numbers of young men who had no affiliations or but light ones. His later taking into his Cabinet such Republicans as Henry Stimson and Frank Knox was from a different motive. He had no thought that they would cease to be Republicans but thought that, under the exigencies of foreign troubles, they should represent that party in a bipartisan defense program. Moreover, his admiration for Theodore Roosevelt and some of his progressive Republican policies was so little concealed that it sometimes annoyed his old-time Democratic followers.

The early days of the New Deal saw no drive to get rid of rank and file Republicans in the non-policymaking offices in Washington. In the numerous offices that I held, I was never asked or encouraged to, and never did, discharge a man, ask his resignation, or give him embarrassing or humiliating assignments because he was a Republican. I saw much evidence that the same practice prevailed in most of the other departments. However, new agencies were being created that provided new jobs for those whom it was politically expedient to take care of and, therefore, the pressure was less than upon some administrations.

The President did desire to rid the Administration of men in policymaking positions who disagreed with him as to policy and of whom he suspected a purpose to sabotage the work of his Administration. This, within those bounds and as to posts that are strictly executive, I believe is justifiable. That is what we have an election for—to determine whether there will be a change of policy. Where the people vote for it, I have sympathy with neither Democrats nor Republicans who whine because the will of the electorate is translated into action.

Roosevelt went, as the Supreme Court held, rather beyond those limits with his policy clean-out when he attempted to remove William E. Humphrey from the Federal Trade Commission.[1] It was not an executive agency but an independent one possessing quasi-judicial powers. President Roosevelt asked Humphrey to resign, stating that their minds did not go along together in matters of policy. He wanted to appoint his own trade commissioner. Humphrey refused to resign and the President removed him. The removal was after he had obtained an opinion, I believe from James M. Landis, then Dean of Harvard Law School, as well as from his regular legal advisers, that he had the right to do so.

Humphrey contested the removal but soon died, and his estate brought an action against the United States in the court of claims to recover his salary. The Supreme Court supported Humphrey and held that the Federal Trade Commission was an independent agency, not wholly in the executive department, and that the tenure of office was not at the pleasure of the

President but was a term fixed by Congress.² Humphrey could not be removed for anything except causes specified in the statute. The cause of the President's removal admittedly was that the President disagreed with the decisions that Humphrey was making and his policy of administering the Federal Trade Commission Act.

Of all the decisions of the Supreme Court of that era, I think the one that stayed his hand in removing Humphrey was the one that Roosevelt resented most. He thought it was aimed at him personally and was contrary to the position of the Court when it sustained the power of President Wilson to remove a postmaster.³ There was, however, a substantial difference in the nature of the offices, which was the purported, and I have no doubt the real, basis of the Court's reaching opposite conclusions in the two cases. I think most lawyers would agree that the two cases were not parallel and the decisions not inconsistent.⁴

The President later consulted me as to his power to remove Arthur E. Morgan as head of the Tennessee Valley Authority. It was a purely executive agency for the performance of certain construction and operational functions. It was not adjudicating the rights of parties where the decisions of the commissioners were supposed to represent independent judicial judgment, like those of the Federal Trade Commission.

There were three members of the TVA and there developed a very bitter feud among them. The President was much concerned about it. It was a scandalous public disagreement between Morgan against the other two. Morgan was chairman, which made the disagreement more difficult.

The President took a hand in the matter after Morgan had publicly charged dishonesty and want of integrity against his fellow directors. He was asked by the President to supply the proof of his charge. If true, they would have warranted removal of the other members. Morgan did not come forward with proof. The President then asked Morgan to appear before him. The President put to him questions about the charges. Morgan refused to answer. He took the position that he would only answer a committee of Congress and generally that he had no obligation to the President.

That precipitated the question of whether the President had the power to remove Morgan, whose conduct in making these charges and refusing to sustain them was obviously very demoralizing to the Tennessee Valley Authority. Attorney General Cummings was down in Pinehurst, North Carolina, on vacation when this matter came to a crux in 1938 and the President asked for my written opinion. My recollection is that I talked with Cummings on the telephone before I sent my opinion over to the President, who wanted it and wanted to get busy with it. My opinion tried to distinguish between the cases of Humphrey and Wilson's postmaster and advised the President that he could remove Morgan because the function of his position was purely executive.[5] The President removed Morgan, citing Congress to my opinion as his authority. Dr. Morgan later sued to contest the removal but he never recovered and eventually abandoned the effort.

The whole thing was a sad chapter because Morgan had been a very able and useful man and had given a great deal to the Tennessee Valley Authority. The President acted, I think, with very genuine regret.[6] But he thought Morgan's conduct was contemptuous and contemptible. The President thought that he was entitled to have the man whom he had appointed, and who had made charges against his other appointees, back up his statements. Morgan flatly refused. His position was that his only responsibility was to Congress and that the President had nothing to do with it.

Congress at that time would not move. The matter was involved in politics. There were congressional enemies of the TVA who were delighted that the Authority was in a feud. There were friends of Morgan who, while regretting the feud, took his part in it. There were enemies of David Lilienthal, a very able man, who was one of the parties to the feud. There was some anti-Semitism in the attitude toward Lilienthal. Harcourt A. Morgan, the other director, had his friends, of course, and if the disagreement were left to Congress to straighten out, it would be going yet. So Arthur Morgan was removed by the President. The feud was ended and the TVA went its way. But as a result of the *Humphrey* decision, some other men held office during his Administration who I think would have been dropped had it not been for fear of adverse Court action.[7]

The attitude of the President toward his own party was that of a patron, not of a slave. He was not averse to making appointments or taking positions for reasons of party strategy. But he was not willing to allow the party organization in the nation to become a duplicate of the corrupt local machines which he always had fought. He made that clear shortly after his Administration began. Several members of the Democratic National Committee had set up quickly prospering law offices in the City of Washington and were specializing in various governmental matters. There were ugly rumors of influence, of favoritism and hints of corruption. President Roosevelt lashed out at this practice and demanded that the members of the Democratic National Committee either retire from the law practice in Washington or resign from the Committee. There was deep resentment within the Party organization. I took keen interest in it because one of the lawyers involved was Robert Jackson of New Hampshire, a man with whom my name was often confused in my early days in Washington.[8] After Roosevelt cleared out this situation there were occasional accusations of influence or favoritism but very little suggestion of corruption.

I was in offices sensitive to such matters because the offices involved taxation and money. I never had reliable evidence of but one employee who accepted a bribe. On receiving that information, he was suspended and committed suicide the following day.[9] My observation in those days was that there was very little money influence upon officers in the Administration; if some lawyers or agents pretended to possess such influence, they were cheating their clients. And my experience in the Bureau of Internal Revenue convinced me that political bribery is less common than commercial bribery—purchasing agents, corporate officers, and local labor leaders are more subject to bribery than public officers are. But the disposition to favor one's friends as against strangers, one's partisans as against one's opponents, is one that I expect to see as long as politics is politics.

It would not be fair to appraise the Roosevelt Administration's attitude toward patronage and corruption without recognition of the good influence of James A. Farley, a Chairman of the Democratic National Committee. This is a matter on which a concrete example is worth a thousand pages of abstractions. I knew Mr. Farley well because I had worked and traveled with him on campaigns. He had endeavored to interest me in coming to Washington and endorsed my appointment as General Counsel for the Bureau of Internal Revenue. When I took over there, I found, among appointments under consideration but not consummated pending investigation of the applicants, one of an attorney from my own state. Among his letters of recommendation was an enthusiastic one from Mr. Farley. A delicate factional situation prevailed in the city in which the applicant lived involving relations between President Roosevelt and Governor Smith. The appointment was designed by Mr. Farley to help ease that situation of growing concern in the party. But the Intelligence Unit investigation showed a man who had been arrested for being drunk and disorderly and for a number of other minor offenses. I had had a little experience with the Intelligence Unit and did not wholly rely on them.[10] I called an old friend, a Democrat but one who practiced law without much attention to politics in that city. He confirmed all that the report said and added that the applicant was a man I would not employ for my own work.

I packed that file under my arm and went over to see Farley. I said that I did not want to start my work in Washington by turning down his recommendation but the investigation showed this aspirant to have a bad record. At once he said, "Then you shouldn't make the appointment." He went on to say that his letter recommending an applicant meant that politically he was clear and desirable from the point of view of the organization. He said that if I followed his commendation and got into political trouble on the Hill with a congressman or a senator or with the organization, he would go to bat for me. But he added, "that doesn't mean the man is fit for a particular job in your office. It is up to you to keep your office fit and clean and if you don't do that, I will be the first man to jump on you." I suggested that, me being new in Washington, perhaps he would think my standard of qualifications was too severe and that I would like him to look at the file and see if my judgment was right. He glanced through the report and tossed it back to me and said, "You certainly should not take a man on in face of that report."

I have always remembered that conversation because it was private advice, given to a novice in the Administration by the Chairman of the Democratic National Committee. I think it revealed the true Jim Farley. Never did he ask me in any office to do an act that would reflect discredit. He never tried to interfere with a prosecution or to fix a case. Sometimes he called and asked me to see some friend of his on official business. He always added, "I know nothing about the merits of what he is going to put up to you, that is up to you," or words to that effect. I always took him to mean it. The same general attitude characterized Frank Walker as National Chairman during 1943 and 1944. Especially in the lower levels of an administration, the demands of a national chairman have great influence. I have no hesitation in giving to Mr. Farley and to Mr. Walker credit for a good deal of the general atmosphere of integrity which pervaded the Roosevelt Administration during their chairmanships.

It will be asked, then: What about the power of the bosses of the big city organizations of the Democratic Party? What about Pendergast, Hague, Tammany Hall, and Kelly? Did they not render valuable service to Roosevelt in conventions and elections, and did he not favor them in return? This is a fair question. But one must distinguish between the influence of these men over matters in their own localities and their influence in Washington. Completely in control of the machinery of the party in their sections, they also were individually and collectively powerful in the National Convention. It is quite possible that if the early days of his Administration had not dramatically established Roosevelt's popular leadership—had it been a normal administration—these organizations might have had much more effect in Washington. But the fact was that Roosevelt quickly established a devoted following in the precincts of these bosses, which made them more dependent upon him locally than he was dependent upon them.

The President was not a dreamer. He recognized that by virtue of local conditions, these men were entrenched in leadership of their organizations, and that these were entrenched in power by virtue of local votes. How much those organizations influenced their congressmen or senators, I would, of course, be unable to say, but probably considerably if they wanted to remain in office. Recommendations or actions that came from those quarters were always appraised accordingly. In some instances, Roosevelt recognized local organizations with local patronage. In some, he did not. Some of his appointments they liked and some they resented but had to swallow. But as for direct influence on the policies or personnel of the Administration in Washington, I saw little evidence of it.

Certain it is that Tom Pendergast, the Democratic boss of Kansas City, did not have enough influence to save himself from prosecution and conviction. That case had long been in the making in the Treasury before it was publicized. Pendergast and his associates knew they were under investigation and that prosecution was likely, and they exerted all the powers they had to prevent it.[11]

Frank Hague of Jersey City, apart from strictly local matters, seemed not only without influence in Washington but to be rather shunned. His acres of diamonds were his own backyard, and he was more interested in his City Hall than in anything he could get from Washington. Only once did he ever call on me officially. After I became Attorney General we were investigating the conduct of Judge Davis of his State of New Jersey, and I received word, while in Florida, that Mr. Hague was on his way to my hotel room. My son chanced to be with me. When Hague came in he introduced himself, for we had never met before, and I introduced my son. Hague asked, with a delightful Irish brogue, "What are you going to make of the boy?" "Well," I said, "I hope he will make something of himself." That seemed to go over his head for he replied, "I made a judge out of mine."[12] Then he told me he wanted to talk about the Judge Davis matter and what he said amounted to this: Hague knew very little about the facts but hoped we would not "persecute" Judge Davis; Hague was interested because Judge Davis used to be a Protestant minister before he was a lawyer and, since he became a judge, he goes a lot of places and speaks where a political speaker could not go, and Judge Davis always says the right things to the right people. Hague did not indicate that he enjoyed any judicial favors from the Judge and doubtless would not have indicated it if he had. I told him that the case would have to take its course. It did, and Judge Davis was twice tried, but the jury disagreed in each case. Apart from this, Mr. Hague never made any approach to me nor through anyone else, to my knowledge.

I reported to Roosevelt on this. I told him about the Hague conversation, which gave him a laugh. I kept him informed of what we were doing in a matter of that importance, but we never had any discussion of the policy because it was obvious what I should do. There was no objection from any source. It was routine, really, and I treated it as such.[13]

With Mr. Kelly the case is very similar. He never came to me but on one case, that of a prominent politician that we had indicted in his city of Chicago. All that he had to say about it may be summarized in this: "I am not asking you to do anything about this case itself. Whatever the evidence shows, it will have to show. But if you send out prosecutors of the kind that sometimes come out from Washington, they will give out a lot of press releases that are not based on evidence and make a lot of wild charges. I just want you to have responsible men in charge of the prosecution and try their case in court." I told him that so far as possible I intended to follow that course in all cases.[14]

Mr. Kelly told me that shortly before I became Attorney General, he had gone to the White House and pounded on the President's desk and told him with a good deal of heat that he demanded one thing from a Democratic Administration, that his Attorney General, Frank Murphy, either stop issuing press statements that reflected on him or indict him so that he could defend himself. That's all he asked. He said, "If he's got any case against me, let him present it. Then I can defend. But I can't defend against a press conference." Kelly told me that so far as he personally was concerned, that was all he had to ask of me. It may have been bravado, or good tactics, but he never took any other attitude with me. He said Roosevelt had told him that he was entitled to one or the other. I later confirmed this with the President, who did not think Mr. Kelly had been treated fairly in the matter. The President told me that Kelly was furious about it, and he thought Kelly had a point.[15]

As the fall of 1939 wore on, the President called me more and more on matters relating to the Department of Justice. Then suddenly came the death of Pierce Butler, a Justice of the Supreme Court. Butler was a Catholic and the only Catholic on the Court. It was logical that his successor should be Catholic. Attorney General Murphy was a Catholic. As Attorney General, it was not illogical that he should be promoted.

The President told me that he intended to appoint Mr. Murphy to the Court and me Attorney General. I said, "Mr. President, I don't think that Mr. Murphy's temperament is that of a judge." The President said, "Well, probably not, but there are a number over there who can keep him straight. It's the only way I can appoint you Attorney General. I can't remove Secretary of War Woodring at this moment. If I could, I wouldn't dare appoint Murphy Secretary of War. So it's the opportunity to put this Department in your hands, where I want it to be." So I said no more.

On leaving the Attorney Generalship for the Court, Murphy saw fit to give some intimations that there were pending in the Department important tax fraud or other cases against political leaders and he regretted that he could not stay to make sure they were prosecuted. The intimation was insidious, although he denied it was intentional. However, I got very angry about it, I am frank to say. I knew from the men in the Criminal Division, the Tax Division, and the Federal Bureau of Investigation that there were no cases in the Department against men such as Mayor Kelly of Chicago. There had been intimations that they had protected gambling, which, of course, was not a federal offense in any event unless there was some income tax angle to it. I ascertained from the Tax Division that there was no tax case pending. It looked to me quite unfair for Murphy to leave the office with the intimation that he had these cases and then, when nothing would develop, the opposition press would be in a position to say that Murphy had them but I had killed them off.

I was at my apartment at the Wardman Park and I received an early morning telephone call from the President. He said, "What do you suppose is the latest?" I said, "I don't know." He said, "Frank has given out another statement." The President had seen the newspapers and I had not. We talked on the telephone about it and he asked me to come down. I went down. I showed him a letter I had prepared declining the office unless and until Murphy cleared this matter up. I knew that if I refused to take that office, Murphy would not be appointed to the Supreme Court. At least, I felt that way. He would then have to face the collapse of his own stories. The President read it over hurriedly, handed it back to me and said, "Don't leave that with me. We'll work this out."

I took a position that the only way it could be worked out was for the President to insist that Murphy file with him a report as to what cases he had against important political figures, because I had made diligent inquiry in the Department and could not find any cases pending against or even remotely concerning them. The President sent Tom Corcoran to ask Murphy for such a report. Murphy immediately said, "Well, if it's misunderstood, I will make a statement to the press." It was not a statement to the press that I wanted. It was a record as to what cases, if any, he had. Any statement that he made to the press was likely to make the matter worse. However, he and Corcoran worked on some kind of statement.

I gave the President another memorandum about the subject on the desirability of a report to him. However, in spite of all that could be done, Murphy held a press conference and told the press that he did not have any cases against Mayor Frank Hague and he did not have any cases against Mayor Kelly. The manner in which Murphy did it, or the disposition of the press to attribute something of the kind, led to the immediate suggestion that he had been threatened or pressured into making the statement, and that the statement was not true. In other words, he made a bad matter worse. My position with regard to this was known in wide circles—many men in the Department knew, because of my inquiries, and others in the White House group knew.

The President then said that he wanted to have the swearing in ceremony at the White House as soon as the confirmations. "Well," I said, "Mr. President, Frank really should be sworn in over at the Court. All of the Justices have always been sworn in at the Court." He said, "Bob, don't raise any technicality. I want to get him sworn in before he can hold another press conference and I want to make the arrangements myself and do it fast."

So Murphy and I were sworn in at the same time at the White House. I was detailed, among other things, to invite Chief Justice Hughes, who had a very strong view that justices of the Court should be sworn in at the Court. He turned me down extremely coldly, as I expected he would, but he knew that I was merely transmitting an invitation. He said he would not be present.[16]

In his draft autobiography (1944), Jackson described how he and the President had been discussing FDR's plans for Murphy, Jackson, and the Department of Justice since late 1938:

Murphy told me that he really did not want to be Attorney General, but that he really wanted to be Secretary of War—that he naturally was an executive and felt that he belonged in the War Department. He said he was only taking the Attorney Generalship by arrangement with the President as an interim appointment. The President had told him, he said, that in any changes he made in the Department he was to consult me, for I was to be Attorney General to follow him in six months, and he would go to the War Department.

I told the Attorney General that I was not accustomed to counting my chickens until they were hatched, and that while I had not the slightest doubt about the good faith of the President in making his plans, I did not count on its happening, and that I thought that he, the Attorney General, would be very unwise if he communicated that plan to a single human being. I said that although the President had told me the same thing, I did not intend to take even my best friends in on the information, for there was nothing more certain to stop a plan in Washington than to have it announced. He, too, agreed that he would not tell anybody that such a plan was afoot. Had he stuck to this resolution, I think he might well have become Secretary of War.

The impression that Democratic political leaders were highly influential was assiduously cultivated by the opposition press. During the Democratic National Convention of 1940, members of the Cabinet, along with other of the leading delegates and figures of the Party, were invited to an official dinner given by Mayor Kelly of Chicago. When we got there, Harold Ickes, Henry Wallace and myself, and I think one or two others, found ourselves placed at Mayor Kelly's table, at which Mr. Hague and other prominent Democratic machine politicians were seated. Photograph after photograph of the table were taken and circulated throughout the country, with titles which suggested that we Cabinet members were like peas in a pod with these leaders, with whom, as a matter of fact, we were less acquainted than were some of the leaders among our critics.

These leaders and machines clung to Roosevelt—not that they always wanted Roosevelt, but they needed him. In 1940, they would have personally preferred James Farley or some other presidential candidate. But Roosevelt's name and influence had struck so deep into their own local followings that they did not dare desert him. They announced themselves for him early and sought to force him to accept the nomination because they did not want their voters to have the slightest suspicion that they were against the President. They were his captives—he was never theirs.

A President's relations with his Cabinet is often indicative of his political prospects, for it not only is the most important adjunct of his office but part of his political apparatus. Only a short-sighted Executive would overlook, in selecting a Cabinet member, that he is choosing not only an adviser and administrator in whom to put trust, but also a spokesman whose words, whether rightly or not, will be regarded as inspired or approved by the President himself. His personal relations with individual members, always an object of gossip, may vary from intimacy to mutual suspicion and dislike.

But the Cabinet as an institution is one of the most talked of and least understood in our whole system of government. Not provided for in the Constitution and apparently unanticipated by the Founders, it came into existence almost immediately, as of necessity. It is often assumed to have an importance as a body apart from the weight of the individuals who compose it. But it was not during my time and, so far as I can learn, never has been a deliberative or collegiate body. It adopts no resolutions and takes no formal actions. Sometimes a consensus of opinion would be reached on some general subject and sometimes disagreement was evident. But the very nature of the body as a gathering of specialists from separate departments makes real debate usually impossible. Who could debate with the Secretary of State on most issues of foreign policy if he has not the background information and seen the relevant recent dispatches and reports that give authority to the views of that officer? Who would engage in disagreement with the Secretary of the Treasury on a financial matter without the aid of technical studies by the experts? No department head really has time to master the affairs of his own department, let alone become a critic of another. The one exception was the Department of Justice, because many Cabinet members were lawyers and all had solicitors or counsel who supplied them with legal opinions. But except on very general subjects, or on matters concerning several departments, there was nothing that could be called a Cabinet decision.

Sometimes the President would raise questions. Perhaps he had read in the newspaper a criticism of some department. Or perhaps someone else had conveyed to him some criticism. He would remind the Cabinet member of the complaints he was getting on this or that subject. Sometimes matters were brought before the Cabinet as a matter of protection to the member, who felt that they were likely to break out into the press and wanted his Cabinet colleagues to be forewarned as to what the facts were.

Apparently the Cabinet never has been a deliberative body, but it has always been a meeting of the President's staff. Its history has been little explored, but in his book *Democracy in the Making* (1938), Hugh Russell Fraser relates that after John Tyler became President in 1841 following the death of President William Henry Harrison, Daniel Webster, Tyler's inherited Secretary of State, suggested at the first Cabinet meeting that the President should carry on the ideas and customs of his predecessor. Webster told Tyler, "It was our custom in the cabinet of the deceased President, that the President should preside over us. Our custom and proceeding was that all measures whatever, however, relating to the administration were brought before the cabinet, and their settlement was decided by a majority—each member, *and the President, having one vote*."[17] Tyler is reported to have replied that as President he was responsible for his Administration and would hope to have the cooperation of the members of the Cabinet, but that he could not "consent to being dictated to" and if the members thought otherwise, their resignations would be accepted.[18]

All I can say is that in the days of President Roosevelt, if any member had put forward a proposal of this kind, he should have accompanied it with his resignation. The President did not regard the Cabinet members, and should not in my opinion, as co-equal authorities, but as the staff of his Administration. They were partners in a sense, but he was still the President. Now and then he would make a very peremptory decision on some matter that was pending in one of the departments, and he expected it to be carried out.[19]

The President usually appeared slightly bored at Cabinet meetings and brought with him often an early edition of the *Washington Evening Star*, chuckling over and showing us the latest cartoon by his friend Clifford Berryman, although they were often at his expense. Beginning with the Secretary of State, the President went around the table and asked the members in order of rank if they had matters to bring up. Sometimes he would make a statement about some development, political or governmental, or bring up some problem that was on his mind. This was more often in the nature of information or instruction for us than in the nature of debate. Unless matters concerned some other department, the members rarely brought up their problems. They would say, instead, that they had a matter they would like to take up with the President after the meeting. These after-Cabinet interviews were not especially welcomed by the President and often meant that someone was trying to get a hasty commitment from him. If a distasteful subject or one in which ill feeling was apparent between members was brought up, he was likely to end the discussion with a joke or some light comment. It did not solve the issue but postponed it. He was a difficult man to force into a discussion of any subject toward which he wanted to close his eyes.

Jackson's oral history recounts FDR using humor, at Jackson's expense and in his defense, during Cabinet meetings:

Sometimes the President would have some preliminary remarks about some personal affair of a Cabinet member. One who had just been on a trip might be asked some question. On one occasion I remember that my son had been in difficulty up at Yale. He had been arrested for lugging a bus sign back to his room.[20] There was a good deal of publicity that day about it. As I came into the Cabinet, the President looked up, smiled and said, "It's all right, Bob, I've got some boys too." He would very often open the meeting with some bit of humor, or a story that he had heard.

On leaving one Cabinet meeting I found that my hat was gone. In place of it was the hat of the Apostolic Delegate. It seems that he had called on the President. We both had Homburg hats. He had taken my hat and left his. It was the only ecclesiastical headgear that I ever wore. That story came up in the Cabinet, which in Roosevelt's day was a very human institution. If anything happened to anybody that could be laughed at, it was laughed at. As a matter fact, I do not think the President ever cared too much for Cabinet meetings, or took them too seriously.

. . .

The meetings were not always congenial, although the sharp disagreements were confined to a very few members. Harold Ickes was the center of a great deal of difficulty. He was always very sharp in his method of dealing with people. If he had a disagreement with the Department of Justice over a title to land, he was very likely to write a letter to the President saying that the Department was holding him up and delaying matters unduly. I remember such a case over the Vanderbilt title in Georgia. Ickes was very impatient. If he wanted an opinion from the Attorney General, he was quite apt to make it known to the world that he had asked for such opinion. Sometimes it appeared it was for the purpose of putting the Attorney General on the spot and forcing him to deliver the opinion that he wanted.

I remember one Cabinet meeting when I had been the victim of some such experience. As I went in, I met Jesse Jones. I said to the Cabinet afterward that Jones was one man who knew how to get along with an Attorney General. I related what happened, which was that Jones said to me, "Bob, here's a piece of paper. On it is a question. Here's another piece of paper and on it is the answer that my solicitor says he thinks the Department of Justice should give to this question. If you can give that answer, I want to ask you for a formal opinion. If you can't, I just want you to let me know and tear up the other paper."

Most of the departments were very considerate of each other and tried to get on. Ickes, while he was irascible and sharp, was the center of a good deal of fun in the circle. Not infrequently the President was ribbing him about one of his feuds with somebody.

The President always reminded me of an old lady up in my neighborhood who said she always enjoyed her religion more if there was a little deviltry going on in the choir. The President never seemed to mind a certain amount of deviltry going on in his official family. The meeting was sometimes very pleasant and very relaxing.[21]

Jackson also described, in his oral history, FDR's penchant for constant, often private, meetings:

The serious matters between the President and departments were usually taken up privately. For my own part, I had lunch with him frequently, and during the lunch hour we discussed his problems and mine. Oftentimes also I went over at the close of his day, and also I went frequently to his bedroom in the morning while he had breakfast. He did business at all hours of the day and night. You might say that Roosevelt was never closed for business.[22]

Toward his sub-Cabinet and minor officers, the President was peculiarly cordial. He attended dinners of the Little Cabinet, was on an informal first name basis with most of them, and appeared anxious to know them and the details of their work. On one occasion, he told us how disappointing and difficult it was for him as Assistant Secretary of the Navy because he so seldom could see President Wilson.[23] Roosevelt told me once, when I was Assistant Attorney General, "I've seen you more times this month than I saw Wilson during a whole year." Perhaps because of this experience, he was generous in granting appointments to those in lower ranks of his service.[24]

FDR's fondness for and generosity toward Jackson may be best demonstrated by the President's efforts, albeit unsuccessful, to orchestrate Jackson's election as New York's Governor in 1938. Serving as New York's Governor from 1939 forward would have positioned Jackson to seek, with FDR's support, the 1940 Democratic presidential nomination to succeed Roosevelt, who planned to retire to Hyde Park after his second term. In his oral history, Jackson recounted his dealings with FDR on this topic:

The fact was that the President did want me to consider running for Governor of New York. In 1937, I think in November or perhaps a little earlier,[25] I went to see the President and told him that I must resign my office within the next few months and return to private practice. My practice was going to be dissipated if I stayed away much longer. It was costing me more to live in Washington and keep up my home in Jamestown, dashing back and forth between the two, with two children about to be in college and all the rest of it. I told him that I was going to have to resign. I could not stay the rest of the Administration. I would time it when it was agreeable to him and Attorney General Cummings.

That talk took place at his bedside in the morning. He said, "Well now, I can see your position about this, but, Bob, you can't leave now.

You're in this thing. You can't quit. I want to talk with you about the New York situation. I think that you are the logical man to run for Governor of New York. I don't think Herbert Lehman is going to stand for another term." He was then a little annoyed at Herbert Lehman because Lehman had come out against the 1937 Court-packing plan at a time when it was particularly harmful to the President.[26]

We had quite a long talk about the governorship. He said, "If you can be elected Governor in '38, you would be in an excellent position for the Presidency in 1940. I don't intend to run. Every once in a while somebody suggests that I'm going to run, but I want to get up to Hyde Park." He went on and told me his plans for Hyde Park and how he wanted to lead his life up there as sort of an elder statesman—Thomas Jefferson in retirement was as near as I could think of. I think he was entirely sincere in that.

He went on to say that he had tried to get his son Jimmy to live in New York State. If Jimmy would just go up on the farm, stay up there, and establish himself as a resident of upstate New York, the time would come when Jimmy would be nominated for Governor, because he said, "You know, they have to have, every once and so often, an upstater. They have to get one who isn't a Catholic and who isn't a Jew. When those times come, there are so few that any man who is at all outstanding is just in the line. You're in the class that's got to be chosen. I think that you will have to be considered."

I said that I did not know that to be Governor was a particularly desirable thing in itself. As I understood it, it always had left everybody who had had it broke. While I was not doubtful that I could at any time make my living at the bar the rest of my life, I was not sure that it was a very attractive office. He insisted that it was a great office and so forth.

I said, "Well, Mr. President, if we're thinking about doing something of this kind, shouldn't I talk with Jim Farley about it?"

"No," he said, "you don't need to talk to Jim. I think Jim and I have a very thorough understanding on the subject. Jim's got to make some money. Bess wants Jim to be rich. She's very much annoyed that other people have more things than she has. She wants Jim to make some money. Jim is not financially in shape to run for Governor. I think Jim ought to if he's thinking about the Presidency. Jim, according to some of his friends, is thinking about the Presidency in 1940. He doesn't seem to see that if he would run for Governor of New York and serve a term, he would establish an independent record as an administrator. He could then go before the people as an administrator, a governor. But now he's a national political party chairman and a Postmaster General. I don't think the people would elect a national chairman president. He ought to establish an independent record. But Jim isn't in a position to do it. He's not going to do it and I wouldn't go to him about it at this time."

So I said, "All right." That ended that.

The President talked with various other people about it. By and by it became rumored that he was backing me for that place. The result was that some of the people in New York who wanted to be sure they were on the right side of things also started doing things about it. There was a Jackson Day dinner at New York at which the President wanted me to speak.[27] That was an unfortunate move, I think, because what they did was to invite as speakers everyone that they thought was a possible candidate for Governor. Of course, I did not have the organization that John J. Bennett had, for instance—he was Attorney General and had a large staff in New York. While the meeting went off very well, it was not a good thing to do. It was rather premature and weak.

Then the Young Democrats arranged to give me a dinner, which, at the time I accepted, I did not think would develop into what it did. But that is one of the difficulties in political matters. You never can tell what will develop from small things. I accepted their invitation to be their guest of honor at a dinner.

Then the legend grew very fast that the President was backing me for Governor, that I was the candidate of the extreme left New Deal, and that this would put Farley out of the picture. Unfortunately, the thing was brought forward as an anti-Farley movement. That is why I never blamed Jim Farley for being against me. Jim himself, long before, had said to me, "Some day you're going to have to run for Governor." I would have had every expectation of at least friendly relations with him on the subject if I had gone to him and talked with him about it. I am not sure that he would not have said, "Why yes, I will bring it forward." When it was brought forward as an anti-Farley move, however, it was a matter of self-defense for him to stop it.

In connection with this Young Democrats dinner, Morris L. Ernst, Tom Corcoran, and Ben Cohen spent all one Sunday with me. Morris had a proposition from Edward L. Bernays, the publicity man.[28] Bernays wanted to take up my case. He wanted to manage the publicity for this Young Democrats dinner, the build-up and all that went into the making of a candidate. I just could not agree to it. The program sounded to me just like the kind of a build-up that Wendell Willkie later got in 1940, when they all turned in a high-pressure publicity campaign. It was then that Morris Ernst went away and said that he guessed I did not want to be Governor very bad or I would do some of the things that were necessary to get it.

It was suggested by many of the newspapers that this governorship program originated with Tommy Corcoran. The fact is that Corcoran was active in carrying out the President's wishes in connection with this and many other political matters. Corcoran had won the President's confidence by his keen wit, his quick intelligence, his complete devotion to the President, and his readiness to undertake any kind of task. Corcoran was a legman for a man who had no legs of his own. He did all kinds of errands. He made many suggestions and at times influenced the President, not because the President bowed to Corcoran, but because he bowed to a good idea when Corcoran presented it.

The difficulty with Corcoran's position was that he did not have any position. I said to the President once, "If you put Tommy Corcoran in a recognized job of any kind, put him in an office and put his name on the door so people will know that that's Corcoran's door and all, this mystery about him will disappear. He's now a mystery man because he comes in the back door and he doesn't have any office and he can't be found."

There was a great deal of truth in that. Those who hated Roosevelt hated Corcoran because he was Roosevelt's agent. I do not think that Corcoran ever, to my knowledge, disobeyed the President's instructions or tried in any way to carry out a plan that the President did not want.

The President knew the New York State political situation up, down, and sideways. It was not Corcoran's idea. It was Roosevelt's. I don't mean to say that Corcoran was not for it. He certainly was. He did an immense amount of work and raised and spent money in carrying out the President's instructions. He telephoned a lot of people, contacted many people, was present at a great many conferences, and did a great deal of work. The only power back of the move, however, was the President. It was not a movement by a group. It was distinctly the President's project.

The President resumed the discussion with me on a fishing trip in late November 1937. The fact that he took me on a trip with him at that particular time was taken as notice that he might be favoring me. The President's argument was the same as it had been before, except that he said that he had considered other possibilities who could be the New York Democratic Party's 1938 gubernatorial nominee, that there was a possibility of Fiorello La Guardia, but that La Guardia was not a Democrat and it would be very difficult to get the Democrats to support him. He felt that the Party was in some danger in the state and that if La Guardia took the American Labor Party nomination and went off in the other direction, he would beat the Democratic Party.[29] La Guardia was in a strong position to bargain.

The President wanted me to get busy with the New York people and see what I could do. He thought that Senator Robert F. Wagner would have to run for reelection and stay in the Senate. The President did not think that La Guardia could be elected Governor, but he would have to work with us, and we with him, in order to hold the American Labor Party. The President thought I had to be the man who had to make the campaign.

The New York situation was that John J. Bennett had been for many years Attorney General. He had a large organization and a host of friends. He was determined, with the support of the Brooklyn organization and some of the Tammany crowd, that he would run for Governor if Lehman did not.

A dinner was given for Bennett in Brooklyn on the same night as this Young Democratic dinner for me at the Commodore Hotel.[30] It was one of the saddest things you ever saw, the way Democratic politicians developed laryngitis suddenly and could not go to either dinner, not knowing which one was going to win out eventually. Those who early on had accepted for mine, when they found the Bennett dinner was going on, were so sick they were unable to come. Some others adopted other tactics. They had to be in Florida—they had sick wives or sick relatives in Florida and had to get out of town. Some others tried to meet the situation by going from one dinner to the other in the midst of the performance. It was very amusing. I think I enjoyed it more than anybody present because of the way the politicians were trying to avoid being counted on either side before they were sure who was going to win. But the dinner was a very large and successful one.

As the move began to shape up, there were several factors that counted. One was that Farley announced his opposition to it. The other was that the organization politicians who did not make any announcement were quietly against my nomination. Tammany, of course, was opposed. The upstate organization of the O'Connell brothers in Albany, Troy, Schenectady, and that area was opposed. The Kelly organization in Syracuse was at least not much favorable. The Dailey organization in Rochester was friendly and probably would have been favorable. The Buffalo organization was not for it, but probably would have come around because it would have been a little dangerous to oppose the President on someone so close geographically.

However, Lehman was then a bit hostile to Roosevelt, and Roosevelt to Lehman. Lehman did not like the prospect of my coming into the picture because he had a feeling that my public speeches in late 1937 had been over-radical.[31] He did not want to see Bennett succeed because both Lehman and Farley had the feeling, which they had expressed many times, that Bennett just was not up to the job. Therefore great pressure was put upon Lehman to run again. A great many people went to Lehman and argued, "If you don't run, we're going to have a battle in the Democratic Party. Bennett's going to be a candidate. He's got a lot of friends and he's got some delegates. The President's going to be for Jackson. If the President pushes Jackson, he's radical, it will make a bad split in the party."

So the matter never came to an issue. If it had, I do not know just what would have happened—whether the President would have considered it wise to compromise on someone other than Bennett, whether he would have insisted that they put me over, I do not know. In any event, Lehman accepted renomination and that settled that.

Despite the fact that I had become Solicitor General in March 1938 and was paying no attention to it myself, as I literally was not, my candidacy kept being speculated about in the newspapers. They attributed my keeping still to a feeling that I had talked too much already.

I think that the President felt that I would appeal to the same general groups that he had and would be able to carry them along. I think that Farley, on the other hand, felt that if I was successful, I would be beholden to groups other than his group and that therefore my election was a bit of a threat to his organization. The organization men felt that they wanted some patronage. They did not see much in my record that would encourage them to believe that they would get it. I had never made political appointments in the offices where I had men to choose. Once in a while we had to take care of somebody for some senator with some definite power over our appropriation or something of that kind, but my appointments were not based primarily on politics. Very few men who were typical organization men ever found a place in my office. That they did not like, and they were probably justified in it.

Also, David Dubinsky passed the word around in labor circles that he had not been successful in what he wanted with me. Of course, we had Dan Tobin who was angry about an anti-racketeering case and some of the longshoremen who were in the longshoreman racket that we broke up. So there were substantial elements that had come to the conclusion that I would not be a good governor for them, and they were right.

Labor as a group did not turn me down. It was Dubinsky individually. The American Federation of Labor crowd generally was friendly. Their policy was not to make open endorsements. The President figured that the American Labor Party, in spite of Dubinsky, would come through because of La Guardia. He figured that some arrangement would have to be made with La Guardia, putting him into something in Washington. He figured that the labor forces in New York generally would come into line. Dubinsky himself would eventually come in line but was against it. That encouraged Farley and added an argument to the Tammany men who were against it: "Why, you see, labor isn't for him—Dubinsky isn't." Others could say, "Labor is for him—Hillman is." So I would not say that labor was against me, but that element was.

The President probably could have gotten my nomination if he wanted to press it, if Lehman had not run. I think he could have gotten labor, even Dubinsky. Sidney Hillman was favorable to me and the AF of L crowd in general was. The opposition knew that if Lehman withdrew, the President could put me across. Their real triumph was in getting Lehman to announce that he would accept the nomination. That kept the door closed so that the thing never really came to a test. That was regarded, at the time, and properly, as a Farley victory because Lehman was regarded as being on the outs with the President.

Lehman was a little fearful of me, although we have always been good friends. I went to the executive mansion in Albany a number of times and spent two or three days there assisting on some of his messages. He named me to that banking scrip commission.[32] We see each other now that he is in the Senate and we have always been very friendly, but he thought then that I was an erring friend. He finally announced at the late September 1938 convention that he would run and that settled the matter. If he was to run, nobody was going to buck him.

Long afterward, I discussed this at length with Jim Farley. Jim and I discussed it two or three times. We met in Rome when I was there in connection with the Nuremberg trials. Jim was also over. We were both at the consecration of Cardinals in February 1946. Jim and I sat down and talked the thing over at length. He claimed that the President never had any talk with him. He said that if the President had talked with him about it, he would have said that I was being pretty radical, but he doubted very much if he would have opposed me. He said that the way the thing came out, it was an effort to defeat his leadership. He was chairman of the state Democratic committee. He was the recognized political leader in New York. It was an attack on his leadership. He had to fight it. I think that's true.

Who was right about that is the problem. My own impression is that Roosevelt did not talk with Farley, but that he thought it was not necessary to talk with Farley. He thought they understood each other well enough so that it was not necessary to talk with him. He may have talked with him on the fringes of the subject and formed his impression that Jim was not able to run. But I do not think they had ever had a frank, candid talk. If the President had sent me at that time to Jim, one of two things would have happened. We would have known how to hold our fire until we were sure that Lehman was not going to run, or we would have known that Jim was ready to back it. If he was, it easily would have been accomplished.

However, I am infinitely more happy that it turned out just as it did, because becoming Governor in 1938 would have been a dead-end street with the situation as it developed in 1940 and 1944. I am so much happier where I am than I would have been there that there's just no comparison.

I do not think this political experience made me cynical. I did not have to have the governorship. The difficulty with so many people in politics is that they get into a position where they're dependent. I had my profession. The advertising had not done me any harm profession-ally. I was in a good professional position. I was fairly independent financially. It had been fun. It was not anything that I had set my heart on having. I cannot say that there was ever a moment of real disap-pointment about it. There might have been annoyance or disgust at some particular individual, but it was all part of the game.[33]

Jackson's oral history also includes the following material regarding FDR's deci-sion to seek a third term and his 1940 reelection campaign:

The President had told me repeatedly that he did not expect to be a candidate in 1940. I had every reason to believe that he was entirely sin-cere in that. He also had told me that it would be necessary that he make no announcement to that effect because he would have to hold in line those who were for him, or who at least would not want to be against him, in order to have control of the convention. In our discus-sions outside of official hours, he had talked of the library he wanted to build, what he wanted to have at Hyde Park, the kind of life he wanted to lead. I think in 1938 he was looking very earnestly to retiring. . . .

The approach of the war in Europe and the complications there were decisive things that were changing his mind. Another was the unwillingness of the Democratic organization to let him bring forward anybody that he wanted to. He was annoyed that the organization had not gone along with me in New York State. It was becoming increasingly apparent to the rest of us, as well as to him, that he was not going to be able to name somebody that he could be sure would carry out his general attitude to government.

I think that Roosevelt was definitely of a mind to retire and rest on his laurels—he accomplished a great deal—if it had not been for the war. With the war coming, he was not willing to see a war economy turned over to somebody else, for example, Senator Carter Glass of Virginia, for whom he had great respect in his way. I think that his feeling was sincere. I recall at one time he was telling me about something he had said to Wilson. Wilson was pressing for some measure to be passed. Roosevelt said to him, "Mr. President, wouldn't it be well to keep this back and make this fight in your second term?" He said that Wilson said, "Roosevelt, in the first place we don't know that we'll have a second term. Many things may happen. In the second place, my observation of American history is that Presidents only accomplish things in their first term. Second terms are always conservative terms compared to first terms. The movement has exhausted itself. What we don't get in the first term, we're not likely to get."

That impression was in Roosevelt's mind, more or less. He felt that the momentum of the New Deal would exhaust itself, and perhaps some of its errors would catch up with it, because there were conflicts in it, as he knew. It was timely for him to retire after two terms. I think it was a very wise decision based on conditions internal.

· · ·

In general I would not have favored a third term, but the change in foreign affairs and the unwillingness to allow the President to name a successor who would carry on the tradition seemed to indicate that a third term was inevitable. My reason for not favoring a third term for a president is not that I am afraid he would become a dictator in his second term, or third term, or fourth term. It is that I do not think he would amount to much in the third or fourth terms. I think that was proved in the case of Roosevelt as far as domestic policy was concerned. A man in the Presidency can make his contribution in one term. He certainly can make any contribution that he is capable of in two terms. Thereafter, he is not likely to bring forward much that is new, or to get it by his own party if he tries to. Parties in power tend to become inert and interested in remaining in power, which means maintaining the status quo. That happened with the Democratic Party in those days. But the foreign situation presented a quite different problem.

. . .

I did not have a very active part in the 1940 campaign. It was not a very intensive speaking campaign. People wanted to hear Roosevelt and they wanted to hear Willkie but they did not want to hear others. Secondly, in New York State, where I might be expected to be most active, the organization was in the hands of Mr. Farley and his friends. I was asked to speak at three or four relatively unimportant places in New York State, and I complied. I spoke at Oswego, in Yonkers, and Jamestown, but for a member of the President's Cabinet in a crucial state, I did very little. Radio had come into such wide use that people were not interested as much in second rank speakers as they were in times past. They were only interested in hearing the candidates. The days of the campaign orator were drawing to a close. It was not what others said about the candidate that people were interested in; it was what the candidate himself said.

Roosevelt, of course, had his press conferences at any moment he wanted to. There's a tremendous advantage in being an "in" because a President can do things that the papers cannot fail to take note of. They are official. They are dramatic. They are power moves. The "outs" can just run around and talk about it. Roosevelt was extremely skillful in doing things that focused attention on his purposes, so he did not need to do so much speaking. He made some speeches, as the history of the campaign shows. His enemies charged, and there was a good deal of truth in it, that he was campaigning all the time. Any Cabinet meeting, any press conference, any executive order was in a sense a part of his campaign in that it was conveying to people an idea of what he was trying to do.

The campaign, of course, ran into difficulty because Roosevelt was trying to do two things, I believe, very sincerely. One was to keep out of the war. The other was to prepare for a war in case we had to have it. Every step that he made to prepare, such as the conscription bill, cast a certain doubt on the sincerity of his desire to keep out of it. Every time he made a speech declaring a purpose to keep out of it, it lessened the enthusiasm for his measures of preparedness. That made it difficult to carry on both policies.

Of course, Willkie was under some of the same difficulty. He was making absurd promises about keeping out of the war if he was elected, which he later brushed off as campaign oratory. That ended any possibility of Willkie as a leader, because a real leader cannot brush off his promises that way. Roosevelt did not live up to his promises that the country would not become involved in war, but he was not cynical about it. He was able to point to a changing scene, which necessitated changing policies.

Roosevelt and I talked about the campaign frequently. Willkie had an enormous buildup at the time of the convention. He looked like a very formidable candidate. The buildup kept going on and on and on until his acceptance speech, which was to be the great speech that would inflame the country and scourge Roosevelt out of office. It was oversold, tremendously oversold. No man could live up to the expectations that were aroused in the hearts of the people opposed to Roosevelt. They expected a messiah. Then Willkie got up at Elwood, Indiana, in August 1940 and made, as his acceptance of the Republican nomination, a very ordinary campaign speech.[34] It deflated terribly. I happened to hear that speech up in the country with Republican friends. We went over to the old farm at Spring Creek, Pennsylvania, to broil steak out in the woods. I turned on the radio in the car, half expecting some powerful message. It went flatter and flatter. My spirits went higher and higher, and my Republican friends' lower and lower. I got the full force of the deflation. Everybody felt let down. It was oversold in advance. The actor just could not live up to the billing.

Throughout the campaign Willkie's course was steadily downward. The President's confidence rose constantly. But I think no candidate ever feels secure until the votes are counted, and the President was nervous up to the last. He had been nervous in 1936. He never overlooked or discounted the possibilities of defeat.

The destroyer-bases deal, which was taking place then, did not last long in the campaign. The people approved the transaction and by and large they did not question the methods much. The fact was that the people realized that Congress would debate the thing for six or eight months before they would ever come to a policy. They were tired of debate. Roosevelt could have gone much farther in disregarding Congress, as Lincoln went much farther in disregarding Congress in the face of emergency, and could have gotten away with it as far as public sentiment was concerned. Congress is not a particularly popular body. I think the people rather felt glad that he had decided the matter and ended the controversy. There was no serious issue over the destroyers.[35]

Republicans kept talking about the third term issue, but nobody was taking that seriously. That had been exhausted before Roosevelt was nominated. Willkie on foreign policy was more "internationalist" than Roosevelt. Willkie was promising not to undo any of the social gains. He had opposed them constantly in the past and the hope of those who nominated him was that he would bring all this New Deal business to an end. But he promised to do it bigger and better. There was not much of a campaign, really.

The President was very happy at his election. He was happy at the vindication. He liked to be President. I think he liked the Presidency better than any man I have known who has occupied it. I have not known many Presidents, but I think he liked it better than Truman, Hoover, or Eisenhower. Here was a man who had such physical disabilities that there were not many things that he could do, but he could be President. He enjoyed the part.

The New Deal itself by this time was substantially at an end. In some of the administrative agencies perhaps it was carried on, but it was not extended. The President, as far as domestic policy was concerned, gave all that he had to the country in the first four years, really. There was not much in the second four—a little, but not much. There would have been no justification for a third term, except for the foreign situation. The President's leadership in domestic affairs had accomplished everything that he could accomplish—everything that was in his bag of tricks had been pulled out and exhibited. I do not think there would have been any justification for a third term on the basis of his domestic program. It was the foreign affairs only that warranted it.[36]

At the July 1940 Democratic Party convention in Chicago, FDR was nominated for a third term and Henry Wallace, who had served as Secretary of Agriculture during the first two terms, was nominated as his running mate. In Jackson's oral history, he recounted FDR's perspective and the White House response in general to the prospect that some bizarre letters that Wallace had written would become public during the fall campaign:

Shortly after we returned from Chicago, I was summoned to a hurry-up evening meeting at the White House. Hopkins was present, as were the President, General Watson, Stephen Early, I believe Bernard Baruch, I think Jimmy Byrnes, and it seems to me Senator Robert F. Wagner. Hopkins reported that Paul Block, publisher of the *Pittsburgh Post-Gazette*, had succeeded in buying a series of letters written by Henry Wallace in which there were very many derogatory statements about the President. They were a series of letters that Westbrook Pegler has since published in part. Hopkins had obtained photostatic copies of the letters. How Hopkins had obtained them, I never knew. That was not explained and I asked no questions. The letters had been written sometime past. There had been rumors that there were such letters in existence, but I do not think those rumors had reached the President. Apparently the woman and parties involved had attempted to market them before. Block had finally bought them. They were of a religious character and were thought to be very damaging. Block was the man who had exposed Hugo Black's membership in the Ku Klux Klan after his appointment to the Supreme Court. His power as a promoter of publicity was considerable and there was real anxiety about what to do about it.

I did not have copies of the letters. There was only one copy and that was a photostat that Hopkins had obtained from some source. The letters were not read. They were voluminous. Hopkins summarized their content, insofar as he felt they were damaging. There were references by code names to Secretary of State Cordell Hull, the President, and some other members of the Cabinet in the early days of the New Deal. They were concerned with matters of government and some occultism, mysticism of an Oriental nature, which, it was understood, Wallace had investigated and inquired into in Tibet and elsewhere.

The most serious things from a campaign point of view were intimations about the mental health condition of the President—very personal comments, as I understood it. Their publication at that time, if they were authentic, would have put both Wallace and the President in a very difficult spot.

There were all manner of suggestions as to what to do at this White House meeting, none of which seemed workable. Baruch suggested the possibility of an injunction. That, obviously, would have insured publicity for the letters. Even if it kept the letters themselves from being published, it would have added mystery to damage, which would have made it even more damaging.

The problem was thrashed over at great length. There were discussions as to whether they could be bought. Wallace, of course, was not there. He was up in the West campaigning. We did not know for sure whether the letters were authentic, although there was a general belief that they were. I think the conclusion of everyone in the group was that Wallace had written them. I think that was assumed. There was some handwriting that appeared to be his. I do not know that there was proof of authenticity, but it was assumed. The woman to whom many of the letters were written was a religious cult leader—a cult in which Wallace had had some interest. I was designated to see Mrs. Wallace and to see that she did not make unfortunate responses if she was interviewed, which I did. She did not seem to question that that there had been such correspondence.

Wallace, however, was shown the letters up in Wisconsin or Minnesota—somewhere where he was campaigning—and was asked about them. He said that for several years certain parties had been trying to blackmail him with them. For some reason the letters were never published in the campaign, although we expected momentarily that they would be.

I think those letters left a rather deep impression on Roosevelt, however, and I am not sure that that was not one of the reasons that he was willing to abandon Wallace four years later when Harry Truman was nominated in his place as Vice President.

Finally, at this White House meeting, when all courses had been explored, the President more or less laughed the thing off. He said, "Bob, you've got the FBI. Can't you find Henry in bed with this woman? Can't you turn this into a romance—this writing of letters? Everyone would understand that, but nobody would understand the writing of this kind of letters without any romance in it." We broke up more or less laughing about it in that tone. However, the possibilities of the use of those letters overhung the whole campaign. They were regarded as serious and I have never known why they were not used. I've never known how they could have been met if they had been used. I've never known why they should have been written nor understood the whole problem that they posed as to the personality and mental traits of Wallace. They were a most mysterious element.

So far as I know, the President never brought them up to Wallace. I'm inclined to think that he never did. If they had broken into print, it was not unlikely that newspapers would have harassed Mrs. Wallace about them, and I went to their apartment and talked to her about it. She showed no surprise and no annoyance at my suggestion, and was thoroughly cooperative in agreeing that she would not have given out any statements or any interviews if they had appeared in the paper.

So far as I know, no one connected with the Administration ever confronted Wallace with those letters. I never talked with him about it and I never knew anybody who did. He was not a man with whom people were on terms of great intimacy. He was a rather lonely man, given to speculation and interested in the occult and esoteric. He was something of a mystic.

There is a possibility that Block decided not to publish these because of the fear it would lead to attacks in recrimination about Mr. Willkie's private life. The President was determined that no use of that kind of material should be made. All of us recognized that that kind of campaigning was not only likely to be unfair and injure innocent people, but that it was also bad politics. I never knew why they were left unpublished.[37]

In 1952, Jackson received an inquiry seeking his comments, for a historical publication, on a late 1944 letter in which FDR had recorded his thoughts about seeking a third presidential term in 1940. FDR had written the following:

I hate the fourth term as much as you do—and the third term as well—but I do not worry about it so much as a matter of principle. It would be a mistake, of course, to establish it as a tradition but I think I can well plead extenuating circumstances! The real meat of the question is not the length of term, but the continued opportunity of the voters of the country freely to express themselves every four years. And there is the further question of the personality of the individual. You and I know plenty of people who love power of a certain type and who, with perfectly good intentions, would hate to give it up. I am not one of this type, as you know. For as far as individual preference goes I would, quite honestly, have retired to Hyde Park with infinite pleasure in 1941.

Then there is the other question of the alternative. Willkie was an anomaly who improved greatly in his general thinking after 1940. But, although I liked him personally, I did not feel that he had much knowledge of the world and that he would had to have learned about the world in the school of hard experience. This would have been a rather dangerous experiment in 1940.

As to the last gentleman who was the alternative [Thomas E. Dewey, who in 1940 was the District Attorney of New York County and, after he was elected Governor of New York in 1942, was the Republican presidential nominee who lost to FDR in 1944], I say nothing.[38]

Jackson's 1952 commentary on FDR's letter was the following:

About all that I have opportunity to say in reference to President Roosevelt's letter . . . is that I think it was an honest statement of his views of a third term.

Personally, I should not ordinarily favor a third term, because it is my observation that a President is able to contribute to the country in two terms anything there is in him and if he cannot, there is little hope that he would do better in the third. And that, I think, would have held true with President Roosevelt, except for the very great change that came about with the approach of war. I have good reason to know that in 1937, 1938, and 1939, he was earnestly planning his retirement to Hyde Park, where he hoped to live as a country squire. . . . It became apparent that the politicians of the party would not permit him to name as his successor someone who, he thought, would carry on his policies and that, if he did not continue in person, the work that he valued in his administration might be undone.

Then, long before he had decided to seek a third term, his adversaries began talking about it and denouncing it until the people had come to accept the idea of a third term. Before he announced, and I think before he had reached any decision to abandon the two-term tradition, his opponents had made it apparent that the people were ready to abandon it. This eased the way to his own decision. The breaking-out of war in Europe made the decision for him finally.

This hastily summarizes conclusions that are based on many details.[39]

Toward Congress, the President's attitude was somewhat mercurial. Congress itself is mercurial. Generally he appeared to regard it as unwieldy, uncohesive, incoherent, and without effective leadership. There were individual representatives and senators for whom he had high regard and others he despised and distrusted. But he did not expect the Congress as a whole to supply the initiative necessary in a swift-moving age—the President expected to supply that, and to have it made effective through the representatives of his party.

When the President could not get members of Congress to cooperate with him, he believed in going over their heads to their constituents. The famous 1938 purge proved that this was, at least in those instances, bad political judgment.[40] Roosevelt, during his terms as Governor of New York, had used the Republican legislature as a target instead of a collaborator. Roosevelt had developed the technique and the habit of mind of regarding the legislative body as opposition and of trying to outmaneuver it. He was always playing checkers with the legislature to corner his opposition.

Men are apt to adhere to the pattern by which they have once succeeded, and when he came to Washington, I think he carried over toward

Congress a good deal of the attitude that he had found advantageous in dealing with the New York Legislature. Roosevelt's whole executive career, up to the time he came to Washington, was in dealing with an opposing party in the legislative branch. He had established a pattern of action, which was to propose something that would put them in a hole and never let them out of the hole. When Congress would not respond to his leadership, he was ready to act and appeal to the country for ratification over the heads of elected local representatives. The Court bill, for example, he sprang on the leaders of Congress, who were of his own party and some of whom were in sympathy with his objectives. But his method put them in the hole. A good deal of the legislation that he proposed was brought out as if the Congress were hostile to him. That tended to make it hostile. I think that some of the opposition that he had in Congress might have been less virulent, at least, if he had been a little more willing to take Congress into his plans earlier.[41]

One instance of Roosevelt's readiness to act over the heads of elected representatives was in connection with the Washington airport. During the early part of the Administration, the only airport in Washington was what was called, in an uncomplimentary fashion, I always thought, the Hoover Airport. It consisted of a pasture intersected by a highway. When a plane came in, they had to close the road to traffic and open it again after the plane had landed. It was dangerous, inadequate, and everyone regarded it as long behind the times.[42]

The President had some vision of the coming of air power. He also had some vision of the unfortunate events abroad. He had tried to get Congress to move. It had long been debating about an airport. The matter came up regularly, but Congress was bogged down by contests between different real estate interests. Some of them wanted the airport in Maryland. Some wanted it in Virginia. Some wanted it in one direction from the city and some in another. No progress could be made and little consideration seemed to be given to aviation needs. No money would be appropriated until a site was settled, and no site could be settled because of the conflicting interests.

Finally I, as Solicitor General, happened to attend a Cabinet meeting in the absence of the Attorney General. The President had had surveys made of the possibility of filling in Gravelly Point in the Potomac to make the land for an airport. At this point the President was pretty much disgusted. He had tried to get his own appointee to build it with PWA funds. He pointed out at this Cabinet meeting how London had its Croydon, Paris had its Le Bourget, Berlin had its Templehof, and Washington had a cow pasture. He was determined to bring that situation to an end and have a decent airport in the national capital. He decided that Gravelly Point presented the fewest problems.

The obstacle was that government agencies, Public Works Administration and Works Progress Administration, had difficulties about their money because of congressional restrictions. Some money could not be spent in the District of Columbia, some could only be spent there, and so on. They had been conferring, but the conferences had not produced anything. There also were personal controversies between different agencies that he wanted to put up some money.

At this Cabinet meeting, the President reviewed his difficulties. He turned to me and said, "Bob, I want you to get Harry Hopkins's WPA legal men together with Harold Ickes's PWA legal men at once and knock their heads together until you get that money knocked out of them. Get this straightened out. I want to break ground at Gravelly Point a week from Monday."

The undertaking, as I saw it at the moment, was one in which I expected to fail. Both legal staffs had been studying the matter, however, and I was able to telephone the President by eleven o'clock the next morning to report that he could depend on the money from those sources. He asked me if he was likely to go to jail as a result of it. I told him all that I could promise was to go to jail with him if that would be any comfort. Therefore, without congressional authorization or appropriation, the present Washington airport was begun.[43] Without that Presidential initiative, Washington probably would have faced World War II without an adequate airport.

The President's action in this matter was an instance in which, although the President acts beyond the Constitution, he invades no private right and therefore is probably not subject to injunction by a court. Here was a case where he took nobody's property. He spent some public money, but the Supreme Court long ago held that that could not be enjoined.[44] There was no basis on which anyone could stop him, even though he was perhaps exceeding the powers of his office. But I do not say that he was exceeding the powers of his office—I would certainly go a very long way to find authority to sustain that kind of an exercise of power where the congressional process seemed stalled.[45]

He did the same thing with the destroyers in exchange for bases, as I shall later relate,[46] and when Congress dawdled and diddled about his request for authority for the FBI to tap wires of aliens and persons engaged in sabotage, he simply ordered that it be done.

Looking back on it, I am sure that the Roosevelt technique is the only way that a party leader and the head of state can sometimes deal with the Congress. Congress is so local in its viewpoint—its members have only local constituencies, and their interests often conflict—that its aggregate characteristic is inertia. In addition, it is bogged down with the seniority system, which brings to the top some of the best and some of the worst. In our form of government, initiative, if it is to exist anywhere, perhaps can come only from the executive.

It seemed to be Roosevelt's philosophy that the head of state must be protected. He believed that lower echelons, in the Congress as well as in the executive branch, were expendable and should bear all blame. I never heard him put this in words, but I think he acted upon it and I believe he was right in doing so. No man should enter an administration who is not willing to sacrifice himself politically for it, if it becomes necessary to do so.

An example of what I mean occurred while I was representing the Treasury before the Finance Committee of the Senate in support of the Tax Bill of 1935. It proposed, among other things, a heavy increase in the estate taxes. Senator Pat Harrison of Mississippi, Chairman of the Committee, was not pleased with it. I was in his office when he told the President on the telephone of his dissatisfaction and proposed a compromise by which the tax increase would commence at a considerably higher bracket. Distinctly I heard the President's voice say, "Yes, Pat, that will be satisfactory. We'll accept that if you can get it." I was surprised, for I thought the President was giving away more than he realized.

Evidently that was the case. When the Senate convened on June 25, Senator Harrison stated that he had talked with the President and the President had agreed to that modification, which was welcome to many of the senators. The Treasury then got busy at the White House, and at his later press conference the next day, the President denied the understanding. Senator Harrison was left "holding the bag," as the expression goes, and he cheerfully admitted that perhaps he was mistaken in saying that the President had agreed to it.

I was quite new to Washington and more than little surprised when Senator Harrison assured fellow Senators that he had misunderstood and that the President was undoubtedly right. The President had blundered. But Harrison told me he considered it his duty to take the blame for a misunderstanding rather than to expose the President to loss of prestige through his hasty agreement on the telephone.[47] Senator Harrison was that kind of a soldier. From the point of view of party organization and statecraft, I think he was right, but few of the liberals would have played the game that way.[48]

The Roosevelt attitude toward the judiciary and the struggle it brought on can hardly be condensed into a few paragraphs. While he began life as a lawyer in the office of the famous Carter, Ledyard, and Milburn firm, his mental processes were not those of a lawyer, for legal education is really schooling in a way of thought.[49] He did not really like the judicial process with its slow movement, its concern with detail, its insistence on primary evidence, its deliberation. He wanted short cuts. His favorite Justices of the Supreme Court were Holmes, Brandeis, Cardozo, and Hughes, yet he told me he had agreed to appoint Senator Joseph Robinson, their exact antithesis, if he got the bill through that would give him a vacancy.

Jackson's 1944 draft autobiography includes the following account of President Roosevelt's 1937 Court-packing plan:

The period of my service in the Antitrust Division marked my maximum activity in political and legislative matters, and I became involved in things of the kind far deeper than I had ever wished to be. In 1937, my time was much occupied with three legislative projects. First of all, there was the fight over the reorganization of the Supreme Court, which was precipitated by the message of the President on February 5, 1937. I had spoken at the annual meeting of the New York State Bar Association in January and had made a speech sharply critical of the Supreme Court.[50] It was widely circulated and commented upon, generally—I may say—adversely. Coming so close to the President's message, many jumped to the conclusion that I had acted as a sort of trial balloon to test out public sentiment. As a matter of fact, I knew nothing about the message until I read it in the newspapers on the afternoon it was sent. I was on the train returning from New York, and at Philadelphia a paper purchased aboard the train told the story. I was as much baffled by his proposals as anybody. It is unnecessary here to discuss the weaknesses or character of the proposal, which I have made the subject of separate study.[51] While the proposal seemed to me in many respects unsatisfactory, once the President had become committed to it, it was the only proposal that had a chance, and there was genuine need of some kind of reform in the Supreme Court. Some writers, including Charles Michelson, who was the Democratic Party's chief publicist, have attributed to me a part in the formulation of the plan, and Michelson says that I was a member of the board of strategy.[52] In the first place, I doubt that a strategy board ever existed by any designation of the President. And if such did exist, I was not a member of it.

My first expectation of taking any part in the Court fight came when Senator Henry Ashurst of Arizona, Chairman of the Judiciary Committee, called me and said he would like me to appear as the second witness in favor of the plan, Attorney General Cummings to appear first. I told him that I would do so if my appearance was approved by the President. He intimated that he had called me at the suggestion of the White House and therefore I had no doubt that I would appear. The Attorney General was then in Florida, having gone there for a vacation almost immediately after the bombshell was exploded. He remained there during the critical period and returned only in time to testify. Because he was the person chiefly responsible, I have always had some difficulty understanding how he was willing to commit the prosperity of his brain-child to others. The Attorney General and Mrs. Cummings were at our house for dinner with journalists Barnet and Naomi Nover and Roswell Magill, Under Secretary of the Treasury, somewhat later. He told us with evident pride that the plan was his own and that very few men knew anything of it. He intimated that in the Department only Solicitor General Stanley Reed and Cummings's special assistants Alexander Holtzoff and Carl McFarland knew of it. He was specific in saying that neither Ben Cohen nor Tommy Corcoran knew anything about it. Yet while his plan was being torn asunder, he was vacationing in Florida—a vacation no doubt much needed, but unfortunately timed.

I did not intend to testify without some understanding with the President. I discussed the matter with Solicitor General Reed, who was Acting Attorney General in the absence of Mr. Cummings. We went to the White House and talked with the President. I told him that I could not support the claim that the petitions for writs of *certiorari* were not being properly handled for, in my opinion, the Court was doing a substantially satisfactory task in that respect. I told him, furthermore, that I did not think that he could ever base his fight against the Court on criticism of handling of *certioraris*, for most of the people who would support the President did not know what a *certiorari* was. He said, "It is a pretty terrible platform to stand on, isn't it?" I also told him that I did not think it expedient for me to discuss the matter of the Justices' ages for, in the first place, I had some doubts whether age was the only thing that ailed the Court, particularly in view of the fact that Brandeis was one of its oldest members and also one who Roosevelt would be the last to say needed an alternate. He agreed to that. I told him that in my judgment he should make a straight attack on the doctrine of the Court as embodied in some of its most objectionable decisions and establish that there was a responsibility on Congress for it. He agreed with this line of attack.

Another problem had greatly troubled his supporters. He was to leave on a fishing trip and planned to speak to the country on the subject of the Court fight when he returned. I, in common with many others, felt there was great danger that sentiment would crystallize before that time, and that if his speech was to have any influence it must be delivered promptly. In fact, there were indications that sentiment was already tending to be solidified against the plan. Knowing that I had an appointment, Thomas Corcoran and Herman Oliphant, General Counsel at Treasury, urged me to impress upon the President the necessity of speaking at once. I waded into it and told him I was afraid public sentiment would form against him in his absence, that the sentiment of the bar was almost unanimously against him, and that the bar was the best-informed group existing in every community, while those who naturally favored his program were in the main laymen. I pointed out that his original message did very little to arm these laymen for a discussion and that before he left, he must put in the minds of his lay followers the answers to the questions that were certain to be asked. He made no commitment, but within a half hour after I left the White House, it was announced that he would speak on March 9.[53] He did so, and I was among those who supplied suggestions for that speech. I adopted a quite different treatment of the subject and in my testimony made a frontal attack on the Court's philosophy and attitude toward the problems of the country.

I did not at any time engage in any lobbying for the bill. Thurman Arnold, then a Yale professor and a Wyoming native, and I had lunch with Senator Joseph O'Mahoney of Wyoming and discussed the problem with him, urging, of course, the President's point of view. Stories were rife that promises of patronage were being made. If that was true, I did not know of it, and I doubt very greatly the authenticity of the stories.

I prepared my statement on the Court plan. I went over it with Ben Cohen, Tom Corcoran, Herman Oliphant, and some of the younger men in my own organization. It was never submitted to the White House nor to the Attorney General. It was delivered on the second day of the hearings, March 11, 1937, before a packed hearing room, and a hostile press conceded that it was the strongest presentation of the President's case.

I did not help any other person prepare testimony, nor did I ask any other person to testify. But at the end of about a week it was plain that the case for the President was not going to be greatly strengthened by additional names.

There is no doubt that at this period the Administration suffered a bad attack of over-confidence. Postmaster General Farley was talking about its being "in the bag." Joseph Keenan, who was assistant to the Attorney General, was confidently reporting that the votes were available to pass the bill and that they would not budge. Under these circumstances, the case for the bill was rested and the hearings turned over to the opposition.

Meanwhile, a series of dramatic overrulings of decisions took place in the Supreme Court. I was much interested in the cases in which attacks were made upon the constitutionality of the unemployment compensation and the old-age-benefit provisions of the Social Security Act. After those cases were decided in our favor on May 24, 1937,[54] I saw the President. At that time it had become clear that the original bill could not pass. The strength that had been counted upon had either never been present or had faded away. It had then become a proposal that two members be added to the Court.

I had a long discussion with the President in his study in the evening. I advised him strongly against accepting the compromise of adding two judges to the Court, but urged him instead to avoid a vote by sending a message pointing out that the Court had reconsidered its attitude on many of the questions that had concerned him so greatly, had announced new doctrine in accordance with the contentions of the Administration, and that he withdrew his recommendation, for the time being at least. I pointed out to him that he was in a position to claim the victory in the Court if not to claim one over the Court, and that bitterness which was developing dangerously could be terminated.

The President told me that he thought that would be the wiser thing to do, but that he could not do it at that time. He said candidly that he had promised to appoint Joe Robinson to the Court and that he had committed himself to accepting the proposition of two additional Justices. I argued even further against the plan. I pointed out that if he added Robinson and one other who, I assumed, would be of a more liberal school of thought, the two appointments would offset and he would have made no change in the balance of power on the Court. I told him bluntly that the only excuse that history would accept for packing the Court was that a packing was needed and that it was successfully done, and that to have the odium of packing it and have it fail would be, I feared, the outcome of accepting two additional Justices.

Fate took the matter out of his hands, however. Senator Robinson died on July 14. Without his support, even this compromised plan collapsed, and the President's proposal was defeated. Out of this came great bitterness and there were attempts to purge or defeat in the 1938 Democratic primaries or at the elections some of the senators responsible for the defeat of the Court plan, notably Senators Walter George of Georgia, Millard Tydings of Maryland, and Guy Gillette of Iowa. I took no part in that effort.

During this fight over the Court bill, Senator George came to my office with Archibald Lovett, later judge of the United States District Court for Georgia, and other members of the Georgia Bar Association.[55] The Senator asked me to go to Georgia and speak to the State Bar meeting. I reminded him that he knew my position on the Court plan and that I knew his, that the Court plan was about the only subject the bar was interested in at the time herein discussed, and that if I made a speech in Georgia on that subject it would be construed as an attack upon him. Senator George said simply, and I felt with entire sincerity, "The people of my state are entitled to hear both sides of this question. A good many of them, perhaps most of them, will agree with you. I shall not be surprised if the position I have taken means the end of my political life, but I do not feel that I could do any differently, no matter what it meant to me. I want you to go to Georgia and speak, as the Bar there want to hear you, and I want you to say to them just what you think without regard to its effect on me." I went to Georgia in late May to make the speech, but I did not mention the Court plan directly.[56]

It is not realistic to hold the President or his Attorney General responsible for appointments to the District Court benches without recognizing that under our constitutional system they have lawfully become senatorial patronage.[57] This is due to the custom of senatorial courtesy, under which a senator, by making personal objections, can prevent the confirmation of any appointee to his District Bench.

The President challenged and tested this practice in Virginia, by making a district judge appointment in the summer of 1938 without consulting Senators Carter Glass and Harry Byrd, but I think after consultation with Governor James H. Price, who was at odds with the senators. That man, whose name was Floyd Roberts, was admittedly a competent man to hold the position, but because of the failure of the President to consult them, Senators Glass and Byrd opposed the confirmation.[58] It became very plain that the President could not get that man confirmed. The President was plainly defeated. It was a stalemate. He would not withdraw the nomination. The post was vacant.

One day we were down on the President's yacht over a weekend, fishing and relaxing. The President said, "I've got a job for you, Bob, and for 'Pa' Watson. I want you to go down to Charlottesville and see if you can't get Armistead M. Dobie, the Dean of the University of Virginia Law School, to accept the appointment as district judge. I think if I send his name to the Senate, the Senators from Virginia will not dare to turn him down." He thought Glass and Byrd would support Dobie and thereby break the deadlock without loss of face to anybody.

It was plain that the contest at that point had become one of personal prestige, and the President wanted to put one over that they would not dare resist. This was when I was Solicitor General, not Attorney General. He was apparently handling the matter quite independently of Attorney General Murphy. He said that there was a vacancy coming up on the Fourth Circuit Court of Appeals, and that if Dobie accepted the appointment to the district court, we could say that the President would feel that he should be promoted to the Court of Appeals when the vacancy occurred.

So "Pa" Watson and I took a White House car and made an appointment to meet Dean Dobie at the Farmington Country Club in Charlottesville. We sailed forth. When we got in the vicinity, "Pa" Watson, in his genial southern way, said, "Now, Bob, you handle the heavy thinking in this, and I'll go out and get a bottle of bourbon." I talked with Dean Dobie while "Pa" took a little trip. When "Pa" came back, I introduced him to "Judge" Dobie. The Dean had agreed to accept the appointment. About ten o'clock, after we had had dinner and duly induced the Dean to accept, we telephoned the President that we had met the enemy and he was ours. The President immediately sent his name to the Senate, and there was a prompt announcement from Senators Byrd and Glass that they would vote for his confirmation.[59]

During the 1940 campaign, the President told me that Christopher Sullivan, leader of Tammany Hall, had complained that Tammany had gotten no federal judicial appointment, that it had good men, and that it had been discriminated against in the Southern District of New York. Now, Tammany Hall did have some good men. The head of the Tammany law committee for a long time was John Godfrey Saxe—he's not now (1952) living—an eminently able man. If the Tammany organization would have allowed him to choose, he could have named any number of competent, honest, reputable men. The President told me, a little sheepishly, that he had promised Sullivan that he could decide who should fill a federal judgeship in New York. He said "You know, Christy claims that I have done nothing for Tammany Hall and that the judgeships there, as well as most of the other posts, have gone to his enemies." But he added quickly, "I have told him, however, that whoever he suggests must have the approval of the Bar Association. You know," he said, "when I was Governor, I found that was a great protection. The rest is up to you, Bob."

Sullivan submitted name after name. Some were so obscure that they were unknown to the bar committee or to the Judges. Some had records so bad as to preclude their appointment even if the Bar Association had recommended them. This was inexcusable in an organization that numbered many able lawyer members of high standing.

On and on it dragged and name after name came up until one day, in sheer disgust, I said that we must fill the place. I thought we had given Sullivan chances enough. The President talked with District Attorney John Mack of Poughkeepsie, the President's original political sponsor and a man in whom he had great confidence. Mack proposed that John Bright, an upstate lawyer from outside of Sullivan's bailiwick, be named.

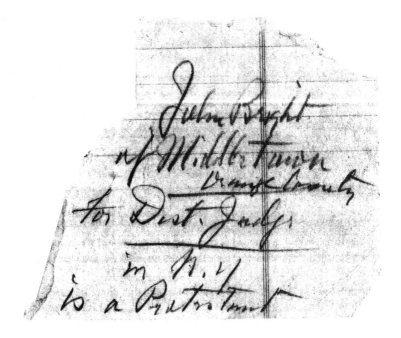

I called Bright on the telephone and asked him if he would accept the appointment. He was completely astonished that he was being picked out.[60] We sent his name to the Senate and he was confirmed. He made an excellent judge, but unfortunately he did not live long. Sullivan was of course very much annoyed to think that he had not gotten a Tammany man named. Tammany thought it was double-crossed. It was—by the stupidity of its leader.[61]

Such was Roosevelt the party leader, the holder of the nation's highest political office. Political life is a succession of making and breaking friendships and alliances, of taking and receding from positions on public questions. But one who expects to find the real source of Roosevelt's great power in his management of party machinery or manipulation of the checks and balances of government will be disappointed. Here he was skillful and experienced, but his underlying strength was not with Congress, nor was it with the party leaders. It was with the great masses of warmhearted people who saw in him a champion and enlisted in his cause.

3

THAT MAN AS LAWYER

WHILE ROOSEVELT was labeled a Wall Street lawyer at the time of his debut in politics as a New York State senator, it is plain that he was born for politics, not for the law. I doubt if he ever liked the drudgery and detail of the law, and he was always impatient of the slow and exacting judicial process.

His attitude toward the law and the lawyers was indicated by his preference in 1931 for Raymond Moley, a political scientist, rather than a lawyer, as head of the New York commission to investigate the administration of justice. It was also clear when the Walter-Logan bill[1] was passed by Congress in 1940 and he asked me to prepare a veto message. There were many defects of a rather technical character in the bill. It carried some unintended consequences. I outlined these in a letter to him and he attached it to his veto message.[2] But the message itself spoke strongly in favor of the administrative process as against the more legalistic rules applied in judicial review.[3] The Walter-Logan bill represented the way lawyers felt about administrative agencies. Congress had gone to extremes and would have destroyed the administrative process. All of this was gone over with Roosevelt carefully and the veto message reflected his own attitude. It was true, however, that the legal profession is and always has been a conservative influence. And on the whole, its function in society is such that its contribution will necessarily be on the side of conservatism in the balance of social forces.[4]

Roosevelt was a strong skeptic of legal reasoning and criticized many attitudes of lawyers and members of Congress for being legalistic. He found great enjoyment in a story, a true story, that I told him of an experience in the Bureau of Internal Revenue. The question became important in the application of tax law as to just when a marriage was effected. The question was referred for an opinion to a young man just out of law school. He found the rule that the law does not recognize a fraction of a day. He also found a rule that in the service of process, the first day is excluded and the count begins on the day after the date of service. Combining these two, he came up with the conclusion that a marriage is legally effective on the day following the date of the ceremony. Needless to say, this impractical conclusion was not issued as an opinion, but it does illustrate how by the use of perfectly good premises, a very farfetched conclusion can sometimes be reached that will have every appearance of good legal reasoning.

I was unable to agree with the President as to the function of the Department of Justice in the government. It was my idea to keep the Department purely a law office and not have it engage in the administration of legislation. This was based on my view that the best quality in a lawyer's advice is disinterestedness, that he is never disinterested where he is himself a litigant, and that if the Department were in a detached position, it would often be able to prevent ill-advised litigations from getting into the courts with unfortunate results. But he did not share that feeling.

When he decided to remove the Bureau of Immigration and Naturalization from the Labor Department, he insisted that it come to the Department of Justice.[5] This matter began on May 14, 1940, when Sumner Welles, the Under Secretary of State, had lunch with me in my office. For some time, Welles had been sponsoring a suggestion that Immigration should be transferred from the Department of Labor to the Department of Justice. The President intimated that he had it under consideration. Other agencies, including a good many of the committees of Congress concerned with immigration and naturalization problems, had favored it.

Personally, I did not want it. In the first place, I did not think that the Department of Justice and the Federal Bureau of Investigation were adapted to the alien problem. To mix the pursuit of criminals with the control of aliens seemed to me to have unfortunate implications. Another thing I was concerned about was that I did not want the Department of Justice to become itself a litigant in the courts over these matters. It seemed to me that the value of legal counsel is in the detachment of the adviser from the advised, and that if we put these departments under the administration of the Department of Justice, it immediately would lose its detachment and have no detached advisers. It would itself become a litigant defending its own acts, and the unhappy result would be that the Attorney General would lose his standing for disinterestedness before the courts.

Those objections the President rather laughed off as being theoretical. Welles also did not give them much consideration. It became plain to me that it was going to be handed to us. The President, in one of our discussions of the subject, said "Why, Bob, you're the only man in the government who isn't coming to me asking for more employees, more money, and a bigger department. Half my time is spent settling fights between Ickes and Wallace and Hopkins and Ickes over extensions of their jurisdictions. Here you are resisting taking a whole bureau that I'm trying to give you." Of course he laughed when he said it. He knew perfectly well that the transfer was one that I did not welcome.

There was another reason. I did not feel that the criticisms of Frances Perkins and her handling of the Labor Department were justified. It is true she made mistakes, but in general I had a very high opinion of Frances Perkins's motives. I had complete confidence in her loyalty and a feeling that the fact that she was not getting a fair deal from the public, the press, and Congress for what she was trying to do was probably a foretaste of what would be awaiting me if I took over that bureau. I found that it was.

Welles prepared a memorandum, dated May 18, 1940, to the President about the transfer of the departments and submitted it to me. It was a very competent job. But I had previously notified Welles by letter on May 15 that I did not want the responsibility for the Bureau of Immigration and Naturalization, that I should like some further time to make some studies of it, and generally demurring to the proposition.

On May 21, the President asked me to lunch and abruptly handed me an executive order that proposed immediate transfer of the Bureau of Immigration and Naturalization from the Department of Labor to the Department of Justice. As I noted at the time, "he turned to his soup and left the move to me."[6] He knew that it was unwelcome news to me.

I read the order and we then had a discussion of the thing, which followed lines that we had discussed previously. I told him that I did not think immigration could be handled acceptably by me any more than it had by Frances Perkins. Of course, his move was more or less necessitated by the 1940 campaign. There was a feeling of distrust of the Department of Labor. It was probably necessary politically for him to make some move that would tend to shield him from that criticism and from the suggestion that the Bureau was not being vigorously administered.

I told the President that there was, in my opinion, somewhat the same tendency in America to make goats of all aliens that in Germany had made goats of all Jews, and that it was going to be very difficult to maintain a decent administration. I favored a stronger border control and stricter supervision of aliens in the country than we had had in the past, but I was opposed to a policy of persecuting or prosecuting aliens just because of alienage. Of course, he agreed with all this.

I then suggested that he ought to set up a separate agency as a part of the national defense to handle the matter of alien control, sabotage, espionage, and subversive activities. These matters were more nearly allied to defense than to the ordinary administration of justice and the methods of handling them should be preventive rather than remedial.

The President was not, however, persuaded—my suggestion was rather peremptorily turned down. He said that, at least for the time being, the Bureau must go to the Department of Justice. It was the only place that was adequately prepared to handle it. I had already talked with Solicitor General Francis Biddle, who was rather willing to undertake administrative work as I had not been when I was Solicitor General. I had arranged that if we had to take the Bureau, Biddle would supervise the transfer.

I then held a press conference on May 23, 1940, and tried to break the news of our policy as gently as possible. The aliens had a very strong feeling that they should not be under the supervision of the Federal Bureau of Investigation. This was because they did not feel they were criminals and the FBI was regarded as an arm of the criminal administration, and quite rightly. I therefore pointed out that this Bureau of Immigration and Naturalization would not be under, nor mingled with, any existing division or bureau, but would be a separate bureau with an administrative status similar to the FBI or the Bureau of Prisons. That tended to allay some suspicions that we were going to treat aliens as suspected criminals. I also announced that Solicitor General Biddle would handle the integration of the new bureau with the Department of Justice.[7]

One of the first steps to undertake concerned the list that was available of aliens who had entered the country subsequent to January 1, 1939, as visitors. It had been suggested in the Welles memorandum that they be checked. The job was entirely beyond the capacity to do quickly and so we undertook spot checking of the visitors to determine whether they had departed in accordance with their visas and what their mission in this country apparently was.

By May 29, 1940, we had made some studies on the subject of immigration and naturalization and the cost of the work that would be put upon us in connection with it. The appropriations that had been made available to Madame Perkins were entirely inadequate for the intensified border patrol, the additional checking of aliens, and so forth.

So I went to the President to point out that we must have an estimated

$9 million for the additional work of the Bureau of Immigration and Naturalization. The President was in a very bad mood. He exploded in what I described at the time as "the worst fit of temper I have seen in his public life," and I had seen him in some very vexing circumstances.[8] He said that the War Department had just sent estimates of its needs in excess of those that he had communicated to Congress in the defense message, which put him on the spot. If he did not actually send the message to Congress, it would leak out and he would be accused of not giving the Army adequate backing. If he did send it, it would be said that his defense message had not been adequately considered and would give his enemies ammunition in the campaign. He did not relish this dilemma.

This was a rather unhappy introduction for the request I was about to make, which fell under about the same heading. So I took it head on. I told him I had the same kind of thing to present to him. I had to ask for $9 million more than had been estimated in the budget, due to expansion of work beyond anything that we had calculated, or that had been calculated by the Department of Labor. Of course, inasmuch as the Bureau had just been wished on to me, I was not responsible personally for the former estimates. As I had taken it very unwillingly, he was not in a very good position to deny my request, but he did not give me a very prompt answer.

The President instead went on to the subject of his irritation with French Ambassador René St. Quentin, who had come out of the President's office as I came in. The Ambassador had seemed cheerful, and, from everything that one could gather from his appearance and from our brief discussion, he had had a pleasant interview. He took a surprisingly optimistic view of the news that Germany had attacked France. The President's view was quite the opposite. He damned St. Quentin as a dumb career diplomat. The President had asked him what would be done if, as seemed possible, the Germans overran France and similar questions. To all, the Ambassador had answered, "The French people will never live under such conditions"—all of which seemed very unrealistic to the President.

Eventually, however, the President mellowed up, and I got the necessary funds.[9]

We took over the immigration bureau bodily from the Department of Labor, except for the commissioner, who was James Lawrence Houghteling. Lawrence Houghteling was married to a Delano girl and was related to the President. Houghteling did not come over to the Department of Justice. A good deal of the criticism, which I thought had been unjust, had centered on him, and it was necessary in connection with the move, as the President felt, and I was agreed, that a new commissioner replace Houghteling. We eventually got Lemuel Braddock Schofield of Philadelphia to act as commissioner. He was suggested by Biddle, who knew him. Schofield had been police commissioner in Philadelphia. He was a lawyer, and the Schofield family came from Warren County, Pennsylvania, so I knew his forebears by reputation.[10] I had a view that he would be an effective commissioner in two respects. One was that he would be a vigilant man in doing his duty. The other was that he would impress the congressional committees as such.

We had a very considerable problem with the rising tide of feeling against all immigrants and a suspicion of all kinds of misdoings on their part. We had to present Congress such an administrative program that there would not be a lot of hostile legislation passed, which was threatened in many sources. I think Schofield won the confidence of the committees and was quite effective in his office in most respects.

We had to employ the Federal Bureau of Investigation to do some of the checking of aliens because they had the existing force and we did not have it in any other form. We built up within the Bureau of Immigration, however, an investigative staff. It clashed with the FBI at some points. There were some disagreements, but we endeavored to maintain and to begin the creation of a separate bureau, because the objections to having an alien investigated by the FBI seemed very legitimate. The mere matter of inquiry among an alien's neighbors as to what he had done, what he was doing, if it was conducted as an immigration matter, was one thing. If the FBI went into an inquiry as to an individual, it raised suspicions about him that were very objectionable. We endeavored to handle immigration as an entirely separate matter from the criminal investigations. It was very difficult, and sometimes they overlapped.[11]

Although the alien property problem—what to do with enemy property in the United States once war began—was only foreseen (it had not yet arrived) when I left the Department of Justice in 1941, it was the President's insistence that that too should be handled in the Department, even though there again the Attorney General was a litigant. I also did not desire the Department of Justice to be the agency to conduct hearings for conscientious objectors under the Conscription Act, but here again I was overruled.[12]

After I left the Department and we were at war, I was a guest with the President on a weekend in April 1942 at General Watson's Charlottesville home.[13] The President asked me what I would think of his appointing a White House Counsel to be his always-on-hand adviser on matters of law. I told him I thought very little of it, because the Attorney General of the United States is by law his responsible legal adviser[14] and to put another lawyer between the President and the Attorney General could not have good administrative results. If there was disagreement between them, the Attorney General would still be the responsible officer, although not the one closest to the President. If they agreed, the post was superfluous and, in any event, likely to result in a great deal of delay. I suggested that if he did not trust his Attorney General to be his adviser, he ought to make a change in that office. I went so far as to say that if I were the Attorney General, I would resign if an officer were put in that position. The President did not agree, however, and told me that he had already spoken to Judge Samuel Rosenman about acting in that capacity. Of course Judge Rosenman, with his tact, handled the situation without conflict with Attorney General Biddle and, by reason of his long association and intimacy with Roosevelt, became the most potent of legal advisers.[15]

It so happened that during the legal battles over the New Deal, I was twice with the President when he had occasion to express his views of cases pending in court. One was on the night of January 10, 1935, when we were discussing the tax message. The Attorney General, Homer Cummings, had that day been arguing the *Gold Clause* cases resulting from the devaluation of the dollar.[16] Some very disturbing questions had been put to him from the bench and these the President viewed as an indication that the devaluation policy might be held unconstitutional, with disastrous results to the Treasury.[17] It would have enormously increased the obligations of the government and would have caused a good deal of chaos in the nation's finances. Naturally the Secretary of the Treasury, Henry Morgenthau, was very much concerned about it. The President asked what could be done in case the Court decision went against the government, how the government could be protected against the chaos that would follow. Outright defiance of the Court was possible.

The President was greatly concerned about the possible outcome of that case and was quite determined that he just could not accept an adverse decision. He frankly asked about methods of overcoming an adverse decision. I had read and mentioned to him an article by Ratner in the *Political Science Quarterly*, which pointed out that President Grant had named two additional Justices to the Supreme Court for the purpose of reversing the Court's previously announced decision on the legal tender issue.[18] We discussed the possibility of enlarging the Court. Two days later, on January 12, 1935, I supplied a memorandum to the President reminding him that a simpler method might be to protect the Treasury by invoking the doctrine of sovereign immunity and refusing to give consent to actions against the United States growing out of the devaluation measures.[19] The statute of consent was limited so as not to permit any claim growing out of the destruction or taking of property during the Civil War. I suggested that it would be possible to protect the Treasury from a multiplicity of litigations by amendment of that statute to provide that no claim could be prosecuted against the United States growing out of the gold proclamation and the devaluation. Even if the United States would wish to meet the obligations that an adverse decision might impose upon the Treasury, there should be some procedure by which the amount should be determined outside of court. Later I discussed this with the President and I think this plan would have been adopted—a withdrawal of consent to be sued. None of these steps became necessary at the time because the *Gold Clause* cases were so decided as not to increase the liabilities of the government. But an adverse decision of those cases would, in my judgment, have precipitated a controversy at that time between the Executive and the Courts.[20]

I also happened to be in a midday conference with him on May 27, 1935, with other members of the Treasury when the telephone rang and he received the news from Don Richberg, General Counsel of the National Recovery Administration, that the *Schechter* case had been lost and the NRA held unconstitutional.[21] The conversation at the President's end of the line ran something like this: "You mean it was unanimous against us? Where was old Isaiah?" This was a favorite characterization of Justice Brandeis. He then asked, "What about Ben Cardozo?" He then told us that the decision had gone against the government by all members of the Court. It was this feature that shocked him most. But he was already in political trouble over the NRA and the chances of getting the extension of its life depended on the outcome of a bitter political battle. We suggested to him that perhaps he had been relieved by the Court of a serious problem. He seemed inclined to agree with that view of it and I was somewhat surprised to read some days later of his press conference remarks, which were construed as being rather bitter, about the decision taking us back to the "horse and buggy" days.[22] I attributed the interview to the influence of some partisans of NRA, perhaps Richberg. Although I have no direct evidence of that, I suspected that Don, who felt very much annoyed at the defeat, had convinced the President that it was really a disaster after all. The NRA had reached the point where it was doubtful if it was not fostering monopoly in this country. Most of the people in Washington, who held somewhat the Brandeis negative view of "bigness," of monopoly, and of concentration of power, had come to fear NRA. A considerable number of senators held a similar view. As a temporary economic revival measure, it had, in my judgment, served a very important and useful purpose. As a permanent or long-continued policy, it seemed heading in the wrong direction.[23]

The President's battle with the Supreme Court never interfered with cordial personal relations between him and Chief Justice Hughes. Both had been Governor of New York and both evidently had enjoyed the experience—each addressed the other as "Governor." Despite many differences, they respected each other. This was obvious to one who saw the two men together. An incident will indicate the easy relations between them. After the election of 1940, I, as Attorney General, was invited to accompany the Court when it paid its annual visit of respect to the President. The President and the Chief Justice were discussing their days as Governor where they had had somewhat similar battles. Roosevelt had never concealed his admiration for the Hughes administration of that office. Finally, with a twinkle in his eye, the Chief Justice said, "I hope you won't mind, after I administer the oath to you the third time, if I lean over and quietly ask, 'Governor, is this getting to be a habit?'" They both broke into hearty laughs at the kind of passage that could only occur between men who had no deep-seated enmities, even if they had differences of opinion.

Jackson expanded on his admiration for Chief Justice Charles Evans Hughes, and thus indirectly on the similar qualities Jackson saw in FDR, in his 1944 draft autobiography:

Purely apart from their abilities or attainments, merely as personalities, Chief Justice Hughes and the President outshone every other presence. They were quite different, but when they were together, as I saw them several times when the Court called upon the President and as Solicitor General I accompanied them, one saw two magnificent but very different types. The Chief Justice had an external severity that contrasted with the President's external urbanity. But Hughes was one of the kindest men, and no person who saw him preside over the Supreme Court will ever have any other standard of perfection in a presiding officer. He was firm and prompt, dignified and kindly. He rarely interrupted counsel but gave them every opportunity to discuss their cases as long as they stuck to the point. He tolerated no personalities or wanderings from the issue, and he could sum up in two or three questions a whole lawsuit. He never used his position on the bench to embarrass counsel or to heckle them, and if counsel were frightened or timid or incompetent, he often went out of his way to make sure that their position was fully brought out. He was a model of dignity.[24]

As a lawyer-president, Roosevelt was not the strong champion of so-called civil rights that some of his appointees on the Supreme Court became. The only case that I recall in which he declined to abide by a decision of the Supreme Court was its decision that federal law enforcement officers could not legally tap wires. Wire tapping had been used in the Department of Justice by my predecessors. After the decision in *Nardone v. United States*[25] came down in late 1939, I as Attorney General quickly issued an order to discontinue all use of the interception of wire communications.[26] This was in the days preceding the war, however, when every effort to spy upon our preparations and to retard production that might be helpful to the allies was taking place. Without wire tapping, the Federal Bureau of Investigation was unable to cope with the problem of espionage and sabotage.

The President discussed the matter with me and said he could not believe that the Supreme Court could mean that the enemies of this country could use its communication system and not be detected. He did not see the tapping of wires under such circumstances as an invasion of civil rights. We tried in vain to get legislation to authorize it but Congress bogged down in debate. All efforts to obtain legislation failed, and finally, as the situation grew more desperate, the President's patience failed. On May 21, 1940, after going over the situation carefully, and after consultation with me, the President sent a memorandum to me in which he said that he agreed with the broad purpose of the Supreme Court decision relating to wire tapping, and that in general it was a sound practice as wire tapping might lead to abuse of civil rights. But, he said, that he was convinced that the Supreme Court never intended to apply the rule to grave matters involving the defense of the nation. He said it was too late to do anything about it after fifth columns had succeeded in sabotage and that

> You are, therefore, authorized and directed in such cases as you may approve, after investigation of the need in each case, to authorize the necessary investigating agents that they are at liberty to secure information by listening devices direct to the conversation or other communications of persons suspected of subversive activities against the Government of the United States, including suspected spies. You are requested furthermore to limit these investigations so conducted to a minimum and to limit them insofar as possible to aliens.[27]

I had not liked this approach to the problem. It seemed to me that wire tapping was a source of real danger if it was not adequately supervised, and that the secret of the proper use of wire tapping was a highly responsible use in a limited number of cases, defined by law, and making wire tapping criminal outside of those purposes or limits.

The memorandum of the President limited the cases in which we were authorized by his authority to use wire taps. It fixed the responsibility pretty clearly for seeing that those limitations were observed. So far as I know, during my time there, FBI Director J. Edgar Hoover was careful to remain within those bounds. He reported to me regularly the taps that were made and usually obtained authorization in advance. There might have been some circumstances under which I was not available and he did not. But I had regular reports and was pretty closely in touch with that sort of thing to make sure that it was not abused. I think that Hoover had no desire to abuse it. He was interested in those major offenses, and not in minor ones. The fact that he refused to go into labor matters at the request of the War Department and supervise labor conversations showed a restraint in the use of his powers for which, I may say, he was never given credit outside.

I tried to get authority from Congress for wire tapping limited to espionage, sabotage, extortion, and kidnapping cases. The President supported that, but a House resolution sought generally to authorize FBI wire tapping "in the interests of national defense." I filed a letter with Congressman Emanuel Celler, who was heading the House investigation, pointing out the need for specific authorization with safeguards. This proposal was supported by Alexander Holtzoff, the special assistant to the Attorney General, but it was opposed by Lee Pressman, the General Counsel of the Congress of Industrial Organizations who, it since appears, was at one time a member of a Communist cell. It was also opposed by the American Civil Liberties Union, by Alexander F. Whitney of the Brotherhood of Railroad Trainmen, and others of liberal persuasion, including John L. Lewis.

While I was on the boat with the President on a fishing trip in the spring of 1941,[28] I learned that James Lawrence Fly, Chairman of the Federal Communications Commission, had gone before the Judiciary Committee and made a very vigorous attack on the legislation which the President had supported and which I was supporting.[29] The President was quite annoyed at his action in doing it and we attempted to obtain a copy of his testimony. It was with the greatest difficulty that we obtained any copy, since his testimony had been given in executive session. He had followed the line, however, which most of the so-called liberals had taken, that there should be no wire tapping, and which, as an ideal, is quite a different thing than the practice that had prevailed. At any rate, no action was taken.[30]

The President was also severe in matters of deportation. He wanted the Princess Stephanie von Hohenlohe,[31] a close associate of German government officials, deported regardless of the fact that papers for admission to another country could not be obtained. She was in this country and carrying on a great many activities. According to our information, she went back and forth a great deal between Sir William Wiseman, of the British intelligence staff in this country,[32] Captain Fritz Wiedemann—Wiedemann being the German consul in San Francisco and a friend of Hitler's—and others. His relations with Hitler were unusually close. She was here on a visitor's permit that had expired. We declined to renew it. There were many, many reasons to believe that she was active in a type of espionage, or at least was concerning herself with matters that were none of her business.

She was, however, a citizen, I believe, of Hungary. The State Department was applied to, as usual, to obtain a passport on which she could be returned. They were unable to get one. They were unable to get a passport to admit her to any other country.

For some reason—I never knew the source of the needling of the President—the President had a particular dislike for the Princess Hohenlohe and her activities. He rode me rather hard about it when it was perfectly obvious that I could not dispose of her, except if the State Department got the passport. It seemed to me that his criticism should have been of the State

Department rather than of me. His criticism was always good natured, but usually took the form of kidding me for not wanting to part with "that Hohenlohe woman" or my "girlfriend."[33]

She finally was before the United States courts on writ of *habeas corpus*. I again applied to the State Department to get some passports so that we could deport her, but as long as I was Attorney General we were never able to deport her. What became of the lady after that, I do not know.[34] There was considerable agitation in the press about it. She seemed to become sort of a symbol of the alien who was suspected of disloyal activities to this country. I could not say that her activities amounted to espionage. It was not at all certain that there were not some kinds of negotiations between Sir William Wiseman and Fritz Wiedemann, in which she was a go-between. It was never entirely clear to me what her activities really were. She, of course, claimed that they were not hostile to the United States and that she was not engaged in any kind of espionage.[35]

Perhaps the sharpest instance of the President's limited commitment to civil rights was a disagreement between the Department of Justice and the War Department over methods of investigating labor matters. It was reported to me that the President had given a "green light," as it was said, to methods of investigations that had long since been prohibited to the Federal Bureau of Investigation as unethical. Such methods were apparently not precluded to Army Intelligence or Navy Intelligence, and they believed that the FBI should be as ruthless. A very sharp correspondence ensued,[36] but the President himself was apparently intent to let the methods of the military prevail.

The President had directed the FBI to take care of espionage and sabotage, but of course the War Department and the Navy Department claimed particular jurisdiction over naval and army installations. They claimed particular jurisdiction to obtain military or naval intelligence. We made no effort to obtain military or naval intelligence. They had their own military police and their policing, in a sense, of the plants that were working for them and the labor. We had a number of strikes that were Communist-inspired, undoubtedly. At least they were led by Communists. Harold Christoffel in the Allis-Chalmers strike and Harry Bridges in the North American Aviation strike were examples. The Army and the Navy felt that because the responsibility for production was put upon them, it was their affair if there was a slowdown or sabotage of any kind in these plants.

The matter of other agencies doing the work of the FBI came to the attention of the President. J. Edgar Hoover frequently sent reports to the President—often directly to the President, although sometimes through

me. Sometimes the President conferred with Hoover. He was very much
concerned about his jurisdiction because he did not want conflicts with the
other departments. It was impossible to delineate a very exact line. It had
to be worked out from time to time.

Hoover had told Assistant Secretary of War John McCloy that he could
not conduct any investigation in reference to labor relations that involved
wire tapping or other unethical practices in reference to labor relations.
McCloy had said that he intended to seek a conference with me for the purpose of determining whether it could not be worked out that the FBI
would be instructed to disregard technicalities and investigate these cases in
a vigorous manner.

The following Monday, April 28, 1941, Under Secretary Robert Patterson
and McCloy of the War Department called on me. I sent a memorandum
of the call to the President because they said that the President had given
them a "green light" to the proposition. The proposition, as I understood
it, was that the labor disturbances were to be investigated by methods quite
different than had prevailed in the Department of Justice. They frankly
complained that investigations were confined within the limits of the law.
They thought that they should be unrestrained in wire tapping, stealing of
evidence, breaking in to obtain evidence, conducting unlimited search and
seizures, use of Dictaphones, and all other methods of the kind.

I took a very strong position against it, both with the President and with
them. I told them that such methods would demoralize the Department of
Justice and bring it into disrepute with the other departments, that we did
not have the type of men who would handle these things and did not want
them in the Department, and that whether such a unit should be set up
somewhere also was not for me to say, but that I did not want it in the
Department of Justice. I thought that while our methods were slower, we
would eventually get whatever evidence there was of any serious sabotage.
There was no situation that warranted us in departing from our methods.

I talked with Hoover and he agreed fully with the letter that I sent to
the President. I then advised Secretary Patterson and McCloy that we could
not set up such a unit in the Bureau and we could not loan the men elsewhere.

A reply was made to me by Assistant Secretary McCloy in which he
thought that I had interpreted the suggestion as primarily one to investigate labor leaders through use of illegal methods. He wanted it understood
that it was not to investigate labor leaders, as such, but to investigate anyone who they thought was causing stoppages, slowdowns, strikes, or unrest
in the plants. It seemed to him that in an emergency, the government

should take all measures necessary to detect and suppress activities, even though such measures include interception of messages by mail, wire, and so forth. He felt that all of that was desirable and that the government could not avoid responsibility for taking such measures.

I replied to that, perhaps rather sharply, and rejected the proposal. I told him that there was no possibility of going along with him. I had been urging the committees of Congress to amend the law that forbade the use of intercepted messages. I had met bitter opposition and I had not had the help of any men from any department of government, except from the President of the United States. I said that these efforts to broaden our powers so that we could do the things McCloy was asking us to do had not been supported by other branches of the government. Meanwhile, I did not propose to engage in the practices that he suggested without authorization. I said that our men were not trained for that kind of work and that I did not want men about who were. I added that "[t]he man who today will rifle your desk for me, tomorrow will rifle mine for someone else. I just don't want that type of fellow in my outfit."[37]

The War Department replied, saying that they would help all they could with the legislation, but nothing was ever done that was at all effective. The legislation died. It never was enacted.[38]

Fortunately, when the war came, the Communist was soon the subject of the Nazi attack. The Communists then became more patriotic than the patriots. It was the Communist underground that we had chief reason to fear, for the Nazis never had an extensively organized espionage or sabotage ring in this country. The Communists, on the other hand, had planted their men in strategic positions in the labor movement. Had the war continued with Russia on the side of Hitler, there is no doubt that there would have been espionage and sabotage on a large scale, and there is no doubt in my mind that President Roosevelt would have taken most ruthless methods to suppress it. He had no patience with treason, and he did not share the extreme position about civil rights that some of his followers have taken.

In his oral history, Jackson explained that FDR generally refrained, once he had appointed Jackson to the Supreme Court, from questioning him about the work of that independent branch of government:

Roosevelt was often accused of packing the Court and of attempting to get judges who would decide cases his way. I voted to decide cases against the administration and for the administration, without any reference to what he might think. After I came on the Court, he never mentioned but one decision to me. We had a case here in which a mutiny had occurred on board a ship. The seamen had gathered and refused to take orders. It was a strike. They claimed that they had the right to strike, that they could take that kind of action, and that they were protected by the National Labor Relations Act in doing so. I had voted that they could not. There had been a very strong dissent.[39]

One night we were playing cards and the President said to me, "By the way, Bob, how did you vote on that question of the mutiny on ship-board?"

I was a little annoyed because I thought he was going to criticize me.[40] "Well," I said, "I voted that those fellows had no right to have a strike on shipboard. The captain had a right to order them to their posts. When they disobeyed, they were in trouble."

He said, "My God, I don't see how anybody could take any different view of it." Instead of being critical of me, he was critical of the people who took a different view of it. That is the only decision of the Court that he ever asked me about or discussed with me as long as he lived, and I saw him quite frequently in a social way."[41]

Jackson's oral history includes this general conclusion regarding FDR and law:

The President had a tendency to think in terms of right and wrong, instead of terms of legal and illegal. Because he thought that his motives were always good for the things that he wanted to do, he found difficulty in thinking that there could be legal limitations on them. The President was not a legalistic-minded person. He was not an economic-minded person. He was a strong thinker in terms of right and wrong, for which he frequently went back to quotations from the Scriptures. Certain things just were not right in his view.[42]

THAT MAN AS COMMANDER-IN-CHIEF

THIS WAS HIS constitutional role and it was one that he liked. As the war in Europe became more likely to involve us, he devoted more and more time to activities that fell under that rubric of authority. I was not with his Administration during the war, having gone on to the Supreme Court in June 1941. It is not mine to recite on this subject beyond rather casual observations made when I saw him on social occasions thereafter.

Despite this disclaimer, Jackson was, as Solicitor General and then as Attorney General, involved during 1939–1941 in many of the preparations for war. On Thursday, September 7, 1939, Jackson dictated for his files a memorandum that described his presence at the White House and some of his dealings with the President as the war in Europe began:

After some six weeks' family vacation, in which I had driven to the west coast and back, I planned to go to Jamestown, New York, to visit my mother and to remain a week or so after Labor Day 1939.

The imminence of war in Europe overshadowed everything else in importance. As I was about to leave, Under Secretary of State Sumner Welles called me (in the absence of Attorney General Murphy, who was vacationing at Narragansett) to say that matters in Europe were looking very bad. In spite of the fact that the President was out of town, Welles thought it advisable for the Department heads to get together and establish a method for dealing with the problems that would arise if war should be declared. After talking with the Attorney General by telephone, and after Mr. Welles advised that there was little except preliminary consideration to be undertaken at these meetings, I decided to go ahead with the Jamestown trip. Assistant Attorney

General Thurman Arnold of the Antitrust Division was designated to attend the sessions.

Matters in Europe became constantly blacker during the time I was north. On Thursday, August 31, General Watson, the President's appointments secretary, called me at Jamestown and said that the President was in a mood for a social evening with a few close friends, and that it was being arranged for Saturday night, September 2. Watson said the President wanted to forget all about the war for one evening and had asked that I be invited. He urged me to come in spite of conflicting arrangements.

I left Jamestown on Friday night. I drove back and arrived in Washington on Saturday morning, conferred with Attorney General Murphy, and went to the White House at 6:45 P.M. Mrs. Roosevelt was out of the city. We were having dinner upstairs in the living quarters.

We went to the President's study where, at his desk, he was mixing cocktails. Everybody was in a jovial mood, but there was a trifle of the air of one who is jovial to conceal the fact that he is sad about the occasion. Those present were the President; Interior Secretary Harold Ickes, who was an expectant father; physician Admiral Ross McIntire; press secretary Stephen Early; General Watson; and me. Justice Bill Douglas, who had made the seventh on prior occasions, was unable to attend, but he enlivened the occasion by sending a note with amusing reference to Chief Justice Hughes as "Charles the Baptist."[1]

We had a simple early dinner served in the apartment and the war was rarely mentioned. The President did tell us of the ominous turn things had taken in Europe. He was in constant contact by telephone with Ambassadors Bullitt in Paris and Kennedy in London. Of course, it was general information that every wire in Europe was tapped and that in all probability every communication that the President had with both Bullitt and Kennedy was known in every chancellery in Europe within ten minutes after it occurred. There is little doubt that the President, knowing this, said some things in confidence in the hope that they would promptly be repeated. He was a master at that kind of strategy.

We then spent the evening playing poker in the President's study. Admiral McIntire, who is the President's physician, said the game must end at 11:00, but the President begged for and obtained an extra three quarters of an hour. The President seemed to relax under the stimulus of the game and for the moment we forgot the war.

The President's usual good luck was not with him, but it was with Ickes, who declared he had won enough so he could afford to have a baby,[2] and with Pa Watson. The President, Steve Early, and I all contributed diverse sums, with the President the heaviest loser. None of it ran into money as poker games go, however, and only once did the war descend upon our games. A message from Joseph Kennedy, Ambassador to St. James's, was received from the State Department about 10:00. The President sadly said, "Gentlemen, by noon tomorrow, war will have been declared." The event justified the prediction, but we parted that night feeling that the President had had his first relaxation in many days.

I spent Sunday, September 3, writing an article considered to have some importance if war did not overshadow the political situation, working at my apartment at the Wardman Park, and I was joined for dinner by Tom Corcoran, his secretary Peggy Dowd, and Viola Bartz, who was assisting me.[3]

Labor Day was spent in the office because it had been arranged that I would meet Attorney General Murphy, but he did not arrive during the morning as we were informed that he was riding. I spent it in the study of the statutes governing war powers.

There was a Cabinet meeting at 2:00. About 4:30, the Attorney General returned from it and gave me a file of proclamations that had been prepared by the State Department. The Attorney General said it was desired to have them passed upon by the Department of Justice. The task was delegated to me and to Ben Cohen. When we examined the file, we found that Attorney General Murphy, Secretary of State Cordell Hull, and Acting Secretary of the Treasury John W. Hanes had already approved the whole thing in writing and had so advised the President. The documents constituted the proclamations of neutrality that the President later issued, one under international law and one under the Neutrality Act.

These had been approved with the countries that were to be at war. I discussed with Assistant Secretary of State Adolf Berle the formula by which these powers should be named. He felt that it should include the United Kingdom and its dominions beyond the seas, which meant Canada. I questioned whether Canada should be included, as its own Parliament had not declared war and it was not subject to the disabilities of the Neutrality Act unless it were bound by the declaration of Great Britain.

Tuesday, September 5, 1939: I was to see the President at 10:30. I mentioned to him, among other things, the question as to whether Canada should be included in the declaration of neutrality. Having lived close to the Canadian border, I knew how strongly Canadians felt as to the Statute of Westminster establishing their independence.[4] His response was immediate and emphatic that Canada should not be included in the declaration. We awaited the arrival of Secretary Hull, Under Secretary Welles, and Assistant Secretary Berle, who brought with them the proclamations for execution.

These conferences took place in the President's bedroom, where he in pajamas was trying to overcome a bad head cold. He took the proclamation and said, "Well, now here in the very opening paragraphs is a question as to whether Canada should be included. Has she declared war yet?" He asked in detail for the latest information as to Canadian action. He did not indicate that I had raised the question, for it would likely be regarded by some of the State Department officials as none of my business.[5] We engaged in considerable legal argument as to the situation. The State Department advised that there was no declaration by the Canadian Parliament, but they felt Canada was bound by the act of England. The President said, "I am thinking of this as it will affect relationships over the years. If it is a question between the Canadian government and the British government, I should favor Canada. I feel we should not declare Canada bound unless she considers herself bound. Why isn't the simple thing to do to call Mackenzie King and see how the Canadian government feels about it?"

This simple and informal solution met with everyone's approval and a telephone call was made to Mr. King, the Prime Minister of Canada, at Ottawa. Secretary Hull, addressing him as "Mr. Prime Minister," made a rather formal statement of the problem and was very quickly told that Canada did not wish to be included in the proclamation, that her own parliament would act on Thursday, September 7, and that until then she was free. The effect of the Neutrality Proclamation would be to suspend trading between the two countries in many commodities, and it was desirable both from our point of view and from that of Canada that the commerce be uninterrupted as long as possible.

The President then took the telephone and said, "Hello, Mackenzie, it's pretty tough, isn't it?" With a few words of personal good wishes and a suggestion that they keep in touch, he closed the conversation.

The President then with his pen struck out "dominions beyond the seas" and inserted "New Zealand and Australia," which had meanwhile declared war. The proclamation was executed, and Secretary Hull left to affix the seal and give it to the world.

I went and had lunch with Secretary Ickes, Tom Corcoran, and Ben

Cohen, and we engaged in some rather doleful exchanges about the effect of the war on the social program of the President and the general tendency of the reactionary and moneyed interests to move into positions of importance as the situation became warlike.

At 4:30, we returned for the execution of the second proclamation, which was under the Neutrality Act and had the effect of an embargo upon shipments of many commodities to the powers at war. These were duly executed, along with subsidiary proclamations and executive orders.

I was then instructed by the President to complete a study, which had begun, of the powers he might have and exercise upon the proclamation of an emergency. This had been started by Judge Newman

Townsend, Acting Assistant Solicitor General, who had not been given a clear impression of what was desired.

Today I took the memorandum to the President and we reviewed the powers that might be obtained by proclamation.[6] To some he said, "No," and to others, "Yes," and I noted them on my memorandum.[7]

We then discussed the issuance of a proclamation. I pointed out to him that the chief powers he wished to obtain did not require a proclamation. However, he was desirous of issuing one, and as we discussed it, he wrote out the terms of a proclamation in the rough and gave it to me as the basis for one wish he wished me to draw.[8] He also wanted executive orders drawn that would increase the enlisted men in the Navy and Army and Marine Corps but still not be enough to bring them up to their authorized peace-time strength. He also asked me to proceed with a study of the control of profiteering and outlined a tax plan that he had in mind, making in longhand a memorandum by which profits above 6 percent on a base that he fixed should be taxed 99.9 percent.[9]

He also discussed declaring an embargo prohibiting sale for export of certain commodities, such as copper, if profiteering developed.

I asked for and obtained authority to get the assistance of Randolph Paul on taxes, of Leon Henderson and Jerome Frank on economics and planning generally, and of Ben Cohen on the law and draftsmanship.

I took his memorandum back with me and called into conference Townsend and several of the young men of the Department of Justice who had been working on the neutrality problems. Not one word could be found that could be usefully added to what the President in extemporaneous fashion had written, and not one thing could be substituted to advantage. We used the body of the proclamation exactly as he had written it and put on the preamble and the final clauses and it was issued.[10]

In his oral history, Jackson described the political difficulty of FDR's position as a military policymaker in the years leading up to World War II:

The President was under the peculiar difficulty, all the time, that if he made any move that looked like getting the country ready for war, he was charged with being a warmonger. But he felt obliged to take some steps that would prevent us from being caught unawares. He had a dual policy. One was a policy of peace. The other was a policy of preparing for war. Each step that he took in favor of one of those policies was construed as an abandonment, or perhaps as insincerity, concerning the other. So it was very difficult for him to move.[11]

Roosevelt was not over-awed by military or naval rank and did not feel any sense of inferiority in the presence of a general or an admiral. He knew that the winning of a war is not all seamanship or generalship but is in large part politics and economics. He often repeated that war is too important a matter to be left to the generals.

The Navy was his special interest, and at Cabinet meetings we sometimes referred to it as his branch of the service. He had the general conception of naval power that was set forth in the late nineteenth century by Admiral Alfred Thayer Mahan,[12] but he was not blind to the significance of the growth of air power. He knew that that opened a new chapter and called for new techniques. He was interested in the most minute developments of new weapons and new strategies, even new tactics. My impression was that Roosevelt had no lack of respect for the training, judgment, and advice of his generals and his admirals on the special subjects that were within their technical competence, but that as Commander-in-Chief he was more apt than most presidents to assert his personal authority over the military, naval, and air authorities.

This is an important subject but one best left to those whose opportunities of observation were more extensive and knowledge of the subject is more accurate.

On Tuesday, September 3, 1940, FDR announced to Congress and the American public that he had agreed to provide substantial military assistance to Great Britain. Roosevelt revealed that the United States would support the beleaguered British navy in its war against Germany by sending Great Britain fifty World War I–era American destroyers, and that Britain had agreed to give the United States long-term leases for bases on British territories in the western Atlantic and the Caribbean. FDR made this announcement in the midst of his campaign seeking reelection to an unprecedented third presidential term and, in that time more than a year before Pearl Harbor, to a Congress and country of strong isolationist sentiment.

Twelve years later, Justice Jackson—with research assistance from one of his law clerks, William H. Rehnquist—began to write about Jackson's significant involvement as Attorney General in the events that culminated in FDR's announcement of this exchange. Following Jackson's death in 1954, his son, William E. Jackson, and the Justice's final law clerk, E. Barrett Prettyman, Jr., intermittently edited Jackson's unfinished manuscript about the "Destroyer

Deal." The following text is Jackson's manuscript, including his notes, as Bill Jackson and Barrett Prettyman left it when they last worked on it in 1957:

The Exchange of Destroyers for Atlantic Bases

From the middle of May to the first of September, 1940, was a critical period in American history and in the government of Franklin D. Roosevelt. During this period, the Administration deliberated upon and rejected a series of proposals by Great Britain to buy, borrow, or obtain as a gift our over-age destroyers for wartime service. Out of those negotiations eventually grew an American proposal, which was accepted and consummated, to exchange destroyers for naval and air bases in the Atlantic. That period also saw a change in the Roosevelt internal policy. Originally it was to submit any proposal to Congress for specific authorization. It shifted to one of independent executive action.

When the President announced the completed transaction to Congress and the country, he could not prudently disclose to the world all that had influenced his decisions. This left the field open to exploitation by myth-makers, some of whom wield pens that by long usage have become skilled in the arts of defamation. More recently, however, the parts played by some of the participants have been made public, mainly as incidents of their personal memoirs.[13] But these require fitting together, like the pieces of a jigsaw puzzle, to present a complete picture, and when this is attempted we find that the accounts do not in all respects match each other. The result is an impression of the events that is dim, fragmentary, and confused.

My purpose is not to argue the wisdom or appraise the consequences of the exchange or the policy of aid to the allies that it foreshadowed. No one in our time has the disinterested perspective to judge it, least of all one who then sat in the President's Cabinet. However, only those who were within his councils can bear witness to the evolution of his policy and the reasons for some of his decisions. I profess to do no more than add what I may to the pool of information that will be preserved for dispassionate students of the period's history when they arrive at the scene.[14]

It may aid analysis of the material, though at the expense of some repetition, to reserve the question of internal policy *vis-à-vis* Congress and first to trace the course of British-American negotiations. These negotiations have already been disclosed to some extent, through the correspondence of Ambassador Lord Lothian with his Foreign Office;

some other sources not likely soon to be available would throw important light on many details.

The negotiations divide readily into two phases: (1) the period that lasted from May 15, 1940, through June and July, during which Churchill urged and Roosevelt refused the sale or loan of destroyers to Britain; and (2) the period following an American proposal to exchange destroyers for bases, quickly agreed upon in principle but delayed throughout August by the reciprocal stubbornness of both Churchill and Roosevelt, each persisting in untenable demands upon the other. Whether the facts as related here leave any credibility in the "conspiracy" theory advanced by critics of Roosevelt will be for the reader to judge.

I. The Period of Pleas and Rebuffs, May–June–July 1940

The first appeal for American destroyers was made by French Premier Reynaud on May 14, 1940, four days after the German forces invaded France.[15] Winston Churchill, then Prime Minister for less than a week,[16] added his plea by cable to President Roosevelt on the following day. He urged a proclamation of "non-belligerency, which would mean that you would help us with everything short of actually engaging armed forces." He listed five immediate needs, the first one being "the loan of forty or fifty of your older destroyers to bridge the gap between what we have now and the large new construction we put in hand at the beginning of the war. This time next year we shall have plenty. But if in the interval Italy comes in against us with another one hundred submarines, we may be strained to the breaking-point."[17]

President Roosevelt immediately refused the pleas of both Reynaud and Churchill. He was unwilling to impair our own defense requirements in this hemisphere and in the Pacific. He reminded both Churchill and Reynaud of his lack of specific authority from Congress and the untimeliness of any present request for such authorization.[18]

Reynaud renewed his request on May 31.[19] He was again advised that the transaction would be inexpedient because of the enormous sea area we had to patrol, and he was reminded of a lack of congressional authorization.[20] The President sent a memo to Under Secretary of State Welles so advising him, and adding that the destroyers could not be sold as obsolete because all of them were in commission or in the process of being commissioned. He thought building destroyers here "most inadvisable."[21]

It would be impossible adequately to understand the changing atti-

tudes of the Administration without taking into account the contemporaneous developments in Europe, for events were making their own
terms with theories and preconceptions. The swift collapse of Western
defenses had indicated that at best an addition to the French navy
would be futile, and at worst our aid might ultimately be added to
Hitler's strength. But this was not all that gravely concerned Roosevelt.
The impact of war events had shaken his confidence in Britain's capacity to win the war and perhaps even to survive. Then and throughout
the negotiations, he feared she might be tempted or driven to bargain
for peace by a surrender of her navy, which would assure Hitler mastery of the seas.

In conversation with Lord Lothian concerning the first appeal for
destroyers, Roosevelt candidly expressed his worries, and the British
Ambassador put the problem of satisfying this anxiety to Churchill. The
presidential state of mind was not easy for Churchill to deal with as disaster after disaster beset his nation's forces. He made valiant efforts at once
to convey the strongest impression of Britain's desperate need while at
the same time stopping short of confirming any sense of hopelessness.
By cable of May 20, he stoutly denied any need to dwell on such ideas,
but nonetheless asked to be excused for "putting this nightmare bluntly."
If defeat came to Britain, Churchill's administration would be finished,
and others would come in "to parley amid the ruins." Then the "sole
remaining bargaining counter with Germany would be the Fleet, and, if
this country was left by the United States to its fate, no one would have
the right to blame those then responsible if they made the best terms
they could for the surviving inhabitants."[22] As we shall see, the thought
of this catastrophe haunted the negotiations to the very end.

Churchill repeatedly renewed his pleas for a loan or purchase of
destroyers as grim events put new instruments of persuasion into his fer-
tile mind. By June 11, the British Expeditionary Force had escaped annihi-
lation by the miracle of Dunkirk. The German armies were rushing,
through feeble resistance, upon Paris. Italy had joined what appeared to
be a victorious ally, and Roosevelt responded by making his "stab-in-the-
back" utterance at Charlottesville.[23] Against this gloomy background,
Churchill again begged a loan of destroyers, promising that they or their
equivalent would be returned "without fail, at six months' notice if at
any time you need them." The Italian entry into the war made it necessary "to cope with a much larger number of submarines which may
come out into the Atlantic and perhaps be based on Spanish ports. To
this the only counter is destroyers."[24] Roosevelt did not yield.

By June 15, conquest and demoralization had so far subdued France that the French fleet, under the ambiguous Admiral Jean François Darlan, seemed likely to be surrendered and thus added to the German and Italian navies. Churchill again cabled Roosevelt urging that thirty-five destroyers be sent[25] and calling attention to the revolution in sea power that might follow German victory. Roosevelt also was alarmed, but either not enough or too much to part with the destroyers.

The specter of overwhelming German naval power, added to her seemingly irresistible air and land forces, deeply troubled the President. If the Germans should capture the French fleet, it—with Germany's own and that of Italy, and with probable cooperation from Japan—would leave the United States to face alone a most formidable naval and air power. But in the early days of July, Britain, defying what seemed to be forces as inexorable as fate and risking alienation of the French people, boldly attacked and largely disabled the French fleet so that it could no longer be of substantial service to Hitler. Britain won not only our admiration for her courage and audacity but our gratitude as well.

The bloody and depressing days wore on. German armies goose-stepped under the Arc de Triomphe; the heart of France was in their hands, the rest of it theirs for the taking. Theirs, too, was the whole coastline across the narrow channel from England, from which they could assault her cities with robots, attack them from air bases, send out submarines to cut her life lines, and even launch an invasion. The fall of France and the Low Countries left exposed the jugular of the British Empire.

The last days of July saw Britain standing alone as the last obstacle between the United States and a powerful and malignant combination of Nazi–Fascist–Communist forces. That last barrier was being mercilessly pounded by air while her fleet—her very sustenance—was being sunk by submarines in the exposed sea lanes. We then suspected, as we now know, that her invasion and destruction were being planned by Hitler's High Command.[26]

In a letter on July 31, Churchill reiterated in most urgent terms his appeal for the loan or sale of destroyers, motor boats, flying boats, and numerous military items. England's force of destroyers was being sunk at the rate of one a day. He candidly said, "We could not sustain the present rate of casualties for long."[27]

This plea brought to an end the first phase of negotiations. At no time during May, June, or July was there any mention of Atlantic bases. The British proposals, which Roosevelt consistently considered unacceptable, were invariably couched in terms of a loan or sale. This, of course, to the extent that they were useful to them would detract from our own naval strength. But if the British propositions had not awakened a changed response, the progress of the war had.

II. The American Proposal of Exchange for Bases

With the success of Germany's drive to the West, and the manifest feebleness of Britain's land and air defenses, the President began to consider whether the greatest usefulness of destroyers to the United States might not be to put them at the service of Britain. What was going through his mind became apparent to me when, during the battle over France, I went to the President with some matters of my department. He brushed aside discussion of them. He was in a grave mood that June afternoon and asked, "Do you know the problem that Churchill is wrestling with this afternoon?" I did not. He continued in substance, "The question is, what part of the Royal Air Force will he commit to the battle over France? If he throws it all into this fight on the Continent and it is lost, as it well might be, Great Britain will be left utterly defenseless against air attack. If he withholds it for defense of his Islands, France will accuse him of letting his ally down, and the British will reproach him for failing to employ his full resources to win while he still has the help of the French and while the battle is over French territory." There was little I could contribute as we discussed this dilemma at length and he said, as I left, "We'd better be thinking about this. It is not much different than the questions *we* may have to face if things continue as they are going now."

The continuing disasters of the summer brought about a shift of American sentiment in favor of aid to England. Even those who loved England least felt that it was one thing to grumble and thrust at her in her moments of pride and power but quite another to see her blotted out by the Fascist-Communist coalition. On the selfish side, there was a growing realization of the strangling position which that coalition, if it succeeded, would hold on the United States. By the end of July, the American public was thinking of our destroyers in much the same terms as the Churchillian dilemma that Roosevelt had described when the fate of France was in the balance.

Another change occurred with the fall of France and the threat in the Pacific that seemed to follow the curve of Nazi success in Europe. For some time—a year and a half to my certain knowledge—the President had desired to replace Secretary of War Harry Woodring.[28]

Charles Edison, the Secretary of the Navy, had taken his portfolio with notice that the President might want to name a Republican to that position. On June 19, the President requested the resignation of Secretary Woodring[29] and on the following day announced the appointment of Henry L. Stimson as Secretary of War and Frank Knox as Secretary of the Navy.

On August 2, President Roosevelt and his reconstituted Cabinet engaged in what Mr. Stimson, out of long experience with presidential Cabinets, described as "one of the most serious and important debates" he ever heard on such occasions.[30] It was precipitated principally by the Churchill letter of July 31, and its diplomatic follow-up. Unfortunately, there was no Cabinet secretary, no transcript of the proceedings, and no formal action. The discussion is recorded only in accounts by participants prepared after the event, and they differ somewhat in substance and much in emphasis.

Secretary Stimson, an understanding and meticulous witness who usually dictated his diary entry on the following morning, recites that Secretary Knox opened the discussion by relating how Lord Lothian had pleaded with him for the destroyers on the previous evening. Knox had countered with an inquiry whether the British had ever considered selling parts of their Atlantic and Caribbean possessions. Lothian said they had not. This, so far as I know and so far as I can learn, was the first mention of an American need for bases in connection with the British need for destroyers.

Mr. Stimson continues that Secretary of State Hull then raised the question whether such acquisition by us might not violate the hemisphere-defense agreements that he had just finished negotiating with the American Republics. The President admitted that possibility but suggested, recalling some precedents, that the United States might lease bases from the British. The idea of acquiring some such rights met with general concurrence. Discussion then turned to ways and means, especially in regard to securing the necessary legislation and reaching some agreement with Mr. Willkie, the Republican presidential nominee, so that it would not be made an issue in the campaign.[31] Mr. Farley, Postmaster General and Democratic Party chairman, considered this last proposal an excellent one.[32]

The President himself must have regarded the discussion as of unusual importance, for late that night he reduced his recollection of it to a memorandum, which it was not his custom to do. Strangely, he makes no mention of bases or of any proposal to obtain them in exchange for destroyers. He says the discussion was "in regard to devising ways and means to sell directly or indirectly" the destroyers. The only *quid pro quo* he mentions is found in the suggestion that the British be approached through Lord Lothian to discover whether they would give and allow to be published, positive assurance that the British navy would not in any conceivable circumstances fall into the hands of the Germans. The President adds that all those present agreed legislation was necessary to accomplish any sale. He also notes that Willkie's help would be sought to obtain agreement from Congress.[33]

Why did Roosevelt fail to mention a matter now so obviously important as the possible acquisition of bases? I think the likely answer is that at the moment he considered it something of a hobby of Knox's to which he did not expect British agreement. Knox, long before he entered the Cabinet, had been pointing out in his newspaper, the *Chicago Daily News*,[34] that United States defenses urgently required naval and air bases, particularly in the Caribbean to protect the Panama Canal. I believe he had even advocated seizing them, if necessary. In bringing this matter before the Cabinet, he received no encouragement that such a transaction would meet with British approval. It seemed at the time like one of the many good ideas that would die aborning. Certainly for Roosevelt's Administration to acquire these much needed bases not only would strengthen our defenses but would be a dramatic achievement, and no one can accuse Roosevelt of being slow to pick up his cue in the drama of politics. The difference between his narrative and Stimson's, in my opinion, reflects their different hopes about the possibility of accomplishment.

Another consideration may have led the President to underestimate the possibilities of the project. Secretary Hull obviously was not happy at the initiation of such a negotiation by the impetuous Knox and seemed doubtful of the wisdom of acting without seeking the consent of the other governments in this hemisphere—a course that necessarily involved substantial delay. Knox's launching of the proposition surely was irregular and rather symptomatic of the informality of the times. President Roosevelt himself often did not observe "channels," nor was he likely to hold their disregard against his subordinates, but it was not hard for him to see that the path of such a proposition through his State Department was not clear.

Another question may perplex the reader. Since the President had evidently reached the conclusion that Britain ought to have the destroyers, and since the ultimate transaction was accomplished by executive action, why the general agreement that congressional action was necessary? There are two answers. For one thing, the President was still considering a proposal of gift, loan, or sale of the destroyers. This, I had informally advised him, could not be accomplished without amendment of the existing law. An exchange that would add strength to our own defenses would stand in very different legal light, but the President had not yet come to accept that outcome as probable. Moreover, the President, at the time, was laboring under two kinds of "necessity": one dictated by law, and the other by the exigencies of his reelection campaign. As the proposition then stood, the President clearly had not as yet seriously entertained the idea of making the destroyers available to Britain on any basis without specific authority from Congress.

On August 3, the day after this Cabinet meeting, the whole aspect of the negotiations took a sudden and decisive turn. Churchill cabled Lothian that to grant bases in British possessions was "agreeable, but we prefer that it should be on lease indefinitely and not sale. It is understood that this will enable us to secure destroyers and flying-boats at once. You should let Colonel Knox and others know that a request on these lines will be agreeable to us."[35]

Mr. Hull records that on August 4 Lothian called on Hull and formally offered the bases.[36] Mr. Hull's reception must have seemed cool compared to the enthusiasm of Knox. Hull told Lothian that the bases would have to be for the benefit of all the American Republics, that legal difficulties were involved, that amendment of statutes "may be necessary," and that such procedures move slowly. He also reminded the Ambassador of possible opposition in Congress.[37] This must have sounded like a tolling bell to the hard-pressed Britisher, but at least the proposition was legitimatized by being brought into diplomatic channels. Despite his caution, Secretary Hull favored the transaction and prepared a bill for introduction in Congress to authorize it.[38] The President was quick to approve, and all seemed in readiness for swift action—Congress permitting.

With the exchange of destroyers for bases approved in principle on both sides of the Atlantic during the first week of August, there occurred an amazing interlude of bickering between the statesmen who headed these great nations. Each seemed determined to attach a condition that could not possibly be accepted by his opposite number. Churchill became shy about what Mr. Hull calls a "swap" and wanted the matter handled as reciprocal gifts—grandiose gestures of friendship and unity—with the United States making a present of the destroyers to Great Britain and Great Britain making a gift of the bases to the United States. Churchill gave cogent reasons why he did not want the exchange to be viewed as a bargain. In terms of the actual values involved, it was not a good bargain for Great Britain, a fact to which he did not want to attract British attention by having the transaction weighed there as a business one.[39] Churchill was firmly seated and as a practical matter possessed the treaty powers of both King and Parliament.[40] He seemed not to comprehend the very different constitutional and political position of President Roosevelt, who was bound by a written Constitution separating executive from legislative power and putting in Congress the control of disposal of government property.[41]

The President told me of a communication with Churchill (as I recall, a transatlantic telephone conversation) in which he attempted to make that admirable but obdurate statesman understand that the President simply could not make gifts of American property. He chuckled as he told me the Britisher thought the trouble must be in the Attorney General rather than in the Constitution. Before I could say anything to that, he added, "But what Winston can't get is that even if I had the legal power, it would not be politically possible now just to make a gift of these destroyers."[42]

So the transoceanic argument went on over the merits of reciprocal gifts as against a bargain of exchange until August 25. Then out of the conferences between the State Department Legal Adviser Green Hackworth and the Justice Department's Newman Townsend came a formula to let each leader have his own way—to split the bases into two groups. Churchill would make us a gift of one, and we would trade destroyers for the other. The President agreed, and the formula was tried out on the British and accepted.[43]

Roosevelt, on his part, was determined to obtain a promise that the British navy would never be turned over to the Germans or sunk, even if England surrendered or was defeated. Of course, as some of his advisers urged, the promise was unnecessary if England survived and worthless if she went down. Moreover, the request misapprehended Churchill's position about as badly as Churchill misapprehended Roosevelt's. Churchill had forcefully pointed out that it was impossible for him to enter into an engagement with the United States that would publicly suggest that he was considering even the remote possibility of surrender. Nonetheless, he had made an effort to satisfy Roosevelt's doubts on June 4 by telling the House of Commons in general terms that the fleet would, if necessary, go abroad to guard the empire beyond the seas.[44]

This was as far as he reasonably should have been expected to go. Many of Roosevelt's advisers agreed with Mr. Stimson, who urged that to ask Churchill to go further "would be merely an indication of mistrust" and highly detrimental to the morale of Britain and the Commonwealth that supported her.[45] And yet, while the perilous month of August wore on, the President was adhering to this demand. Indeed, he did not, until the very final hours of the negotiations, yield on it.

Thus a transaction that if done at all should have been done quickly was agreed upon in principle in the first week of August and not consummated until the first week of September. However, the events of the intervening month brought about vital changes in internal policy, changes that probably expedited the ultimate exchange by more than the month of seemingly useless international argument. The rest of the story may more appropriately be treated by a discussion of these internal developments.

III. The Decision Not to Seek Congressional Approval

Any decision by a Chief Executive to act on a matter of this magnitude without specific approval of Congress is likely to involve two considerations—whether he has the power, and whether it is politic to exercise it. The latter consideration assumed an especially large place in the Administration thinking due to the forthcoming elections. The myth-makers have spun the fable that Roosevelt decided from the beginning to bypass Congress, and that he obtained a made-to-order legal opinion to justify his decision.[46] Such was not the case.

I can say with assurance that as long as the negotiations involved a gift, loan, or sale of a portion of our naval strength, the President never entertained the idea of proceeding without the specific approval of Congress. The assumption that congressional approval would be sought even persisted for some time after an exchange had been proposed.

I cannot fix an exact day or hour when the President made the decision to bypass Congress, and I suspect that he could not either, for it was not a flash decision but a growth to which several factors contributed. I am sure the decision was not reached earlier than August 15. On August 13, he was fully committed to the concept of an exchange, but he was advising Churchill that such assistance "would only be furnished if the American people and the Congress frankly recognized that in return therefor the national defense and security of the United States would be enhanced."[47] As late as August 22 he was writing Senator David Walsh of Massachusetts, who chaired the Committee on

Naval Affairs, "I do hope you will not oppose the deal. . . ."[48] He would
not have decided to bypass Congress without the approval of Secretaries Stimson and Knox, in view of their representation of the Republican Party in his Cabinet, their immediate responsibility for the defense
services and their previous relation to the negotiations. Yet on August
14, Mr. Stimson was telling Lord Lothian that the exchange presented
"an attractive proposition for the President to make to the Congress."
On August 17, Secretary Knox was publicly declaring that the question
was one for Congress to decide.[49]

There were various factors that influenced the determination to
close the exchange by executive action. It had been decided at the
important August 2 Cabinet meeting to approach Mr. Willkie, the
Republican candidate, through the Emporia, Kansas, newspaper editor
and progressive Republican supporter of U.S. aid to Great Britain,
William Allen White, in an effort to win bipartisan support for the
transaction. Mr. Willkie's biographers, and apparently his papers, throw
little light on what was an important negotiation. The Barnes biography of Willkie,[50] despite its general objectivity, contains two serious
errors. It says "Winston Churchill had written to Roosevelt on July 31,
outlining the swap of British bases for overage U.S. destroyers substantially as it was finally accomplished."[51] As I have pointed out, the desperate July 31 cable did not mention bases.[52] Whether the proposition as
put to White and Willkie was a sale, loan, or exchange for bases, I am
unable to make out. Barnes also states that the President "knew,
although he did not tell White, that he was not even going to try to get
Congress to authorize the deal."[53] The error in this is the assumption
that Roosevelt then knew that he was not going to Congress with the
matter. It is clear from the evidence that he then contemplated no other
course and that his failure to obtain a satisfactory commitment from
Willkie played a large part in his decision to bypass Congress.

The most that the President understood Willkie to do was to say
that he himself would not make a campaign issue of the destroyer disposition.[54] Others have put it a little stronger. Mr. Hull reports his conversation with White, who said that Mr. Willkie "agreed in principle
with our methods for aiding Britain."[55] Mr. Stimson records that he,
too, communicated with White, "who was finally able to assure him
that the Republican candidate, Wendell Willkie, would in general support the plan."[56] What plan is not made clear.

The President's memorandum made the night of August 2 states
that a mere personal approval was not what he sought. I doubt if he

was fearful of the issue in the campaign. (The Gallup poll published on September 6, after the plan had been announced by Roosevelt, showed that 60 percent of those who expressed an opinion favored transferring the destroyers (bases were not mentioned in the poll).[57]) But he was fearful of delays and obstructions in Congress. He told this to White, and when White replied that Willkie's attitude was the same as Roosevelt's, the President records, "I explained to him that that was wholly insufficient, and that Willkie's attitude was not what counted but that the Republican policy in Congress was the one essential."[58]

White is authority for the statement that Willkie refused to help with the party leaders in Congress. White says Willkie "ducked" because legislation had not been introduced, and "he feels a natural diffidence about assuming Congressional leadership before his ears are dry."[59] Willkie in this negative way powerfully influenced the decision to bypass Congress. It left any congressional proposal exposed to the obstructive tactics of Republicans who came from constituencies so strongly isolationist that it would be advantageous, or from those so heavily Republican that it would be safe, to oppose the plan. This attitude, added to a formidable opposition from the President's own party, made certain that long delay was the best that could be expected from submission of the proposal to Congress.

Meanwhile, evidence accumulated that it was politically safe to proceed by executive agreement. The proposition had shifted to exchange for bases, which would be a dramatic and popular stroke and probably politically helpful. But what of the President's power?

IV. The Question of the President's Power

It will disappoint those who imagine that the President decided to go it on his own and ordered the Attorney General to turn out a sustaining opinion to learn that the Attorney General advised some time before the decision itself that existing law gave the President the necessary power. The legal opinion, far from being the result of the President's decision, was a contributing factor in reaching it, as may be inferred from the fact that the opinion was sent to Congress and the country to accompany the message announcing the exchange.

It must be understood that there were proposed transfers of ships of two different classes to the British that encountered legal complications. The two classes sometimes are confused. The first included small motor torpedo boats and submarine chasers of various experimental designs that were under construction by private contractors for the

Navy. In 1940, the Navy agreed to defer these deliveries and receive instead a later design that would give it a superior boat in several respects, including doubled firepower and increased speed. This freed the shipbuilders to dispose of the boats under construction, the plan being to complete the boats for the British. The Navy's position was that such a transaction would concern only the contractor and the prospective purchaser.

About the middle of June, these facts became public with no small amount of exaggeration, and criticism followed from congressional and other sources. The proposal was not, as in the later case of the destroyers, that the government sell these boats to Britain, but that it allow the private builders to complete, outfit, and deliver them. When this matter came up at the Cabinet meeting of June 20, I expressed the view that the shipbuilders would violate a 1917 statute that prohibited fitting out and arming vessels in our country for a belligerent[60]—a statute passed to forestall such a breach of international law as that that formed the basis for our successful "*Alabama* claims" against Great Britain after the Civil War.[61] I never knew to what extent, if any, government officials had encouraged this shipbuilding transaction, but the matter appeared to have proceeded so far that my opinion was embarrassing. Harry Hopkins, as the Cabinet went on to other matters, passed me a note:

> Bob: Assuming we are in a jam over those ships to the British—is this a way out?
>
> The British tell the Navy that for some appropriate reason they do not want the ships.
>
> Harry.

The President, however, appeared to agree with me. The law seemed plain, and it was supported by detailed studies in the Department of Justice. Although no written opinion was rendered, on June 24 I made public my informal opinion that, even if released by the Navy, these ships could not lawfully be completed in American yards for the British.

Later, these same small boats were included with destroyers in the British list of requests in exchange for bases. In my formal opinion on the destroyer exchange, I repeated the view, with supporting reasons, that the builders could not complete these boats for Britain without violating the statute.[62] They were not, therefore, included in the exchange with Britain.

Whether my informal June opinion would also preclude the government from transferring over-age destroyers, the President did not then ask, no doubt because he did not regard their loan or sale as feasible. Under date of July 19, however, Benjamin Cohen, at the request of Secretary Ickes, submitted a twelve-page opinion to the President quite properly pointing out that the statutes that the Attorney General had advised would preclude private contractors from completing ships under construction would not apply to government sale of over-age destroyers. He continued with a well-reasoned opinion that destroyers could be legally "released" by the President to Great Britain under existing law.

Up to this time, no exchange for bases had been proposed, and Cohen did not indicate what, if any, return would be required. But the President was skeptical. He sent the opinion to Secretary Knox, just entering his Cabinet, with the observation, "This memorandum from Ben Cohen is worth reading. In view of the clause in the big authorization bill I signed last Saturday which is intended to be a complete prohibition of sale, I frankly doubt if Cohen's memorandum would stand up." He added, "Also I fear Congress is in no mood at the present time to allow any form of sale." He suggested that Knox consider the possibility of trying to get Congress to authorize their sale to Canada "on condition that they be used solely in American Hemisphere defense. . . ."[63]

Cohen sent me a copy of his memorandum, which I examined with the care due to a well-thought-out opinion by an exceptionally competent lawyer. Then I referred it for study and report to Acting Assistant Solicitor General Newman A. Townsend, a hard-headed, conservative, and forthright former judge, on whose judgment I placed much reliance.

On August 11, a legal opinion to the same effect as Cohen's appeared in the form of a letter in the *New York Times*, signed by Charles C. Burlingham, Thomas D. Thacher, George Rublee, and Dean Acheson, names that carried weight in the legal profession.[64] If this group had learned that the proposition was being reshaped into one by which the United States would obtain bases in exchange for destroyers, the opinion did not show it. Regardless of any exchange, they thought there was ample power to transfer the destroyers. The President saw the letter and asked what I thought of it, but gave no indication that he desired any particular answer. Indeed, at this time I think he feared possible embarrassment as much from having a power that he did not think it expedient to use as from finding that he was without it. I told him the subject was being studied and that I would let him know the results, but that the Cohen opinion and the *Times* letter each made on its face a strong case.

On August 13, Judge Townsend, with a caution typical of his work, concluded that there was a basis in existing statutes probably sufficient for Presidential disposition of the over-age destroyers. His study, like those of Cohen and the *Times* group, did not contemplate an exchange for bases, which was a far stronger case in my view than a sale. Of course, I told the President of this development. Mr. Green Hackworth, Legal Adviser of the Department of State, was collaborating with Judge Townsend, and on August 15 they prepared a summary of their conclusions to the effect that the destroyers could be released under existing statutes and sent to the British without the violation of domestic or international law. There was one reservation: "There is some question whether the transaction would not be in violation of the provisions of the Hague Convention." Judge Townsend accompanied the draft with a memo saying "[t]he Hague Convention provisions and their application have not been fully thought out. . . ."

The following forenoon I went over the statutes, texts, and precedents with Townsend, Solicitor General Biddle, my assistant Gordon Dean, and Cohen, to satisfy ourselves that nothing had been overlooked and to verify the conclusion. I lunched with Secretary Knox and gave him a copy of the one-page summary of conclusions. At 2:00 the Cabinet met, and the results of our study were announced. The President then asked me to put them in a formal opinion to have ready if he should decide to act on it. There is evidence that by the next afternoon he told Prime Minister King of Canada that he would act on it.[65]

At the Department of Justice, we resumed conference after the August 16 Cabinet meeting to prepare a formal opinion. We were joined by Admiral Stark, the Chief of Naval Operations, who had opposed a sale or loan of the destroyers. His certification was essential under our view of the law, and he still was skeptical about taking the responsibility of making a certificate.

The first difficulty in preparing a formal opinion was that there had as yet been no meeting of top minds as to the form of the transaction, though they were in accord as to its substance. Roosevelt was still making the plan turn on the declaration that Churchill rejected as defeatist. Churchill was still, and was long thereafter, bombarding Washington with objections to a contract and insisting on reciprocal "spontaneous acts" of gift.[66] But to me, form was substance. While Cohen, the *New*

York Times letter, Townsend, and Hackworth had thought there was a sufficient basis in existing statutes for transfer regardless of the nature of the *quid pro quo*, I knew, before I was called upon to accept their conclusion that the *quid pro quo* would be bases. To sell the destroyers and receive their equivalent in money would weaken our defenses and not materially strengthen American finances. To exchange them for bases would give us far more than their equivalent in actual defense facilities. On this basis, it seemed to me, the Chief of Naval Operations could certify that the destroyers were "not essential to the defense of the United States," and thus the transaction would conform to the conditions of the Act of June 28, 1940.[67] A strong and plausible effort had been made to show that this could be certified on the ground that transferring the destroyers to Britain's defense was the same as using them in our own,[68] but even so ardent a friend of Britain as Mr. Stimson later wrote that "[i]t was not readily apparent how Admiral Stark could give any such certificates for his destroyers,"[69] except for an adequate *quid pro quo*.

We were obliged, therefore, to assume a hypothetical case, based on the assumption that Roosevelt would prevail and Churchill would yield on their points of difference. Welles, with Admiral Stark and others, had worked out drafts of letters to be exchanged between Lord Lothian and Mr. Hull, if that should occur.

Mr. Welles on behalf of the State Department, Mr. Stimson, and General Marshall for War, Mr. Knox and Admiral Stark for Navy, and Judge Townsend and myself for Justice met in my office on the evening of August 21, in the endeavor to settle on a procedure that would not at the last minute meet objections from some quarter. We had a draft of an opinion ready. Admiral Stark and General Marshall were ready to certify. There was a long discussion of details and alternatives, including that suggested once by the President of a transfer to Canada instead of to Britain. An outline of procedure to accomplish that end had been prepared. It was agreed, however, that this would only be chasing the devil around the stump with no legal advantage. No obstacle to immediate action appeared.

August 22 was a critical and busy day. I attended White House conferences with the different groups concerned and showed the President a draft of my proposed opinion. He read it carefully and said that he was persuaded he had the power to close the deal, and that if he did so, he might want to send my opinion to Congress along with a message informing Congress of the action taken. In view of that possibility, which I had not anticipated, we went over the document together, line by line. He wrote on my draft "his own suggested changes," or "the changes he would like made," and I noted a few changes that occurred to me as desirable.

Only one change was of legal significance. The President placed a big question mark in the margin opposite a citation of a precedent that he regarded as of dubious value. Further study proved that he was right. Another change was that he deleted from my recital of the agreement the statement that "Great Britain to make declaration regarding the use of British fleet for Empire defenses including Western Hemisphere." He had become convinced that it would not be advisable to make public, even in language designed to be innocuous, his insistence upon a declaration that the British fleet would not be surrendered. He also changed some expressions that offended his nautical sense, such as my reference to the small boats as a "mosquito fleet," for which he substituted "mosquito boats."

Conferences on this subject went on at the White House all day. The American end of the bargain was rapidly taking shape, but all again was unsettled by the cable of that day from Churchill renewing his objection to any bargain, and by a memorandum from Lothian asking for additional materials. Mr. Welles, who had handled the affair for the State Department to this point, dropped out of the conferences and began a well-earned vacation, while Mr. Hull, who had been on vacation, took over in his stead.

The following day the Cabinet met again. It was plain that the President was taking increasing pleasure in completing, all on his own, an exchange so obviously advantageous and popular.

With my aides in the Department of Justice, I was revising the opinion in view of the President's intimation that it might be sent to Congress. The opinion did not rest on broad and easily understood constitutional generalities. It based the President's power wholly on a series of congressional acts. Changes to make this opinion on a technical subject of statutory interpretation more nearly intelligible to the lay public were debated and discussed by members of our staff, including Judge Townsend, Gordon Dean, and others.

A Cabinet meeting had been called for Tuesday, August 27, after which the President was to leave Washington for several days. The opinion was completed, dated that day, and before the meeting again reviewed hurriedly with the President, who suggested no changes. He was fully set to proceed. Letters consummating the transaction would be exchanged the following Monday (September 2) between Secretary Hull and Ambassador Lord Lothian, unless some new objection came from Churchill. The President would send a message to inform Congress that the exchange had been made, without asking approval, and attaching my opinion as his justification for executive action. The President said to me, with a chuckle, "They will get into a terrific row over your opinion instead of over my deal, but after all, Bob, you are not running for office." His reputation as a political prophet did not suffer from that prediction.

Completion of the details of the letters of exchange[70] was left to Secretaries Hull and Knox, and it appears they devoted a large part of the night to working them out with Lothian. One deletion, however, was directed by the President. A paragraph in the proposed letters that first came to me read:

> The British Government, in terms of the leases to be agreed upon, will grant to the United States for the period of the leases all the rights, power, and authority within the bases leased, and within the limits of the territorial waters and air spaces adjacent to or in the vicinity of such bases, which the United States would possess or exercise if it were the sovereign of the territory and waters above mentioned. However, individuals other than citizens of the United States who may be charged within the area of the bases leased with crimes or misdemeanors amenable to the laws of the British colonies within which such bases are located shall be delivered by the appropriate United States authorities to the duly authorized authorities of the colonies in question.[71]

Mr. Hull says that originally both Roosevelt and he favored having Great Britain cede to the United States the lands needed for bases. However, it was my understanding that the President, from the first, favored leasing. Mr. Stimson attributes to Roosevelt the suggestion of a lease basis when the proposition first came before the Cabinet on August 2.[72] Leasing seems to have been one of the alternatives that Knox, in originating the negotiations, first put to Churchill and the one the latter favored.[73] So far as I know, cession of the bases was never seriously considered on either side.

In my view, the difference between cession and leasing was vital to the President's power to act independently of Congress. Cession would extend the area of the United States, impose upon us the responsibility for governing the ceded territory, and make persons born within it citizens. So to expand the boundaries of the United States, in my opinion, would require an Act of Congress or a treaty ratified by the Senate and would commit us to extensive and indefinite future obligations. What we eventually acquired, however, was an option to establish naval, air, and military bases on British territory, and this, as my opinion emphasized, did not commit the United States to anything unless Congress approved and appropriated money for construction of the bases. Leasing did not take territory or persons into our constitutional system.

The President's reasons for preferring leases to cession are significant and, I think, have not been fully disclosed. According to Mr. Hull's version, it was the "penurious condition of the native populations of most of the islands."[74] The President wrote to Senator Walsh, Chairman of the Naval Affairs Committee:

> Naturally, knowing the situation in all of these places intimately, I do not want the United States to assume control over the civilian population on these Islands. In the first place, they do not want to live under the American flag, and, in the second place, the civilian populations would be a drain on the national treasury, would create all kinds of tariff involvements in the Senate and House, and give future generations of Americans a headache."[75]

Because of the bearing of the question on the President's power and on the terms of specific leases to be taken under the general agreement, I had occasion, more than once, to discuss with him the nature of and the limitations on the rights to be acquired by the United States. Over and above all of the foregoing reasons, the President warned me that we must not in any way assume any responsibilities for government of the bases that could involve us in race relations there. He thought the British had shown admirable ability to govern the inhabitants without fostering racial tensions between the white and colored such as unhappily obtain in some parts of this country. On the islands, there was not legal discrimination and in fact very little of any kind. If the United States assumed sovereignty and continued the British policy, it would be in sharp conflict with southern practice and sentiment and would precipitate a row with southern representatives in Congress. If the United States should attempt to change insular practice to conform to its own racial pattern, it would cause grave unrest in the islands. Therefore, he wanted the powers and the responsibilities of the United States confined strictly to military installations and personnel, leaving civil government of the territory entirely to the British.

While preparation of the diplomatic documents was not my business, I felt constrained to point out to the President that this sovereignty clause in the early draft of the letters might conflict with his purpose. To assume all the power and authority that the United States would have if sovereign might be hard to distinguish from the assumption of sovereignty itself. We thought the clause might meet objections from the British, though whether it actually did, I do not know. At all events, the President now directed that the sovereignty clause be eliminated. The final letters granted to the United States only power and authority within the bases and their vicinity "necessary to provide access to and defence of such bases, and appropriate provisions for their control."[76]

Hardly had announcement of the President's exchange reached the country when we learned that a serious blunder had been committed. The President and the British Ambassador were both greatly embarrassed by it. How it occurred is not explained by Mr. Hull's memoirs or by Mr. Churchill's text, but Mr. Stimson attributes it to "sheer inadvertence."[77]

The schedule of items to go to the British included a quantity of military materials, in addition to the destroyers that I advised could be exchanged, and the torpedo boats that I held could not. These materials were airplanes, rifles, and ammunition to meet the threatened invasion of England. The final letters of exchange dropped out all these items. It is not difficult to explain what may have happened. Mr. Hull had returned from his vacation just before the final papers of transfer were drafted, and Mr. Welles, who had been handling the diplomatic phases of the matter, left on his vacation. The discussion of the President's power had centered attention on the destroyers and torpedo boats, which tended to obscure in everyone's mind the uncontroversial equipment. The final documents were settled on a hot evening cruise down the Potomac, the American hosts being Secretary Knox and Admiral Stark. The Army was unrepresented, and the items dropped were Army items. Lord Lothian represented the British on the occasion, and the oversight on his part can only be understood if one realizes what a weary and harried man he was in those days.

From the telegrams published by Mr. Churchill, it is apparent that this omission startled London. Mr. Churchill, on September 5, asked what was being done about these items, saying, "I consider we were promised all the above, and more too. Not an hour should be lost in raising these questions. 'Beg while the iron is hot.'"[78] The anguished Lothian carried out instructions. The President called a meeting of those who had participated. Everyone recognized the intention on both sides to include these items in the exchange. Mr. Stimson urged a public admission of error and a statement that the materials would be supplied at once. Most of us, however, disagreed. The President was placed in a difficult position. He had made public what purported to be all of the transaction. If it now appeared that other undisclosed transfers were involved in the same transaction, he would be charged with deception, and doubt would be raised as to the extent of his commitments. This might well be injurious to his campaign, for his adversaries were increasingly charging him with sacrificing American interests to aid Britain. Therefore, it was decided that no public statement should be made. I understood later that Secretary Knox and Secretary Stimson, through what the latter calls a "compensatory transaction," saw to it that the British promptly obtained the promised material.

The bargain itself was so manifestly advantageous to the United States that there was little criticism of the trade. Roosevelt, however, had shown uncanny foresight in expecting my legal opinion to draw the heat away from his deal. The opinion became the focus of much of the public controversy that ensued, and opposing quarters with equal extravagance threatened the Attorney General with everything from immortality to impeachment.[79]

Many opposed the transaction as a violation of international law and especially of the Hague Convention.[80] I have already noted that at the outset Judge Townsend had reserved that question as not having been thought through. In the same manner he had added, "I understand (from State Dept.), however, that the President is not greatly worried about either international law or the Hague Convention." The Attorney General's opinion was not sought on those subjects.

The President's unconcern did not, in the light of what I knew, indicate disregard of international law. His attitude and that of his Cabinet were settled on that large subject too clearly and firmly to require technical legal advice.[81] It was a subject the President had discussed with me several times.[82] At the time the Hague conferences were held and most conventional international law was written, each state was regarded as having the legal right to resort to war against any other state at any time for any reason or for no reason at all. Since all war-making was a legal right, a third state that wished to claim the immunities of a neutral had to abstain from many forms of assistance to either of the equally lawful belligerents. But following the First World War, nearly all of the nations, including Germany, agreed unequivocally by the Kellogg-Briand Treaty to forgo war as an instrument of policy. This treaty, and many others that Germany had entered into, left no vestige of legal right for her to resort to a war of aggression. From the beginning, Roosevelt, Hull, Welles, Stimson, and I had been in agreement that Hitler's war was one of naked aggression, that by contemporary international law it was an illegal one, and that other powers were under no obligation to remain indifferent but instead had the right, if not a duty, to vindicate the rule established under these treaties by assisting the victims of such unlawful aggression. This view had been too often discussed and too fully agreed upon to need repetition within the official circle. Whether, at the time, it might not wisely have been explained to the public is another question.

It was upon this legal basis that Secretary Stimson and Secretary Hull espoused the Lend-Lease program before Congress. It was amplified and documented in my speech to the Inter-American Bar Association at Havana on March 27, 1941, for the information of the legal profession of the other American Republics.[83] This concept of the Nazi attack on the peace of the world as an illegal enterprise was the basic premise for the Nürnberg international trials of the Nazi war criminals. It was the fundamental assumption of the whole aid-to-England policy of the Roosevelt Administration. Of course, it was not consistent with the older Hague concept of neutrality, which had been made obsolete by the later outlawry of aggressive war.

Such is the story as it is known to me. That other details will appear from as yet unpublished accounts by participants, I have no doubt. That nothing, however, will alter the essential features of the transaction as outlined here, I am confident. Judgment upon its wisdom is for history.

In his oral history, Jackson described FDR's and his Cabinet's attitudes and information before and after the attack on Pearl Harbor:

On December 7, 1941, I was at home at Hickory Hill in McLean, Virginia, and was reading with the radio going. I think I had been listening to a musical program, which I sometimes do as I read. Suddenly the news of the Pearl Harbor attack was broadcast. Of course, the radio hummed with it from then on. There was a deep sense of shock, although I had known that we were not far from war. Still, I was shocked by the boldness of the attack as well as by its success. I was amazed that we had not been better prepared for it, because there was so much awareness that we were on very dangerous ground—I could not imagine military and naval people in an outlying base being as unprepared as they apparently were. Then, of course, it was followed up by the disasters at Manila,[84] which were even less excusable in my view because they had more notice.

. . .

I had heard repeatedly in Cabinet meetings that a war with the Orient would not amount to much, that our Navy would "knock Japan out of the water" in no time. I think Secretary of the Navy Frank Knox had said a number of times that it would only take maybe six months. At any rate, when questions had arisen such as stockpiling rubber, Knox, with great assurance, had said that our naval forces in the Pacific were so superior to those of Japan that we would have a very brief interruption of our rubber supply. Of course at Pearl Harbor the losses were very serious, much more than the public realized. The naval force was very much reduced. But even so, I was surprised that we were faced with such a serious problem in the Pacific. I did not know the extent of the losses at Pearl Harbor at the time, of course.

. . .

The President told me some weeks after the attack the extent of our losses. I was frightened by it. It was shocking. But he said it had not delayed us as much as we might think. Even with those ships, we could not have swung into action much before we did. While the losses were serious, from a strategic point of view, he would not have been able to have made an attack in the Far East that would have been very much more effective. I remained unconvinced about that—that if our naval forces at Pearl Harbor had not been badly depleted, we could have done no more in the Philippines.

. . .

I think Pearl Harbor was a great shock to the President—that with all the war talk there had been, he did not believe Japan would make a surprise attack. Of course it was a great embarrassment to him. It reflected on his Administration. His appointment of Supreme Court Justice Owen Roberts and the commission to make an investigation indicated his concern about it, and his concern with the reaction of public opinion. After all, we had been talking for some time—many, many months—about preparedness. We had been talking about surprise attacks. Here, on an exposed perimeter of the country, nobody apparently was anticipating any difficulty. I think it was a great jolt to him.

. . .

How long the war would last and what the prospects were, I did not have much opinion. I was baffled. Our intelligence had proved to be wrong on nearly everything. American intelligence services let us down at every point. I had heard in Cabinet discussions the views that had come from our intelligence services. We had enormously underestimated the strength and striking power of Hitler. We had overestimated the staying power of France. We had overestimated the strength of England. We had overestimated the attitude and stamina of Belgium. We had terribly underestimated Japan, at least her immediate striking power. We had terribly underestimated the power of Russia. When she was attacked by Hitler, I heard the highest military authority say, and the common expression around Washington was, that the German armies would move through Russia like a hot knife through butter. I heard General Marshall express the most doubtful views of the power of the Russians to resist. The conquest of Russia was expected to be a very short matter.

Based on such information as I had, it was a very dark prospect indeed. I was very pessimistic about it. It looked like a very long war and a war that would be terrifically costly in lives because Hitler would have to be dislodged from the position that he held. We had to wage a war of attack. The foolish optimism that had prevailed, such as the invincibility of the American navy and this and that, all went out of Washington very fast. In place of it, a very deep pessimism came in. There was talk about a war of a decade and all that. In the early part of December and the following months, spirits were pretty low here.

· · ·

I have never doubted that the President was utterly sincere in his desire to stay out of war and that he had hoped in the early stages that he would be able to succeed with that policy. He was trying to pursue a policy that was inconsistent, in a sense, and one that looks perhaps more inconsistent than it was—one, to avoid involvement in a war, and two, to be strong defensively so that we could not be taken unawares and would be successful in case we were involved in it. Every step taken in execution of one policy tended to reflect on his sincerity in the other.

· · ·

Even if we had not been attacked, there was the great problem of how long we could stand by and see the last bastions of Western civilization wiped out. I just do not know. There has been a certain amount of talk that some of the Roosevelt Administration wanted war. I think those people were more impressed with the danger to us rather than being more eager for war. I do not think anybody in that Administration wanted war. Some were convinced that it was inevitable, and that being inevitable it was useless to delay it. I was one who wanted to take the last clear chance for peace.

Some men, like Mr. Stimson, had used language that might sound as if they were trying to get up a war. Stimson's statement that our problem was to get Japan to fire the first shot[85] has been seized upon by some people as an indication that Stimson wanted the United States to have a war. I think what he meant, knowing him as I did, was that he recognized that war had become inevitable and that the United States would not start it. Being inevitable, the commencement of it must await Japan's movement. His statements, I think, are overdramatic and overemphasize what he meant.

However, Secretary Stimson, Secretary Knox, Secretary Morgenthau, and Secretary Ickes were much more convinced that war was inevitable and they were much more ready to meet it on the basis that it was inevitable than some of the rest of us, and more, I think, than the President himself. He thought it was avoidable much longer than did some of the others. Roosevelt had a great confidence that something would happen to bring things out right. He felt that by some stroke of diplomacy, or some other stroke, it will come out all right.[86]

Once World War II had begun, Justice Jackson in effect tried to enlist in the cause—he told the President that he was willing to leave the Supreme Court and return to service in the executive branch. In his oral history, Jackson recounted an April 1942 conversation of this type, including FDR's declination of the offer and his thoughts at that time about what to do with Germany following her inevitable defeat:

After the attack on Pearl Harbor it was impossible for one who had recently been active to serve on the Court without feeling a certain sense of frustration and dissatisfaction. That, I think, influenced Justice James F. Byrnes in leaving the Court and going with the President.[87]

There came a time when I offered to do the same thing. We spent a weekend on a very delightful house party down at General Watson's in Charlottesville, Virginia.[88] I had been invited to ride down with the President and to ride back with him. We discussed many phases of the conflict and the problems that it was going to raise in the future. Some of them we had discussed before.

The proposition came up as to the future of Germany. We all assumed, of course, that there was no question that eventually the

United States, with its allies, would win. How long it would take, no one was in a position to say. The President long before that had said to me what he now repeated—that he thought Germany would have to be broken up to its pre-Bismarkian small states. I had argued against that. It seemed to me that peace in the world could never be advanced by atomizing large units, but would rather come by consolidating them and reducing the occasions for friction. During our weekend trip, the President again was back on that thesis that Germany ought to be broken up. We discussed that at some length.

We also discussed the role and attitudes of various people in the war effort. I told the President that on the Court, I felt I was in sort of a back eddy. I was not doing anything that promoted the war effort and not much that seemed to be very important in contrast with the great issues at stake in the world. I said I thought there were a good many men who were entirely capable of performing the function on the Court with satisfaction, and if there was anything in the war effort he thought I could be more useful in, I would be quite ready to resign and take it on. I had to admit, and to say, that there were a very limited number of things in which I could be of use in a war effort, being anything but a warrior.

The President said that he did not think there was anything at present. He thought the work on the Court had permanent importance, even though temporarily it did not seem to be important. He thought I ought to stay there and that there were further prospects in connection with the Court, which I took to be a reference to the Chief Justiceship. He said that it was quite possible, however, that when the peace came and the time for the settlement arrived, there would be important things that I was particularly qualified to do. What it was he did not say, and of course I did not ask. The matter dropped at that.[89]

In early 1943, President Roosevelt publicly demanded the "unconditional surrender" of the Axis powers. Ten years later, after Jackson had served as the chief American prosecutor of Nazi war criminals at Nuremberg, he reflected in his oral history on the meaning and consequences of FDR's demand:

The President announced his unconditional surrender formula at his January 1943 meeting with Churchill in Casablanca.[90] Just what unconditional surrender involved, no one knew. I later learned how the uncertainties of that proposal contributed to the propaganda of Josef Goebbels and his machine. They claimed it meant virtual slavery. There was no doubt that the phrase was entirely consistent with the idea of complete submission by the German people, as well as the state, to the will of the conqueror. It was not difficult for Goebbels to persuade the German people that the will of the conqueror would be shaped by a desire for vengeance, which would be very oppressive to them.

What the unconditional surrender formula would mean in terms of individual lives and private property was very vague. It was a phrase, the full implication of which I was later—when the Nuremberg tribunal was dealing with the Nazi defendants—obliged to confess I did not understand. Its legal effect was hard to determine, but it doubtless made the ending of the war more difficult.[91] It seemed to be a departure from the Wilsonian tactic, which had succeeded so well, of driving a wedge between the German people and the government by insisting that he would make peace with the people if they got rid of the government. "Unconditional surrender" operated rather the other way in that it made the people feel a strong sense of solidarity with the Hitler government.

I think that the "unconditional surrender" formula in the United States was rather pleasing. In the first place, it sounded like U. S. Grant. But Grant had used unconditional surrender in reference to an army, not a state.[92] There was, except in academic circles, very little consideration of what was involved when a whole state, with a complicated economic and social system already badly demoralized, surrenders. What does that mean in terms of the extent of submission of the inhabitants? What does that mean in terms of responsibilities assumed by those who accept the surrender? Those who take over prisoners of war assume certain responsibilities toward them. If you take over a whole state as captive, what responsibilities do you assume?

The story of the first announcement of the unconditional surrender formula has been told by Winston Churchill. Apparently, from his account, the phrase was used by the President without very much consideration and no consultation. Churchill did not expect it to be made public, so he now says. It is a shorthand phrase for total victory and complete submission. In the context in which it was announced, I think that the President had in mind encouraging and stimulating the overrun peoples to exert their utmost in helping to overcome the Nazi power—that he was thinking of bucking up our Allies rather than announcing a political program after the war. I doubt if he gave very much consideration to its implications in terms of international law or ultimate responsibility. It was good propaganda. I think that is the origin of that phrase. Perhaps in that respect it resembles Wilson's Fourteen Points,[93] although it is somewhat different. After peace came, it had quite a different connotation.

The sentiment of the United States brightened up very much when the unconditional surrender demand was announced. The unconditional surrender formula, so far as the public was concerned, raised no questions. People thought of it as meaning that the Germans were completely counted out. The complications that it implied gave the general public no sleepless nights at all. They thought it meant that we just were not going to have any appeasement—there had to be a complete collapse of the Hitler regime. If there had been a proposition by Roosevelt equivalent to Wilson's Fourteen Points—that is, a peace agreement—people would have reacted that the agreement would not be worth anything. This country, probably, was not in a mood to have a peace that depended on an agreement of the German government. In that sense, people were ready to go to the limit to destroy the German government because they felt that they had once made peace with it and it did not last. In that way, I think Roosevelt's unconditional surrender formula was popular here. It said, "This time we aren't going to do what we did before." To that point, the formula was acceptable.

Then too there was a very large Jewish influence in public sentiment. That favored a very strong or severe peace, to which unconditional surrender was preliminary. The unconditional surrender formula was less subtle than Wilson's method of driving the wedge between the Kaiser and the people, and perhaps it aroused a bit more expectation of a rather vengeful peace than Wilson's formulas of "making the world safe for democracy" and "A war to end war" and that sort of talk. There was no suggestion of compromise in the Roosevelt formula.[94]

Jackson also discussed, in his oral history interviews, FDR's views about prosecuting war criminals following World War II, and his connection to what became, after Roosevelt's death, President Truman's decision to send Jackson to Nuremberg:

I think that the policy, so far as the war criminals were concerned, had already been pretty well settled by President Roosevelt before he died in April 1945. Judge Rosenman, who had become White House counsel, was in Europe at the time of President Roosevelt's death. Rosenman described in his book that he was to carry on discussions with the Lord Chancellor and others in London to make arrangement for the trial of war criminals. He found that the officials of Great Britain wanted to dispose of the six or seven top Nazis without a trial. They

feared that an open trial would provide a sounding board for Nazi propaganda. Roosevelt was determined that a speedy but fair trial should be
accorded to the war criminals. Judge Rosenman advised them of that
and opposed the execution without trial, pointing out that a tradition
and legend would grow up about them as it had about the memory of
Napoleon, and that the President insisted that there be a documentation of their crimes and of their steps.[95]

Just as Judge Rosenman's negotiations were coming to an end, the
President died and a change in the presidential office was made. My
information is, however, that President Truman decided to carry on the
policy that was already made by Roosevelt, which was a speedy but fair
trial of these men. He more or less delegated Rosenman to put into
effect the Roosevelt plan in that respect.

I have always assumed, although I have no definitive information to
that effect, that Roosevelt had had some talk with Rosenman about des-
ignating me in that connection, which would have been in keeping with
my former role in his Administration. The trial of these persons for illegal precipitation of war would also be entirely in keeping with the philosophy of Lend-Lease that I had espoused, with the destroyer
exchange, and the aid to Britain.[96]

*Jackson's oral history also includes this summary observation about FDR as a
wartime president:*

Inevitably war exalts the executive function. It did in the Civil War.
A wartime President, who is a maker of day-to-day policy and commander of the armed forces, is just bound to grow in the public vision
and fill the public eye much more than the senators. The nation is at
stake. The President is the only officer who represents the whole
nation. All the rest are elected from some little part. No man in the Senate represents the United States. The President is the only man to
whom the whole United States is a constituency. Naturally they look to
him as the representative of national unity and national power. His post
is exalted by the hazards of war.

I think Roosevelt tried to fulfill his functions within the Constitution.[97]

THAT MAN AS ADMINISTRATOR

WE HAVE DWELT UPON the subjects in which Roosevelt excelled. But not all of his activities fall in these classes.

Roosevelt certainly was not accomplished as an administrator and in normal times, when his office demanded only an orderly and efficient administration of settled affairs, it is doubtful if he could have been a distinguished President. He was just not a routine executive.

He had one quality of a good administrator. He inspired an intense loyalty nearly everywhere in his administration. Young and ardent idealists, old and tired politicians, professors, even businessmen who joined up with him were ready to work at all hours of the day or night to carry out his bidding. But often it was hard to find out what his bidding was.

There was always considerable conflict of policy within the Administration and different factions favored different courses. The New Deal was not a reform movement. It was an assembly of movements—sometimes inconsistent with each other. It was not an infrequent occurrence that one of those whom the President trusted would take to him a document, such as an executive order, and obtain his approval before he had consulted with other persons affected. Roosevelt then would find himself in trouble. There were always those who were trying to get him to commit himself in a hurry, and too often he yielded. The remedy, instead of squarely backing up and undoing what he had done, was to promulgate some sort of compromise. He was reluctant to dismiss or demote anyone he liked, and he liked nearly everybody. Instead of dismissing a person who was pursuing a course inconsistent with his policy, he would create an additional layer of authority, which usually merely complicated matters.

In his oral history, Jackson described how this "layering" continued to occur, and worked, during World War II:

I think the situation as the war developed was somewhat like Churchill's organization of a War Cabinet, apart from the other departments of government. In wartime, a War Cabinet is pretty nearly a necessity. Roosevelt set it up informally. When some particular agency failed, Roosevelt was a great hand at setting up some other agency over it to control it, instead of abolishing it. His agencies by and large had real logic in their creation, however.

His inability to destroy an agency, but to pyramid one on top of another, was a good deal temperamental on his part. Roosevelt would deliver speeches in which he made quite an attack on individuals, or groups and classifications of men. But he did not like face-to-face quarrels with people. He did not like to dismiss people from his service. He thought dismissals usually involved some element of injustice to a man, particularly if he had tried hard and failed through causes other than disloyalty. It was just easier, and the path of least resistance, to set up overriding authority.

An exception was his treatment of William Knudsen, later on, which I think was pretty rough.[1] Of course he eventually fired Commerce Secretary Jesse Jones. But he found it easier to set up a new agency than he did to reconstruct an old one. That was the man's way.[2]

Roosevelt had a happy disregard of channels, ranks, and priorities and often would confer with or give instructions to lower-string men about subjects he should have taken up with their superiors. He once asked me, as Attorney General, to get Secretary Hull and Secretary Morgenthau together and settle their disagreement about a foreign financial policy. After the Cabinet meeting, I pointed out to him that it would be impossible for me to arbitrate between two men, both my senior in years, both my senior in Cabinet rank, both my senior in service there, and who, moreover, both had sources of information on the subject matter that I could not possibly have. Only one man could possibly settle that difficulty, and that was the President himself, but he shrank from doing so. He ultimately had to take up the task.

It was sometimes charged that he let his own people down, and the 1933 London Conference is cited as an example.[3] It sometimes happened, but on the whole I think he was more likely to stand by his subordinates in their errors than are most superior officers. I never had occasion to feel that he

THAT MAN AS ADMINISTRATOR

had let me down, even when action that I had taken, without consultation with him, may have caused embarrassment. The files of contemporary newspapers will show that many others in the Administration, although subjects of the most serious and widespread criticism, retained his confidence and support.

In late 1937 and early 1938, Jackson, as Assistant Attorney General heading the Antitrust Division, gave a series of public speeches that attracted national media coverage, much of it critical. Jackson argued that a small number of wealthy families and monopolies were responsible for the economic depression and promised antitrust prosecutions. Interior Secretary Harold Ickes also made similar allegations in a prominent speech during this period. More than fifteen years later, Jackson explained in his oral history what he, Ickes, and like-minded colleagues had been up to on FDR's behalf, and his supportive reaction to their efforts:

We decided, finally, to do some speech-making. . . .

For quite a time, nobody paid very much attention to our efforts. It was a great surprise to us when all of a sudden it caught fire and burst into a conflagration. I had been asked to make a speech on the radio, I think of fifteen minutes duration, the night after Christmas 1937. I had not the slightest premonition that it was to be an important speech. Among other things, I discussed steel prices and contended that steel had priced itself out of the market. As a matter of fact, that expression did not come from New Deal economists Isidore Lubin or Leon Henderson or any of the so-called radicals. In a visit that I had made just before the radio speech to Jamestown, where I was pretty much in touch with the industrial conditions and where the industries relied on steel for the making of metal furniture, partitions, doors, and the like, the expression that "steel had priced itself out of the market" was made by the president of the bank with which I was connected, as an observation on the industrial situation in Jamestown, New York. It struck me as a very good expression. I used it without credit.

It seemed that the expression caught attention and, to my surprise, the *New York Times* the following morning picked up this radio speech as a front page item.[4] That, of course, called it to the attention of everybody who was interested industrially and the reaction began violently. It was denounced as an extreme, radical, socialistic, communistic speech. The newspapers were full of it.

Either directly or through Tommy Corcoran—I am not sure which it was—I learned that the President was pleased with the speech and that he felt that events had been going too far the other way and too

fast. His word was to go ahead and do some more of it. I had not submitted this radio speech to the White House for clearance, chiefly
because I did not regard it as of very great importance.

. . .

During this period I talked with the President. He told me candidly
he was delighted. He thought it was arousing the people who were
really for the New Deal and was checking the movement against it.
There were great hopes of many Democrats, however, that because of
the outcry in the newspapers, which was of the most vigorous kind, the
President would find it expedient in his message to Congress to repudiate us. I remember that the *Washington Star* ran a cartoon showing Ickes
and myself out on a limb. The question was whether the President
would saw it off.[5] To their great chagrin, when the President's message
came in late April 1938, there was a paragraph in it, not, of course, referring to our speeches by name but plainly indicating his approval.[6] We
did not think he would let us down, and he did not.

. . .

In the course of the discussion I made a speech at Syracuse, I believe
more or less in response to one by former NRA administrator Don Richberg.[7] Richberg and I had opposite views. While we were always good
friends personally, we were making pretty pointed remarks about each
other's philosophy. Before I made the speech, I had talked with the President, but I did not submit any of these speeches—and I believe Ickes did
not—to the White House for clearance. We did not know what the reaction would be to them, and, as I have already stated, we thought that it
was better that the President be in a position to say that they had not
been read or cleared at the White House. We would take the responsibility for what we said and pay the penalty if necessary. But the general
lines of the speeches I discussed with the President and had his approval.
The only interference I had from Attorney General Cummings was
after the Syracuse speech, which was rather sharp at Richberg, who was
his close friend. I knew that Cummings felt that I had gone too far in
some of the things I had said—I knew instinctively that that was the
way he would feel. He said to me, "Bob, have you ever gotten the
approval of these speeches at the White House?" "No," I said, "I
hadn't." I did not say to him that the President had approved the general line of the speeches. "Well," he said, "I think you're in danger of
being repudiated. These speeches are pretty extreme. They're clever. I
enjoy reading them. But I think you're going pretty far and I think
you're exposing yourself to a good deal of danger." I said that I sup-

posed that was true and that I would have to take the consequences. But he did not forbid me to make them or ask me not to.

In a sense, we felt that the President was using our group as a stalking horse. That is what we had set ourselves up to be. We knew the risks. None of us were novices, exactly. We knew that we were plowing into dangerous ground. All of us were more or less of the belief that the head of state should be saved, that he should be protected—that if our speeches backfired in a bad way, we should take the gaff. That is one of the reasons why none of our speeches during that period was submitted to the White House for approval—so that the President could, in good faith and all honesty, repudiate what was said if it became necessary. I think it is sound policy that the head of state has got to be protected.[8]

In a private letter written almost two years after FDR's death, Jackson summarized Roosevelt's unregulating and tolerant approach on the subject of administration officials making public statements and speeches about policy matters:

There was no rigid rule during my tenure of office that all speeches or statements must be cleared with the President or with anyone else. If I made a speech or statement relating merely to the work of my Department, I rarely if ever cleared it with anyone. If, on the other hand, I made a speech or statement affecting the general policy of the Administration, I sometimes cleared it if I thought it might be out of harmony with the President's position and did not bother to clear it if I was pretty sure of my grounds. Frequently I discussed in advance with the President invitations I had received and the general subjects that I might discuss. In such cases, sometimes I would send him a manuscript of what I prepared, and sometimes I would not.

On one or two occasions—notably my speech at Havana discussing neutrality and the obligations and rights of neutrals in the war[9]—I cleared my speech with the State Department to avoid any possible conflict.

I can only generalize that under President Roosevelt I was quite free to voice my views. I sometimes thought he was too tolerant, for the good of the Administration, of individuality in matters that really required team play. The President to a large extent relied on the good faith and good sense of people about him not to precipitate needless controversies within the Administration. No one, so far as I know, was ever asked to give public support to any proposal with which he was not in agreement.[10]

There were feuds within the Administration, too, and on those his disposition generally was to let them fight it out. Harold Ickes and Harry Hopkins had a long-standing disagreement over their respective functions and jurisdictions, which the President never definitely settled. But despite their quarrels, he frequently invited the two of them to go on trips with him. No evidence of their disagreements ever marred the occasions.

He respected the personality, individuality, and integrity of his assistants and did not require them to do things that in their opinions they ought not to do. An instance was the May 1938 request of Dr. Hugo Eckener for helium, a non-inflammable light gas, to experiment with in his lighter-than-air balloons.[11] The *Hindenburg* had recently burned at Lakehurst, New Jersey, and the inflammable gas being used was a great menace to lighter-than-air navigation.[12] The amount of helium sought was enough to continue the zeppelin experiments. It was obtainable only in the United States. The National Munitions Control Board had been created, but the statute had given the final word on control of helium to the Secretary of the Interior. Secretary Ickes opposed giving any helium to the Germans and was determined upon that course. The State Department, on the contrary, desired to see us aid the lighter-than-air experimentation. The military and naval authorities said that the quantity sought by Dr. Eckener would be of no military consequence.

A long conference was called in the office of the President on May 12, 1938. He was rather disposed to aid the experimentation. The military authorities—Army Chief of Staff General Malin Craig and Chief of Naval Operations Admiral William Leahy—were present. Mr. Ickes was asked to state his attitude, and he stated his opposition to the delivery of helium gas to the Nazis.[13] General Craig and Admiral Leahy assured the President that there was no military hazard involved in the transfer. That seemed to be what Ickes was waiting for. He opened his briefcase and whipped out testimony given by military and naval representatives before one of the committees of Congress that seemed to contradict the conclusion of General Craig and Admiral Leahy. Ickes announced that so long as his approval was necessary, he would not agree to it.

The President had earlier talked with me and asked me to investigate the statutory authority over helium. He thought that perhaps he had final authority in the matter. The act, however, was very clear. The approval of the Secretary of the Interior was indispensable to any exportation of helium. I so advised the President.[14]

After Mr. Ickes had put the military and naval authorities back on their heels, the President turned to me and said, "Now, what can I do about this?" The situation was rather tense. Tempers were under control but obviously present.

I said, "Well, Mr. President, I don't see that you can do anything about helium unless you do something about your Secretary of Interior first. As long as you have such a stubborn one, I don't see how you can transfer helium under the statute."

The President laughed heartily, as did all the rest, but that ended the matter—the President would not give a preemptory order to his Secretary that went against the latter's judgment. Eckner was notified that he could not have the helium and was much disappointed.

Ickes stood his ground and many times afterward told me how proud he was of the fact that he did not let the Nazis get hold of helium. He felt that if he had done so, when the bombardment of London was on it would have been charged that Americans had provided the Nazis with some of the means. Ickes received a good deal of condemnation and an equal amount of praise for the position that he took in the matter. Whether he was right or wrong, I never knew. It was just another day in the life of a Solicitor General whose duty was with the law, not policy.[15]

Despite his hard and constant work at the job and his extensive knowledge of government procedures and personnel, it must be admitted that the President was not a master executive. Administration was not his strong point.

6

THAT MAN AS ECONOMIST

MANY OF THE LITIGATIONS and other matters that presented legal aspects were also economic matters. It always seemed to me that the President was at his weakest in dealing with economic or business problems. He had not engaged in business as my law practice had compelled me to do, and he had no personal knowledge of its methods or its problems. He tended to think of economic matters as personal rather than impersonal forces. He was much inclined to think about economic matters in terms of rights and wrongs. He was inclined to think that we were prosecuting a group of businessmen because they had done some moral wrong, and that if he talked to them and made them see that their course was morally wrong, they would do something about it.[1]

When we were considering the commencement of Department of Justice actions in 1937 to dissolve the motion picture combines, I went to the President and told him that I wanted to start an action against them. The President said, "Well now, of course, they've been doing wrong, but do you really need to sue these men? If you would bring them in here and let me talk with those fellows, don't you think they would change their practices? I think they can be straightened out." My answer, of course, was that these men were in a sense victims of their practices as well as perpetrators of them. It was a system that had grown up to where no one man or group could break it up without the intervention of government. Even if they all decided they ought to break it up, they could not do it. It was not a moral problem. It was not a right and wrong problem. It was a social and antisocial problem that did not reach moral concepts. What the President found difficult to envision was that they were caught up in a course of business practices that they were as powerless to escape from individually as if they were prisoners.

The President was not given to thought in economic terms, nor did he think of the problem in terms of men who were enmeshed in a system of business in which they were not entirely free agents. This was often the fact. He still thought of the antitrust, in a way, as punishing a conspiracy, thinking of a conspiracy as a dark cellar operation in which evil men got together in masks and plotted to do something. He never got what seemed to me to be the problem, which was that while these men were perhaps only acting in self-preservation, the aggregate of the measures they were taking were bad for the economy of the country. They could not be talked out of it. Many of them would admit that the practices were bad practices. They said, "What are we going to do? Here are the conditions. How can we change this?"[2]

I took over the Antitrust Division of the Department of Justice in 1937. It must be admitted that the economic philosophy of the Administration at that time was bogged down in conflict and confusion. The National Recovery Administration had been the most dramatic and intensive experiment of the Administration. It was based on a philosophy almost exactly the opposite of that of the antitrust law. The antitrust policies espoused by Woodrow Wilson were based generally on the belief that business would be self-regulating if competition were kept free and that the function of government could be limited to keeping open the channels of competition. The NRA was a reversion to the Theodore Roosevelt philosophy that business should be allowed to become big but regulated, that industrial policies should be permitted even if they restrained trade, provided the government had an overseeing or regulating hand. A source of confusion was that many people never knew the difference between antitrust laws and the NRA. They thought they were both anti-business, or in the nature of business regulations, and therefore they were for either one or the other without much regard to the merits. I must say that as time progressed and the work advanced, I came to be convinced that the President was not too clear on the difference between the two, their implications, and their means of execution.

During the NRA experiment, there had been a pretty general suspension of antitrust law activities, and practices were encouraged that were misunderstood by some businessmen to authorize what constituted violations of the antitrust laws. As I worked with the problems, it became very clear that there was urgent need for reconsideration of the antitrust legislation. I discussed the subject with the President a number of times.

In October of 1937, he wrote to me that the problem of "the inadequacies and defects in our anti-monopoly laws, which I have often reviewed informally with you and others," required attention. He asked me to assemble the important facts bearing on success or failure of present laws, the economic and social results of the legislation, and the necessity for revision or amendment, together with the different proposals or alternatives worthy of practical consideration and the advantages and disadvantages of each.[3]

THE WHITE HOUSE
WASHINGTON

October 22, 1937.

My dear Bob:—

      One of the problems that continues to require attention is the inadequacies and defects in our anti-monopoly laws, which I have often reviewed informally with you and others. I want to ask you to undertake, with the help of such others in the government service as you wish from time to time to enlist, to assemble for me the following:

      1. The important facts bearing upon the success or failure of our present anti-monopoly laws, their economic and social results, and the necessity for revision or amendment.

      2. The different proposals or alternatives worthy of practical consideration, with the advantages and disadvantages of each.

      You are, of course, authorized to call upon other officials for data and suggestions to make your report complete.

      I will look forward to receiving this information at your early convenience.

      Very sincerely yours,

Hon. Robert H. Jackson,
Department of Justice,
Washington, D. C.

Franklin D. Roosevelt

I began the work at once with a number of others from my own staff and from the other economic agencies of the government. At the end of November, I was invited to accompany the President on a fishing trip and took my materials with me. We discussed the subject extensively while on the trip.

I was urging the President to send a message on monopoly in general in order to get a thorough-going congressional consideration of the policy that should underlie our antitrust action. It seemed to me that the basic policy itself was unsettled. Part of the law looked to protecting business from interfering with competition. Another part of it looked to protecting it from competition. It was pretty difficult to draw the line where the two things met. The Robinson-Patman Act was on the books, but it was presenting great difficulties of interpretation.[4]

The President suggested that I prepare a draft of the message. We had a discussion of the need to carry this matter into some practical effect.

When we came to the framing of his monopoly message, the draft of which I had worked out with Ben Cohen, Leon Henderson, Herman Oliphant, and others who were in the Antitrust Division, it went to the President and came back in a few days with a paragraph added that proposed to allow industries to agree on volume of production for a given year. What he had in mind, as he explained to me, was to even out the peaks and valleys of employment through a fixed production schedule. He used the example of the automobile companies. He said, "I don't see any harm in Ford, Chrysler, and General Motors getting together and agreeing on a production schedule that will maintain employment on an even basis over a given period of time."

I said, "Mr. President, the difficulty with that is that the quantity to be produced is related to price. An automobile at $1000 has one market. An automobile at $1200 has a different market. (Those were not ridiculous figures at that time.) Therefore, the moment that you say that these men may sit down and plan production, they have to plan price. They have to allocate territory. In other words, every evil that we fight under the antitrust laws will come in under schedulized, agreed production."

"Yes, I guess that's right. I guess we can't do it," he would conclude.

The President, however, always was torn between the Theodore Roosevelt theory of regulated bigness and the Wilsonian-Brandeis theory of free competition and retention of the smaller units. He never seemed very clear as to what distinction he would make or where he would draw the line between the two. He knew the difference between the two philosophies, but as to which was preferable and whether there was not some way by which you could have the best parts of each, he was never quite clear.

By the next year, 1938, I had become Solicitor General.[5] The President went to Warm Springs, Georgia, for a much-needed rest. He suggested that we get a draft of a message to Congress and meet his train at Atlanta on his return so we could work on it on the train coming back. Ben Cohen and I went to Atlanta on April 2, worked on a draft in the hotel, boarded the President's train, and spent the day and evening working with him on it in his private car. The matter drifted along until April 28, at which time the President assembled several of us in his study for the evening and took all of the matters that had been submitted and started to dictate his message to his secretary. About 11:30, he had completed his dictation and gave it to us for minor editing. He told us if it was finished, he would send it to Congress on the following day.[6]

Ben Cohen, Tom Corcoran, and I went to the Cabinet room. About 1:00 we had some sandwiches sent up from the White House kitchen and we worked on until 3:30. About 3:30, the draft seemed in as good shape as we could put it. The only thing left was to cut stencils and get it mimeographed so that it would be ready. I was to be on hand the following morning and present it to the President before he left his bedroom.[7] It was quite a custom of the President to look over matters of that kind in bed as he had breakfast.

I went to the White House, arriving about the time he had his breakfast sent up, and had coffee with him. He read the message over very lightly, having been over it pretty thoroughly the night before. I called his attention to the principal changes we had made. He signed it and told me to take it down and have it sent. The message went to Congress that day.[8]

But until the very last, I was not certain whether it would take the direction of the Woodrow Wilson theory or of the NRA theory in dealing with the monopoly problem. Donald Richberg, a trusted adviser, had submitted a number of proposals looking to the NRA plan and he had supported them effectively in personal conversation and by memoranda. I would argue against them, as I was of the Wilson school. I would apparently convince the President and the paragraphs suggested by Richberg would be laid aside. The next time I would talk with the President, they would be in again.

A contest between Richberg and me ran throughout the preparation of the message. Richberg was an advocate of the NRA, and when that was held unconstitutional,[9] he urged strongly upon the President that a system be set up by which businessmen could be allowed to make certain agreements that would be in restraint of trade with the approval and under the supervision of an administrative body. I was opposed to this course. I believed that in three months' time the businessmen would dominate the body and that it would prove a bulwark to monopoly rather than a bulwark against it. However, the President was much impressed with the idea, as he had always been favorable to the NRA.

Richberg during the early months of 1938 supplied the President with memoranda, one of which dealt with the steel industry, urging that it was not monopolistic and that its basing point system for charging customers was not unfair.[10] Richberg was out of the city during the period that we were putting the finishing touches on the message. On April 23, he wrote frantically from San Francisco because he had read in the newspapers that the President and Senator William Borah of Idaho, a Republican Senate leader, were in agreement. Richberg said: "The philosophy of the fanatic trust busters, their hostility to all large enterprise, their assumption that cooperation is always a cloak for monopolistic conspiracy—this philosophy is wholly inconsistent with the New Deal." On the other hand he contended that the NRA was not inconsistent with the New Deal.[11] Had he been in town to press his views personally, I am not sure that he would not have prevailed, for I do not think the President ever took the time to think through fully the conflict between the antitrust law philosophy and that of the NRA. He genuinely felt that there was some way by which well-intentioned men would be able to get advantages of both.

The President plainly had no firm convictions and expressed no very dogmatic views about the monopoly problem. He knew that there were evils in the suppression of competition and that there were evils in competition itself, and where the greater evils were he never fully decided.

I do not set myself up as one to appraise the mental processes of the President, but they did not impress me as being grounded in economic theory or practice. He had keen political judgments and social philosophy, but I think he had never devoted himself to much study of the economic processes of the country.[12]

When I arrived in Washington in February of 1934, the first legal battle in which I found myself involved was the Andrew Mellon tax case.[13] The Department of Justice, contrary to the advice of myself and others at the Treasury, had presented the matter as a criminal one, and on May 7, 1934, the grand jury had refused to indict him.[14]

The grand jury's refusal to indict Mellon left the question for the Treasury as to assessment of the tax and the more difficult question as to whether a fraud penalty should be assessed in addition. This was not a simple question of law but also involved some questions of policy. Mr. Mellon had been a Republican Secretary of the Treasury and it was easy to charge that he was being persecuted for that reason. The criminal proceedings had failed and brought considerable criticism. The evidence of fraud was that he had sold stocks at losses, in sales that lacked the element of good faith. This reduced his tax substantially, but the stocks were in fact transferred to other corporations or members of his family where he would not lose control of them. It was, however, more or less of a system that the Treasury tolerated not only in Mr. Mellon but in others. The issue also would have to be tried before Judges of the Board of Tax Review who came to office during the Mellon regime at Treasury.

I recommended that fraud not be charged and no fraud penalty be assessed. I later learned that, had this course been followed, the taxes would have been paid. I recommended this not because I was convinced on the merits of the matter, but as a matter of trial strategy. Under the statutes, if fraud was charged, the burden was on the government to prove it, while if we only charged a tax to be due, the burden was on the taxpayer to show that it was not. This may seem a technical point, but it is a very important matter of trial strategy.

The Department of Justice was opposed to my recommendation and the matter was taken to the President. I was not present when it was discussed and my memorandum was not read by him. He never reached the question of strategy. When Attorney General Cummings had told him of the details of some of the Mellon transactions, the President closed the discussion, I was told, by holding his nose and saying that we must proceed with the fraud charges.[15] Before I left for Pittsburgh to try the *Mellon* case, however, I had a long discussion of the trial strategy with him. I think it illustrated the tendency to make snap judgments on insufficient information, for when it was explained, he understood the difficulties of our position.

Arthur Krock, the influential columnist who ran the *New York Times*'s Washington bureau, suggested in 1934 that the President "knew nothing in advance of the move to indict Andrew Mellon for income tax evasions."[16] I would doubt that statement. I doubt that any Attorney General would start criminal proceedings against a former Secretary of the Treasury, former Ambassador to the Court of St. James's, and leader of the opposition party without the President's knowledge.

The President never told me that he did not know of it, and I discussed the case with him just before I went to Pittsburgh to try the civil case a year later. I told him at that time that even in the civil case, we were going to be in real difficulty if Frank Hogan, Mellon's lawyer, started his case with technical corporate reorganization issues. I also told the President what evidence we had, and gave him a general briefing on the case.[17] The President did not indicate to me that he did not know about the *Mellon* criminal case, although he realized that the Administration was in a very bad way with it. One of the things that he hoped I could accomplish in the civil case—one of the things that I hoped I could accomplish—was at least to make a case from which the public would understand that the charges were not wholly unfounded, that it was a legitimate tax claim, and that the government ought to have pressed it. Whether it should have been prosecuted as a criminal suit was a different question. But at least there was substance to the charge that Mellon was a tax evader. If that could be established, it would save the Administration's face. It was pretty much in need of being saved after the grand jury refused to return an indictment against Mellon.

The President may have sought to minimize his own responsibility for the mistake and intimated to somebody that he did not know too much about it. But I think as a matter of fair history, he did know about it.[18]

Late in 1934, the President requested a study of the tax system, to include consideration of changes to strengthen the economic structure and to conform more nearly to the social objectives of the new Administration. The President, like the rest of us, was discontented with the system of taxation. He felt that it was unduly burdensome to lower incomes, and that the hopes of the income tax as a measure equalizing the burden had not been achieved. He generally favored the revision of the tax structure. That was necessitated by the fact that appropriations were large and there was a necessity for increasing the revenues. During the Depression, the income tax revenue had very much dried up. People generally did not have the income. Some who made good profits during that period were able to handle their affairs in such a way that their profits were not taxable.

The program for revision of the tax structure of the United States was the subject of study for more than six months. It was the most important matter, apart from the *Mellon* case, into which I was thrown after coming to the Treasury. Looking back on it, there is no service in this period that gives me greater satisfaction than the work I did in connection with it.[19]

The government was confronted with the fact that a considerable number of taxes enacted as a more or less temporary matter were expiring on June 30, 1935. Included were taxes on toilet articles, photographic films, bank checks, insurance premiums, electric light bulbs, and various other things. The result was that the government would suffer a large loss of revenue. At the same time, it had become plain that the program of the Administration of relief and welfare work had to be curtailed, or that additional revenues had to be produced from some source. So study of the tax structure began in dead earnest.

A study was prepared by Mr. Herman Oliphant, counsel for the Treasury; George Haas, statistician for the Treasury; and myself, covering inheritance, estate, and gift taxes, a proposed intercorporate dividend tax, a graduated tax on corporations scaled according to size, and several other features of the tax laws.

Early in December of 1934, this was the basis of a conference with the President. It was held in the evening in his study and we reviewed it in some detail and discussed the economic situation. I have always remembered his statement on that evening, that he could relieve unemployment in short time if he would resort to methods that Hitler and Mussolini were using of relieving unemployment by building up their armaments. It was really the first time that I had thought of their solving their economic problems in that way. I suppose I had not been paying much attention to it. It was somewhat startling. He thought there was some need for us to improve our armaments, but that the country would not support any substantial rearmament program. At that time I felt strongly opposed to that method of relief of unemployment, for I thought it would result in another arms race. I said then that I hoped he did not consider doing that because it would be a tragic way of solving the Depression. He agreed.

After the conference, the task of preparing a message was delegated to me and on January 7 I completed it. Mr. Haas worked on a separate draft and his was completed on January 10. On the night of January 10 we held another conference with the President, and then I again prepared and on January 15 submitted a proposed draft of a message embodying the result of our further discussions. I went to Pittsburgh at about this time to try the *Mellon* case and nothing of substance was done during my absence except that studies went on and some discussions were held. The President took our joint Treasury draft with him on a trip down the river on the *Sequoia* and a photostat was returned to me showing many changes in his handwriting and certain suggestions noted over the initials "R.M." His conferee on that subject had been Raymond Moley, and thereafter Moley's draft of a proposed tax message was sent to us.

Following the Moley draft, we in the Treasury—the same group, the work being done largely by Oliphant, Haas, and myself—prepared another draft, which was ready on June 15, 1935. The President took our draft and revised it considerably, mainly in its wording, to give it greater clarity and less technicality, and to make it more acceptable and understandable to the public.

I left for Pittsburgh for the trial of the *Mellon* case and the matter dragged until another conference on the evening of June 16, 1935, at which were present Secretary of the Treasury Henry Morgenthau, Mr. Oliphant, Mr. Haas, and a man I never before had met, Professor Felix Frankfurter, who was the guest of the President at the White House. The President read the proposed message from beginning to end and noted various changes and suggestions. The President put forward his settled convictions that additional taxation must be resorted to. He also stated that the burden of it must fall largely upon the upper brackets of income and not interfere with the purchasing power of the masses, who keep the economic machine running by spending their income instead of investing it in additional capital. The problems, of course, were the techniques for accomplishing these ends. It was left to Mr. Oliphant and me to put the draft into final form. I spent a great deal of time at work on it, having several consultations with the President.

On June 19, 1935, the President sent the result as a special message transmitting his views on the broad question of taxation and tax policies.[20] Generally speaking, it proposed increases in the taxation of inheritances and estates, a graduated tax, heavier on large corporations than on small ones, and suggested a study of a tax on dividends paid by one corporation to another, which theretofore had been tax-free. This message made a number of suggestions for important changes in the tax structure intended to produce more ample revenues without discouraging enterprise and to distribute the burden of taxes more equitably. The studies that we had made had proved that a great deal of the wealth of the country was escaping taxation through various devices—devices that were legal, that the tax laws had permitted.

In the hearings that followed, it was delegated to me to present the support for the President's message, and in Senate Finance Committee sessions lasting two days, I did so. The results are a matter of record.[21] His enemies promptly labeled it a soak-the-rich program. It is no part of my present purpose to argue the merits of it, but upon returning to my office I found a highly complimentary letter written in longhand from the President on the presentation.[22]

The President was keenly aware of the effect of taxation on the lives of the people and on their standard of living. He knew that any tax, no matter how devised, would have social consequences, and he frankly desired to shape the tax to achieve desirable instead of what he considered undesirable social consequences. But he viewed the taxation problem perhaps too exclusively as a social problem and not sufficiently as one in economics. As I have suggested, economics did not appear to be his long suit.[23]

In 1937, the President sent a tax message to Congress in which he

THE WHITE HOUSE

Robert Jackson Esq
Treasury

THE WHITE HOUSE
WASHINGTON

Aug 7
1935

Dear Bob —

My congratulations & thanks to
you for that wholly excellent
presentation before the Senate
Committee — It was a grand
performance —

As ever yours

Franklin D Roosevelt

Robert Jackson Esq

attacked the tax evasion or avoidance methods of various taxpayers and proposed a congressional investigation.[24] I was no longer in the Treasury and knew nothing of the message until I read it in the newspaper. Treasury Secretary Henry Morgenthau and General Counsel Herman Oliphant proposed that I conduct the investigation. The idea was that it would be something like the Pecora investigation of banking that a Senate committee had conducted in 1933 and 1934.[25]

I advised that I did not wish to do so. I told them that I did not want to undertake it. It was out of my line of work at the time and, furthermore, I did not see how it could be conducted very successfully. If the taxpayers were using illegal methods, it was the duty of the Treasury to prosecute them and to collect the tax being illegally evaded, and if the Treasury had failed to do so after our Administration had been in power for four years, it was not in a very good position to complain. On the other hand, if the taxpayers' methods were legal ones that Treasury approved, I could not see justification for pillorying taxpayers who had employed them. After all, there was no obligation to pay taxes that the Treasury was not under obligation to collect. I was told, however, that it was the President's wish that I should do this, and that he would communicate with me. I was able to present what seemed to be good objections to my participation.

The next thing I knew was an invitation to spend the weekend with the President on a cruise on the Potomac. I suspected from the information that I had received from the Treasury that I would be urged to conduct the congressional investigation. I had thought the matter over and was somewhat prepared, but nothing was said about it. We spent the afternoon in visiting and fishing and the evening in gay conversation on general topics, and not until Sunday afternoon as we were coming up the river did the President mention the matter to me. He then said in substance, "Bob, Henry thinks it would be a nice thing if you would conduct the investigation that he has going of the income tax dodgers. Do you want to do it?" I replied, "Mr. President, frankly, I do not want to do it." I told him I was fearful that it could not be successful. In fact, I said it might very well be turned into an investigation of the Bureau of Internal Revenue, for if illegal evasions are not being prosecuted, somebody is delinquent. I also suggested that I did not see how I could conduct a congressional investigation unless I was engaged by the congressional committee. The President dismissed the whole matter by saying, "I don't think it is a job that you better get into anyway," and we left it at that.

I advised the Secretary and Mr. Oliphant that I had declined it. The opening of the investigation as scheduled was very close at hand. I received

Democratic Party vice presidential nominee FDR on a campaign visit to Jamestown, New York, October 21, 1920. (Photograph by Black; from the collections of the Franklin D. Roosevelt Library, Hyde Park, New York, and the Fenton History Center, Jamestown, New York.)

Vice presidential candidate FDR, speaking on a railroad siding near Jamestown, New York, October 21, 1920. (From the collection of the Franklin D. Roosevelt Library, Hyde Park, New York.)

New York Governor FDR and Jamestown lawyer Frank Mott prepare to leave Mott's cottage at Driftwood on Chautauqua Lake for Chautauqua Institution, July 13, 1929. Standing behind the automobile are George Brill, Robert Jackson, Walter Jackson (no relation), Daniel Scannell, Elliott Roosevelt, and an unidentified New York State trooper. (From the collection of the Fenton History Center, Jamestown, New York.)

President FDR, in the White House, working on his stamp collection, May 5, 1936. (From the collection of the Franklin D. Roosevelt Library, Hyde Park, New York.)

FDR delivers his "I Hate War" speech in Chautauqua Institution's Amphitheater, August 14, 1936. Assistant Attorney General (Tax Division) Robert Jackson is seated in the second row, on the left side of the aisle. (From Chautauqua Institution Archives, Chautauqua, New York.)

FDR delivering the "I Hate War" speech at Chautauqua Institution. Jackson is next to the microphone pole at FDR's left elbow. (From Chautauqua Institution Archives, Chautauqua, New York.)

Following the "I Hate War" speech, FDR, Chautauqua Institution president Arthur Bestor, and Jackson are driven from the Amphitheater to a reception at Dr. Bestor's home. (From Chautauqua Institution Archives, Chautauqua, New York.)

"Come along. We're going to the Trans-Lux to hiss Roosevelt."

Peter Arno's cartoon, published in *The New Yorker* on September 26, 1936, captures the social status and sentiment of at least some of the Americans who, with deep loathing, referred to FDR as "That Man in the White House." (© The New Yorker Collection 1936 Peter Arno from cartoonbank.com. All rights reserved.)

The *Washington Star*'s front-page editorial cartoonist, Clifford K. Berryman, depicts, on September 19, 1937, "That Man" shocking a sedate Congress by calling for urgent action. President Roosevelt had, two days earlier, used his nationally broadcast radio address on the occasion of the 150th anniversary of the signing of the U.S. Constitution to describe a "crisis in American affairs that demands action now." FDR said that the American people were insisting on economic and social security and a higher standard of living, and he described public "illusions" that dictatorship would, because it could accomplish these objectives, be preferable to democratic government. He called for action on his legislative program and, just weeks after the defeat of his Court-packing plan, reiterated his view that the Constitution is a "layman's charter" that permits necessary national government action. (© 1937, The Washington Post. Reprinted with permission.)

FDR on the rear platform of the presidential train, about to leave Union Station in Washington, D.C., for Miami and then a fishing trip off Florida, November 27, 1937. Assistant Attorney General (Antitrust Division) Robert Jackson stands to FDR's right and Secretary of Commerce Daniel Roper is to his left. (Bettmann/Corbis.)

THE MOST POPULAR RADIO FEATURE FOR 1937!

After Jackson gave a number of prominent, nationally broadcast speeches blaming a small number of wealthy families and monopolies for the economic depression and promising antitrust prosecutions, Clifford Berryman depicted FDR on December 30, 1937, as the ventriloquist who was responsible for Jackson's utterances. (© 1937, The Washington Post. Reprinted with permission.)

After FDR stated in his January 1938 state of the union address to Congress that businessmen and bankers intend to be "good citizens," Berryman depicted the President as undercutting vocal business critics Jackson and Interior Secretary Harold Ickes—to the amusement of other administration figures who had not joined in their public remarks. (© 1938, The Washington Post. Reprinted with permission.)

OUT ON A LIMB!

As FDR's aspirations for Jackson's political advancement became quite public in early 1938, Berryman depicted Jackson as poised to jump from the Solicitor Generalship (to which he had just been nominated) to FDR's former office and then to his current one. Berryman inscribed his original drawing and gave it to Jackson as a gift. (Reprinted courtesy of Nancy R. Jackson.)

FDR congratulates Jackson in the White House study following his taking the oath as Attorney General, January 18, 1940. (Gift from Jackson to Gordon Dean; reprinted courtesy of Deborah Gore Dean.)

As Attorney General Jackson watches, new Solicitor General Francis Biddle is sworn in by Justice Felix Frankfurter, January 22, 1940. (Bettmann/Corbis.)

FDR, in the House chamber, asks a joint session of Congress to appropriate more than one billion dollars to build up American air defenses. The front row audience includes, from left, Sen. Harry S. Truman, Agriculture Secretary Henry Wallace, Assistant Secretary of the Navy Lewis Compton, Commerce Secretary Harry Hopkins, Secretary of State Cordell Hull, Treasury Secretary Henry Morgenthau, Secretary of War Harry Woodring, Attorney General Robert Jackson, and Interior Secretary Harold Ickes, May 16, 1940. (Acme; courtesy Bernard L. Douglas, Jr.)

FDR pins the Distinguished Service Cross on General John J. Pershing, commander of the American Expeditionary Forces in World War I, on his eightieth birthday, in the White House study, September 13, 1940. Congress had voted in 1922 to award Pershing this honor for a 1913 act of heroism in military action in the Philippines, but he refused to accept it. In September 1940, Roosevelt was particularly grateful to Pershing for his August 4 public statement, which was broadcast nationally by radio, urging what became FDR's decision to deliver fifty over-age U.S. naval destroyers to Great Britain. Watching are, from left, Secretary of War Henry Stimson, FDR's military aide and secretary General Edwin ("Pa") Watson, U.S. Army Chief of Staff General George Marshall, Treasury Secretary Henry Morgenthau, Attorney General Robert Jackson, and Secretary of Labor Frances Perkins (obscured). (Bettmann/Corbis.)

FDR attends the state funeral of the late Speaker of the House Rep. William B. Bankhead (D.-AL), a devoted New Deal supporter, in the House chamber, September 16, 1940. Rep. Sam Rayburn, the new Speaker, is at the podium. Present in the front row are, from left, former Commerce Secretary Harry Hopkins, Secretary of Agriculture Claude Wickard, Interior Secretary Harold Ickes, Attorney General Robert Jackson, Secretary of War Henry Stimson, Treasury Secretary Henry Morgenthau, Secretary of State Cordell Hull, President Roosevelt, and, across the aisle, Sen. John H. Bankhead (the late Speaker's older brother), Mrs. Florence McGuire Bankhead (the late Speaker's widow), and, mostly obscured, actress Tallulah Bankhead (his younger daughter). (Bettmann/Corbis.)

FDR, holding a mason's trowel and the arm of General Watson, dedicates Washington National Airport, September 28, 1940. (From the collection of the Franklin D. Roosevelt Library, Hyde Park, New York.)

Clifford Berryman, in a cartoon that the anti-Roosevelt *Washington Star* published on Halloween 1940, depicts Uncle Sam as reacting angrily to the prospect of "That Man's" impending reelection and many more years in office. (© 1940, The Washington Post. Reprinted with permission.)

Attorney General Jackson, speaking in his adult hometown of Jamestown, New York, and on a nationwide radio broadcast in support of President Roosevelt's 1940 reelection to a third term, acknowledges applause from his audience. (WJTN photo archive, Jamestown, New York. Reprinted with permission.)

Lend-Lease program director Harry Hopkins, Attorney General Robert Jackson, FDR, General "Pa" Watson, Interior Secretary Harold Ickes, and Navy Rear Admiral and presidential physician Ross McIntire stand on the dock in Port Everglades, Florida, in front of the USS *Potomac* after their cruise, March 30, 1941. (Bettmann/Corbis.)

FDR aboard the USS *Potomac* in Port Everglades, Florida, with, from left, General Watson, an unidentified Navy officer, Robert Jackson, Harry Hopkins, Harold Ickes (seated), and Dr. Ross McIntire, March 1941. (From the collection of the Franklin D. Roosevelt Library, Hyde Park, New York.)

FDR at his knickknack-covered desk in the Oval Office with his secretaries (from left) Grace Tully, Stephen Early, and Missy Le Hand, May 22, 1941. (From the collection of the Franklin D. Roosevelt Library, Hyde Park, New York.)

FDR, having just signed Jackson's commission following his oath taking in the Oval Office, grins as he shakes the hand of the newest Associate Justice of the Supreme Court. Mary M. Jackson (daughter) and Irene G. Jackson (wife) beam as they watch, July 11, 1941. (From the Library of Congress photographic collection.)

FDR signs a family Bible before new Attorney General Francis Biddle and Associate Justice Jackson, September 5, 1941. (© AP / Wide World. Reprinted with permission.)

FDR delivers his fourth inaugural address from the south porch of the White House, January 20, 1945. Secret Service agent Charles Frederick, James Roosevelt, and General "Pa" Watson look on. (Bettmann/Corbis.)

Dignitaries leave the White House following FDR's funeral in the East Room, April 14, 1945. Those pictured include the late President's military chief of staff, Admiral William Leahy (far left); former Chief Justice Charles Evans Hughes (white beard, in the left-center front); his wife, Antoinette Carter Hughes; Commerce Secretary Henry Wallace (to the left and rear of Hughes); Emir Faisal, son of King Ibn Saud of Arabia (behind Wallace); U.S.S.R. Ambassador to the United States Andrei Gromyko (to the right of Mrs. Hughes); Attorney General Francis Biddle (behind Gromyko); Irene Jackson (in profile, in the second row, right of center, wearing a black hat); Justice Felix Frankfurter (next to Mrs. Jackson, partially obscured); and Justice Jackson (back of head, to the right of Frankfurter facing the woman in the white hat). (From the collection of the Franklin D. Roosevelt Library, Hyde Park, New York.)

President Truman presents General Watson's posthumous Distinguished Service Medal to his widow, Frances Nash Watson, in the White House rose garden, June 8, 1945. FDR had, shortly before his own death, decided to award the Medal to Watson after the return trip from Yalta on which he had died. Former First Lady Eleanor Roosevelt, shrouded in mourner's black, looks on, as do her daughter Anna Boettiger (behind Mrs. Watson) and, to the right of the pillar, Justice Jackson, Irene Jackson, and Justice Frankfurter. (From the Library of Congress photographic collection.)

a call asking whether Morgenthau, Oliphant, and Under Secretary Roswell Magill could see me at my house. I was then living in the country on the River Road in Maryland. They drove out in the midst of one of the worst thunderstorms I have ever seen. They came, they said, at the suggestion of the President, who wanted me to open the investigation and conduct it for two weeks. Then I would be relieved and someone else of my choosing would take over. This, they said, the President had just requested them to tell me.

I had an idea that the plan had not originated with the President, and I had a strong suspicion that he had merely nodded his amiable head when it was put up to him. I felt under a good deal of obligation to the President, and I did not want to turn him down, at least without a chance to give him my reasons, but I said, "Has anybody discussed this with Senator Harrison?" Senator Pat Harrison of Mississippi, who chaired the Finance Committee, was scheduled to preside at the hearing. No one had even mentioned this plan to him. I asked, "How do you expect counsel to conduct a congressional investigation except as chosen and authorized to do so by the committee itself?" I pointed out to them that the committee might not even permit him to appear. I knew Senator Harrison and some other members of the committee were not too cordial toward the President's message and the plan. I also told them that even if the Committee did consent, I would not be able to undertake it for only two weeks, because once being in it I could not withdraw without opposition papers saying either that I had been fired because my services were not satisfactory or that I had quit because I disagreed with somebody in the Treasury. It was an utterly impractical scheme.

They got the President on the telephone from my house, and on talking with him I found that he was not very much concerned about whether I did it or not. There was a tone in his voice that did not seem to be urging me very hard. The fact was that the Treasury officials had gotten themselves in a jam and they were desperately insisting that I take over and take responsibility. They were not prepared to conduct the hearings, which were scheduled less than a week away. It seemed to me that the President had hurriedly signed a proposal that had gotten him into a dilemma and I told him so quite candidly. The President did not insist that I undertake the job and suggested that Magill go at once to Senator Harrison and discuss the matter with him.

When I got to the office next morning, I learned that Under Secretary Magill had made an appointment with Senator Harrison for me and Mr. Magill for 12:30. They also proposed later to make an appointment with the

President. I declined to go to see Senator Harrison unless he wanted me to
be present. Senator Harrison then asked me to come, and of course I went.
He was completely opposed to the Treasury plan of operation. He pointed
out all of the difficulties that I had and some more. He said frankly that
even if the committee were to employ counsel, he would not employ me.
He went on to say that he felt great friendship for me, in which I believe he
was completely sincere for in several later matters he demonstrated it. But
he said that if there was an investigation of the kind, it should not be conducted by a former officer of the Bureau of Internal Revenue. I agreed that
he was completely right about it. He said that he expected the Treasury to
be present with some witnesses who would testify as to the facts on which
the tax evasion was based and to demonstrate what legislation, if any, was
needed.

It was next proposed that I be a witness and that I declined, for it was
obviously impossible for me to prepare anything in such a short time and,
second, I did not like the Treasury plan of proceeding. I did not like the
idea of disclosing the names and affairs of particular individuals and criticizing them when you had to wind up admitting that what they had done
was within the law and was approved by the Treasury. Thurman Arnold
was working with me in the Antitrust Division, and it was arranged that he
should go into conference with Treasury people and assist in preparing
their statements. He reported that almost nothing had been done about
getting material for the hearings, but he hurriedly threw together statements for the Secretary of the Treasury, the Commissioner of Internal Revenue, and others.

The investigation is a matter of public record. The criticisms of it were
insistent and bitter. It has always seemed to me to have been one of the
major mistakes of the Administration, alienating a good many members of
Congress and embittering unnecessarily and justifiably a great many people. I was glad that I had nothing to do with it, and it appeared to be a situation where the President had relied too heavily on the advice of others. It
was a case where excessive zeal had gotten the President in a hole. I could
not have gotten him out. The most that I could have done would have been
to get into the hole with him. Nothing about me would have made that
very consoling to him.[26]

The President's lack of aptitude for economic matters was also evident
in the consideration of the studies of inflation, prices and price controls,
and other economic subjects connected with the emergency that arose
after Hitler had made his attack on Poland. One day in September of 1939,
the President handed me a weird plan for excess profits taxation in connec-

tion with the request that I confer with various others and devise a real excess profits tax law. He had put his formula, God knows from where he had obtained it, in the form of a short memorandum. It was, in brief, to add the book value of a corporation's plant to its present appraised value, the cash capital of the company, and its earnings averaged for five years. Taking that total and dividing it by four would give the base for the tax. He would allow a 6 percent return on that base and tax all over that at 99.9 per-cent.[27] I am sorry to say that none of the experts in the Administration whom I consulted gave his memorandum respectful attention.

The President was not at his best on the business side of government. He needed strong economic and financial advisers on whom he could rely. His interest was in the personal rather than in those impersonal forces that make up our national lives.

THAT MAN AS COMPANION AND SPORTSMAN

IT WAS HERE THAT Roosevelt was irresistible and inimitable. He liked people, almost any people. He liked their company, liked to pick their minds and see what they were thinking, liked to know the details of their lives and their problems.

I know nothing that illustrates the contrast between him and Woodrow Wilson, the previous Democratic President, better than their attitudes toward Henry Ford. I lunched with journalist George Creel one day, who told me the difficulty they had with Wilson in the early days of World War I, getting him to confer with American businessmen to gain their cooperation in the war effort. He refused to see most of them, saying they were specialists who had nothing to teach him with his general problems affecting the whole nation. Finally they prevailed upon him to see Henry Ford, and after the interview, Creel entered and said to the President, "What do you think of Henry Ford?" Wilson impatiently answered, "I think he is the most comprehensively ignorant man I ever met." He had complete contempt for Ford.

Two or three days after that lunch with Creel, I noticed that Ford was President Roosevelt's luncheon guest. I happened to be at the White House that afternoon late and opened the conversation by saying, "Mr. President, I see you had lunch with Henry Ford." "Yes," he said, "I had a grand time with Uncle Henry." He then described the conversation enthusiastically and with gestures. He said he tried to discuss with Ford the problem of an annual wage for workmen. Roosevelt described how he edged him up to the subject, and when Ford saw what he was leading up to, he would draw back, then he would work him up to it from another angle and Ford would draw back, and he said he spent his whole luncheon hour playing chess with "Uncle Henry," as he called him, trying to get him up to the subject. Roosevelt said, "You know, I never got him to it." But he liked Ford and respected him for the things in which he was able and had none of the contempt that characterized the Wilsonian attitude.[1]

Roosevelt took frequent weekend trips on his Presidential yacht down the Potomac. They were not free from work, for often the company for the trip was chosen with a view for certain work to be done while away from the hectic interruptions of Washington. My first invitation illustrates something in the President's makeup.

The President's secretary, Missy Le Hand, called. My secretary, Mrs. Grace Stewart, a Washington secretary of long experience who practiced the Washington habit of listening to the conversation and later reminding me of any engagements or promises made, was on the phone.[2] Miss Le Hand said the President would like Mrs. Jackson and me to go with him on a trip on his yacht the following Saturday and Sunday, starting about 11:00 Saturday morning. I replied that ordinarily I would be very glad to do so, but that I would not be able to go on the coming Saturday morning.

At this point my secretary dropped her telephone and exclaimed, "You can't do that, you can't do that, it just isn't done. An invitation from the President is a command." Despite her appeal I finished the explanation. I said that my son was graduating from St. Albans School that morning, that the exercises were to be at 11:00, and that I would not want to be absent. Miss Le Hand said she understood and regretted the circumstances, and that ended the chapter for a few moments, except for the lecture that I received on Washington etiquette from my well-advised and distracted secretary, who felt confident that I was forever outside of the Presidential goodwill.

A few moments later there was another call. Miss Le Hand said that the President wanted to congratulate me on Bill's graduation and that, of course, I ought to attend the exercises. He thought he might be somewhat delayed in getting away and would be glad to wait until 1:00 if it would be possible for me to make it at that time. That I said I could do.[3] That is exactly what I would have expected of him, for a more considerate man or one less inclined to stand on the position that a presidential word was a command, particularly as against the little things that mean a good deal to other people, never was President. In the many weekend trips that we spent on the Potomac thereafter, it never escaped notice how he had attempted to set his schedule and make arrangements to convenience others.[4]

I was fortunate enough to take fishing trips of some duration with him in the fall of 1937, in the late fall of 1940 after the election, and again in the spring of 1941. The first of these was to Florida and along the Keys as far as the Dry Tortugas,[5] the second was down the Potomac and the Chesapeake Bay, and the third was to Florida and the Bahamas. His means of recreation were limited and fishing was one that he could enjoy. But on the fishing trips there was much reading, much sleep, much discussion, much work, and much play. Twice a day, dispatch bags arrived containing all manner of documents that demanded his attention. The radio was constantly bringing news of the world and there was no relief from the fact that twenty-four hours a day he was President of the United States.

Before dinner we usually had martini cocktails made by the President's own hands, but any impression that the President was given to any considerable amount of drinking—which may arise from the fact that his son's account of some of his trips abroad appeared in form condensed except as to the cocktails, which were always mentioned[6]—is a mistake. I never knew him to take more than a couple of cocktails, nor did he want anyone about him who drank to excess.

We usually played poker after the dinner table was cleared, but it was a pastime, not a passion. The limits were small, so small, indeed, that I look back over the log and notice that on my first trip my total losses were a trifle over $7.00 and my total gain a little over $4.00, making a net loss of $3.00 for several days of playing.[7] Harry Hopkins, particularly, used to be impatient at the small limits, but the President would never let the game become one of substantial amount. His luck was phenomenal. Always, however, the game ended one round after 10:00. He retired early and wanted others to do the same.

Jackson apparently kept a journal during his late 1937 trip with the President and others by train to Miami and then by ship through the Florida Keys to the Dry Tortugas. Shortly after their return to Washington, Jackson used his notes to dictate the following eighteen-page memorandum for his files:

CONFIDENTIAL
Memorandum of a Fishing Trip with President Roosevelt
Leaving Washington, D.C. on Saturday, November 27, 1937
and Returning on Monday, December 6, 1937

The background of the trip was that the President had been ill from the effects of an abscessed tooth, the drawing of which was too long delayed. It had caused a temperature running up to 103, had confined him to his bed for several days, and resulted in general upset.

There were depressing conditions in the country. Business activity was showing a marked recession. Congress, called into special session to enact the Farm Bill, the Reorganization of Government Bill, and the Wage and Hour Bill, was failing in all three.

Tom Corcoran advised me that the President would like to have me accompany him, and this was confirmed by James Roosevelt, who asked me to come to the White House at 10:00 Saturday evening and join the President.

I went to the White House at 10:00 and waited in the red reception room about thirty minutes, after which I was taken to the ground floor by the stairway, and the President—in his chair—came down the elevator. He greeted me cordially, and accompanied by Mrs. James Roosevelt and Miss Le Hand, we entered the limousine waiting at the south entrance and started for the train.

The President was not in high spirits. His jaw was visibly swollen. There was not the customary quickness of reaction, and he talked somewhat discouragingly of having to get back perhaps in the middle of the week because of the foreign situation, which was acute—particularly on the Far Eastern front, where Japan was vigorously invading China. He referred to the need for rest and hoped to avoid having to return. We talked about the economic situation on the way to the train. Commerce Secretary Dan Roper was there with several little matters that he pressed upon the President. We entered the car after being photographed on the rear platform and were soon joined by James Roosevelt, who had attended the Army–Navy football game in Philadelphia and had been delayed in arriving.[8] As all were weary, I went to my compartment in an adjoining car. The train got under way about 11:30.

Sunday, November 28, 1937

On Sunday morning Harry Hopkins joined the train in North Carolina, accompanied by Bernard Baruch who, however, did not join the traveling party.

Secretary Ickes had boarded the train at Washington, and John Biggers, a delightful and competent businessman from the central northwest,[9] was also aboard.

I had lunch with Colonel James, the general passenger agent of the Atlantic Coast Line, in his private car, along with Marvin McIntyre, secretary to the President; Colonel Watson, the President's military aide; and several others.

I was notified that the President had invited me to join him for dinner. Others in the dinner party were James Roosevelt and Mrs. Roosevelt, Miss Le Hand, Harry Hopkins, and Senator Claude Pepper, who had joined the party. Senator Pepper was particularly anxious to be identified with the President as he was a candidate for reelection in Florida and opponents of the President's plans, especially the lumber companies that were bitterly opposed to the wage and hour policy of the Administration, were giving him a bitter battle.[10]

The President was far below par. We discussed business conditions and policies, particularly questions relating to the monopoly problems and the patent problem, together with the policies affecting Senator Pepper's campaign.

At Jacksonville, Scott Loftin, former president of the American Bar Association and receiver for the East Coast Railways, had his private car attached and also invited me to dinner, which I was obliged to decline.

I spent a large part of the day reducing my notes on the monopoly problem to orderly form for discussion with the President, which he had indicated he would want to have as early as he felt disposed on the trip.

Monday, November 29, 1937

We arrived at Miami, took our places in waiting cars, and drove between great lines of people to the pier. They cheered the President enthusiastically, and he carried Senator Pepper with him to make manifest his friendship and support of his candidacy. We arrived at the *Potomac*, many pictures were taken, and with a profound sense of relief, we cast off and put out to sea.

The party consisted of the President; James Roosevelt; the President's personal physician, Dr. Ross McIntire, a delightful and scholarly gentleman; the President's naval aide Captain Walter Woodson, a methodical naval officer of wide experience; the President's military aide Colonel Watson, a charming southern gentleman of most entertaining type; and Secretary Ickes, Harry Hopkins, and myself.

We had lunch on the stern deck and, about fifteen miles out, after all had changed to informal clothing, slowed down about six knots and began trolling along the keys and reefs. The next event of consequence was that the President got the first fish, a mackerel weighing about twelve pounds, and his pleasure at the catch was marked. Colonel Watson next caught a grouper. His language as he tried to reel the resisting fish into the boat was picaresque and caused great merriment. He was successful in landing him, and as there were no further strikes, we finally resumed speed and headed along the keys for Dry Tortugas Islands.

We dined in the cabin. Conversation was light and the President's spirits were improved. He told us something of the history of Fort Jefferson located on Dry Tortugas Islands. There was considerable discussion of the Fort, the President having been there before, as had also Secretary Ickes and Harry Hopkins.[11] Colonel Watson, the President's military aide, professed great chagrin that he was not aware of the status of Fort Jefferson. The President protested solemnly that he had not been receiving salutes that he was entitled to and said that he trusted that at Fort Jefferson he would be saluted as the office he held deserved. Colonel Watson was reminded that it was his duty to wire to the commanding officer our time of arrival so that preparations could be made. A radiogram to the commanding officer, notifying him of the arrival, was duly prepared, signed by Colonel Watson, and sent.

Colonel Watson was, however, more than half onto the joke. The twinkle in the President's eye might have warned him. When we arrived the next morning, we found that there was no commanding officer, no garrison, no mounted gun, and nothing but a ruined fort. The whole thing had been transferred to the Department of the Interior as a national monument and was in the charge of a Cuban caretaker and a colored cook. Watson never heard the end of it, and the President was delighted to have so good a joke on him. Ickes, thereupon, charged Watson with trespassing upon his grounds and we held a mock trial at which the President, of course, presided and I was appointed to defend Watson. He always charged that I not only pleaded him guilty to all he was accused of, but informed the court about several things that had not been brought up. The President, of course, found him guilty.

After dinner we enjoyed a small game of poker. The President did not play, for he had brought along a large amount of reading matter and he immersed himself in it. Luck ran with me and when we prepared to retire at 10:00, I was some $7.00 ahead of the game.

We maintained our speed during the night against some sea.

Tuesday, November 30, 1937

We awoke at anchor off the Dry Tortugas, located in the Gulf of Mexico some seventy miles off Key West. Captain Clark of the *Potomac* ordered boats lowered and asked me if I cared to join the exploring party. We went in the channel, took soundings, and went along the docks to determine whether it was safe to bring the *Potomac* in. There was some sea but we found a completely sheltered harbor that Captain Clark determined to be a safe haven for the *Potomac*. We returned to the ship, which was then brought in and tied to the dock at Fort Jefferson.

We were convoyed by the *Selfridge*, a destroyer that had left Miami with us. She took up her post outside and within visible signaling distance.

There was the landing dock, which was in fair shape and to which we tied. There were also two old coaling docks in a bad state of dilapidation, both timber and steel beams falling into the sea. Fort Jefferson was a hexagonal fort, three stories in height, beautifully constructed of brick. It was surrounded with a moat perhaps thirty feet in width and six or eight feet in depth. It had served as a Civil War Federal prison, having always been in Federal control. When used as a prison, the moat was kept filled with sharks and escape was pretty hopeless.

Dr. Mudd, who aided in the treatment of John Wilkes Booth after the assassination of President Lincoln, had distinguished himself there for his care of yellow fever sufferers.

The fort was started in the 1840s. After some fifteen years in construction, it was found to have become obsolete through the perfection of the rifled gun.

There was considerable exploring of the tiny island to which we were anchored and there was some fishing, but I had no luck. We had enjoyed the President's mackerel for breakfast, and Colonel Watson's grouper was served at lunch in a soup made according to the President's recipe. It made a delicious luncheon dish.

After dinner the President read until 9:00 when he joined the poker game, which resulted in an exchange of much conversation but little money. Colonel Watson contributed a large share to the fund. He announced that he was one of the Virginia Watsons and that they never quit under fire. It often cost Colonel Watson money to stay, and whether he stayed or dropped out, his comment was always rare. The President was a winner by a very small amount and my luck appeared to have deserted me but not seriously.

I had the imprudence to sleep with a port open at the head of my berth, which resulted in an attack of neuritis that remained with me throughout the trip, causing me considerable inconvenience and pain.

Wednesday, December 1, 1937

Wednesday broke a fair and windy day. We still had fresh mackerel for breakfast. I roamed about the fortress and did some work on papers that I had brought along. The event of the morning was the arrival of the mail, which was brought in a naval plane from Washington. It landed with a quantity of mail that the President went through, referring some of the communications to various aides who assisted in disposing of them. The return mail closed and we had lunch.

About 2:30 the President had a whale boat with a crew of three prepared for fishing and invited me to accompany him and Jimmy. We started trolling and the first catch was a barracuda by Jimmy, who landed his fish successfully. We each got strikes and Jimmy landed a second fish. Then the President caught one, landing him with great skill. We kept on with rather indifferent luck until close to sundown. The President had said we would make one more trip around the harbor and, if we had no luck, we would quit.

Scarcely had these words been spoken when Jimmy had a strike. He began to reel. Just then the President had a strike and he too began to reel. Jimmy lost his fish but a barracuda broke water at the end of the President's line. I began to reel in to get out of his way so he could land his fish. In reeling in, I suddenly had a strike, and it was at once apparent that it was a big fish. The President began to neglect his own in order to give me instructions, for I was a novice. I was somewhat excited and probably did the wrong thing on all occasions. Some of his instructions were: "Don't let him get your pole on the gunwale—he will break it," and "Give him a poke with your pole, and then relax it and reel him like this" as he demonstrated his own method. The result of it all was that, in helping me, he lost his own fish. When mine came along side and was gaffed and brought in, it was the biggest catch of the trip—a barracuda weighing twenty-five to thirty pounds. Meanwhile, we had a convincing demonstration of the fighting character of the barracuda. One of Jimmy's fish had been tied to the boat with a rope passing through his gills and out the mouth. He had been expected to die but apparently his vitality had been underestimated. He had bitten a half-inch rope in two and disappeared with a section of it in his gills.

We put back to the *Potomac*.[12] We had fished with a small price for each boat—$1.00 for the largest fish and $1.00 for the most fish. The others had had good luck and felt confident. I laid a side bet with Colonel Watson, who was pretty happy with his own catch, but when he saw my own he conceded and promptly paid. The $1.00 that our boat had won for the largest fish was solemnly distributed as follows:

To the President	.34
" Jimmy	.33
" myself	.33
	$1.00

It was apparent at dinner that the President was feeling decidedly better. The swelling in his face had pretty much disappeared, his spirits were high, and we had great sport swapping fish yarns and making unappreciated remarks about each other's skill.

Our usual evening diversion was the little poker game, which the President joined at the beginning. The wind, and effort, and neuritis combined to make me a pretty dull player. Twice I laid down my hands when called and announced my hands incorrectly; both times, however, fortunately for me, I had understated my hand and was corrected by Captain Woodson or other players. One of these corrections resulted in taking a pot away from Colonel Watson. He announced that he always played by the Powder River rules and that it was settled practice to shoot any man who announced his hand incorrectly. Hopkins was uniformly lucky and played his cards for everything there was in them. Secretary Ickes, like myself, was not a particularly colorful player. Watson was a rather careless player, bent on thorough enjoyment of the game rather than on results. Dr. McIntire was a keen player and thoroughly intelligent. Woodson was a very careful, calculating, and accurate player. Jimmy was a good player, mixing fun with shrewd betting.

The President studied the players as much as he did the cards. We sometimes caught him bluffing but throughout the trip there was a marked peculiarity in his playing. Invariably he lost the early part of the game and we would have him down several dollars. Invariably he made it up in the last three or four hands of the evening. We finally told him that the only way we could beat him was to break up the game and we were going to arrange to have a fire call about four hands before the finish.

Thursday, December 2, 1937

Thursday morning broke with a stiff wind. I walked the top of the fort, being told later I was lucky I had not been stung by scorpions as they were plentiful. Ignorance had made the walk comfortable even if not safe. I also walked the sea wall as far as possible, for it was breached in three places. I worked on some of the matters brought with me. The President still had no spirit for work after he did the necessary work of the day—answering the dispatches, which was a constant process—and considered the matters thrust upon him by radio.

We had lunch on deck with much lighthearted talk of affairs of state, of fishing, of business, of politics, and of personalities. Comments were frank, informal, and quite inclusive, and they are better unrecorded.

After lunch the President, Dr. McIntire, and Secretary Ickes took a whale boat and started out to do still fishing. Jimmy and Hopkins took another boat and Colonel Watson and I another, and we entered into competition. We made bets on our respective boats to catch the largest number of fish and the largest fish. The wind was high and the weather rough. Colonel Watson and I cruised about making several knots up and down to run ahead. We had no luck and finally Jimmy proposed that we discontinue for an hour or so and go in. Colonel Watson, in scorn, declined to quit. Jimmy replied in words that would have meant fight except for the smile. We cruised on and on until dark and came in only to find that while we had no fish, Hopkins had one about eight inches long—some variety of tiny fish that seemed more ornamental than useful. It was enough to win the bets, however. Colonel Watson and I protested vigorously and with strong suspicions that this fish had come to its untimely end in some illicit manner, but they had the fish and we had to settle. The President adjudged us the losers and suggested that we were not good losers at that. We grudgingly made a settlement with many remarks that indicated our suspicion as to that fish.

Secretary Ickes had some martini cocktails and Colonel Watson a bit of sherry, and in Colonel Watson's room we indulged in a drink before going up to the cabin where the President was waiting for dinner. It was not an infrequent thing that we showed him the great discourtesy of keeping him waiting, but he did not seem to mind and courtesies were waived all around. The President resumed work after dinner and joined our game about 9:00. It was not a good evening for Watson, Ickes, or myself, but the President came through in the last game without losses.

Friday, December 3, 1937

Friday was a clear day but not a particularly warm one. My neuritis was bad and I did no fishing. Dr. McIntire gave me some aspirin, looked me over, and advised me to have my teeth x-rayed, suggesting that it might prove serious.

The last mail was to arrive and the President had wanted to discuss the monopoly problems and papers that I had brought along. We did not get to it. We did, however, have some discussion of New York State politics.

The President said he had come to the conclusion that there were only three men who could save the Democratic Party in the gubernatorial campaign. They were Jackson, Senator Robert Wagner, and Mayor La Guardia. While the latter would not be a Democratic Party nomination, rather than lose the cause of liberalism, the President would accept it. Farley had told him he was not a candidate. Wagner was needed in the Senate. It would be hopeless for our Party unless we could get the American Labor Party endorsement. He thought I should make some speeches pretty steadily in New York City, particularly in the near future.

We had lunch in the cabin because of the chill wind and Captain Clark of the *Selfridge* joined us. There was much talk of naval affairs, naval history, and naval construction.

The President and Dr. McIntire went fishing in one boat while Hopkins, Watson, and Jimmy tried their luck in another. Secretary Ickes and I remained aboard the *Potomac*. It could carry only three days' supply of water and, accordingly, it obtained its supply from the *Selfridge*, which had a water distilling plant. Captain Clark took us for an inspection tour on the *Selfridge*. That was most interesting to me, who knows so little about naval construction. The fishing was not good and my record catch was undisturbed.

The President was in high spirits at dinner, and in the game that he joined at about 9:00, he lost pretty consistently until the last two or three hands, which brought him back even with the game.

Saturday, December 4, 1937

We were to depart at 1:00 and there was no fishing. The President inspected the fort. We then settled down for a long discussion of the problems of monopoly, including antitrust legislation. We reviewed the O'Mahoney-Borah bill, just introduced to strengthen the Federal Trade Commission, and reviewed my own notes on the subject.[13] We discussed the regulation of trade associations among small businessmen in the interest of enabling them to have a clearer definition of what was permissible and what was not, and the possibility—among other things—of affording price protection for the public against those industries where monopoly was an accomplished fact.

We cast off at 1:00, headed eastward into a fairly heavy sea. Hopkins and Ickes went below and "sought the seclusion that the cabin grants." I sat in the sun on the deck and visited with Dr. McIntire.

The President was in fine spirits and after dinner we had the usual little poker game. It was a good evening for me, bringing my winnings up to about $7.00 and leaving my losses for the trip only $4.70. The President, as usual, went way down and in the last four hands came back. It seemed to be his luck, for there was no discernible difference in his technique between the early and late evening. It must have been just that undefinable thing known as Roosevelt luck. He was the winner by about $18.00 in the last few hands in which everybody was rather reckless and the stakes were far higher than had been usual.

Sunday, December 5, 1937

We had breakfast about twenty miles out from Miami, then slowed down to about six knots and began trolling. There were strikes but no fish.

We had lunch aboard and discussed the conduct of Congress, particularly of some of the members who had sought the President's aid in being elected only to betray him. The President showed no bitterness, but I cannot say that the rest of us were similarly charitable.

The Coast Guard cutters took our extra radio man borrowed from the *Selfridge* back to his ship and brought Secret Service men who had been aboard the *Selfridge* to the *Potomac*. We docked at about 1:30. Mrs. Roosevelt,[14] Miss Le Hand, and secretary McIntyre joined us and the President held a brief press conference in the cabin. We then went to the train amid long lines of cheering people. One fairly well dressed woman insisted on getting by the lines of the police in order to present two bottles of medicine. She said they contained oils and extracts that, if the President applied the contents of one bottle to the inside and the other to the outside, would work a very prompt cure. The bottles were delivered to Dr. McIntire.

Receiver Loftin of the Florida East Coast Railway was in his private car ahead behind the engine and the President's private car was on the rear of the train. Colonel Watson, secretary McIntyre, and myself joined Loftin for dinner and I then retired early.

Monday, December 6, 1937

As we sped northward, we had many conferences. Lister Hill of Alabama, who was running for the Senate against Tom Heflin, joined the train in order to get the benefit of the President's blessing and make manifest his friendship for the President. We discussed various political problems during the day.

Dr. McIntire said that the President wanted me to join him for lunch. The luncheon party consisted of Dr. McIntire, Colonel Watson, James Roosevelt, Mr. Hill, Mrs. Roosevelt, Miss Le Hand, and myself. The luncheon time was spent largely in discussing Mr. Hill's difficulties in his campaign.[15]

After luncheon, the President said he wanted to talk with me, and the others left. Our discussion was then of New York politics. He suggested that I see Governor Lehman. Roosevelt said he felt that the Democratic Party was in some danger in the state. La Guardia had enrolled with the American Labor Party, thus breaking completely with the Republican Party. This loyalty to the Labor Party would doubtless be rewarded with the gubernatorial nomination if he sought it. La Guardia's presence as a third party candidate would beat the Democratic Party. He was therefore in a very strong position to bargain, and as Senator Wagner had to run for reelection, La Guardia would be able to demand support for himself in return for support for Senator Wagner.

There was also a possibility that Governor Lehman would want to run for senator, with Senator Wagner running for Governor.

The President also suggested that he would like to have me get in touch with the Rochester organization headed by Don Dailey and urge that it make peace there, and also see whether there was any possibility that the party could be put on a sounder basis in Buffalo, where it had had a series of misfortunes.

We discussed the monopoly matter and I was to prepare suggested material for his message by December 15.

I expressed my gratitude for being included in the party and departed with his declaration that he wanted to see me often and keep closely in touch on both the matters of the monopoly drive and the political matters that concern me.

Contrast between the man who went out on Saturday night and the man who headed the luncheon table as we returned to Washington was striking. He had done a great deal of work. Every morning we received about ten pages of radio news, which was picked up and multigraphed on the *Selfridge*. It included most of the important news of the day and was a very acceptable substitute for newspapers. Its items constituted an interesting theme for conversation. In addition to this the President had two big mails daily, constant dispatches—many of them of a confidential character—and he was always living under the burden of being President. Notwithstanding this, he had rested. Life had been most informal in dress and in conduct. He was of course treated respectfully by all, but with perfect informality. In fishing contests, playing cards, and conversation, he was and wanted to be an equal. He asked no favors and granted none. He played the game on its merits. He was able to avoid all pose. He was away from curious eyes. We were completely isolated.

While the cavity had not completely healed and there was a prospect that a curetment would be necessary, it had ceased to annoy him. It was a President in high spirits and good health who returned to Washington at the end of the trip, which was not marred by any clash of personalities—and no irritations. It had been one of the delightful experiences of life.[16]

A striking example of Roosevelt's concern for others' rest was on our 1941 trip to the Bahamas. There was a high wind and the sea was rough, so we decided that we would spend an easier night at the Fort Lauderdale wharf than out in the open sea. Therefore, Steve Early and Harry Hopkins showed up about dinnertime in dinner clothes, a very unusual thing on our trips. The President asked why and was told that Harry and Steve proposed to go to Miami and make something of an evening of it. The President said that he had nothing to say as to Steve, for he was a well man, but he lit into Harry Hopkins like an angry father with a wayward son. He reminded Harry that he had been ill and told him that he brought him along on the trip to get some rest and restored health. He told him bluntly that if he went to Miami and stayed out, as he would do if he went, that he would not take him on another trip. Sheepishly, the dinner coats came off and we spent a quiet evening, retiring early. It was the only incident on which I ever heard an angry word directed at one of his associates.

One must read all of Roosevelt's deeds with knowledge of his penchant for humor and fun or he will misunderstand him. The dangers of humor to a public man are those of misunderstanding, but Roosevelt enjoyed pulling the legs of over-serious persons, particularly those not sophisticated.

My experience with humor is that it is impossible with a public man in a public place. I could give instances of attempts to be humorous that back-fired every time. For example, I made a statement at an off-the-record luncheon, thinking it was something humorous, that Roosevelt possibly seeking a third term was not really an issue because the Supreme Court had invalidated the first term. Everybody present laughed and it was regarded as a joke by those who could see my face and hear my voice. But when it came out in the papers as a serious contribution to the third term discussion, I was considerably embarrassed by it, because it seemed obviously an attempt to be humorous. It was not humorous at all.[17] You just cannot be humorous in American public life. You have just got to be a stuffed shirt. The President understood how that happened. They had picked up things that he said, that he thought were funny, the same way. It is not safe to be a humorist.

An incident is told by Mr. Churchill of the concluding dinner at the Teheran Conference, when Stalin proposed to round up and shoot 50,000 German officers and leaders without trial.[18] Churchill objected and insisted that they should be tried. Elliott Roosevelt joined with Stalin in suggesting that they be shot. The argument was becoming very hot and unpleasant when President Roosevelt intervened and suggested a compromise, that they shoot only 49,000 of the German leaders. This, of course, brought the thing to a close and avoided a disagreeable situation. How frequently I have seen him close controversies in the same inconclusive way, but at least it tided over the unpleasantness for the moment.

On another occasion, General Watson and Secretary Ickes had an argument as to whether Josiah Bailey, Senator from North Carolina, was a lawyer. Ickes insisted he was not, the General that he was, and the dispute was to be left to the President to arbitrate. When the President came out from his room, he decided that Bailey was a lawyer but Ickes would not pay the bet—he appealed and said that he would get better information when he returned to Washington. Some weeks later I was in the outer office and General Watson, who handled the President's appointments, said, "What am I going to do, I can't get this fellow Ickes to pay that bet." He said he would like to engage me to collect it. I said, "Well, if you will follow my advice you will get your money." I said, "You are keeping the door, aren't you, and he is coming in this afternoon because he wants something from the President?" I said, "Get your money before you open the door." This amused him immensely and he collected in that manner. When I returned to my office I sent him a bill for legal advice of $100.00. He took the whole thing to the President who promptly made up a memorandum suggesting an opinion from the Solicitor General as to whether I should be removed for practicing law in the White House. Such was the spirit with which the President dealt with his associates.[19]

In private notes that he dictated contemporaneously, Jackson recorded FDR's reflections at a May 1940 private dinner away from the White House:

In the evening the President was the guest of Mr. and Mrs. Sumner Welles at their magnificent estate at Oxon, Maryland, and we were invited. Other guests were Lord Lothian, the British Ambassador; Mr. Norman Davis, Chairman of the Red Cross, and Mrs. Davis; and Governor and Mrs. O'Conor of the State of Maryland. When the President arrived his humor had changed. He announced that he had bawled out everybody he had met until 4:00 P.M., when the humor of the situation dawned on him. I reminded him that it was only 1:00 when I met him last and confirmed his impression that his mood had been terrible.[20]

After cocktails we went into dinner, and the President discussed experiences he had had in Harlan County, Kentucky, as a younger man and some of his experiences during the World War.

After dinner the ladies left and the conversation turned to American history and to Sandburg's *Lincoln*. The President told Lord Lothian of the incident of the British Ambassador during the Civil War. He related that Seward, leaving the White House late one night, went along by Lafayette Park, which was then separated by a high fence. As he walked along, his attention was attracted by a call from the inside. To his astonishment, the British ambassador appealed for help to get the gate unlocked. He explained that his predicament was most embarrassing, inasmuch as he had been locked in the park with the Spanish ambassador's wife when the park was closed for the night.

Seward did not know where keys might be found or who had charge of the park, so he walked back to the White House and around to the gatehouse on the southerly side. He ran into Lincoln, who was taking a walk before retiring. Seward related the incident to Lincoln, who was greatly amused. Lincoln said he did not know who took care of the park, but he thought there was a ladder around the White House. They found one, and the President of the United States and the Secretary of State lugged the ladder between them over to the park and rescued the British ambassador and the Spanish ambassador's wife from the enclosure.

We insisted that it was the duty of the British ambassador to uphold the tradition of his office. Lothian then explained that the officer during that period was his uncle.

We discussed Lincoln's difficulty conducting the war, the embarrassments placed in his way by the industrial interests of the North as well as the rebellious interests of the South, and we drew parallels with present conditions.[21]

In his 1944 draft autobiography, Jackson recounted another unusually striking recollection of FDR—a memory of the President at work (politics) and also at play, in the privacy of the White House pool:

The Solicitor Generalship proved the happiest and most satisfying of my public offices in the Executive Department. The work was purely professional. There was no interference with my work from the Attorney General, although we frequently discussed its problems.[22] The office was removed from political activity by tradition and from the fact that it was regarded as an adjunct of the Supreme Court. Members of the Solicitor General's staff had rarely been active in the political side of government beyond making an occasional speech.

Nevertheless, I did not take office without a period of suspense and considerable publicity. There still hovered over the situation a possibility that I would be a candidate for Governor of New York, and there were Republicans and Democrats both who, because of that, were particularly interested in stopping my confirmation. Objections were made by Senator Warren Austin of Vermont on behalf of the Republicans, and by Senator William King of Utah on behalf of the Democrats.

Senator Austin asked for time to study my speeches and public utterances, which apparently he had known only by headlines and reputation. I could not have had more honorable opposition than his. After he had had time to make some study of my speeches, he privately expressed surprise that they seemed to have nothing more than the conventional antagonism to monopoly and did not indicate the subversive and radical views that they were supposed to contain. He examined me about my views in several sessions, which were widely reported and which served to clarify matters in which I had been misrepresented.

Senator King was less intelligent and less considerate. I am sure he had only a second-hand knowledge of the content of my speeches, but he was much more bitter, although a Democrat, than my Republican adversary. He announced that no Socialists had done as much harm to the American form of government as my speeches had.

While this was going on, the President asked me to come over and swim with him. It was his habit to take his afternoon swim in the pool that had been installed in the White House, as that was one of the few exercises possible for him. Conferring while swimming has its disadvantages. As we swam back and forth, I reported what King had said, and the President said, with his mouth half under water, "Isn't he an old bastard?" The last word produced a spray that was so funny he tried it again and again, each time producing a considerable spray by saying the word "bastard" half under water. We disported like a couple of small boys and decided that the battle over my confirmation was about over.[23]

It was. The vote was taken within a day or so. Senator Austin made a speech that was complimentary rather than otherwise, but voted against me, the total votes against the confirmation numbering four. The incident never produced any personal ill will between Senator Austin and myself, and he voted for my confirmation each time my name was thereafter before the Senate. Senator King likewise voted to confirm me for Attorney General, but the voters of Utah had retired him by the time I was nominated for the Supreme Court.[24]

Even at the last dinner that I ever attended with the President, on March 17, 1945, he was in the same spirits. It was both St. Patrick's Day and the fortieth anniversary of Mr. and Mrs. Roosevelt's wedding. They asked us in to a small dinner. Besides the President and Mrs. Roosevelt, the guests included only the Princess Juliana of the Netherlands, who was a guest in the country, Assistant Secretary of State and Mrs. Nelson Rockefeller, the President's daughter Anna and her husband, John Boettiger, Mrs. Kermit Roosevelt,[25] one of the ladies accompanying Juliana; the Netherlands Ambassador and Mme. Loudon,[26] and the Van Houtens, he counselor of the Netherlands Legation.[27]

The President had just returned from Yalta and seemed to be in fine spirits. He mixed some martinis and we discussed the events of the day. The war was moving well, and the President was cheerful.

As they started to wheel the President into the dining room, one of the three dogs that had greeted us in the Red Room was lying in the path, and he jocularly said, "Somebody move the dog—but not by air." This caused a good deal of laughter, for the newspapers had just been filled with criticism of Elliott Roosevelt for shipping a dog via air.[28] The President had a wonderful sense of humor and incidents like that of Elliott's dog were tossed off that way. The President had a profound self-confidence that carried him through a lot of things.

We went in to dinner, and the President was flanked on his right by Juliana and on his left by Mme. Loudon. I sat next to Juliana, and Irene sat across the table next to the Netherlands Ambassador. The table was covered with St. Patrick's decorations—pipes, green hats, shamrocks, and all that goes with a typical Irish observance of St. Patrick's Day. With mock gravity, I turned and, speaking across the Princess, said, "Mr. President, you have made the first diplomatic error I have been able to detect." He said,

"How is that?" I said, "Here you are, entertaining the House of Orange and you have the shamrock and the Irish decorations." He said, "Oh, what a blunder!" He laughed and made a great deal of it, explaining to Juliana at great length the realities of American politics and the influence of the Irish and how important it is for an American politician to make no failure in observing St. Patrick's Day. We had a great deal of fun about it. Juliana seemed to appreciate the situation thoroughly.

Mrs. Rockefeller was engaged at home in fixing her hotbeds and asked my judgment of the relative merits of hen manure and horse manure for hotbed purposes. We fell into a lively table discussion, which must have been overheard by the Princess, and I rather hope she did not think I had initiated it. We had a good laugh later at the subject of dinner conversation, but both the Jackson and Rockefeller hotbeds have flourished, as I have since learned, despite the difference in treatment.

After dinner, we went downstairs, where a moving picture screen had been arranged. We gathered in the front seats, and the servants of the household gathered in the rear ones. The pictures that were shown consisted of a ghastly movie, The Suspect, with Charles Laughton and Ella Raines in the leading roles. It was an English life movie, involving several murders, and the President remarked that it might spoil his sleep.

The interesting feature of the movies, however, was the showing of pictures, taken by members of his own family and staff, of the Yalta conference and trip. They showed, in color and with some amateurish touches about the photography, the trip over and the President's ship zig-zagging to avoid danger of submarines; the arrival in various ports, Algiers and others; the trip on the island of Malta; and the various scenes at the Yalta conference. He made humorous comments on many of the pictures.

Then, too, there were movies of the entire reception of King Ibn Saud, the King of Egypt, Haile Selassie of Abyssinia, and the Oriental potentates. The President told us a good deal about Ibn Saud and his forty-five sons, and apparently he found him an intensely interesting character. He commented on the fact that he was not allowed to have any cocktails or to smoke while the King was aboard his ship, and he was for four hours without a cigarette. This was out of deference to Ibn Saud as head of the Mohammedan Church. Also, no women were allowed aboard the ship while the King was there. Accordingly, women members of the family were taken off for the occasion. I told him that, interesting as his account of the King was, I would be much more interested in hearing the King's account of him. This thought seemed intriguing, and he began to speculate on whether he could ever obtain through diplomatic channels or otherwise the reactions. It was, I believe he said, the first time that the King had ever been on a warship.

We broke up about 10:30. As we drove home, Irene said to me, "I do not think we will ever see the President alive again." I said, "That's damn nonsense!"—that despite the weariness of his appearance, I thought he was in no danger. But she insisted that she had sat opposite him while I had not had the full view of his face. She said that she could see that "the moment he isn't thinking of it, his face looks awfully bad," and that she had drawn her impression in part from comments that the President had made during the moving pictures that followed dinner.

She was right—we never saw him alive again. I saw him briefly at the White House Correspondent's dinner on March 22, 1945,[29] but I did not see him closely. He appeared in good spirits, but weary, and if he was not when it started, he must have been when it finished, for it was one of the dumbest programs that I ever saw devised for a public dinner. It consisted of radio features. One of the speakers had a long story about where he was born and "the little house out back of the big house." The first time he got the line off was amusing, but about the seventh or eighth time it became a little sickly. But he rambled on and on.

I got tired of the thing, left the dinner, and did not hear the President's speech. The price of listening to cheap and tawdry radio features in order to hear the President was too great to pay and I went home, reflecting on the high price one has to pay for being President.

In a few days he had passed away.[30]

In April 1945, Jackson wrote the following notes regarding these and other incidents that showed the President's declining health in his last year:

The President's health had been the subject of anxiety to his friends for a considerable period of time. I first noticed it sharply in August 1944, when the President entertained the President of Iceland.[31] I was asked to the stag dinner at the White House, and as I greeted the President, he introduced me to the President of Iceland as his Attorney General. One could never quite tell when the President was joking or ribbing one, and I said something to the effect that I was not much of an Attorney General—meaning that I had ceased to be. It was plain that the President thought of me, however, as Attorney General.

Later in the evening, he made an informal speech at the table after dinner. Among other things, he remarked that three members of his Cabinet were present. The only members of his Cabinet present were War Secretary Henry Stimson and Commerce Secretary Jesse Jones.

Jones, who was near me, turned and said, "Where is the third?" I did not say what I felt sure was the fact: that the President was still counting me as a member of his Cabinet. I did not repeat the incident to anyone for, if passed out, it might easily have confused the campaign against him. However, it was clear to me that, for the moment at least, he was so immersed in world problems that he really had not kept up with what was going on domestically.

I did not have much contact with him from then until after the 1944 election. At the Inauguration ceremony, we stood a few feet from him and he looked pale and worn, despite the rest he had taken. Mrs. Roosevelt asked my son Bill and his wife (and her cousin) Nancy to go in and see the President afterward, and he had a pleasant chat with the young people.[32] He was in fine spirits, but there was an inescapable atmosphere of weariness about him.[33]

I do not think death was unkind to him. At the Department of Justice on the next afternoon, I was asked to speak to those who had been associated with me in that Department. I could not refrain from expressing sentiment that death had been kind. His great work was done. If he was not going to be able to carry on, he would not have desired life.[34]

I do not expect to see his like again. The two greatest personalities of my time were Franklin D. Roosevelt and Charles Evans Hughes.[35] Merely as personalities, these men were eloquent before they spoke. There was about them, something that commanded attention, which took the eye. They had no rivals in their respective spheres and as personalities they have left no successors.

8

THAT MAN AS LEADER OF THE MASSES

IT WAS NO GREAT TRIBUTE to his skill, under the circumstances, that Roosevelt won a majority in the 1932 elections. But it was a tribute to his leadership that he made a normally Republican country into a normally Democratic one. He was even able to take their following away from labor leaders when they opposed him, as John Lewis learned.[1] He broke the firmly established two terms tradition. No President had obtained from Congress so much legislation it did not want as he had been able to do. How was it done?

There are those who think the sole secret is the "Santa Claus" theory.[2] There is no denying that his Administration met with an extraordinary opportunity to extend government aid to an extraordinary number of persons, and that he took full advantage of the opportunity. Banks, railroads, and businessmen were aided through the Reconstruction Finance Corporation. Labor unions and their leaders were strengthened by enactment and administration of the National Labor Relations Act. Unorganized and inefficient labor was given the advantage of the Minimum Wage and Maximum Hour Act. Unemployment was relieved through a program of public works, and unemployed and aged persons received direct relief by the aid of the federal government. It bypassed the state governments and dealt directly with the municipal and local authorities and thereby established loyalties among local officials, who were enabled to solve their problems by direct contact with Washington. It would be idle to deny that these measures built up a strong popular following for the President based on benefits received.

It would be a mistake to overlook, however, that these measures had many offsetting disadvantages. No such burdens had ever been placed upon the taxpayer, both large and small. Taxes were even imposed on the wage envelope that subtracted from the take-home pay of labor. Powerful and articulate interests were antagonized and the program was so novel that it caused genuine and not unreasonable concern among many elements that could hardly be called reactionary.

In his oral history, Jackson described the bottom-up nature of FDR's popularity at the 1940 Democratic convention that nominated him for a third term:

I think that on the part of the laboring masses of people—the labor unions (including most of the labor leaders) and the minorities, such as the Negroes—the feeling was genuine and very deep that they wanted Roosevelt. They did not want any change. They felt that he was their friend.

On the part of the politicians at the top of the heap, I think it was pretty pure expediency. Recognizing this feeling among the masses and recognizing that it was a great asset to them in their own local campaigns, they wanted Roosevelt. He had a popular following that nobody could discount and nobody could separate from him.[3]

During the ensuing war years, of course, FDR's circle of supporters became virtually the whole nation:

From the point of view of an observer on the sidelines, the way that the pieces in the puzzle that make up American life changed places was quite remarkable. Businessmen who had been the sworn enemies of the President enlisted under him in various posts. People who had distrusted him became his followers. The opposition pretty much melted out. Many of the things that I had feared of war did not occur, partly because of the President himself, and partly because of his advisers.[4]

Had Roosevelt not possessed an extraordinary degree of leverage on Congress through his popular support, he would have failed in the efforts to obtain his legislation. But the masses are still moved by a leader's communication of ideas and emotions. It is plain that Roosevelt got across to the people something that stirred them as few leaders could do.

Speech today, as always, is a primary asset in politics. Public speaking is not an outmoded political weapon, although its style had been changed. Roosevelt was not an orator by the standard of Bryan, Burke, Cockran, and Ingersoll.[5] His speeches lacked that indefinable literary quality and finish that we attribute to Wilson's polished State Papers. Roosevelt could not beat on a big drum so constantly and effectively as his great wartime collaborator Churchill. It is true that he had a certain felicity in tossing off phrases such as the "horse-and-buggy" age, the "Four Freedoms,"[6] "unconditional surrender"[7]—and a certain readiness with epithets such as "Copperheads"[8] and "economic royalists."[9] But where Roosevelt excelled over his contemporaries and had the advantage over his predecessors was that he was the first real master of the new technique in mass communication necessitated by widespread use of the radio. The man who listens to his radio at the fireside, alone or with his family, seems to feel with Queen Victoria, who is said to have asked Prime Minister Gladstone not to speak to her as if he were addressing a public audience. The radio listener liked the way Roosevelt just conversed by microphone. Others might orate, but he would simply talk as to a neighbor—the country sat at its receiving sets, and each felt that he was being talked with. The fireside chat was just that.

The amplifier may work magic, but it is still necessary to have something of substance to be amplified. A fireside manner of delivery is not enough. The radio can convey something of one's personality, but that does not help if the personality is colorless and insipid to begin with. It may bring the minds of the followers into contact with the mind of the leader, but that does not help if the leader's mind is vacant and his thought is unappealing.

Our mechanics of communication have developed a capacity for transmission greater than the development of worthwhile ideas or productions to communicate. Public men are besought to provide all kinds of interviews, statements, and speeches for use by those who have means of communication at their disposal but are short in something to say. The result is a great demand for canned products, prepared by persons facile in the use of language and resourceful in the production of innocuous ideas, which will serve to get one's name before the public. The ghostwriter has become a public institution. But the ghostwriter has depreciated the product by which he lives. More than a few public men stumble through prepared texts, hesitating as though reading them for the first time and blundering over the pronunciation of unfamiliar words.

Roosevelt was different. He employed the talents of others, but he employed others of talent. I was not habitually employed in producing material for his speeches or messages, but I worked upon several of them and had a chance to observe his methods. I think the secret of his success was that whatever resources he drew upon, he completely mastered them and made any speech that he delivered so much his own that it was what he might say in conversation. He never seemed to be reading to an audience. Neither did he seem to be reciting.

If he needed an official document or message on a specialized subject, he would refer the matter to one or perhaps two or three qualified aides to prepare drafts for submission to him. These he would revise, cut, supplement, and edit until he had a draft that suited him.

On other occasions, he would give the general subject upon which he expected to speak or write and would ask that relevant ideas, expressions, or quotations be handed in to him. When the materials were assembled, there was likely to be a conference of those who had contributed, sometimes a half-dozen or so, as he went over the items, rejecting this and accepting that and supplying additional material until the substance suited him.

At such time, complete candor and freedom of criticism prevailed. I recall an occasion when a group of us were working with him on a Jackson Day political speech, and it was his idea to include a humorous note by inviting the Republican leaders to attend. He asked what we thought of it. Miss Le Hand, a most intelligent and understanding secretary, spoke up and said, "Mr. President, I think it's cheap, really cheap and it isn't sincere. I don't think it is good." She spoke the feelings of most of us and no one disagreed with her. But nonetheless he decided that for the purpose of lightening what otherwise might be a rather heavy speech, he would go ahead and use it.[10]

Then there was the matter of style, and here his ideas were rather fixed, although particular items were always open to argument or suggestions. First of all, he eliminated all long, unfamiliar foreign or technical words and brought the thought into simple, plain words, of Anglo-Saxon origin if possible. He knew the forcefulness of plain Bible English with the American people. He eliminated complicated and involved sentences and used short, simple, and direct ones. He sometimes blue-penciled some of my contributions, remarking, with an impish grin in my direction, that they were too legalistic. Then too he never used abstract terms where he could be concrete. When someone suggested that he criticize Republican congressmen in the abstract, he preferred a concrete attack on "Martin, Barton, and Fish."[11] He knew the impact of a concrete statement is far greater than that of an abstract statement. But he never "talked down" to the people, as some leaders have made the mistake of doing. He knew that voters who listen to Presidents and would-be Presidents are self-respecting and quick to detect and resent the condescension that seeks to prove by profanity and vulgarisms that the speaker is just a plain everyday fellow. Voters do not want everyday fellows to take up the responsibilities of high office.

Press conferences were a means of communication that he utilized effectively, albeit one of dubious value. Much has been written to show how skillful Roosevelt was in avoiding subjects at the press conference that he did not wish to discuss and in bringing up subjects that he did. It is always a dramatic spectacle to see the head of state interrogated by reporters, friendly, indifferent, and hostile. The interrogators love it, extol its value, and claim it as a right. But the President realized that these press conferences conveyed to the country only a blurred impression of what he was really driving at. After he had tried clearly to state his position, the account that would appear in the *New York Times* would be very different than the impression that would be given by the *Chicago Tribune*. A comparison of the reports by the major press services would show great discrepancies, if not in what they reported, at least in what they emphasized. The fact was that when he had a message to give to the country, unless it was very simple, short, and dramatic, he lost all control of the emphasis of his message if he gave it out at his press conference.

At one time, serious consideration was given to substituting at regular intervals a radio interview or a talk directly to the American people in place of attempting to reach them indirectly through the press. The President was much annoyed at some sections of the press, which he indicated by declining to attend some of the press functions. There were, of course, difficulties in the way of the proposal. The coming of the war led to its abandonment.

The "serious consideration" that Jackson mentions included discussion that he led at a Cabinet meeting on November 11, 1938. Jackson, who was Solicitor General at the time, attended the meeting as Acting Attorney General in lieu of Attorney General Cummings. Upon returning to the Department of Justice, Jackson dictated the following memorandum for his files:

Armistice Day Cabinet Meeting

The President brought up the problem of how those of the administration are going to make their case plain to the people when the newspapers take speeches and interviews and misrepresent them through abbreviating or through headlines. He suggested the possibility of having someone write to each paper each time such a thing occurred.

Before the Cabinet meeting, I had discussed the same problem with Ickes and Hopkins, and while we had come to no conclusion, we had thought the following plan worth discussion.

I suggested to the Cabinet that if we are going to fight the newspapers, it was obviously impossible to fight them through the newspapers—

that they would always have the last word and always be in a position to use or not use our rejoinders. I suggested that consideration be given to an administration hour on the radio at the same time each week in which, for probably one-half of the time, the President, or some person designated by him would report to the people of the United States. It would be particularly justifiable by the conduct of the newspapers and would enable us to give an authoritative statement directly to the people. Further, it would be justifiable to discontinue the press conferences upon the grounds that they are published under misleading headlines and often distorted and, in any event, news that belongs to the whole people is used as a vehicle for building up circulation and selling advertising by private newspaper interests. The shift of emphasis by the Administration from press conference to radio would have a marked effect in bringing newspapers to realize their responsibility.

Mr. Ickes supported the suggestion warmly.

The President suggested that the difficulty in the way of it was the amount of time it would take to prepare for it each week. Mr. Ickes suggested that the time now devoted to press conferences would pretty nearly provide for that.

Notwithstanding the objection, the President was greatly impressed with the suggestion, and the whole thing wound up in a burst of laughter when he announced that, if it were done, he would call the broadcast "My Week."[12]

It cannot be denied that for the head of state to submit himself to interrogation by hostile reporters in the presence of foreign correspondents is a dangerous if not reckless practice. Even Roosevelt, with all his skill, made some bad mistakes. To decline to answer may convey implications as serious as to answer a tricky or embarrassing question. An extemporaneous answer to a carefully thought-out and involved question is a dangerous thing for any executive, especially near the end of a tiring and hectic day. Any subject on which the President of the United States comments becomes at once important. Any subject that is important enough for his comment deserves deliberate and considered comment. Not only should the substance be carefully weighed but its phrasing should be considered to avoid over-statement or understatement that oftentimes is misunderstood, especially abroad.

However, Roosevelt enjoyed the catch-as-catch-can press conference. He thought himself to be the master of it, and while he was probably the most masterful manager of the conference that had ever occupied the

White House, I doubt if he was as much a master of it as he thought he was. An unbiased study of his use of the press conference would show that a good many serious blunders were made. He was also a master at retrieving a lost position. But on the whole, I believe he left an evil example to his successors in submitting himself to the wide open press conference, one that is very hard for them to break but very dangerous for the country for them to try to follow in time of stress.

It may be safely said that Roosevelt was the President of the United States best understood by the masses of the people. He was best known to them. Others had gone to speak to such audiences as came to hear them. Roosevelt, by virtue of the wide ownership of radios, went to wherever people were. Others, when they communicated with persons beyond the reach of their eyes, reached only the relatively small reading public. Roosevelt spoke directly to the listener with a vibrant voice and a simple tongue and obtained a sympathetic response from more people than any predecessor had been able to do.

With his personality, he probably would have been as great or greater a master of the newly devised television. That opens to his successors even larger possibilities for the communication of personality, sincerity, and thought.

EPILOGUE

In the days immediately following President Roosevelt's sudden death on Thursday, April 12, 1945, Justice Jackson wrote two accounts of those days and that man. The first, written on Monday, April 16, is a journal of the previous four days. The second, which Jackson wrote at Hickory Hill, his McLean, Virginia, home on the morning following FDR's death, is the text that Jackson delivered in the Great Hall at the Department of Justice at its April 13 memorial service for the President.

This generation yesterday laid its President to rest, and today President Truman speaks to a joint session of Congress and a new regime begins. Everyone is conscious that an era has come to an end. For us it is more like the death of a father than of an official.

News of the death reached us casually and accidentally late Thursday afternoon. I had spent the day working with my secretary, Ruth Sternberg,[1] on a speech for the American Society of International Law and on Supreme Court cases. She had left on the 5:30 bus, and I went to the stable. Our handyman, Stuart Loy,[2] who had returned from town, came up with his face glum and said, "Did you hear the bad news?" Thinking it was something about the war, I said, "No. What is it?" He then told Irene and me that the President was dead, that he had died very suddenly, and that it had been announced by radio.

It took a good time for the fact to penetrate. All that evening we listened to the radio, stunned, although not greatly surprised.

Friday it was difficult to concentrate on Court work and so I was at work in the garden when I received a call from Attorney General Biddle, saying that the Department wanted to hold a short memorial service at 4:00 and asking me to come and make a brief address. I dropped the garden work and fell to preparing an address in longhand, which Irene typed, and at 4:00 I delivered it before a full auditorium. The Great Hall of the Department of Justice was packed. I got through it until the last paragraph but then faltered, and I doubt if many heard the conclusion.[3] It was published in full in the *Washington Post* on Sunday. The International Law Society had decided to proceed with its meeting for Friday night, and I went to the meeting and delivered the address previously prepared—somewhat as if in a trance.[4]

Plans for the funeral had been somewhat chaotic, contradictory announcements being published and broadcast. On return home on Friday, Irene had received a call from Mrs. Helm, the White House social secretary, saying that she expected both of us to go to the train at 10:00 the following morning and meet Mrs. Roosevelt and the President's body. She thought the request had been mailed to us, but might not have reached us.[5] She said it was Mrs. Roosevelt's wish, and that they also wished us to join the funeral party and go to Hyde Park for the burial. We had previously been notified that the Court would attend the funeral in a body.

On Saturday morning we went to the Court. Justice and Mrs. Black and Justice and Mrs. Douglas joined us in our car and drove to the station. A great crowd had gathered, a silent and solemn crowd, with many moist eyes. The train drew in and Stephen Early stepped off. A number of senators and representatives, most of the Court, and the new President were present. I shook hands with President Truman. Early called his name and asked him to go aboard. Mrs. Roosevelt, in the next to the last car, was receiving persons who had been asked to the occasion. We passed through the line and shook her hand. Then the procession formed and moved slowly up Constitution Avenue between great lines of sad people, leaving the party at the White House, where only the family entered.

The funeral service was at 4:00 and we returned to the White House for it. The ceremony was simple, short, and Bishop Dun was magnificent.[6] I took occasion to tell him so after the service.

We went to the station at 9:30 P.M. under the direction of the marshal of the Court and found our place on the funeral train, arriving at Hyde Park the following morning. It was a beautiful morning—such a day as would have gladdened the heart of the Squire of Hyde Park. In Army cars, we were driven up through the woods to the garden spot selected for the President's burial. There the group assembled, together with some I had not seen at the funeral services in the White House. Among these was Jim Farley,[7] and I was glad to see him present. The burial service was short, and immensely impressive. We were driven back to the train and resumed our trip to Washington.

On the return trip, politics began to buzz. There was much rushing about by those who had political axes to grind. Conferences were numerous and prolonged. We had dinner and visited with Justice Roberts, Justice Reed, Chief Justice Stone, and Justice Frankfurter. Brother Douglas was sent for by former Vice President Wallace for a conference and was exceedingly busy on conferences. The subdued tone of the train changed considerably on the return trip. The loyalties of politicians shift quickly.[8]

★

Mr. Attorney General and friends in the Department of Justice:

I am touched, that in this hour you remember me as one who has shared with you the privilege of serving under President Roosevelt, and as one who would share your grief in his sudden death. No other event could bow so many human heads in a common sorrow and a sense of personal loss. Throughout the land, by countless humble firesides, people feel less secure today because he is gone; for, while he walked with Kings, they knew that he never lost the common touch; that he was their friend and advocate; that while he lived there would be no forgotten man. Neither sea nor land stretched far enough to get out of range of his sympathy and understanding. During these recent years I, like the rest of you, have watched with growing anxiety as he spent himself so freely in the cause in which he believed. But he brushed aside all warnings—all of his caution was bestowed upon others, and he thought of no human being but himself as expendable.

This is not the time to dwell upon his place as one of the most commanding figures of world history. No Alexander, or Caesar, or Hannibal, or Napoleon, or Hitler ever commanded such an aggregation of physical force. But Power was never an end to him, it was a means—a means to a better world where men might live their chosen lives, rear their families in decency and security, safely think and speak their thoughts, and better their material conditions. His office was the symbol of the greatest of organized physical forces. But it was the moral forces and spiritual aspirations of mankind that he really typified, and they never were so passionately concentrated around a single person. As History will look back on our time, above the other men who made up its scenes, the figure of Roosevelt will stand "like a sharply cut rock in the midst of a shapeless sea."[9]

President Roosevelt had an interest in this Department second only perhaps to that in the Navy, to which we often jokingly referred as "the President's branch of the service." As a lawyer, he often was critical of our profession, of its backward-looking tendencies, its preoccupation at times with red tape to the injury of what he thought were more vital interests. He threw upon this Department from time to time constantly expanding responsibilities, which sometimes were more welcome as evidence of his confidence than for the duties they carried. But he was deeply interested in all of its problems. He wanted us, as attorneys for the government, to live up to the best tradition of our profession, to shun shoddy work, and to do equal justice under the law.

Before me are many men of whose work, either in general or in particular cases, I had occasion to talk of with the President, and many whom he knew by name—usually by the first name.

We cannot avoid a somewhat personal note. Toward us in the Department he never was an exacting or critical overlord. I have had, on more than one occasion, to try to explain to him why things went the way they did, instead of the way I had told him they would go. Peals of hearty laughter would smother my embarrassment. His patience with blundering was sometimes past understanding—but it was mighty comforting when the blunder was your own. How he found time to pen in his own hand the innumerable little chits, telling, or asking, or commenting about this and that, I do not know. No father could be more solicitous of the personal and family welfare of those in his circle. No one worked harder—and no one made you so feel like working hard yourself—and no one knew better the proper proportions in which relaxation and laughter must be mixed with all well-balanced work. He loved the simple things. He could make either a king or a countryman feel at ease in his presence. His personality, his serene self-confidence, and his gentle firmness were gifts of the gods.

I think President Roosevelt would be pleased that we have paused today in his memory. This is not because he would have wanted a personal tribute. But he would have seen it as a sign of our dedication to the things he stood for, and that would gladden him. And not the least of his great services to our times was to inspire us all with his personal courage in the presence of handicaps of life and the mysteries of death. Despair of defeatism among men or nations vanished at his touch. He would want no disheartening note now. After we have paused and renewed our courage through each other's counsel, he would expect us to pick up the burden and carry on.

All of us will agree that for the interests of all that we have and are,

President Roosevelt's death is untimely. How much his passing affects the destinies of mankind, we can never estimate. Certainly, when the New World meets the Old in council, this hemisphere can no longer send a personality so appealing, a mind so richly endowed and informed, a heart so warm and understanding, a spirit so unconquerable.

But we cannot say that Death dealt unkindly with him. In many ways, his sudden passing comes as a fitting climax to life. We are glad that he lived the high moments when he could see that his efforts have led our country to the very threshold of victory both in Europe and in the Orient. It is as though the President had sent his best-loved friend, General Watson, to prepare the way,[10] and now he has followed to the Peace which shall have no end.[11]

On the first anniversary of FDR's death, Jackson—who then was serving before the International Military Tribunal in Nuremberg, Germany, as the American chief prosecutor of accused Nazi war criminals—delivered what was in substance his final eulogy for President Roosevelt. Jackson delivered these remarks on April 12, 1946, at a Roosevelt Commemorative Ceremony that was arranged by the American Institute of Czechoslovakia and the City of Praha (Prague). This ceremony, hosted by Czechoslovak Republic President Edvard Beneš, Minister of Foreign Affairs Jan Masaryk, and Lord Mayor Peter Zenkl, occurred in the Smetana Hall of the Representation Building in Praha. Following speeches by the Lord Mayor and the American Ambassador, Masaryk spoke from a prepared text. He then said, in English, that he was glad Jackson was present because in many ways he had been "FDR's right hand man." The "spirit of FDR is here tonight," Masaryk said, and "I know it says, 'Bob, I'm glad you are there.'"[12] Jackson then gave the following speech extemporaneously:

Mr. President, Mr. Foreign Minister, Lord Mayor, and friends who meet in memory of President Roosevelt—

It is an honor and privilege to speak to the people of Czechoslovakia who desire to meet in respect for Franklin Delano Roosevelt. It is the anniversary of a sad day in the lives of all of us who were permitted to serve under him in his government. I could tell you, if I were more gifted, of his kindness toward us and his thoughtfulness of the men about him. I could tell you of the fatherly interest he took in the young men whom he brought into public life, and I could speak very feelingly of his unfailing charity toward our mistakes. His attitude toward us was more nearly that of an indulgent parent than that of an exacting chief. Today is also a sad anniversary in the history of the struggle of human freedom.

This man is missed and mourned wherever men suffer oppression, privation, or injustice. He was temperamentally on the side of those who suffered wrong. From the very beginning he instinctively knew that there was no basis upon which the democracies of the world could bargain with Hitler. He instinctively understood that Nazism was the evil thing with which there could be no compromise. The planned barbarities of that system offended his sense of justice.

President Roosevelt was a firm friend and admirer of Czechoslovakia. It is a gracious act, deeply appreciated by the American people, that President Beneš and Foreign Minister Masaryk, out of regard for their old friendship for him and his deep sympathy with them, have come tonight to this memorial meeting.

President Roosevelt's sympathy and his understanding were always with the people of this country during their hours under the Nazi yoke. One of his great interests was that the war criminals who had overrun this and other countries and inflicted such barbaric treatment on the inhabitants should be identified and punished—not because of mere vengeance, but chiefly because he felt that punishment was one way that repetition of this sort of thing could be prevented or made less likely. Because his feeling and determination were shared by President Truman, I was sent to Europe, and that gives me the opportunity to be here tonight.

I shall not speak of the fate of the Nazi war criminals on trial at Nuremberg. The guilt and punishment, of course, is for the court to judge and not for me. But I would like to remind you of something that impressed me strongly as we have proceeded with the trial at Nuremberg. I speak of it because it concerns the attitude of the German people and the future dealing with them in the interests of the peace of Europe.

I have yet to hear one of these men say that he regretted he had a part in starting the war. Their only regret is at losing it. Not one sign of contrition or reform has appeared, either in public testimony or private interrogation of the twenty-one men in the dock. Not one of them has condemned the persecution of the Jews or of the Church—they have only sought to evade personal responsibilities. Not one has condemned the creation of concentration camps; indeed, Hermann Goering testified they are useful and necessary. Not one has indicated that, if he were free and able, he would not do the same thing over again.

From their testimony, it is apparent that they would expect the support of most of the German people in the same program again. The testimony of Goering is the strongest argument I yet have seen that

Nazism is unregenerate and virulent, and he himself says only the sternest measure can succeed with the German people. This practical fact shown up at the Nuremberg trial must not be overlooked in dealing with the German people. This practical fact shown up at the Nuremberg trial must not be overlooked in dealing with the German problem.

The world councils that must deal with these problems will miss the presence of Franklin D. Roosevelt. He was a great man—a man, as Mr. Masaryk has pointed out, disciplined by illness. He never lost courage— never for one moment in the darkest hours of the war was there a doubt in his mind of the outcome. And there were some dark hours on our side of the Atlantic too. President Roosevelt had the precious gift of inspiring the courage of others. When he died, the victory for which he had struggled was in sight. He was one of the casualties of the war.

But if he is no longer among us, we can still take courage from his example when dark days face us. We must remember that right has a strength of its own. No end will justify wrong as a means; instead, wrong means will defeat the best of ends. There is a right and a wrong about the conduct of men and of nations that is not merely a matter of expediency, and the man or the people who ceases to make justice its standard of conduct is lost.

Many ideas and institutions that we thought were good and perhaps served well in their time have been rendered obsolete by the war. Much that we have known will pass away. There will be many changes in all our countries. But we must never forget that right dealing is never outmoded, justice is never obsolete, true democracy is vindicated by the victory.

We can face these things and face our problems as he faced his— with courage and belief in the triumph of freedom from arbitrary power and of justice between man and man. We must live in the spirit of the poet who said:

> Though all we know depart
> The old commandments stand: —
> "In courage keep your heart,
> In strength lift up your hand."[13]

BIOGRAPHICAL SKETCHES

Thurman Wesley Arnold (1891–1969) was an Assistant Attorney General and a federal judge under FDR. Arnold began his law career in his father's law practice in Laramie, Wyoming. In 1921, Arnold was elected to the Wyoming legislature. One year later, he was elected Mayor of Laramie. In 1927, he became Dean of the West Virginia University Law School. In three years, his work to upgrade the school and West Virginia's courts built his reputation nationally. After joining the Yale Law School faculty in 1930, Arnold wrote two influential books, *The Symbols of Government* (1935) and *The Folklore of Capitalism* (1937), and also undertook special government assignments. In 1938, FDR appointed Arnold, on Jackson's recommendation, to succeed him as head of the Department of Justice's Antitrust Division. After 1941, Arnold grew disillusioned as the government enlisted those he considered "monopolists" to assist in the war effort. In 1943, FDR appointed Arnold to serve on the United States Court of Appeals for the District of Columbia. Bored with judicial work, he resigned two years later to reenter law practice. In 1946, Arnold, Abe Fortas (later a Supreme Court Justice), and Paul Porter formed the Arnold, Fortas & Porter law firm in Washington, D.C.

Henry Fountain Ashurst (1874–1962), a Democratic senator representing Arizona from 1912 until 1941, became Chairman of the Senate Judiciary Committee in 1933. In 1937, Ashurst initially supported FDR's Court-packing plan, then delayed holding hearings on it and eventually helped engineer its defeat. He was defeated in Arizona's 1940 Democratic primary.

Warren Robinson Austin (1877–1962) was a Republican senator representing Vermont from 1931 until 1946. President Truman then appointed Austin the Chief United States delegate to the United Nations, where he served until 1953.

Josiah William Bailey (1873–1946), a lawyer, was a Democratic senator representing North Carolina from 1931 until 1946. Although Bailey did not support many early New Deal initiatives, he supported FDR's reelection in 1936. In FDR's second term, however, Bailey aligned himself with conservative Republicans and Democrats to fight what they saw as the "collectivism" of the New Deal. This opposition culminated in the 1937 defeat of FDR's Court-packing plan, in which Bailey played an instrumental role. As World War II approached, Bailey abandoned his previously isolationist views to support increased defense expenditures, United States aid to England and France, and the Lend-Lease program.

Bernard Mannes Baruch (1870–1965), the noted financier and philanthropist, was a close adviser to FDR despite not holding a government position. Following World War II, Baruch worked for United Nations control of atomic energy.

John James ("Jack") Bennett, Jr. (1894–1967), a Democrat from Brooklyn, New York, was first elected New York State Attorney General in 1930. Bennett was reelected four times and served until 1942, when he ran as the Democratic Party nominee but lost to Thomas E. Dewey in the race for New York Governor.

Adolf Augustus Berle, Jr. (1895–1971) was a lawyer, Columbia University law professor, and expert on corporations who in 1932 became part of the "Brains Trust" that was advising Governor and presidential candidate FDR. After his election, FDR gave Berle various assignments dealing with banking, railroad, and other crises, but he remained in New York and served as Mayor La Guardia's principal financial consultant. In 1938, FDR appointed Berle Assistant Secretary of State. During World War II, he ran the State Department's intelligence network. In 1944, FDR appointed Berle to serve as United States Ambassador to Brazil.

Clifford Kennedy Berryman (1869–1949) was a political cartoonist for fifty years, first for the *Washington Post* and then for the *Washington Evening Star*. He drew every president from Cleveland to Truman. One of his most famous works commented on both a border dispute between Louisiana and Mississippi and a president's refusal while hunting to shoot a helpless animal: Berryman drew Theodore Roosevelt refusing to shoot a woeful cub that a guide had hauled from the woods. This popular 1902 frame, captioned "Drawing the Line in Mississippi," developed into the concept of the "Teddy Bear." A small bear also became a signature feature of many Berryman cartoons. He won the Pulitzer Prize in 1944 for "But Where Is the Boat Going?," a cartoon that showed several influential political figures, with conflicting goals, in the "U.S.S. Manpower," a lifeboat skippered by FDR.

Francis Beverly Biddle (1886–1968), a lawyer, government official, and judge, first became acquainted with FDR when they were young students at Groton. In 1935, FDR appointed Biddle to chair the National Labor Relations Board. After Biddle had briefly returned to private law practice, FDR appointed him in 1939 to serve on the United States Court of Appeals for the Third Circuit in Philadelphia. Biddle resigned from the bench the next year when FDR appointed him to succeed Jackson as Solicitor General. In 1941, FDR appointed Biddle to succeed Jackson as Attorney General when he moved to the Supreme Court. Biddle was Attorney General until President Truman replaced him in 1945. Truman then appointed Biddle to serve as the senior United States member of the International Military Tribunal at Nuremberg, where Jackson litigated before Biddle's bench as the chief American prosecutor.

John David Biggers (1888–1974) was appointed by FDR in 1937 to conduct the federal census and serve on the Department of Commerce's business advisory council. In 1941, FDR made Biggers Director of the Division of Production of the Office of Production Management. He was transferred to London later that year and served as special minister to coordinate production under the Lend-Lease program.

Hugo Lafayette Black (1886–1971) was a private lawyer, a police court judge, and a prosecutor in Birmingham, Alabama, before he was first elected to the United States Senate in 1926. After Black's reelection in 1932, he became a champion of New Deal legislation and an FDR favorite in the Senate. After FDR's Court-packing plan was defeated in summer 1937, he made Black his first Supreme Court appointee. Black served on the Court for more than thirty years, including Jackson's full tenure of thirteen years. Their relationship deteriorated into a feud that Jackson made public in 1946, then improved in later years.

William Edgar Borah (1865–1940) was a Republican senator representing Idaho from 1907 until 1940. He was an isolationist who opposed United States participation in the World Court and in the League of Nations. After FDR became President, Borah generally supported New Deal legislation aiding farmers and opposed measures that related to industry. In 1936, he unsuccessfully sought his party's presidential nomination. A year later, Borah, who was a member of the Senate Judiciary Committee, helped defeat FDR's Court-packing plan. As World War II approached, Borah opposed United States involvement. He supported mandatory neutrality legislation and helped to block FDR's effort to amend the neutrality laws. After Germany invaded Poland in September 1939, however, these amendments passed despite Borah's continuing opposition.

Louis Dembitz Brandeis (1856–1941), appointed to the Supreme Court by President Wilson, served as an Associate Justice from 1916 until his retirement in 1939. Before he joined the Court, Brandeis was a Boston lawyer who gained national prominence by defending civil liberties and attacking concentrated corporate power.

Harry Renton Bridges (1901–1990) emigrated from Australia in 1920, became a dock worker in San Francisco, participated in the 1933 West Coast dock workers strike, and in 1936 formed the International Longshore and Warehouse Union, which he headed for the next forty years. In 1938, the United States instituted deportation proceedings against Bridges for his alleged affiliation with the Communist Party. In 1941, a new deportation proceeding commenced, focusing on his alleged participation in the North American Aviation plant strike and other labor activity. After the court ordered Bridges deported, its ruling was reversed and then, in 1942, reinstated by Attorney General Francis Biddle. After years of legal proceedings, the Supreme Court ultimately decided that the deportation warrant against Bridges was unlawful. Three months later, his application for U.S. citizenship was granted.

John Bright (1884–1948), a native of Middletown in Orange County, New York, who practiced law there for more than thirty years, was a protégé of Judge John E. Mack. In 1941, FDR appointed Bright to the United States District Court for the Southern District of New York, where he served until his death.

Ralph Budd (1879–1962), the President of the Chicago, Burlington & Quincy Railroad and former president of the Great Northern Railroad, was a transportation expert. FDR appointed Budd to the Defense Advisory Commission, to take charge of all transportation problems and prevent potential railroad congestion, which had occurred during World War I.

William Christian Bullitt (1891–1967) became United States Ambassador to France in 1936. He served there until France fell to the Nazis in spring 1940. Bullitt previously served, from 1933 to 1936, as the first United States Ambassador to the Soviet Union.

Pierce Butler (1866–1939), a son of Irish immigrants to the United States, never attended law school, but he became a Minnesota lawyer in 1888 after working as a law apprentice. He primarily was in private practice, representing railroads and utilities and serving as a powerful member of the University of Minnesota's Board of Regents. In 1923, President Harding, acting on the recommendation of Chief Justice William Howard Taft, appointed Butler to the Supreme Court. On the bench, he was known for his conservative, pro-business views and became one of the Justices who voted consistently that various New Deal laws were unconstitutional. Butler served on the Court until his death in late 1939. FDR then appointed Attorney General Frank Murphy to succeed Butler on the Court and Solicitor General Jackson to succeed Murphy as attorney general.

Harry Flood Byrd (1887–1966), a Democrat, was Governor of Virginia from 1926 until 1930 and represented it in the United States Senate from 1933 until 1965. Byrd was an opponent of the New Deal.

James Francis Byrnes (1879–1972) of South Carolina had an extraordinary and varied public career. He represented his state in the House of Representatives from 1911 until 1925. Byrnes then, after a period in private law practice, was elected to the Senate in 1930 and reelected in 1936. He was a strong supporter of FDR during his time in the Senate. In 1941, FDR appointed Byrnes to the Supreme Court, where he and Jackson were rookie Justices together. A year later, Byrnes resigned from the Court to become FDR's Director of Economic Stabilization, and then, from 1943 until 1945, he served as Chairman of the War Mobilization Board. Byrnes was, in effect, FDR's "assistant president" for domestic economic matters during World War II. Under President Truman, Byrnes served as Secretary of State from 1945 until 1947. He then returned to South Carolina and was elected Governor, serving from 1951 until 1955.

Benjamin Nathan Cardozo (1870–1938), appointed by President Hoover in 1932 to succeed Justice Oliver Wendell Holmes on the Supreme Court, served until his death in 1938. Cardozo previously had served as an Associate Judge of the New York Court of Appeals from 1917 until 1926 and its Chief Judge from 1926 until his Supreme Court appointment.

Emanuel Celler (1888–1981), a Democrat, was a member of Congress from New York from 1923 through 1973. He was a strong supporter of New Deal programs throughout FDR's Presidency.

Harold Roland Christoffel (1912–1991), a labor union leader, led the January 1941 strike against Allis-Chalmers' West Allis, Wisconsin, plant. It and he drew national attention when Representative Clare Hoffman (R.-MI) charged, during a speech on the House floor, that the strike was Communist-influenced. Christoffel denied having any ties to the Communist Party. The strike, which lasted more than two months, temporarily crippled warship and airplane production when military industries could not obtain Allis-Chalmers products, including electrical equipment and generators used for mine sweeping. In 1947, Christoffel was convicted and later imprisoned for committing perjury by denying to the House Education and Labor Committee that he was a Communist.

Benjamin Victor Cohen (1894–1983) was Chairman of the National Public Power Committee in the Department of the Interior, a trusted adviser to Secretary Ickes, and a key draftsman of much New Deal legislation. Before he joined the Roosevelt Administration in 1933, Cohen had been a brilliant law student, a protégé of Felix Frankfurter and Louis Brandeis, a negotiator of the Palestine Mandate, and a New York lawyer specializing in corporate reorganizations. Under FDR, Cohen worked with James Landis to draft new securities laws. Cohen next worked under Ickes at the Public Works Administration and then at the Power Committee, but his more important work was his all-purpose collaboration with Thomas Corcoran, which included writing key legislation, writing speeches for FDR, and political plotting (as in the case of Jackson's nascent 1938 New York gubernatorial campaign). In 1941, Cohen left Interior to serve in the United States embassy in London. During World War II, he was General Counsel in the Office of War Mobilization. Following FDR's death, President Truman appointed Cohen legal counsel in the State Department and later a delegate to the United Nations.

Thomas Gardiner Corcoran (1900–1981), known as "Tommy the Cork," was a prominent Washington lawyer and FDR adviser. A protégé of his Harvard Law School professor Felix Frankfurter, Corcoran first came to Washington in 1926 to serve as a law clerk to Supreme Court Justice Oliver Wendell Holmes. After five years in private law practice in New York, Corcoran returned to Washington in 1932 to work at the new Reconstruction Finance Corporation (RFC). Corcoran remained at the RFC following FDR's election later that year and remained there for most of his first two terms. Although Corcoran never held a prominent office in FDR's Administration, he came to be a principal draftsman of much New Deal legislation and many Roosevelt speeches. Corcoran staunchly defended the President's 1937 Court-packing plan and his efforts the next year to "purge" incumbent Democrats who had not supported the President's policies. Corcoran also was an early proponent of FDR's seeking a third term in 1940. These efforts made Corcoran controversial and earned him many political enemies. When FDR declined to appoint Corcoran to succeed Jackson as Solicitor General in 1940, Corcoran left government but remained in Washington, where he built a lucrative law and lobbying practice and remained influential in Democratic Party politics. He married **Margaret ("Peggy") Dowd** (1911–1957), who had been his secretary at the RFC, in 1940.

Malin Craig (1875–1945) succeeded General Douglas MacArthur as United States Army Chief of Staff in 1935. In 1939, General Craig developed plans to rapidly expand the Army. He retired when he reached the Army's mandatory retirement age in August 1939—just weeks before Germany invaded Poland. In December 1941, Craig was recalled to public service as a member of the Secretary of War's Personnel Board, which was responsible for allocating manpower among the armed services and war industries.

George Creel (1875–1953) was a presidential adviser, government administrator, journalist, and author. He was, at various times in his early career, publisher of the *Kansas City Independent* and editor of the *Denver Post* and the *Rocky Mountain News*. During World War I, Creel headed President Wilson's Committee on Public Information, earning the nickname "Uncle Sam's Press Agent." Creel supported FDR early in his Presidency, later criticized his and then President Truman's foreign policies, and by 1952 backed the Eisenhower–Nixon ticket.

Homer Stillé Cummings (1870–1956), a Connecticut native, former United States Attorney, and Democratic Party official, was FDR's first Attorney

General, serving from 1933 until 1939. Under Cummings, the national government's role in investigating and prosecuting crime expanded dramatically as his efforts helped secure passage of legislation that defined such new federal crimes as kidnapping, bank robbery, and racketeering. In 1936, Cummings responded to the Supreme Court's invalidations of such New Deal programs as the National Industrial Recovery Act and the Agricultural Adjustment Act by drafting the "Judicial Reorganization" proposal that FDR announced to the country in February 1937. This Court-packing plan would have permitted the President to appoint an additional federal judge for each sitting judge who did not retire within six months of reaching age seventy-five. Because six Supreme Court Justices were over age seventy-five at the time, the plan would have permitted FDR immediately to enlarge the Court to fifteen Justices, assuming no incumbent chose to retire. The plan, which generated substantial opposition from Democrats and Republicans, eventually was defeated when the Senate returned it to committee in the summer of 1937. Cummings resigned from office in 1939 and spent the rest of his life in private law practice in Washington, D.C.

Donald A. Dailey (1891–1966) was Democratic Party Chairman of Monroe County (including the city of Rochester), New York, from 1934 until 1940. He then was appointed Postmaster of Rochester. Vincent J. Dailey was his brother.

Vincent J. Dailey (1889–1956) entered New York State Democratic Party politics in 1930 as an associate of James Farley, who was chairman of the state and national Democratic committees. As Farley's chief lieutenant in New York, Dailey ran state and national campaigns for him, including FDR's 1932, 1936, and 1940 campaigns. Donald A. Dailey was his brother.

Josephus Daniels, Jr. (1862–1948) was, as Wilson's Secretary of the Navy, FDR's immediate supervisor during his first stint in Washington. Daniels had served previously under President Cleveland, who appointed him chief clerk in the Department of the Interior in 1893. After serving in that position for two years, Daniels returned to his native North Carolina and became owner and editor of Raleigh's *News and Observer*. In 1912, he supported Wilson's presidential campaign. As Secretary of the Navy under Wilson, Daniels worked with Assistant Secretary of the Navy FDR to institute personnel reforms and improve the quality of schooling for sailors. When FDR became president in 1933, he appointed Daniels to serve as United States Ambassador to Mexico.

Chester Charles Davis (1887–1975) was FDR's administrator of the Agricultural Adjustment Administration (AAA). Davis later headed the Defense Advisory Commission's agricultural division, which tried to prevent conflicts between national agriculture policy and the defense program.

John Warren Davis (1867–1945), a former United States Attorney for New Jersey (1913–1916) and a former United States District Judge (1916–1920), was a Judge of the United States Court of Appeals for the Third Circuit when he was indicted and tried twice for fixing cases. In each trial, the jury was unable to reach a verdict. Judge Davis assumed senior status in 1939 and ultimately resigned from the bench in 1941.

Gordon Evans Dean (1905–1958), a Seattle native, began his law career as a professor at Duke University. He joined the Department of Justice during the New Deal and was instrumental in creating modern federal criminal law, first by drafting and working to pass legislation and then by arguing Supreme Court cases that resulted in decisions upholding new statutes. Dean then handled the Department's public relations and was a senior adviser to Attorneys General Cummings and Jackson. In the 1940s, Dean was in private practice, served in the Navy, and then handled public relations and was a key Jackson assistant during 1945 in London and Nuremberg. In the late 1940s, Dean became a member of the Atomic Energy Commission (AEC), and from 1950 until 1953 he was AEC chairman. He was in private business when he was killed in a commercial airplane crash.

Thomas Edmund Dewey (1902–1971), a native of Michigan, moved to New York as a young man, graduated from Columbia Law School, and became a Wall Street lawyer. In the early 1930s, Dewey became Chief Assistant United States Attorney for the Southern District of New York and then Interim United States Attorney. He then worked briefly under Jackson in the Treasury Department's Bureau of Revenue before becoming a state special prosecutor. Dewey gained national recognition for prosecuting organized crime figures, including Charles "Lucky" Luciano. In 1937, Dewey was elected District Attorney of New York County (Manhattan). In 1938, he narrowly lost New York's gubernatorial election, for an office that for the first time carried a four-year term, to incumbent Governor Herbert Lehman. In 1940, Dewey was a leading contender for the Republican presidential nomination that ultimately went to Wendell Willkie. In 1942, Dewey was elected Governor of New York. He ran for president in 1944, receiving the Republican Party nomination but losing to FDR that November. In 1946, Dewey was reelected Governor. In 1948, he again won the Republic presidential nomination but, in a stunning upset, lost a close race to President Truman. In 1950, Dewey again was reelected Governor. In 1951 and 1952, he worked to secure the Republican presidential nomination for General Dwight D. Eisenhower, and for the selection of Senator Richard M. Nixon (R.-CA) as Eisenhower's running mate. In 1955, at the end of his third term in Albany, Dewey returned to private law practice. In 1968, President-elect Nixon offered to nominate Dewey to succeed retiring Chief Justice Earl Warren, but Dewey declined.

Armistead Mason Dobie (1881–1962), a triple graduate of the University of Virginia, was a member of its law faculty for thirty years and its law school dean from 1932 until 1939. FDR appointed Dobie to serve as a United States District Judge for the Western District of Virginia in 1939. Before the year was out, FDR made a recess appointment of Dobie to the United States Court of Appeals for the Fourth Circuit. In early 1940, Judge Dobie's nomination was confirmed by the Senate and he was commissioned a Circuit Judge.

William Orville Douglas (1898–1980), who was born in western Minnesota, grew up in Yakima, Washington, and graduated from Whitman College and Columbia Law School, began his legal career practicing corporate law in New York City. He became a Columbia law professor in 1926. In 1928, he joined the Yale Law School faculty. In 1934, Douglas moved to Washington to work on a study of the newly created Securities and Exchange Commission (SEC). In 1936, FDR, acting on the recommendation of SEC Chairman Joseph P. Kennedy, appointed Douglas to serve as an SEC Commissioner. A year later, FDR appointed Douglas to serve as SEC Chairman. In 1939, FDR appointed Douglas to succeed Justice Louis D. Brandeis on the Supreme Court. Douglas served for more than thirty-six years, the longest Supreme Court tenure in history. Although FDR in 1944 and President Truman in 1948 each considered Douglas very seriously as his prospective running mate, he never ran for political office. As his Court colleague from 1941 until his death in 1954, Jackson came to view Douglas, who had earlier been a friend and Roosevelt administration ally, as inappropriately politically motivated. Jackson also believed that Douglas had acted, along with Justice Hugo Black, to persuade Truman in 1946 not to appoint Jackson to serve as Chief Justice of the United States following the death of Chief Justice Harlan Fiske Stone.

David Dubinsky (1892–1982) rose through union ranks to become President of the International Ladies' Garment Workers Union (ILGWU), a position he held from 1932 until 1966.

Stephen Tyree Early (1889–1951), a public relations specialist, first worked for FDR as an advance man during his 1920 vice presidential campaign. Early then returned to the Associated Press, where he had worked from 1913 until 1917. He remained there until 1927, when he joined Paramount News and Paramount Publix Corporation. In 1933, Early joined the Roosevelt Administration as Assistant Secretary to the President. He became White House press secretary in 1937 and served in that post into the Truman Administration.

Charles Edison (1890–1969), a Democrat, a son of inventor Thomas Alva Edison (1847–1931) and the businessman who ran his father's enterprises, became FDR's Assistant Secretary of the Navy in 1937. Charles Edison became Acting Secretary of the Navy for almost six months in 1939, following the death that summer of Secretary Claude Augustus Swanson (1862–1939). In late December 1939, FDR made Edison Secretary of the Navy by recess appointment and sent his nomination to the Senate, which confirmed him in January 1940. Shortly thereafter, both to strengthen the Cabinet and to serve FDR's political purposes in Edison's home state, FDR persuaded Edison to run for Governor in New Jersey. He announced his candidacy in March 1940 and, after winning the primary, resigned as Secretary of the Navy effective June 24, 1940. Edison was elected Governor that November and served from 1941 until 1944.

Harriet Wiseman Elliott (1884–1947), a professor of political science and dean of women at the University of North Carolina, worked at the Defense Advisory Commission on measures to protect the consumer against skyrocketing emergency prices. Elliott traveled extensively, holding many conferences with retailers, manufacturers, and others to achieve voluntary agreements to hold down prices.

Morris Leopold Ernst (1888–1976), a lawyer, was one of the country's most successful advocates for civil liberties, especially First Amendment rights, during the twentieth century. Ernst's long association with the American Civil Liberties Union (ACLU) began in 1927, when he joined its Board of Directors. He became ACLU Co-General Counsel in 1929 and held the position until 1952. Ernst was an FDR adviser on various policy matters throughout his Presidency.

James Aloysius ("Jim") Farley (1888–1976) led the national Democratic Party during most of the 1930s and was United States Postmaster General, then a Cabinet office, from 1933 until 1940. In 1931, Farley traveled the country and communicated on FDR's behalf with hundreds of prospective presidential delegates. At the 1932 Democratic national convention, Farley, who was Chairman of the New York Democratic Party and running FDR's presidential campaign, garnered the delegates that secured his nomination. In 1936, Farley ran FDR's crushingly successful reelection campaign, but their relationship cooled during FDR's second term as Farley opposed, for example, FDR's 1938 purge efforts against incumbent Democrats who were not New Deal supporters. In 1940, Farley broke with FDR in principled opposition to his third term candidacy and in favor of Farley's own presidential ambitions. Indeed, his name was placed in nomination for President at the Democrats' Chicago convention that summer, receiving a small number of protest votes on the first ballot that produced FDR's renomination. In August 1940, Farley resigned both his Party chairman and Cabinet positions. He then became Chairman of the Coca-Cola Export Corporation, a position he held until 1973. Farley married **Elizabeth A. ("Bess") Finnegan** (1895?–1955), a native of Haverstraw in Rockland County, New York, in 1920.

James Lawrence Fly (1898–1966) was a special assistant to the Attorney General in the 1930s, then head of the Tennessee Valley Authority's legal department, then Chairman of the Federal Communications Commission from 1939 until 1944 and also Chairman of the Defense Communications Board during World War II.

Henry Ford (1863–1947) and FDR had known each other since World War I, when FDR, as Assistant Secretary of the Navy, had dealings with the Ford Corporation, which built Eagle Boats for the Navy. Ford supported the Roosevelt Administration until FDR signed the National Industrial Recovery Act, which created the National Recovery Administration (NRA) that imposed regulatory codes on industry, in June 1933. At the outbreak of World War II in Europe, Ford opposed United States involvement. In 1941, however, he committed to taking an active part in the war effort, providing automobiles, trucks, and other materials required by the military.

Jerome New Frank (1889–1957), a Chicago and then New York City lawyer who specialized in financial issues in corporate reorganization, joined

FDR's Administration in 1933 as General Counsel to the Agricultural Adjustment Administration (AAA). Frank left the AAA two years later over conflicts with administrator Chester Davis. In 1937, FDR appointed Frank to the Securities and Exchange Commission and, in 1941, to the United States Court of Appeals for the Second Circuit.

Felix Frankfurter (1882–1965), who emigrated to the United States from Austria as a boy, became a Supreme Court Justice who served for more than twenty years. After graduating from Harvard Law School in 1906, pursuing private law practice in New York City, and working under United States Attorney Henry Stimson in the Southern District of New York, Frankfurter moved to Washington. He later served in the Department of War under President Wilson. In 1914, Frankfurter became a professor at Harvard Law School, a position from which he built a national reputation over the next twenty-five years as a brilliant and prolific scholar and a civil liberties lawyer. In 1918, Frankfurter was appointed Chairman of the War Policies Board, where one of his colleagues was Assistant Secretary of the Navy FDR. After Roosevelt was elected Governor of New York in 1928, he often sought Frankfurter's counsel. Their close relationship continued after FDR was President, and Frankfurter was the powerful connection through which many young lawyers became parts of the New Deal. In 1939, FDR, acting in accord with the strong recommendations of Solicitor General Jackson and others, appointed Frankfurter to fill the Supreme Court vacancy created by the death of Justice Cardozo. Jackson joined Frankfurter on the Court in 1941 and they were, over the next thirteen years until Jackson's death in 1954, judicial allies and close personal friends.

Walter Franklin George (1876–1957) was a Democratic senator representing Georgia from 1922 until 1957. In 1938, Senator George was one of the members of the President's own party whom FDR sought, without success in this and most cases, to "purge" to retaliate for opposing the Court-packing plan and other New Deal initiatives.

Guy Mark Gillette (1879–1973) was a Democratic senator representing Iowa from 1936 until 1945. He then became Chairman of the Surplus Property Board and President of the American League for a Free Palestine. Gillette was elected again to the Senate in 1948 but was defeated when he sought reelection in 1954.

Carter Glass (1858–1946) was a Democratic senator representing Virginia from 1919 until 1946. In his earlier career, he had been a newspaperman and then represented Virginia in the House of Representatives from 1902 until 1918. Glass resigned from the House to become President Wilson's Secretary of the Treasury, a position he held from 1918 until he was appointed to the Senate in 1920. When FDR became President, Glass actively supported emergency banking legislation, but he broke with FDR over the wisdom of various fiscal plans and opposed his 1937 Court-packing plan. After FDR's 1940 election to a third term, Glass supported United States involvement in World War II and generally praised FDR's foreign policy.

George Casper Haas (1896-19??), an economist, served under Secretary Henry Morgenthau as the Department of the Treasury's Director of Research and Statistics.

Green Hayward Hackworth (1883–1973) had a thirty-year legal career in the United States Department of State, serving as Legal Adviser from 1931 until 1946. The United Nations then elected him to the International Court of Justice, where he served until 1961.

Frank Hague (1876–1956) was Mayor of Jersey City from 1917 until 1947 and New Jersey's Democratic National committeeman from 1922 until 1952. He once boasted, "I am the law in Jersey City," and from his Hudson County base, he effectively was the Democratic boss of New Jersey.

Byron Patton ("Pat") Harrison (1881–1941) was a Democratic senator representing Mississippi from 1919 until 1941. Throughout the 1920s, Harrison was a staunch opponent of Republican fiscal policies. In 1933, he became Chairman of the powerful Senate Committee on Finance. He was instrumental in achieving the passage of many New Deal measures, including the NRA, the Social Security Act, and several tax bills. In FDR's second term, his relationship with Harrison became strained over differences in tax philosophy. In 1937, FDR supported Senator Alben W. Barkley (D.-KY) over Harrison in the race for Senate Majority Leader, which Barkley won by one vote. By 1938, FDR and Harrison had become estranged and he allied himself with southern conservative senators who opposed social reforms, including anti-lynching and anti-poll tax bills. As World War II approached, however, Harrison helped FDR achieve passage of the 1941 Lend-Lease bill.

Edith Benham Helm (1874–1962) was the White House Social Secretary. She first held this position under President Wilson, and during that period she became acquainted with Assistant Secretary of the Navy FDR and his wife, Eleanor. Mrs. Helm returned to the White House at their request in 1933 and served until President Truman left office in 1953.

Leon Henderson (1895–1986) was an economist who advised the Work Projects Administration and became a member of the Securities and Exchange Commission in 1939. He then played a key role in the New Deal's transition from economic recovery programs to mobilization for World War II. At the Defense Advisory Commission, Henderson set up a statistical bureau and directed price stabilization efforts in the raw materials field.

Joseph Lister Hill (1894–1984) was a Democratic senator representing Alabama from 1938 until 1969. In the 1938 Democratic primary, Hill defeated **James Thomas ("Cotton Tom") Heflin** (1869–1951), an ardent racist, who had represented Alabama in the Senate from 1920 until 1931.

Sidney Hillman (1887–1946), who played a major role in unionizing garment workers in New York and Chicago, became President of the Amalgamated Clothing Workers of America (ACWA) in 1914. Hillman became an adviser to FDR during the early New Deal, serving on the NRA's Labor Advisory Board from 1933 until 1935 and on the National Industrial Recovery Board in 1934 and 1935. He also helped form the Committee for Industrial Organization (CIO) in 1935. As a Defense Advisory Commissioner, Hillman was in charge of nonmilitary personnel. His duties included coordinating employment policies in the so-called war industries.

Frank J. Hogan (1877–1944) began practicing law in Washington, D.C., in 1904. During his career, he was widely regarded as one of America's leading trial lawyers. His prominent clients included oil magnate Edward L. Doheny in Teapot Dome cases, the Pan American Oil Company, and, against government attorney Robert H. Jackson, former Secretary of the Treasury Andrew W. Mellon in his civil tax litigation. In 1925, Nelson Hartson, a former Solicitor in the Bureau of Revenue, joined Hogan to handle his firm's growing tax practice. In 1938, they founded Hogan & Hartson, the national law firm that bears their names today.

Oliver Wendell Holmes, Jr. (1841–1935), appointed to the Supreme Court by President Theodore Roosevelt, served as an Associate Justice from 1902 until his retirement in 1932. He previously was a Civil War soldier, a Boston lawyer, a Harvard law professor, and an Associate Justice and then Chief Justice of the Supreme Judicial Court of Massachusetts.

Alexander Holtzoff (1886–1969), a triple graduate of Columbia University, began his law career in private practice in New York. From 1924 until 1945, he was a special assistant to the United States Attorneys General, including Jackson. In September 1945, President Truman appointed Holtzoff a United States District Judge for the District of Columbia.

John Edgar Hoover (1895–1972), a lawyer and criminologist, joined the Department of Justice in 1917. He became Assistant Director of its Bureau of Investigation in 1921. Hoover headed the bureau, later renamed the Federal Bureau of Investigation (FBI), from 1924 until his death.

Harry Lloyd Hopkins (1890–1946) was a loyal friend, confidante, and political adviser to FDR prior to and throughout his Presidency. Hopkins met FDR during his successful 1928 campaign for Governor of New York. During 1931 and 1932, Hopkins served as deputy to Jesse I. Straus, Chairman of New York's Temporary Emergency Relief Administration (TERA). At the start of his Presidency, FDR appointed Hopkins to serve as administrator of the Federal Emergency Relief Administration (FERA), where he distributed funds to those hit hardest by the Depression. In 1935, FDR appointed Hopkins to head the Works Progress Administration (WPA), which replaced FERA. During his tenure at WPA, Hopkins began to battle the serious illnesses that afflicted him for the rest of his life. In 1939, he became Secretary of Commerce for a brief period, but he soon left that Cabinet office to advise FDR on national defense matters. During World War II, despite his failing health, Hopkins was FDR's chief agent and go-between in his dealings with Churchill, Stalin, and de Gaulle.

Louis McHenry Howe (1871–1936), who worked originally as a journalist, ran FDR's successful 1912 campaign for reelection to the New York State Senate. Because FDR contracted typhoid fever during the campaign and could not make public appearances, Howe's efforts were essential to FDR's victory. Howe also convinced FDR to remain in politics after polio crippled him in 1921, trained Eleanor Roosevelt to campaign for her husband, and planned FDR's successful New York gubernatorial campaign in 1928. When FDR became President in 1933, Howe became his appointments secretary, although his status as one of FDR's most intimate and trusted advisers made him much more than that title suggests. Howe, who had battled persistent bad health throughout his life, became gravely ill during FDR's first term and died in April 1936.

Charles Evans Hughes (1862–1948), a Republican, was twice elected Governor of New York and twice appointed to the Supreme Court of the United States. He served as Governor from 1907 until 1910, when President Taft appointed him to the Supreme Court as an Associate Justice. In June 1916, Hughes resigned from the Court to run as the Republican Party's presidential candidate. After losing to President Wilson by an extremely narrow margin, Hughes was in private practice and then served as Secretary of State (1921–1925) and as a Judge on the Permanent Court of International Justice (1926–1930). In 1930, Hughes returned to the Supreme Court when President Hoover appointed him Chief Justice of the United States. Hughes served as Chief Justice from 1930 until his retirement in 1941. FDR then elevated Associate Justice Harlan Fiske Stone to replace Hughes as Chief Justice and appointed Jackson to fill Stone's Associate Justice seat.

Cordell Hull (1871–1955) served as FDR's Secretary of State from 1933 until fall 1944. He previously was a Tennessee lawyer, state court judge and state legislator, a Spanish-American War veteran, and a Democrat who served in the United States House of Representatives (1907–1921 and 1923–1931) and, from 1931 until he resigned to join FDR's Cabinet, in the United States Senate.

William Ewart Humphrey (1862–1934), an Indiana native, found success in business and in Republican politics after he moved to Seattle in the early 1890s. Humphrey became Seattle's corporation counsel, and in 1902 he was elected to the United States House of Representatives. Humphrey served in Congress from 1903 until 1917; he gave up his House seat to run unsuccessfully for the Senate in 1916. In 1925, President Coolidge, seeking to bring the Federal Trade Commission in line with his Administration's policies, appointed Humphrey to serve as one of five FTC commissioners. Humphrey's appointment created a majority bloc on the FTC of three pro-business commissioners, and they swiftly transformed the Commission from an overseer to a partner of the corporations it existed to regulate. In 1931, President Hoover nominated Humphrey to serve another six-year term, and he was confirmed over the opposition of twenty-eight senators. In fall 1933, FDR removed Humphrey from office. Humphrey then filed suit seeking reinstatement and back pay. Although he died while his case was pending, in May 1935 the Supreme Court held unanimously, in its landmark decision *Humphrey's Executor v. United States*, that FDR had lacked constitutional power to remove Humphrey because FTC commissioners were not purely executive officers.

Harold LeClair Ickes (1874–1952), a Chicago newspaper reporter, lawyer, and Republican reform politician before he joined FDR's Cabinet, served as Secretary of Interior for Roosevelt's full Presidency and briefly under President Truman. He also served FDR as head of the Public Works Administration, as oil administrator under the National Recovery Administration, and during World War II as director of the Petroleum Administration for War.

Irene Alice Gerhardt Jackson (1890–1986), Robert Jackson's wife, grew up in Kingston, New York. In 1912, a cousin who was attending Albany Law School introduced her to his classmate Jackson. The Jacksons were married in Albany on April 24, 1916, and became the parents of two children, William Eldred Jackson (1919–1999) and Mary Margaret Jackson Loftus Craighill (1920–1999).

William Eldred ("Bill") Jackson (1919–1999), Robert Jackson's son, was an honors graduate of St. Albans School (1937), Yale University (1941), and Harvard Law School (1944). During 1945 and 1946, while serving as a Navy ensign, Bill Jackson was detailed to work as executive assistant to his father, who was serving as United States Chief of Counsel for Prosecution of Axis Criminality before the International Military Tribunal at Nuremberg, Germany. In 1946, Bill Jackson joined the New York City law firm that is known today as Milbank, Tweed, Hadley & McCloy, where he became a partner, rose to head its litigation department, and from 1979 until 1984 served as the firm's chairman. His clients included domestic and international corporations and prominent individuals, including Nelson Rockefeller. He negotiated complicated transactions and handled civil litigation in courts at all levels. From 1988 through 1994, Bill Jackson also was vice chair of the International Court of Arbitration at the International Chamber of Commerce in Paris.

Jesse Holman Jones (1874–1956), a Texas businessman who succeeded in real estate, lumber, and banking, held several positions in FDR's administrations. He previously had served in national government as President Wilson's Director General of Military Relief for the Red Cross during World War I and on the board of the Reconstruction Finance Corporation (RFC) under President Hoover. In 1933, FDR named Jones Chairman of the RFC. He left this position to become Federal Loan Administrator in 1939. By special act of Congress, Jones continued to hold that position when he became Secretary of Commerce the following year. At the start of FDR's fourth term, new Vice President Harry Truman asked Jones to resign so that former Vice President Henry Wallace could be appointed to the Cabinet. Jones was angry and bitter but complied. He returned to Texas, worked in philanthropy, and supported Eisenhower for president in 1952.

Joseph Berry Keenan (1888–1954), a lawyer, became special assistant to Attorney General Cummings in the early 1930s. Keenan acted as liaison between the White House and Congress, where he lobbied for legislation that expanded federal law enforcement powers to deal with gangsters, racketeers, and kidnappers. Keenan resigned from the Department of Justice in 1939 to pursue private law practice. In late 1945, President Truman appointed Keenan to prosecute Japanese war crimes. The Tokyo trial in which he was a prosecutor resulted in death sentences for former Premier Hideki Tojo and six others who had been high-ranking Japanese government officials.

Edward Joseph Kelly (1876–1950), the Democratic boss of Chicago, served as its Mayor from 1933 until 1948.

Daniel Joseph Kenefick (1863–1949) began his public service career as an Assistant District Attorney in Buffalo, New York, in 1893. He was elected District Attorney of Erie County, New York, the following year and served until he was elected a Justice of the New York State Supreme Court in 1898. Justice Kenefick resigned from the bench in 1906 to enter private law practice in Buffalo. He was President of the New York State Bar Association in 1928. Beginning in 1931, Kenefick served, along with Jackson, on the New York state commission to investigate the administration of justice.

Joseph Patrick Kennedy (1888–1969) was United States Ambassador to the Court of St. James's from 1937 until 1940.

Philip Henry Kerr (1882–1940), the Eleventh Marquess of Lothian, was the British Ambassador to the United States from August 1939 until his death in December 1940.

William Henry King (1863–1949), a Utah Democrat, served first in the House of Representatives and then, from 1917 until 1941, in the United States Senate. He left office following his September 1940 defeat in his party primary and practiced law in Washington, D.C., until he retired in 1947.

William Lyon Mackenzie King (1874–1950) served as Canada's Prime Minister from 1921 to 1930 and 1935 to 1948.

William Franklin ("Frank") Knox (1874–1944), a native of New Hampshire, was a "Rough Rider" during the Spanish-American War and served with Theodore Roosevelt at the Battle of San Juan Hill. During TR's unsuccessful 1912 presidential campaign, Knox was his campaign manager in the West. After serving in the First World War, Knox became influential in Republican politics and journalism in New Hampshire. From 1929 until 1931, he handled business administration for William Randolph Hearst's newspapers. In 1931, Knox took control of the *Chicago Daily News*, where he became a critic of FDR's Administration. In 1936, Knox was the Republican Party's vice presidential nominee, running unsuccessfully with Kansas Governor Alfred Mossman ("Alf") Landon (1887–1987) against FDR and Vice President John Nance Garner (1868–1967). Knox then returned to newspaper editorial work. In 1939, he became an advocate for building up the military, asserting that the United States had to be prepared to defend North and South America. In 1940, FDR appointed Knox to serve in the Cabinet as Secretary of the Navy, where he served until his death.

William Signius Knudsen (1879–1948), the President of General Motors, was appointed by FDR to be the Defense Advisory Commissioner who would command industrial manufacturing of tanks, airplanes, engines, uniforms, and other items.

Fiorello Henry La Guardia (1882–1947), a lawyer and politician who ran for public office at various times on Republican and American Labor Party tickets, began his legal career in New York City in 1910 working closely with labor and immigrant groups. He was elected to Congress in 1916 but took a leave of absence a year later to serve in the Army Air Service. During this time, La Guardia met FDR, who was Assistant Secretary of the Navy. La Guardia again served in Congress from 1923 through 1933. In 1929, he ran for Mayor of New York City but was defeated by Tammany Hall candidate Jimmy Walker. In 1933, in the wake of the Depression and disclosures of Walker administration corruption, La Guardia was elected Mayor. For the next twelve years, he worked closely with FDR's Administration, and New York City became a showcase for New Deal programs. In 1941, FDR appointed Mayor La Guardia to serve as Director of the Office of Civilian Defense, a position that he juggled with his mayoral responsibilities until early 1942. In 1945, La Guardia decided not to seek a fourth mayoral term. In 1946, he served as an ambassador to Brazil and became Director General of the United Nations Relief and Rehabilitation Administration.

James McCauley Landis (1899–1964) joined the faculty of Harvard Law School, his alma mater, in 1926. He moved to Washington in 1933 to become part of the new administration. Along with Benjamin Cohen and Thomas Corcoran, Landis drafted the Federal Securities Act of 1933. FDR then appointed Landis to the Federal Trade Commission to administer the new law. In 1934, FDR appointed Landis to the newly created Securities Exchange Commission (SEC), which he chaired beginning the following year. In 1937, Landis returned to Harvard Law School as its dean, but he also continued to serve FDR's Administration in various part-time capacities. In 1942, Landis succeeded Fiorello La Guardia as Director of the Office of Civilian Defense. Landis also acted, during World War II, as American director of economic operations in the Middle East. Following the war, President Truman appointed Landis to chair the Civil Aeronautics Board. In 1961, Landis became a special assistant to President Kennedy. Landis also came under investigation by the Internal Revenue Service, and in 1963 he pleaded guilty to willfully failing to file federal tax returns, resulting in a sentence of thirty days' imprisonment.

William Daniel Leahy (1875–1959) was named Chief of Naval Operations by FDR in 1937. Admiral Leahy served until he reached mandatory retirement age in 1939. FDR then appointed Leahy to serve as Governor of Puerto Rico. In 1940, FDR appointed Leahy to serve as Ambassador to Vichy France, the collaborationist government headed by Marshal Philippe Petain. Leahy remained in France until 1942, when he was recalled to the United States to protest the ascension to power of Nazi supporter Pierre Laval. FDR then named Leahy Chairman of the newly created Joint Chiefs of Staff and the President's personal military chief of staff. In this role, Leahy participated at the summit conferences at Teheran in 1943 and at Yalta in 1945. Following FDR's death, Leahy served President Truman as military chief of staff until 1949.

Marguerite Alice ("Missy") Le Hand (1898–1944) met FDR in 1920 while she was working for the manager of his vice presidential campaign. After the 1920 election, Eleanor Roosevelt invited Le Hand to the Roosevelt home at Hyde Park to help organize mail that had accumulated during the campaign. When this job was completed, FDR offered her a job as his private secretary. Le Hand lived with the Roosevelt family at Hyde Park and, over time, became a central manager of the household routine. After FDR's election in 1932, Le Hand moved with the Roosevelt family to Washington and lived with them in the White House. She worked as the President's personal secretary and was one of his closest and most important advisers until she was incapacitated by a stroke in 1941.

Herbert Henry Lehman (1878–1963), a Democrat, was FDR's running mate and served as New York's Lieutenant Governor from 1929 until 1933. Lehman was elected Governor of New York in 1932 and reelected in 1934, 1936, and 1938 (the last time to a four-year term). In December 1942, FDR appointed Lehman to direct the State Department's Office of Foreign Relief and Rehabilitation Operations, a planning organization created to prepare for global needs following the end of World War II. The Office later merged into the United Nations Relief and Rehabilitation Administration, and Lehman became its first Director General, serving from 1943 until 1946. In 1949, Lehman defeated Senator John Foster Dulles, who had been appointed months earlier to fill the United States Senate seat from which Senator Robert Wagner had resigned. Lehman was reelected in 1950 and served in the Senate until his retirement in 1957.

John Llewellyn Lewis (1880–1969), a labor union leader, was President of the United Mine Workers Association of America (UMW) for more than four decades, beginning in 1920. In 1935, he joined with Sidney Hillman and David Dubinsky to form the Committee for Industrial Organization (CIO) and served as its first president. Although Lewis assisted FDR's Administration as a member of various labor boards, his relationship with FDR began to sour when the President sought to remain neutral during steel strikes in early 1937. During the next two years, Lewis clashed regularly with the Administration over labor and foreign policy issues, and in the 1940 campaign he supported Wendell Willkie and frequently spoke out against FDR.

David Eli Lilienthal (1899–1981), a native of Illinois whose parents were Czech immigrants to the United States, graduated from Harvard Law School (where he was a star student of Professor Felix Frankfurter) in 1923, practiced utility law in Chicago with Donald Richberg, and then became a member of the Wisconsin State Utility Commission. In 1933, FDR appointed Lilienthal to be a director of the new Tennessee Valley Authority (TVA). In 1936, FDR reappointed Lilienthal despite his regular conflicts with, and over the opposition of, TVA Chairman Arthur Morgan. The Morgan–Lilienthal feud continued until FDR fired Morgan in 1938. Lilienthal himself became TVA Chairman in 1941, and President Truman reappointed him to that position in 1945. In 1946, Truman named Lilienthal to chair a

State Department advisory committee on postwar production and atomic energy. Later that year, Truman appointed Lilienthal Chairman of the new Atomic Energy Commission (AEC), and he chaired the AEC until 1950. After his resignation, he was an investment banker, an international businessman, and a writer on topics of public concern.

Scott Marion Loftin (1878–1953) was General Counsel of the Florida East Coast Railway from 1931 until 1941 and, during 1934, also served as President of the American Bar Association. For half of 1936, Loftin also served by appointment as a United States Senator from Florida, filling a seat left vacant by the death of Senator Park Trammel. Loftin did not seek election to the seat, however, and resumed his private law practice in Jacksonville, Florida, upon leaving office.

Lord Lothian. See Philip Henry Kerr.

Archibald Battle Lovett (1884–1945), a Savannah, Georgia, attorney, was a 1941 FDR appointee to the United States District Court for the Southern District of Georgia.

Daniel Michael Lyons (1886–1971) served as the Pardon Attorney in the Department of Justice from 1936 until 1953. He then served, in 1953 and 1954, on President Truman's Clemency and Parole Board for War Criminals. This board, which consisted of three members, one from each of the Departments of Justice, State, and Defense, investigated and advised Truman on requests by the government of Japan for clemency, reductions of sentence, or paroles for Japanese war criminals who had been convicted and sentenced following World War II by United States tribunals or the International Military Tribunal for the Far East.

John E. Mack (1874–1958) was the District Attorney of Dutchess County in early 1910 when he spoke to FDR, then a junior lawyer at Carter, Ledyard and Milburn, about the possibility of running for the New York State Senate. After thinking it over and checking with former President Theodore Roosevelt, FDR decided to run and thus began his political career. Mack served as Democratic Party chairman in Dutchess County for almost ten years and was one of FDR's closest advisers when he was elected Governor of New York in 1928. In 1930, Governor FDR appointed Mack to fill a New York Supreme Court vacancy, but he was defeated when he sought election to the position six months later. In 1932, Mack made a nominating speech for FDR at the Democratic national convention in Chicago. Mack repeated this role at the 1936 convention in Philadelphia.

Roswell Magill (1895–1963) was an expert in federal tax law. After graduating from the University of Chicago Law School, he taught there while also practicing law. During the 1920s, he joined the Internal Revenue Bureau in Washington and rose to be chief attorney in the Treasury Department. He subsequently practiced law in New York while teaching a pioneering federal tax law course at Columbia University. In 1933, Magill joined FDR's Administration as a special assistant to the Secretary of the Treasury. In 1937 and 1938, Magill served as Under Secretary of the Treasury. He was a member of Cravath, Swaine & Moore from 1943 until his death.

George Catlett Marshall, Jr. (1880–1959) succeeded General Malin Craig as United States Army Chief of Staff and held this position from September 1939 until November 1945, when he retired from military service as a five-star general. Under FDR, General Marshall became one of the President's most trusted advisers, accompanying him to the Teheran, Quebec, and Yalta conferences and designing and organizing the Allied military victory. Following FDR's death and the end of World War II, Marshall served as special presidential emissary to China, as Secretary of State (1947–1949) and architect of the Marshall Plan that revived and reintegrated the nations of western Europe, and as Secretary of Defense (1950–1951). He was awarded the Nobel Peace Prize in 1953 for his European Recovery Program.

John Jay McCloy (1895–1989), an attorney, was an adviser to every president from FDR to Reagan. Under FDR, McCloy served as Assistant Secretary of War from 1941 until 1945. After four years in private practice, he returned to public service in 1949 as President of the World Bank. Later that year, President Truman appointed McCloy to serve as High Commissioner for Germany. In West Germany for the next three years, he worked to create a civilian government, to administer American economic aid, and to rebuild industry and commerce. From 1952 until 1960, McCloy served as Chairman of the Chase National (later the Chase Manhattan) Bank. In 1960, he became a partner in the law firm of Milbank, Tweed, Hadley & McCloy, where his partners included Jackson's son, Bill. McCloy also was Chairman of the Board of the Ford Foundation from 1959 until 1965. In 1961, McCloy became President Kennedy's chief disarmament adviser and negotiator.

Carl McFarland (1904–1979), who initially was special assistant to Attorney General Cummings, served as Assistant Attorney General from 1937 until

1939. McFarland then left the Department of Justice to practice law in Washington, D.C. He later served as President of his alma mater, Montana State University, and taught law at the University of Virginia.

Ross T. McIntire (1889–1959), a medical doctor who rose to the rank of Vice Admiral during his career in the United States Navy, was FDR's personal physician from 1935 until his death in April 1945.

Marvin Hunter McIntyre (1878–1943) served as FDR's secretary from 1933 until his death. They met during the Wilson Administration, when FDR was Assistant Secretary of the Navy and McIntyre was in charge of press relations at the Navy Department. McIntyre handled publicity for FDR's 1920 vice presidential campaign, and between 1920 and 1932, he worked in Washington in public relations and as a contributor to the *Army and Navy Journal*.

Andrew William Mellon (1855–1937) served as Secretary of the Treasury from 1921 until 1932 under Presidents Harding, Coolidge, and Hoover. In 1932, Hoover appointed Mellon United States Ambassador to the Court of St. James's, where he served until the end of Hoover's Presidency. In 1935, the government first sought to prosecute Mellon criminally, and then successfully prosecuted him civilly, for fraudulent underpayment of taxes. Jackson first came to national attention as the government lawyer who prosecuted the civil case.

Raymond Charles Moley (1886–1975), a Columbia University government professor, became an early and influential architect of the New Deal. His work for FDR began in 1928, when Louis Howe persuaded him to work on FDR's first gubernatorial campaign. When FDR was elected President in 1932, Moley and fellow Columbia faculty members Rexford Guy Tugwell (1891–1979) and Adolph A. Berle, Jr., formed the "Brains Trust" that advised FDR on national issues. During FDR's first one hundred days in office, Moley was the President's chief liaison to Congress. FDR then appointed Moley Assistant Secretary of State, with the understanding that Moley would have no official duties and would function only as special assistant to the President. In September 1933, Moley resigned from State over a disagreement with Roosevelt and Secretary of State Cordell Hull over the World Economics Conference in London. Moley had convinced FDR to send him to the conference to join the American delegation, which angered Hull. After Moley spoke to the conference, FDR criticized it and rejected its proposed declaration, which damaged Moley's reputation and led to his final resignation. Moley later worked as an editor for the weekly magazine *Today*, which later became *Newsweek*, and was a columnist. By 1940, Moley was so disenchanted with FDR that he endorsed his Republican opponent.

Arthur Ernest Morgan (1878–1975) was appointed by FDR in 1933, at the creation of the Tennessee Valley Authority (TVA), to serve as Chairman of its three-director board. Morgan, a civil engineer by training, had ceased his formal education without graduating from college. In his early career, he managed a family surveying business, specializing in the field of flood control. Morgan moved to Washington, D.C., in 1907 to work for the Department of Agriculture's Office of Drainage Investigations. In 1910, he left government to form his own engineering firm in Memphis, Tennessee. Three years later, he was appointed chief engineer of what would become the Miami Valley Conservancy District in Dayton, Ohio, where he administered what was, at that time, the largest flood control plan in the country. In 1921, Morgan became President of Antioch College. By 1938, the TVA board had become deeply divided, leading FDR to dismiss Morgan.

Harcourt Alexander Morgan (1867–1950), who was one of the TVA's three directors for its first fifteen years, served a three-year stint as TVA Chairman following FDR's 1938 dismissal of Arthur Morgan. Prior to his TVA service, Harcourt Morgan, a Canadian who immigrated to the United States as a young adult, was a prominent scholar and public speaker who specialized in the problems of southern agriculture. He began his career at Louisiana State University and then moved to the University of Tennessee, where he rose to serve as university president from 1919 until he joined the TVA board in 1933. Morgan retired from TVA in 1947.

Henry T. Morgenthau, Jr. (1891–1967), whose Dutchess County, New York, estate was near Roosevelt's own Springwood in Hyde Park, was FDR's close friend and loyal adviser for many years. When FDR was Governor of New York, Morgenthau served as State Conservation Commissioner and as Chairman of the governor's agricultural committee. At the start of FDR's Presidency, Morgenthau headed the Farm Credit Administration. He became the Acting Secretary of the Treasury later in 1933 and, following his confirmation by the Senate, was Secretary of the Treasury from 1934 until 1945.

Frank Henry Mott (1873–1932) of Jamestown, New York, was a prominent figure in New York State politics and a leader of the Democratic Party in

Chautauqua County. Like Jackson, Mott was born in northwestern Pennsylvania. He moved to Jamestown as a boy, graduated from its high school, and then apprenticed in a local lawyer's office. After completing his studies at Buffalo Law School, Mott was admitted to the New York State Bar in 1899. In 1900, Mott, who was working as political editor of the *Buffalo Times*, was a New York delegate to the Democratic National Convention in Kansas City and became a supporter and friend of William Jennings Bryan. In 1902, Mott won the Democratic nomination but lost the election to become New York's Secretary of State. He subsequently ran successfully for Jamestown's Board of Education. In 1907, Mott was appointed Deputy Attorney General of New York and served for two years. He then returned to Jamestown to resume his private law practice. In 1910, Mott's first cousin once removed, Robert Jackson, became his apprentice in law practice and, over time, his colleague in Democratic political activity. Mott became acquainted with FDR following his election to the New York State Senate in 1910. They remained in contact after FDR moved to Washington to become Assistant Secretary of the Navy, including during the 1913–1915 period when Mott served as Secretary of the New York Public Service Commission, Second District. Mott had further contact with FDR in 1920, when FDR ran for Vice President and Mott was the Democratic candidate for New York State Attorney General. FDR joined with Mott during his campaign visit to Jamestown on October 21, 1920. Both were defeated on November 2, 1920.

William Francis ("Frank") Murphy (1890–1949) was a prominent Democratic politician who rose from his native Michigan to serve in FDR's Cabinet and on the Supreme Court. From 1923 until 1930, Murphy was a judge of Detroit's recorder's court. He was elected Mayor of Detroit in 1930 and held that office until 1933. FDR then sent Murphy to the Philippines, where he was Governor General from 1933 until 1935 and High Commissioner during 1935 and 1936. Murphy was elected Governor of Michigan in 1936, but he was defeated when he sought reelection in 1938. FDR then appointed Murphy to serve as Attorney General of the United States and, one year later, to serve as an Associate Justice of the Supreme Court. Jackson, who was Solicitor General when Murphy became Attorney General, succeeded him in 1940 and then joined him on the Court in 1941, where they served together until Murphy's death.

Barnet ("Barney") Nover (1899–1973) was a columnist and editorial writer for the *Washington Post* from 1936 until 1947, specializing in foreign affairs.

He covered such events as the San Francisco Conference in 1945 and the Paris Peace Conference in 1946, and his column was syndicated in several newspapers across the country. From 1944 until 1947, Nover also broadcast a national radio program, *Washington Views and Interviews*. In 1947, he became the chief of the Washington bureau of the *Denver Post*, where he remained until his retirement in 1971. He and his wife, **Naomi Nover** (1910–1995), then founded the Nover News Bureau in Washington.

Daniel Peter O'Connell (1885–1977) headed Albany's Democratic political machine from 1921 until his death at age ninety-one. He and his brothers Edward, Patrick ("Packy"), and John ("Solly") O'Connell collaborated with Edwin Corning (1883–1934) to take control of City Hall in Albany in 1921. In 1941, the O'Connell machine installed Corning's son, Erastus Corning II (1909–1983), as Albany's Mayor. He was reelected to office nine times, serving forty-two years until his death.

Herman Oliphant (1884–1939) was, in his early career, a professor of law at the University of Chicago, at Columbia University, and at the Institute of Law at Johns Hopkins University in Baltimore. He also served, during World War I, as Assistant Director of War Trade Intelligence and later as Assistant Director of the Industrial Relations Division of the Emergency Fleet Corporation. In March 1933, FDR appointed Oliphant to serve as General Counsel of the Farm Credit Administration under Henry Morgenthau. In late 1933, Oliphant became counsel to FDR's first Secretary of the Treasury, William H. Woodin. Oliphant continued to serve as counsel when Morgenthau replaced Woodin, rising to become General Counsel of the Department. At Treasury and in regular meetings with the President, Oliphant was an architect of much of the New Deal tax legislation and other fiscal measures during FDR's second term. In 1938, FDR appointed Oliphant a member of the Temporary National Economic Committee, where he worked to strengthen federal antitrust policies. He suffered a heart attack in late 1938 and died early in 1939.

Joseph Christopher O'Mahoney (1884–1962), a Democrat, represented Wyoming in the United States Senate from 1934 until 1953 and again from 1954 until 1961. Although O'Mahoney supported much of the New Deal agenda, including federal intervention to destroy trusts, government regulation of large corporations, and measures to aid farmers, he opposed FDR's Court-packing plan, arguing that enlarging the Supreme Court would not restrain its abuses of power.

Robert Porter Patterson, Sr. (1891–1952) became a United States District Court Judge in the Southern District of New York in 1930. In 1939, FDR elevated Patterson to serve as a Judge of the United States Court of Appeals for the Second Circuit. Patterson resigned from the bench in 1940 to serve as Assistant Secretary of War under Secretary Henry Stimson. Six months later, FDR appointed Patterson to serve as Under Secretary of War, a position he held until the end of World War II. Following Stimson's retirement, President Truman appointed Patterson to serve as Secretary of War. Patterson served as Secretary until 1947, when he left government to practice law at the Patterson, Belknap & Webb law firm in Manhattan.

Randolph Evernghim Paul (1890–1956), a tax law expert, was a part-time adviser to the Department of the Treasury for several years before Secretary Morgenthau named him a special assistant in 1941. Paul quickly became Morgenthau's chief tax adviser, and in 1942 he was named General Counsel of the Department of the Treasury.

Thomas Joseph Pendergast (1872–1945), the Democratic boss of Kansas City, Missouri, lived to see a product of his machine, Harry S. Truman, become Vice President of the United States.

Claude Denson Pepper (1900–1989), a Florida Democrat, was elected in 1936 to complete the unexpired term of Senator Duncan Fletcher, who had died. Pepper served in the United States Senate from 1936 until 1951 and in the United States House of Representatives from 1963 until 1989.

Frances Perkins (1882–1965) began her working career as a social worker in Chicago, Philadelphia, and New York. In 1910, she became Executive Secretary of the New York City Consumers' League and lobbied for fire prevention and sanitation in the workplace. In 1911, the devastating fire at the Triangle Shirtwaist Company factory in Manhattan led Perkins to work on industrial and labor regulations issues with influential politicians such as Al Smith and Robert Wagner and prominent union leaders such as Samuel Gompers. In 1919, Governor Smith named Perkins to the Industrial Commission of the State of New York, where she remained until Smith lost his 1920 bid for reelection. When Smith reclaimed the gubernatorial office in 1923, however, he reappointed Perkins to a reorganized Industrial Commission. She became Chair of the Commission three years later. When FDR succeeded Smith as Governor, he appointed Perkins to head New York's Labor Department. In this capacity, she advocated the abolition of child labor, supported legislation to reduce working hours, and emphasized the need for workmen's compensation. After the stock market crash that fall, Perkins persuaded FDR to form a Committee on Stabilization of Industry for the Prevention of Unemployment and brought public attention to the need for unemployment insurance. When Roosevelt was elected President in 1932, he appointed Perkins to serve as the Secretary of Labor, where she served throughout his Presidency. Perkins resigned from the Cabinet on July 1, 1945. Later that year, President Truman appointed her to the Civil Service Commission.

Lee Pressman (1906–1969), a labor lawyer, joined FDR's Administration in 1933 as an assistant to Agricultural Adjustment Administration (AAA) General Counsel Jerome Frank. In 1935, both were removed due to policy conflicts with AAA Administrator Chester Davis. Pressman then served as General Counsel to the Works Progress Administration and the Resettlement Administration. John L. Lewis subsequently hired Pressman to serve as General Counsel to the Steel Workers Organizing Committee (SWOC) and later to the national Congress of Industrial Organizations (CIO). In 1948, shortly after Pressman had resigned from the CIO, he was called to testify before the House Un-American Activities Committee (HUAC) during its investigation of Alger Hiss. When asked about his own Communist activities while working at the AAA, Pressman invoked his Fifth Amendment privilege against self-incrimination. This hearing ended Pressman's public life. In 1950, he returned to private law practice in New York.

James Hubert Price (1882–1943), a Democrat, lawyer, and businessman from Richmond, served as Governor of Virginia from 1938 until 1942. During his term in office, Price was known publicly to differ on issues with Senator Harry Byrd (himself a former Governor), who was Price's political senior and head of their party.

Stanley Forman Reed (1884–1980) was FDR's Solicitor General, and Jackson's predecessor in that office, from 1935 until 1938. As Solicitor General, Reed defended the constitutionality of many New Deal programs, including the National Industrial Recovery Act, the Agricultural Adjustment Act, and the National Labor Relations Act, before the Supreme Court. FDR appointed Reed to the Supreme Court in 1938. He was Jackson's colleague for his entire tenure on the Court (1941–1954) and served as an Associate Justice until retirement in 1957.

Paul Reynaud (1878–1966) had become Premier of France in March 1940. After Germany invaded France in May and it surrendered in late June, Reynaud refused to accept the dictated terms of the so-called armistice. He was arrested and imprisoned for the duration of the war. Reynaud later held several cabinet positions in the French government.

Donald Randall Richberg (1881–1960) was a lawyer who initially made his reputation in the field of labor law. He represented railway unions and played a leading role in drafting some of the labor legislation of the 1920s. Richberg worked for FDR's 1932 campaign and, in 1933, participated in drafting the National Industrial Recovery Act. Later that year, Richberg was appointed General Counsel of the National Recovery Administration (NRA). In 1934, Richberg temporarily served as Executive Secretary to the President's executive council, Executive Director of the National Emergency Council, and director of the Industrial Emergency Committee. Later that year, he reorganized and then became director of the NRA. In 1935, Richberg resigned from the NRA to return to private practice.

Owen Josephus Roberts (1875–1955) of Philadelphia began his career as a local prosecutor, an attorney in private practice, and a law professor at his alma mater, the University of Pennsylvania. He became nationally prominent in 1924, when he was appointed Special Prosecutor to investigate the Teapot Dome Scandals. In 1930, President Hoover appointed Roberts to the Supreme Court, where he served until his retirement in 1945. As a Justice, he was appointed by FDR on December 15, 1941, to head a five-man board that investigated the causes of the devastating Japanese attack on Pearl Harbor. After leaving the Court, Roberts returned to Philadelphia and served as Dean of the University of Pennsylvania Law School.

Joseph Taylor Robinson (1872–1937), a Democrat, had been a United States Representative and Governor of Arkansas before his election to the Senate in 1912. Robinson, the Senate Majority Leader, was an early supporter of the court reform bill that FDR proposed on February 5, 1937. As FDR's plan ran into political trouble that spring, it came to be understood that he had promised to nominate Robinson to replace retiring Supreme Court Justice Willis Van Devanter. In June 1937, FDR agreed to allow Robinson to seek support for compromise legislation. The compromise, which would have allowed the President to appoint a new Justice for each member of the Supreme Court who had reached age seventy-five but at the pace of only one new Justice per calendar year, did not unify the divided Senate. Robinson worked during early July to garner the support of the few undecided senators, presided over angry Senate debates, and sought to forestall a filibuster. On July 14, 1937, Robinson died of a heart attack, and in the days following his funeral, the proposal also died when a group of freshman Democratic senators announced their opposition. FDR subsequently nominated Senator Hugo L. Black (D.-AL) to fill the existing Court vacancy.

Nelson Aldrich Rockefeller (1908–1979), a grandson of John D. Rockefeller, Sr., was appointed by FDR in 1940 to serve as Coordinator of the Office of Inter-American Affairs (OIAA). The OIAA promoted United States cooperation, and thus countered Nazi influence, in Latin America. Rockefeller was promoted to Assistant Secretary of State for Latin American Affairs in 1944. He resigned shortly after President Truman took office in 1945. In 1958, Rockefeller was elected Governor of New York. He was reelected three times and served as Governor until he resigned in 1973. In 1974, President Ford nominated Rockefeller to succeed him as Vice President. His legal representative in this and other matters was Jackson's son William E. Jackson. Rockefeller was confirmed and served as Vice President until 1977. **Mary Todhunter Clark Rockefeller** (1907–1999), who was Nelson Rockefeller's first wife, was an advocate for the nursing profession for much of her public life. The Rockefellers separated in 1961 and divorced in 1963.

Anna Eleanor Roosevelt (1886–1962) married FDR, her fifth cousin once removed, on March 17, 1905. During FDR's governorship and even more so during his Presidency, she was a tireless advocate for people in need, serving as a constant, and perhaps not always appreciated, prod to her husband's conscience. Following FDR's death, President Truman appointed her to serve as a delegate to the United Nations, where she helped craft the Declaration of Human Rights that the UN General Assembly enacted in 1948. During the 1950s, she campaigned enthusiastically for Democratic presidential candidate Adlai Stevenson and spoke constantly to audiences in the United States and around the world. Mrs. Roosevelt gave late but important support to nominee Senator John F. Kennedy in the 1960 presidential race and, during her last years, served and visibly prodded his Administration through her work on two commissions, one regarding the rights of women and the other concerning the freedom struggle by blacks in the American South. At her death, Eleanor Roosevelt was generally regarded as the most important American woman of her century.

Anna Eleanor Roosevelt (1906–1975) was the firstborn child and only daughter of Franklin and Eleanor Roosevelt. Anna had a very close relationship with her father, as a companion and confidante, especially when she lived in the White House during 1944 and 1945. She frequently acted as the President's assistant and as White House hostess during her mother's travels. At FDR's request, Anna accompanied him to the Yalta conference in early 1945. **John Boettiger, Jr.** (1900–1950), a newspaper correspondent and publisher, was her second husband. They married in 1935 and divorced in 1949.

Elliott Roosevelt (1910–1990), the second surviving son of Franklin and Eleanor Roosevelt, enlisted in the Army in 1940. He subsequently served in North Africa and the Mediterranean as a reconnaissance pilot. Elliott and his younger brother, Franklin, Jr. (1914–1988), also served as special aides to their father at the Atlantic Charter meetings with Churchill in August 1941, the Casablanca meetings in January 1943, and the Cairo-Teheran Conference in November 1944. Elliott ended his military career as a Brigadier General.

James Roosevelt (1907–1991) was the eldest son of Franklin and Eleanor Roosevelt. Throughout the 1930s, James held a variety of private sector positions, including laborer, insurance salesman, and Hollywood producer. He worked on his father's 1936 reelection campaign and in 1937 joined the White House staff as an executive assistant to the President. From 1937 until 1938, James was his father's appointments secretary and his point of contact for Cabinet and agency heads throughout the Administration. In 1940, James enlisted in the Marine Corps. He served first as military observer in the Middle East and Far East and then as military adviser to William J. Donovan. In 1946, following FDR's death, James Roosevelt became Chairman of the California Democratic Party. He ran, unsuccessfully, against California Governor Earl Warren in 1950 and, in 1954, was elected to the first of six terms in the House of Representatives. Roosevelt resigned from Congress in 1965 to become United States representative to the United Nations Economic and Social Council.

Elihu Root (1845–1937), a Republican who had served as Secretary of War under President McKinley and Secretary of State under President Theodore Roosevelt, served as United States senator from New York for one term (1909–1915). Beginning in 1911, Root was senior to New York's other senator, James Aloysius O'Gorman (1860–1943), a Democrat who also served only one term (1911–1917).

Daniel Calhoun Roper (1867–1943), a lawyer from South Carolina, began his political career when he was elected to its House of Representatives in 1892. He came to Washington two years later and then held a series of appointive positions—as a Senate clerk, in the Census Bureau, and as an Assistant Postmaster General. As Commissioner of Internal Revenue from 1917 through 1920, Roper was responsible for the initial enforcement of Prohibition. He practiced law from 1921 until 1933, when FDR appointed him Secretary of Commerce. After Roper resigned from the Cabinet in late 1938, FDR appointed him United States Ambassador to Canada. Roper resigned after four months to resume his law practice in Washington, D.C.

Samuel Irving Rosenman (1896–1973) was FDR's counsel when he was Governor of New York. In 1933, Rosenman became a Justice of the New York Supreme Court. He also served, throughout FDR's Presidency, as one of his closest advisers and drafted many of the President's speeches. During World War II, Rosenman also helped streamline and consolidate the many new war agencies and bureaus into single entities.

John Godfrey Saxe (1877–1953), a noted New York City lawyer and an active Democrat (and the grandson of the noted Vermont poet whose name he was given), was appointed by Tammany leader Charles F. Murphy to head its law committee during the 1920s and 1930s. Saxe also had served with FDR in the New York State Senate during 1911 and 1912. At his death, Saxe was partner in his Manhattan law firm, Saxe, Bacon, O'Shea & Bryan, and General Counsel for Columbia University.

William Francis Sheehan (1859–1917) was a lawyer and politician from Buffalo. Early in his career, he served in the New York State Assembly and was elected its Speaker. In 1892, Sheehan was elected Lieutenant Governor of New York, but he resigned the next year amid scandal. Sheehan then became counsel to and director of a dozen public utilities and railroad companies. He practiced law with Alton B. Parker, the Democratic presidential nominee whom President Theodore Roosevelt defeated in 1904 to win election in his own right.

Alfred Emanuel ("Al") Smith (1873–1944) served four nonconsecutive two-year terms as Governor of the State of New York (1919–1921 and 1923–1929); he was defeated in 1920 when he sought reelection after his first term. Governor Smith was a progressive reform Democrat in a period not known for reform politics. His welfare programs included state support for low-cost housing, bond issues to develop an extensive park and recreation system, more funds for state education, and support for state Labor Department enforcement of safety regulations and administration of worker's compensation. In 1928, Smith was the Democratic Party's unsuccessful presidential nominee. Four years later, he competed for the nomination but lost to his successor as Governor, FDR. Although Smith supported FDR's 1932 election, he soon became a New Deal and Roosevelt critic and, in 1936 and 1940, a supporter of Republican candidates Landon and Willkie.

Harold Raynsford ("Betty") Stark (1888–1972), a 1903 graduate of the United States Naval Academy, met FDR during his tenure as Assistant Secretary of the Navy under President Wilson. During that period, when Stark was a destroyer commander, he followed naval regulations scrupulously by refusing to let FDR, a civilian guest on various inspection cruises, take the helm. In August 1939, FDR, who recalled and recounted their early dealings with great amusement, promoted Stark to the rank of admiral and appointed him Chief of Naval Operations. Stark then succeeded, despite strong isolationist sentiment, in improving the Navy's readiness to fight a two-ocean war. He also advocated the "Europe first" strategy—strong offensive force development with Britain in the Atlantic and maintenance of a defensive force in the Pacific—that became the U.S., British, and Canadian war plan by spring 1941. Later that year, the Japanese attack on Pearl Harbor caused grave damage to, in addition to the Pacific fleet, Stark's career. FDR stripped Stark of his command and in March 1942 sent him to England as commander of United States naval forces in Europe, which was largely an administrative position. During World War II, Stark was liaison to the British admiralty and French government in exile and supervisor of logistical preparations for what became the D-Day invasion of Normandy. Toward the end of the war, Stark faced a Navy court of inquiry and also a congressional investigation regarding Pearl Harbor. He retired from active duty in April 1946.

Edward Reilly Stettinius, Jr. (1900–1949) was a Republican businessman who became a member of FDR's Cabinet during World War II. In his business career, Stettinius was Vice President of General Motors before he moved to United States Steel Corporation, where he became Chairman of the Board in 1938. In 1941, FDR appointed Stettinius to head the Office of Lend-Lease Administration. In 1943, he became Under Secretary of State, succeeding Sumner Welles, and in 1944 Stettinius became FDR's final Secretary of State, succeeding Cordell Hull. Stettinius accompanied FDR to

Yalta in February 1945, helped to create the United Nations, and became its chief American delegate.

Henry Lewis Stimson (1867–1950) was appointed by President Theodore Roosevelt in 1906 to serve as United States Attorney for the Southern District of New York. Stimson held that position until 1909, when President Taft appointed him special counsel for federal antitrust prosecutions. In 1911, Taft appointed Stimson to his first Cabinet position, Secretary of War, which he held until 1913. After practicing law in New York City, Stimson served as Governor-General of the Philippines from 1927 until 1929. Under President Hoover, Stimson was Secretary of State from 1929 until 1933, when he returned to private practice. In 1939, FDR appointed Stimson to serve as a member of the International Court of Arbitration at The Hague. In 1940, Stimson, a Republican, became FDR's Secretary of War, a position which he held until his retirement in 1945.

Harlan Fiske Stone (1872–1946) was a former Columbia Law School professor and dean and an attorney in private practice in New York City when President Coolidge appointed him to serve as Attorney General of the United States in 1924. The following year, Coolidge appointed Stone to the Supreme Court. He served as an Associate Justice until 1941, when FDR, acting in a bipartisan manner to promote national unity as war approached, appointed Stone to serve as Chief Justice of the United States.

Jesse Isidor Straus (1872–1936) was part owner of R. H. Macy's and, when it was incorporated in 1919, he became its President. Under Straus's management, Macy's became the world's largest retail merchandiser under one roof. From this position of business prominence, Straus became active and influential in public affairs, serving on numerous committees and boards dealing with such problems as taxation, trade relations, and social and industrial conditions. Straus was an active Democrat and friend of FDR who labored diligently for his election as Governor of New York and was active in the 1932 pre-convention campaign for FDR's presidential nomination. In 1931, FDR appointed Straus to chair New York's Temporary Emergency Relief Agency (TERA). In March 1933, FDR appointed Straus to serve as United States Ambassador to France. He resigned in August 1936 due to poor health.

Christopher Daniel Sullivan (1870–1942), a Democrat, represented New York in the House of Representatives from 1917 until 1941.

William Sulzer (1863–1941), a reform Democrat, began his political career as a member of the New York State Assembly. He then served, from 1895 until 1912, in the United States House of Representatives, where he advocated such progressive policies as the graduated income tax and the direct election of senators. In 1912, Sulzer gave up his seat in Congress to run for the governorship of New York. His campaign was successful and, as the thirty-ninth Governor of New York, one of Sulzer's first initiatives was to investigate Tammany Hall judges in New York City, who were believed to be corrupt. During this investigation, it was discovered that Sulzer had diverted campaign contributions by investing the money in the stock market. He was impeached and removed from office less than a year after his inauguration. Although Sulzer subsequently was elected and served a term in the state assembly, his later campaigns for office were unsuccessful.

Daniel Joseph Tobin (1875–1955), an immigrant to the United States from Ireland, became President of the International Brotherhood of Teamsters, Chauffeurs, Warehousemen and Helpers of America (IBT) in 1907. Although Tobin headed the Teamsters union and ran its national office for the next forty-five years, much of the union's actual power resided in its local leaders, whom he was unable to control. Tobin was an active leader in the American Federation of Labor (AFL) throughout the 1920s and 1930s. He also was an early supporter of FDR, chairing the Labor Bureau in each of his four presidential campaigns. In 1940, FDR briefly employed Tobin as an executive assistant.

Newman Alexander Townsend (1883–1951), formerly a North Carolina superior court judge, served as Special Assistant Attorney General and Assistant Solicitor General under FDR. In 1944, Judge Townsend left government to practice law in Washington, D.C.

Grace George Tully (1900–1984), who worked initially as Eleanor Roosevelt's personal secretary in Albany, also worked for FDR there and then moved with him to Washington when he was elected President. Tully was Missy Le Hand's assistant until 1941, and after her departure, Tully served as FDR's private secretary until his death.

Millard Evelyn Tydings (1890–1961), a Maryland Democrat, was a lawyer, a state legislator, a decorated World War I combat hero, a United States representative, and then, for four terms (1927–1951), a United States senator. Tydings, a conservative, initially supported FDR but broke with him over the government's deficit spending. In 1937, Tydings became a successful leader of Senate opposition to FDR's Court-packing plan. In response, as part of his 1938 "purge" efforts, FDR campaigned against Tydings, but he won renomination in his party's primary and was reelected handily. Tydings also regularly, but with less success, opposed each FDR nomination of Jackson to an executive branch position. In 1941, Tydings testified bitterly and aggressively against Jackson's nomination to the Supreme Court and later voted against him. In 1950, Tydings fell victim to McCarthyite attacks and was defeated seeking reelection to a fifth term.

Robert Ferdinand Wagner (1877–1953), a Democrat from New York, served in the United States Senate from 1926 until 1949. He was an influential architect of modern government, sponsoring such legislation as the Federal Emergency Relief Administration bill (1933), the Social Security Act (1936), and the National Labor Relations Act (1935), also known as the Wagner Act.

Frank Comerford Walker (1886–1959) served in FDR's Cabinet from 1940 until 1945 as Postmaster General. During 1943 and 1944, Walker was also Chairman of the Democratic National Committee.

Henry Agard Wallace (1888–1965) was FDR's Secretary of Agriculture for his first two terms, Vice President of the United States during the third term (1941–1945) and Secretary of Commerce from 1945 until he left office in 1946.

Edwin Martin ("Pa") Watson (1883–1945), an Army officer who rose to the rank of Major General, began serving FDR as the President's military aide in 1933 and became his appointments secretary in 1939.

Benjamin Sumner Welles (1892–1961) was Under Secretary of State from 1937 until late 1943. He had attended prep school (Groton) with FDR and served as Ambassador to Cuba (1933) and as Assistant Secretary of State (1933–37). Sumner Welles and his wife, **Mathilde Scott Townsend (Gerry) Welles** (1884?–1949), built Oxon Hill Manor, a Georgian mansion and estate located on the Potomac River in Oxon Hill, Maryland, in the late 1920s. During the next twenty years, it was the site of many political, diplomatic, and society functions.

Alexander Fell Whitney (1873–1949) became President of the Brotherhood of Railroad Trainmen (BRT) in 1928. He was an active FDR supporter throughout the 1930s and 1940s and served on the Political Action Committee, organized by Sidney Hillman, that coordinated labor support for the President's 1944 reelection campaign.

Philip John Wickser (1887–1949), a Buffalo native and a graduate of Cornell University and Harvard Law School, was a prominent lawyer, a leader in the insurance and banking fields, and an active Republican when Governor FDR appointed him to New York's Temporary Emergency Relief Administration (TERA) in 1931. He later became TERA's chairman, serving until 1932. Wickser also was known nationally for his efforts to improve bar admission standards. He served as a member of New York's Board of Law Examiners, the federal Board of Legal Examiners, and the National Conference of Bar Examiners. At the time of his death, Wicker had been nominated (and, as the only nominee, he soon would have been elected) to become President of the American Bar Association.

Wendell Lewis Willkie (1892–1944) was the Republican Party presidential nominee who lost to FDR in 1940. The son of two lawyers, Willkie grew up in Indiana and went to college at Indiana University. He then was a teacher in Kansas before returning to the university for his law degree. Willkie was a Democrat at this point in his life. He became a successful lawyer, first in Midwestern firms and then in New York, where he moved in 1929. He became President of Commonwealth & Southern Corporation, a public utility holding company that had been his client. He opposed FDR's New Deal and especially the Tennessee Valley Authority, which conflicted with his company. In 1939, he became a Republican. After his 1940 defeat, Willkie supported FDR's foreign policy as war approached, was a presidential emissary on foreign missions, and advocated a postwar international organization that would work for equal opportunities and world harmony.

Harry Hines Woodring (1890–1967) became FDR's Secretary of War in 1936. From 1930 through 1932, Woodring had been Governor of Kansas and a strong supporter of Roosevelt's presidential campaign. After Woodring lost Kansas's 1932 gubernatorial election to Alf Landon—the young governor who became FDR's Republican opponent in 1936—Woodring joined the Roosevelt Administration as Assistant Secretary of War in 1933. In 1936, after FDR's first Secretary of War, George Henry Dern (1872–1936), died in office, the President elevated Woodring to the Cabinet position. By 1939, Woodring was in disagreement with FDR's desire to provide military supplies and aircraft to Great Britain, and in June 1940, FDR dismissed

Woodring from the Cabinet. In 1946 and again in 1956, he sought to regain the governor's office in Kansas but was not successful.

Walter Browne Woodson (1881–1948), Rear Admiral in the United States Navy, served as FDR's naval aide from 1936 until 1938. He then became Judge Advocate General and held this position until his retirement from the Navy in 1943.

John H. Wright (1867–1951) was one of Jackson's leading clients while he practiced law in Jamestown. Wright was President for many years of the Jamestown Telephone Company and three other independent telephone companies in New York and Pennsylvania. Jackson tried cases for Wright and his companies against the Bell Telephone system.

NOTES

Many of the following notes include citations to "Phillips–Jackson Interviews." During 1952 and 1953, Justice Jackson was interviewed extensively about his full life and career by Dr. Harlan Buddington Phillips of Columbia University's Oral History Research Office (OHRO), who audiotaped seventy-four hours of their conversations. To facilitate Phillips's preparation for these interviews, Jackson had made his files on his pre-Court career available for Phillips's comprehensive review. The taped interviews were transcribed at Columbia by OHRO personnel, edited by Phillips, and then edited further by Jackson, who finished editing the 1476-page transcript just eight days before his death on October 9, 1954. Phillips produced a final text of 1649 pages, THE REMINISCENCES OF ROBERT H. JACKSON, in 1955. The excerpts contained in this book are reprinted here with the permission of the Jackson family.

Introduction by John Q. Barrett

1   Typewritten memorandum, 4 pp., no author, addressee, or date, in Container 201, Thomas Gardiner Corcoran Papers, Manuscript Division, Library of Congress, Washington, D.C. This document, which seems to date from late 1937, may have been prepared by Corcoran for FDR.
2   Letter from Justice Felix Frankfurter to Eugene C. Gerhart, 9/27/1955, quoted in EUGENE C. GERHART, AMERICA'S ADVOCATE: ROBERT H. JACKSON 486 n.35 (Indianapolis: Bobbs-Merrill, 1958); *accord* Felix Frankfurter, *Mr. Justice Jackson*, 68 HARV. L. REV. 937, 939 (1955).
3   FDR to RHJ, 1/18/1941, in the Robert Houghwout Jackson Papers in the Manuscript Division, Library of Congress, Washington, D.C. ("RHJ LOC") Box 19. *See also* RHJ to FDR, 1/16/1941, in RHJ LOC Box 19 (Jackson's letter tendering his resignation "effective at [the President's] pleasure" and thanking him "for the honor of [his] confidence").

4   *West Virginia State Board of Education v. Barnette*, 319 U.S. 624 (1943).

5   *Korematsu v. United States*, 323 U.S. 214, 242–48 (1944) (Jackson, J., dissenting).

6   *See generally* REPORT OF ROBERT H. JACKSON, UNITED STATES REPRESENTATIVE TO THE INTERNATIONAL CONFERENCE ON MILITARY TRIALS, LONDON, 1945 (Dept. of State Publication, Feb. 1949).

7   *Everson v. Board of Education*, 330 U.S. 1, 18–28 (1947) (Jackson, J., joined by Frankfurter, J., dissenting).

8   *Terminiello v. Chicago*, 337 U.S. 1, 13–37 (1949) (Jackson, J., joined by Burton, J., dissenting). *See id.* at 37 for the "suicide pact" quotation.

9   *American Communications Association v. Douds*, 339 U.S. 382, 422–45 (1950) (Jackson, J., concurring and dissenting, each in part).

10 *Shepherd v. Florida*, 341 U.S. 50, 50–55 (1951) (Jackson, J., joined by Frankfurter, J., concurring in the result).

11 *Brown v. Board of Education*, 347 U.S. 483 (1954).

12 EUGENE C. GERHART, AMERICA'S ADVOCATE: ROBERT H. JACKSON (Indianapolis: Bobbs-Merrill, 1958). Gerhart later published a second book that focused on Jackson's Supreme Court work. *See* EUGENE C. GERHART, SUPREME COURT JUSTICE JACKSON: LAWYER'S JUDGE (Albany, N.Y.: Q Corp., 1961).

13 *See* THE REMINISCENCES OF ROBERT H. JACKSON (Columbia University Oral History Research Office, 1955). A copy of this unpublished document is contained in RHJ LOC Boxes 258–59. An earlier draft of these reminiscences, which bears Jackson's extensive handwritten edits, is in RHJ LOC Boxes 190–91.

14 In the years between FDR's death (1945) and Jackson's own passing (1954), the "insiders" who published books that were at least in part accounts of FDR included Elliott Roosevelt (1946), Frances Perkins (1946), Jimmy Byrnes (1947), Ed Flynn (1947), Mike Reilly (1947), Henry Stimson (1947), Jim Farley (1948), Cordell Hull (1948), Henrietta Nesbitt (1948), Robert Sherwood (1948), Eleanor Roosevelt (1949), Grace Tully (1949), William Leahy (1950), and Sam Rosenman (1952). Other FDR intimates, including Henry Morgenthau (in September–October 1947) and Harold Ickes (in June–July 1948), published serial articles in magazines and newspapers about their Roosevelt Administration tenures. All of these works are cited in full in the Bibliography.

15 The Sullivan essay—*Frank Sullivan's Story*, THE NEW YORKER, Aug. 14, 1948, at 22–24—was, at least in its title, directed most immediately at JIM FARLEY'S STORY: THE ROOSEVELT YEARS (New York: Whittlesey House / McGraw-Hill, 1948), the then newly published autobiography of former Postmaster General and Democratic National Committee Chairman James A. Farley. *Frank Sullivan's Story* is a chronicle of ingratitude, indignities, and personal slights by FDR toward the writer—whose purported relationship with the President in fact amounted to one meeting and one handshake in a receiving line.

Sullivan's actual view of FDR is recorded in the private letter that he wrote to Robert Sherwood, the noted playwright and FDR speechwriter, following Roosevelt's death: "I envy you; you knew him intimately. I have to be content and will be content with the great solace of knowing that I was in that company, and a good-sized one it is to be sure, of those who knew from the first that he was a great man, and appreciated him. That is something I will be proud of all my life. . . . I registered my faith in him by voting for him seven times and I feel damned proud of that record. If I brag about it too much in the future, or get to seem smug, let them as don't like it do what they know they can do. In the meantime I feel as though I had lost my father all over again and I have some insight into how you who knew him really, must feel." FSS letter to Robert E. Sherwood, 4/22/1945, *reprinted in* FRANK SULLIVAN, WELL, THERE'S NO HARM IN LAUGHING (formerly titled FRANK SULLIVAN THROUGH THE LOOKING GLASS) 162–63 (George Oppenheimer ed., 1970).

16   WEJ letter to RHJ, "Tuesday the 17th" [8/17/1948], RHJ LOC Box 2.

17   RHJ letter to WEJ, "Sunday P.M." [8/22/1948]. Jackson was referring to former Interior Secretary Harold Ickes's serialized memories of FDR. *See* Harold L. Ickes, *My Twelve Years with F.D.R.*, SATURDAY EVENING POST (Parts One–Eight, published June 5, 12, 19, & 26 and July 3, 10, 17, & 24, 1948).

18   *See* James M. Marsh letter to RHJ, 8/16/1949 ("If there is anything I can do to assist you, please do not hesitate to command me. I am particularly interested in your proposed Roosevelt project. . . ."), in RHJ LOC Box 16.

19   RHJ letter to WEJ, "Thursday P.M." [8/25/1949]. The Bohemian Grove, which is located along the Russian River in Monte Rio, California, is the site of the summer encampment of San Francisco's Bohemian Club.

20   *Id.* This book, which Jackson was reading at a friend's recommendation, was the autobiography of Lord Richard Burdon Sanderson Haldane (1856–1928), the 1st Viscount of Cloan. *See* RICHARD BURDON HALDANE, AN AUTOBIOGRAPHY (Garden City, N.Y.: Doubleday, Doran, 1929).

21   RHJ letter to WEJ, "Thursday P.M." [8/25/1949].

22   RHJ letter to WEJ, undated. The postmark shows that this letter was airmailed from Monte Rio, California, on July 29, 1950.

23   *Youngstown Sheet & Tube Co. v. Sawyer*, 343 U.S. 579 (1952). For a comprehensive history of the case, see MAEVA MARCUS, TRUMAN AND THE STEEL SEIZURE CASE: THE LIMITS OF PRESIDENTIAL POWER (New York: Columbia Univ. Press, 1977). For a memoir of aspects of this case by one of Jackson's law clerks at the time, see WILLIAM H. REHNQUIST, THE SUPREME COURT: HOW IT WAS, HOW IT IS 41–99 (New York: William Morrow, 1987). Chief Justice Rehnquist later published a revised account of the case in THE SUPREME COURT 151–92 (New York: Alfred A. Knopf, 2001).

24   *Youngstown Sheet & Tube Co. v. Sawyer*, 103 F. Supp. 569 (D.D.C. Apr. 29, 1952) (granting the steel companies' motions seeking preliminary injunctions forbidding Secretary Sawyer from acting under the purported authority of

President Truman's order) (District Judge David A. Pine), *stayed*, 197 F.2d 582 (D.C. Cir. Apr. 30 & May 2, 1952) (en banc).

25   *See* 343 U.S. 937 (May 3, 1952) (granting the petitions by the steel companies and the government for writs of *certiorari*, staying the District Court order granting a preliminary injunction, barring Secretary Sawyer from unilaterally changing any term or condition of employment in the mills he would continue to run (at least briefly), and setting the case for oral argument nine days hence).

26   *See, e.g.,* Petition of the United States for a Writ of Certiorari, *Sawyer v. Youngstown Sheet & Tube Co.*, No. 745, at 23 n.12 (arguing that "precedents include[] . . . twelve seizures by President Franklin D. Roosevelt" and quoting the June 10, 1941, "statement of then Attorney General Jackson" regarding North American Aviation) (filed May 2, 1952), *reprinted in* PHILIP B. KURLAND & GERHARD CASPER, EDS., 48 LANDMARK BRIEFS & ARGUMENTS OF THE SUPREME COURT OF THE UNITED STATES: CONSTITUTIONAL LAW 384; Brief for Petitioner United States, *Youngstown Sheet & Tube Co.*, No. 745, at 109 n.11 ("The first seizure, of the North American Aviation Plant, was justified by the then Attorney General Jackson as an act within the 'duty constitutionally and inherently rested upon the President to exert his civil and military, as well as his moral, authority to keep the defense efforts of the United States a going concern.' 89 Cong. Rec. 3992") (filed May 1952), *reprinted in* KURLAND & CASPER 716; Oral Argument Transcript, *Youngstown Sheet & Tube Co. v. Charles Sawyer*, Nos. 744 & 745, May 12–13, 1952, *reprinted in* KURLAND & CASPER 877, 919–22.

27   *See* Oral Argument Transcript, *reprinted in* KURLAND & CASPER at 919–20. Justice William O. Douglas also spoke up during the argument to state his agreement with Jackson. *See id.* at 922.

28   RHJ letter to WEJ, 5/13/1952 ("The steel argument ended. [Steel company lawyer John W.] Davis venerable and magnificent, Pearlman [sic] struggling and confused, the Court weary. It is a subject I have struggled with in several capacities. Probably means we will not adjourn [for the summer] as early as hoped").

29   RHJ conference notes, in RHJ LOC Box 176; *accord* THE SUPREME COURT IN CONFERENCE (1940–1985): THE PRIVATE DISCUSSIONS BEHIND NEARLY 300 SUPREME COURT DECISIONS 172–74 (Del Dickson ed.) (New York: Oxford Univ. Press, 2001) (reconstructing Vinson's comments).

Two weeks later, the Court affirmed by a vote of 6–3 that President Truman had no legal authority to direct Secretary Sawyer to seize the steel mills. Jackson voted with the majority and filed his own concurring opinion, noting and explicitly rejecting Perlman's account of what FDR and Jackson had done in 1941:

> The Solicitor General . . . seeks color of legality from claimed executive precedents, chief of which is President Roosevelt's seizure on June 9, 1941, of the California plant of the North American Aviation Company.

Its superficial similarities with the present case, upon analysis, yield to distinctions so decisive that it cannot be regarded as even a precedent, much less an authority for the present seizure.

Youngstown Sheet & Tube Co., 343 U.S. at 648–49 (Jackson, J., concurring in the judgment and opinion of the Court). Jackson then itemized in a lengthy footnote the factual distinctions between the two presidential directives that had resulted in factory seizures. *See id.* at 649–50 n.17.

30 *See* Robert H. Jackson, *A Presidential Legal Opinion,* 66 HARV. L. REV. 1353–61 (June 1953).

31 *See* ROBERT H. JACKSON, THE STRUGGLE FOR JUDICIAL SUPREMACY: A STUDY OF A CRISIS IN AMERICAN POWER POLITICS (New York: Alfred A. Knopf, 1941); ROBERT H. JACKSON, THE CASE AGAINST THE NAZI WAR CRIMINALS (New York: Alfred A. Knopf, 1946); ROBERT H. JACKSON, THE NÜRNBERG CASE (New York: Alfred A. Knopf, 1947).

Alfred Knopf's wife and business partner Blanche Knopf had visited Jackson in Nuremberg near the end of the trial before the International Military Tribunal. In subsequent correspondence, she nudged Jackson to get to work on an unspecified book project. The timing and context of these letters suggest that the book idea could have been a memoir of either Nuremberg or FDR. *See* BK letter to RHJ, 8/25/1947 ("I hope you have had a good summer and wonder what happened to your idea of possibly starting to write that book"), in RHJ LOC Box 15; RHJ letter to BK, 9/2/1947 (approximate date on retyped version of an RHJ handwritten note) ("I have not found time or mood to begin writing 'that book.' Have been preoccupied all summer with clearing up Nürnberg matters that there was not time to do as we went along"), in RHJ LOC Box 15.

32 AAK letter to RHJ, 6/23/1953.

33 RHJ letter to AAK, 7/3/1953.

34 AAK letter to RHJ, 7/10/1953.

35 Typed notations indicate that Jackson's secretary Elsie Douglas typed his introductory chapter on June 16, 1953, and chapter 1, "*That Man* in the White House," on June 30, 1953. The latest date in Jackson's book file, which appears on a typed draft of chapter 2, "That Man as Politician," is a penciled notation "8/14/53."

36 WALTER F. WHITE, A MAN CALLED WHITE: THE AUTOBIOGRAPHY OF WALTER WHITE 104 (New York: Viking Press, 1948). After FDR's and Jackson's times, another race-related variant on the phrase became the title of the first African-American White House aide's journal of his work in the executive branch. *See* E. FREDERIC MORROW, BLACK MAN IN THE WHITE HOUSE: A DIARY OF THE EISENHOWER YEARS BY THE ADMINISTRATIVE OFFICER FOR SPECIAL PROJECTS, THE WHITE HOUSE, 1955–1961 (New York: Coward-McCann, 1963). Editors at the NEW YORK TIMES also used the phrase to refer to former President Clinton. N.Y. TIMES BOOK REVIEW, June 2, 2002, at 27 (calling Joe

Klein's book THE NATURAL "[a] solid, if provisional, overview of That Man, whose every sin made him more popular but was never able (or didn't really try) to accomplish big-deal reforms, though his incremental achievements were substantial").

37   *See* EARLE LOOKER, THIS MAN ROOSEVELT (New York: Brewer, Warren & Putnam, 1932). The author, Reginald Earle Looker (1895–1976), was a Republican, a childhood friend of the Theodore Roosevelt family, and a best-selling book author. *See* EARLE LOOKER, THE WHITE HOUSE GANG (New York: Revell, 1929) (Looker's memoir of his boyhood schoolmates in Washington, D.C., including TR's son Quentin). Looker's THIS MAN ROOSEVELT was based on a series of articles that he wrote for LIBERTY magazine. Looker's writing, which described his extended observations of then-Governor FDR and included the positive results of an independent medical panel's evaluation of him, helped to dispel public concerns about the candidate's physical health during the 1932 campaign. Looker also worked as a ghostwriter on some of FDR's own 1932 articles in LIBERTY and on some of his later books and presidential speeches. In 1933, Looker reused parts of THIS MAN ROOSEVELT when he published a larger book about FDR's life through the first eight months of his Presidency. *See* EARLE LOOKER, THE AMERICAN WAY: FRANKLIN ROOSEVELT IN ACTION (New York: John Day, 1933) (with an Introduction by Colonel Edward M. House).

38   GEOFFREY C. WARD, BEFORE THE TRUMPET: YOUNG FRANKLIN ROOSEVELT, 1882–1905 5 (New York: Harper & Row, 1985); *accord* Henry Steele Commager & Richard Brandon Morris, *Editors' Introduction*, in WILLIAM E. LEUCHTENBURG, FRANKLIN D. ROOSEVELT AND THE NEW DEAL, 1932–1940 x (New York: Harper & Row, 1963) ("Many of Roosevelt's contemporaries reacted to 'That Man'—and to the New Deal—the way the Federalists had reacted to Jefferson and the Whigs to [Andrew] Jackson. They saw dictatorship and revolution where the majority of Americans saw leadership and a democratic resurgence"). For a humorous FDR-era account of these attitudes, see Frank Sullivan, *The Cliché Expert Testifies as a Roosevelt Hater*, THE NEW YORKER, June 18, 1938, at 18–20, *reprinted in* FRANK SULLIVAN, A PEARL IN EVERY OYSTER 88–96 (Boston: Little, Brown, 1938).

I learned directly, albeit decades later, of hostility to Roosevelt from my own grandmother, who will speak his name but only through pursed lips; born in 1908 and an immigrant to the United States, she believes emphatically, based on life experience, that "Democrats get us into wars." So too a friend's grandfather, an Iowa farm owner, who was so appalled to receive annual government checks, beginning after FDR signed the Agricultural Adjustment Act in 1933, for *not* growing corn, and so convinced that FDR had allowed the Pearl Harbor attack that drew the United States into World War II, that the grandfather refused to permit Roosevelt *dimes* in his home in the years following FDR's death.

39   FREDERICK LEWIS ALLEN, SINCE YESTERDAY: THE NINETEEN-THIRTIES IN AMER-
     ICA, SEPTEMBER 3, 1929–SEPTEMBER 3, 1939 233 (New York: Harper & Bros.,
     1939).

40   *See* FRANK KINGDON, "THAT MAN" IN THE WHITE HOUSE: YOU AND YOUR
     PRESIDENT (New York: Arco, 1944) (with a concluding Message by Rex
     Stout).

41   During Jackson's life and for a period of time following his death, Mrs.
     Douglas kept the manuscript in a filing cabinet with his other nonjudicial
     writings. She described this Roosevelt book project as "ESSAYS ABOUT
     F.D.R: Introduction; I. That Man—As a Politician; II. That Man—In the
     White House, etc." and categorized it under "ARTICLES BY RHJ" in her
     card index to Justice Jackson's files. See RHJ LOC Box 250.

42   *See* WEJ letter to ELD, 4/28/1958.

43   *See generally* Edwin M. Yoder, Jr., *Getting Roosevelt Right*, WASH. POST, Jan. 19,
     1982, at A19 (describing JOSEPH ALSOP, FDR, 1882–1945: A CENTENARY REMEM-
     BRANCE (New York: Viking Press, 1982), as "the best short book we have, or
     are likely to have, about Franklin D. Roosevelt").

44   WEJ letter to BK, 4/22/1958, contained in Knopf Papers, Ransom Archives,
     Univ. of Texas, Box 235-10; *accord* WEJ letter to ELD, 4/28/1958.

45   Notes provide specific citations to the Jackson writings that I drew upon to
     create particular passages.

46   These additions are introduced explicitly as inserts and printed as indented
     passages. They also have notes that specify their original locations in Jack-
     son's unpublished writings.

47   One arguable exception is a passage in Jackson's Introduction to this book,
     where he interrupted his discussion of FDR to ruminate on Machiavelli and
     the standards by which history judges politicians and policies to be successful.
     Jackson had recently, at the time he wrote out these paragraphs in longhand,
     read the Lord Acton introduction to Machiavelli's *The Prince* that he (Jackson)
     quotes herein. *See* Robert H. Jackson, "Introduction," in WHITNEY R. HARRIS,
     TYRANNY ON TRIAL xxix (Dallas: Southern Methodist Univ. Press, 1954) (quot-
     ing, in an essay dated February 1954, Lord Acton's "inaugural lecture as pro-
     fessor of history at Cambridge"). I suspect that Jackson would have, as he
     edited and finalized *That Man* for publication, tightened and clarified this pas-
     sage, connected it more explicitly to FDR, and/or deleted it altogether.

48   *See Kingsland v. Dorsey*, 338 U.S. 318, 324 (1949) ("I should not like to be second
     to anyone on this Court in condemning the custom of putting up decoy
     authors to impress the guileless, a custom which . . . flourishes even in offi-
     cial circles in Washington. . . . Ghost-writing has debased the intellectual
     currency in circulation here and is a type of counterfeiting which invites no
     defense") (Jackson, J., joined by Frankfurter, J., dissenting).

49   FDR's secretary Grace Tully began her own memoir with an excellent
     description of this phenomenon: "In reading some of the books my friends

have written about Franklin Delano Roosevelt, I have been struck by the fact that in the second or third chapter the hero of the story often turns out to be the author, while Roosevelt vanishes from sight or is reduced to a small walk-on part. I have been struck by the further fact that if my friends did all they claim to have done, the sum of the things for which they take sole credit would exceed the sum of the whole New Deal. And nothing would be left for which Roosevelt could be credited—except, perhaps, credit for everything that went wrong." GRACE TULLY, F.D.R. MY BOSS xi (New York: Charles Scribner's Sons, 1949).

50   *See* note 22 and accompanying text.

Introduction

1   During FDR's presidential term, North American Aviation (NAA) was a leading manufacturer of military aircraft and other national defense materials. In 1941, however, as it became increasingly likely that the United States would be drawn into the war that already engulfed western Europe, a Communist-led strike at NAA halted its production. Because NAA had a direct contract with the government, the strike was essentially an action against the government, impairing its preparation for war. FDR responded in June 1941 to this strike by issuing Executive Order 8773, which effectively authorized the Secretary of War to seize NAA's Inglewood plant in Los Angeles. This Order permitted Secretary of War Henry L. Stimson to "employ or authorize the employment of [its] employees" and "to take such measures as may be necessary to protect workers returning to the plant." FDR took this action based on legal advice from Attorney General Jackson and others, and without any authorization from Congress. Stimson, acting pursuant to the Executive Order, directed the Army to act immediately. It cleared a line of picketers, opened the NAA plant gates, and made it possible for the workers to resume production.

2   *See generally* NICCOLÒ MACHIAVELLI, IL PRINCIPE (Oxford: Clarendon Press, 1891) (L. Arthur Burd, ed.).

3   JOHN EMERICH DALBERG-ACTON, the First Baron Acton, "Introduction to L. A. Burd's Edition of Il Principe by Machiavelli," in THE HISTORY OF FREEDOM & OTHER ESSAYS 212 (1922 reprint of 1907 1st edition).

4   *Id.* at 223. Jackson, in his draft of this Introduction, included the precise citation to this portion of Acton's essay.

5   FDR was born on January 30, 1882, to James Roosevelt and Sara Delano Roosevelt at Springwood, the family home at Hyde Park, New York. Jackson, ten years FDR's junior, was born on February 13, 1892, to William Eldred Jackson and Angelina Houghwout Jackson on their farm at Spring Creek in Warren County, Pennsylvania.

6   Prior to the ratification of the 17th Amendment to the Constitution on April

8, 1913, each state's United States senators were chosen by the state legislature, not by the direct ballots of the voters. *See* U.S. Const., Art. I, § 3, cl. 1. Although most state legislatures elected the U.S. senators in joint sessions of the state legislative houses, New York treated the selection of a United States senator as an ordinary legislative act that would move concurrently through each house of the state legislature. This selection method, unlike the joint session approach, gave equal roles to the larger state assembly and the smaller state senate, but it was a method that risked deadlock when the houses could not agree on a candidate.

7   Tammany Hall, the Democratic political machine in Manhattan, took its name from the Tammany Society, an association that formed in 1786 (and took its name from Tammanend, a Delaware Indian chief). Its original leaders were Jeffersonian Democrats who opposed the "aristocratic" Federalist Party. During the nineteenth century, however, Tammany came to be controlled by members of the privileged class. By mid-century, "Boss" William Marcy Tweed controlled Tammany, and thus Democratic Party nominations and patronage in New York City. After a brief reform era under Samuel J. Tilden, who sought to end some of the flagrant conduct of "Tweed Ring," the Tammany machine regained power in 1874 under John Kelly. The political "boss" system became firmly embedded in New York City politics and corruption was prevalent. Tammany's power diminished in the late 1920s when Governor FDR initiated investigations, led by Judge Samuel Seabury, that ultimately discredited the machine. Tammany, which supported Al Smith, not FDR, for President in 1932, continued to decline in power when FDR was in the White House and Fiorello La Guardia was Mayor of New York City.

8   FDR was first elected to the New York State Senate in 1910. By that time, his fifth cousin and uncle-in-law Theodore Roosevelt (whom FDR called "Uncle Ted") was two years an ex-President and planning his comeback. In 1912, TR challenged President William Howard Taft for the Republican Party nomination but was not successful. TR then formed the Bull Moose Party and ran in the general election, where he and Taft were defeated by the Democratic Party nominee, Woodrow Wilson.

9   In 1911, Sheehan sought to become the next United States senator from New York. The new senator, who would be chosen by a simple majority of the state legislature, was certain to be a Democrat because that party held 114 of 200 total seats in the State Senate and Assembly. Sheehan was the choice of Tammany Hall and its leader, Charles Francis Murphy (1858–1924), but more progressive elements of the Democratic Party, including freshman state senator FDR, favored Edward M. Shepard, an independent, and others.

10   Elijah Jackson (1772–1840), Justice Jackson's great-grandfather, was born in Litchfield, Connecticut. He resettled in Spring Creek, Pennsylvania, in 1797.

Elijah, the "stiff Democrat," was a supporter of Thomas Jefferson and Andrew Jackson.

Robert Rutherford Jackson (1829–1913), Justice Jackson's grandfather, left the farm in Spring Creek in 1850 to prospect for gold in California—apparently without much success. This Robert Jackson, who lived on the family farm for several years after his return from California before moving his family to Farmington Township in Warren County, Pennsylvania, also was a Democrat throughout his life—Justice Jackson recalled this grandfather stating that he had voted against Abraham Lincoln twice.

William Eldred ("Will") Jackson (1863–1915), Justice Jackson's father, was, throughout his lifetime, an outspoken Democrat in a strongly Republican community. He was involved in horse breeding and racing and owned, at various times, a hotel, a livery stable, a sawmill, and other properties.

When Justice Jackson's parents married in 1884, they were induced to live on and run the Spring Creek farm with the Justice's great-uncle, William Miles Jackson, who had been in possession of the farm after Elijah's death. Justice Jackson described his Uncle William as a "very sturdy and consistent Democrat." According to the Justice, the Jacksons were consistently Democratic during the Civil War, that being the "least extreme of the parties." They were sympathetic to neither the southerners who favored slavery nor the northern abolitionists. They believed that moderate measures could have avoided the war and freed the slaves.

11   Jackson seems to be referring to a trip that he made from Jamestown to Albany with Frank Mott in early 1911. In fall 1911, Jackson moved to Albany and spent the 1911-12 academic year as a student at Albany Law School.

12   On January 16, 1911, FDR led the group of about twenty progressive state senators and assemblymen who boycotted the Democratic legislators' caucus on the upcoming legislative election of a new United States senator. Their absence from the caucus liberated the boycotters from the caucus rule that in subsequent legislative voting, the vote of the caucus majority would bind all who had been in attendance. The political machine candidate, William F. Sheehan, gained only ninety-one votes in the caucus and thus fell short of the majority he needed in the 200-seat legislature. Tammany Hall leader Charles Murphy then persuaded Sheehan to withdraw and proposed a compromise candidate, Judge James Aloysius O'Gorman (1860–1943) of the New York Supreme Court, who had a good judicial record and no embarrassing corporate ties. O'Gorman was acceptable to the holdouts and won the caucus and the legislative election, 112–80. Through his role in this episode, and notwithstanding its anti-climatic ending, FDR won national acclaim as a progressive fighting machine politics.

13   Following Woodrow Wilson's presidential election in 1912, he appointed FDR to serve as Assistant Secretary of the Navy. FDR was sworn in on March 17, 1913.

14   This discussion of Jackson's visits to FDR in Washington during 1913 and
      1914 includes material from the Phillips–Jackson interviews, p. 112.

15   This paragraph includes material from the Phillips–Jackson interviews,
      p. 113.

16   FDR, the 1920 vice presidential running mate of Democratic presidential
      nominee Governor James M. Cox of Ohio, campaigned in Jamestown on
      Thursday, October 21, 1920. After speaking in nearby Falconer that morn-
      ing, Roosevelt traveled to Jamestown by automobile. At noontime, he
      spoke from his car to a crowd in Jamestown's Theodore Roosevelt (formerly
      Brooklyn) Square, discussing the reasons he and Governor Cox favored
      United States membership in the League of Nations and other topics. Fol-
      lowing these outdoor remarks, FDR went inside Jamestown's Hotel
      Samuels, where he spoke around 1:00 P.M. to 300 or so persons at a joint
      meeting of the local Kiwanis and Rotary clubs. He spoke there about issues
      in government management, including waste and duplication among exec-
      utive branch departments and the need for Congress to regularize the
      appropriations process. *See F.D. Roosevelt in Jamestown*, JAMESTOWN MORN.
      POST, Oct. 22, 1920, at 5, 7. On November 2, Republican nominees Warren
      G. Harding and Calvin Coolidge trounced the Cox–FDR ticket.

17   At this deadlocked convention, it took the Democratic Party 103 ballots to
      nominate John W. Davis as its presidential candidate.

18   The 1924 Democratic National Convention was held at Madison Square
      Garden in New York City from June 24 through July 9, 1924.

19   Although FDR, who served as Smith's campaign manager, gave the cele-
      brated "Happy Warrior" nominating speech on his behalf at Madison
      Square Garden on June 26, 1924, the Democratic Party's presidential nomi-
      nation that year went to Davis, a compromise candidate. President Calvin
      Coolidge, a Republican, defeated Davis soundly in the general election that
      November.

20   *See* Western Union Telegram, Franklin B. [*sic*] Roosevelt, Warm Springs,
      Ga., to Frank H. Mott, Hotel Powers, Rochester, N.Y., 9/30/1928 ("Know
      Jackson would be fine for Attorney General but am too far away to know
      whether this would balance with rest of ticket").

21   In the 1928 general election, Hamilton Ward, a Republican, narrowly
      defeated Albert Conway, the Democratic candidate, in the race for New
      York Attorney General.

22   This paragraph includes material from the Phillips–Jackson interviews, pp.
      156–57.

23   Jackson was referring to Governor Roosevelt's July 13, 1929, trip to Chau-
      tauqua Institution. On that occasion FDR, who had spent the previous
      week inspecting schools and hospitals and politicking around New York
      State, spoke briefly to 4500 people in Chautauqua Institution's Amphithe-
      ater about advances in public responses to mental illnesses and mental and

physical handicaps. Regarding "the cripples," FDR spoke words that must have been particularly striking to an audience that had just observed him "walking" to the podium with the assistance of his son Elliott: "A generation ago the crippled had no chance. Today, through the fine strides of modern medical science, the great majority of crippled children are enabled, even though the process may take years, to get about and, in many cases, find complete or practically complete cures. In other words, that large part of humanity which used to be pushed to one side or discarded is now salvaged and enabled to play its own part in the life of the community." *At Chautauqua, N.Y., July 13, 1929*, PUBLIC PAPERS OF FRANKLIN D. ROOSEVELT, 48TH GOVERNOR OF THE STATE OF NEW YORK, 1929 719, 720 (Albany: J. B. Lyon, 1930). FDR and his party had spent the previous night in Jamestown, visited with Frank Mott, Jackson, and others at Mott's house at Driftwood on Chautauqua Lake, and reviewed a Boy Scout troop at another lake location.

24 On August 28, 1931, Governor Roosevelt called the legislature into a special session to consider appropriate measures for meeting the emergency on a state level. Within a month, the legislature passed the Wicks Act. It defined an emergency period—from November 1, 1931, to June 1, 1932—during which state aid was to be extended to municipalities for work relief and home relief through a separate agency, the Temporary Emergency Relief Administration (TERA). An appropriation of $20 million was to fund these efforts. Through the Wicks Act, New York became the first state to provide state aid for emergency unemployment relief. The legislature extended TERA several times and supported it with continuing appropriations until it expired in June 1937.

25 *See generally Roosevelt Signs Court Inquiry Bill*, N.Y. TIMES, Apr. 1, 1931, at 18.

26 Governor Roosevelt first appointed Samuel Seabury (1873–1958), a well-respected former judge of New York's trial and appellate courts and the Democrats' unsuccessful 1916 candidate for Governor, to investigate official corruption in New York City. In 1932, on the eve of the Democratic national convention that would nominate FDR for President, Seabury, who then was serving as counsel to a state legislative committee to investigate New York City government, filed a politically explosive report. Seabury alleged that New York City Mayor James ("Jimmy") Walker (1881–1946), the popular product of the Tammany Hall machine, had engaged in such gross improprieties as accepting bribes and using official influence to obtain lucrative business opportunities for his friends. Seabury's report sought Walker's removal from office under the New York Charter, which provided that the Governor of the state could preside at a hearing to examine charges of improper conduct by government officials and, on that basis, remove mayors and others from office. Pursuant to this procedure, FDR—who by that time was the presidential nominee of the Democratic Party—presided at a

trial to determine whether Walker should be removed from office. FDR was aided by special counsel Martin Conboy (1878–1944), who was, like Walker, prominent and a Catholic—unlike Roosevelt and Seabury, who were Episcopalians. Conboy's involvement refuted claims by Walker supporters that the proceedings reflected anti-Catholic sentiment. As Tammany battled to save Walker, FDR debated the removal question with his advisers. FDR was spared making this decision, and any resulting effect on his candidacy, when Walker resigned abruptly on September 1, 1932. The Walker case was a damaging blow to Tammany Hall and contributed to its defeat in the 1933 municipal election.

27   This fishing trip occurred on the late afternoon of Wednesday, November 13, 1940. *See* White House Usher's Diary entry, 11/13/1940 ("1630- Motor to Navy Yard to board USS *Potomac* accompanied by Harry L. Hopkins, Robert H. Jackson, Frank C. Walker"), in Pare Lorentz Chronology, FDR Library.

28   Moley had been, throughout the then-just-concluded 1940 presidential campaign, an outspoken critic of Roosevelt and the New Deal. These efforts culminated in Moley's scathing speech at an October 23 "No-Third-Term" rally in New York City, which was part of a final effort to sway voters to Republican candidate Wendell Willkie. During the speech, Moley compared Roosevelt to a power-hungry Napoleon, arguing that Roosevelt's first term was "marked by practically all of the social reforms that are now used as arguments for perpetuation" and that "the second term was marked by a continuous effort to increase executive authority." In Moley's summary, FDR had served "[t]wo terms—the first was for the people, the second was for power." Moley said that FDR's second term "drive for power" made up the "four horsemen of autocracy": first, passing "must" bills; second, the desire to "pack" the Court; third, the "purge" of Congress; and fourth, the current "command to perpetuate." According to Moley, FDR had "only two checks upon himself. His own self-restraint is one. That failed in July [when he accepted renomination]. Only one is left. That is your vote in November."

Chapter 1

1   At his May 28, 1940, press conference, FDR announced his intention to use statutory authority that was granted to the President by the National Defense Act of 1916, which was a still-in-effect remnant of World War I. FDR announced that he would, acting pursuant to this law, revive the National Defense Advisory Committee (NDAC) under the Cabinet committee known as the Council of National Defense. The Council, made up of six Cabinet officers, subsequently nominated the seven NDAC members to handle, as presidential appointees, the coordination and mobilization of industrial resources. FDR explained later that the NDAC "was designed to

aid in ascertaining precisely what America needed in the way of defense materials, where she could get them, and what was the best way to obtain them. . . ." Each NDAC member was charged with special knowledge in a certain field in order to handle the growing demands of the War Department. In early 1941, as the national rearmament program expanded, FDR modified and expanded the NDAC's function creating the Office of Production Management. *See* Executive Order 8629 (Jan. 7, 1941).

2   The Cabinet members were Secretary of the Navy Charles Edison, Interior Secretary Harold Ickes, Attorney General Jackson, Treasury Secretary Henry Morgenthau, and Agriculture Secretary Henry Wallace. Also present were Harold D. Smith, who was FDR's Director of the Budget; General "Pa" Watson, the President's military aide; William H. McReynolds, who was one of FDR's administrative assistants; Senator Alben Barkley; and the Speaker of the House, Representative Sam Rayburn.

3   RHJ Nuremberg diary, 6/16/1945 p. 2, in RHJ LOC Box 95.

4   This trip occurred on November 13–17, 1940. *See* RHJ LOC Box 30 (note by RHJ's secretary).

5   Jackson seems to be referring above to the Radio Press News reports that were teletyped to FDR on the USS *Potomac* on November 14–15, 1940. These printed reports, which Jackson subsequently saved in his files, included short bulletins on two nights of British air raids on Taranto, but it was identified only as "the Italian naval base . . . in the heel of the Italian boot." *See* RHJ LOC Box 30.

6   Taranto was, in November 1940, the principal base of the Italian naval fleet. Because it was holed up at Taranto and would not come out to sea, the air arm of the British Royal Navy Fleet had, on the nights of November 11 and 12, launched torpedo plane and bomber attacks from aircraft carriers in the Mediterranean. These surprise attacks, which crippled half of the Italian battleship fleet and damaged a number of other vessels, turned the previous Italian battleship superiority into a relative disadvantage and facilitated further British harassment of Italian military operations south across the Mediterranean and east across the Adriatic.

7   In the above text, Jackson may have confused the November 1940 cruise on the Potomac with a March 1941 fishing trip in the waters south of Florida. Ickes was not present on the November 1940 cruise, which was when the British made air raids on Taranto. He was present on the 1941 fishing trip, and he noted in his diary that he and FDR worked on their stamps on this occasion.

Chapter 2

1   On Humphrey's life and career, his removal from the FTC by FDR and the ensuing litigation that culminated in the Supreme Court's decision against

FDR, see WILLIAM E. LEUCHTENBURG, "The Case of the Contentious Commissioner," in THE SUPREME COURT REBORN: THE CONSTITUTIONAL REVOLUTION IN THE AGE OF ROOSEVELT 52–81 (New York: Oxford Univ. Press, 1995).

2   *Humphrey's Executor v. United States*, 295 U.S. 602 (1935) (holding that, because the Federal Trade Commission is a quasi-judicial, quasi-legislative body created by Congress, its officers are not part of the executive branch and cannot be removed by the President for reasons not specified in the statute creating the FTC).

3   *See Myers v. United States*, 272 U.S. 52 (1926) (holding that, although the Senate must confirm all executive appointments, the President has discretion to remove executive officers without consent of the Senate) (William Howard Taft, C.J., for the Court).

4   This discussion of the *Humphrey* case includes material from the Phillips–Jackson interviews, p. 674.

5   *See* Robert H. Jackson, *Power of the President to Remove Members of the Tennessee Valley Authority from Office*, 39 Op. A.G. 145 (Mar. 18, 1938) (opinion issued by Jackson as Acting Attorney General).

6   At this point in his Columbia oral history interview, Jackson stated that "[t]he President had burn about the way Morgan acted, but I wouldn't say it was slow." Jackson later deleted that sentence when he was editing his transcribed interview. *See* RHJ LOC Box 190, p. 599.

7   This discussion regarding Morgan includes material from the Phillips–Jackson interviews, pp. 674–77.

8   Charles Michelson, a former newspaperman who became a speechwriter for FDR and other prominent Democrats, wrote in 1944 that "[i]n intimate political circles confusion of the names is averted by referring to one as the Good Bob Jackson and to the other as simply Bob Jackson." CHARLES MICHELSON, THE GHOST TALKS 4 (New York: G. P. Putnam's Sons, 1944). The former is the author of this book.

The latter Robert Jackson (1880–1973) was a New Hampshire lawyer. In 1931, he became secretary of the Democratic National Committee (DNC). In 1932, this Jackson established a large private law practice in Washington, D.C., and also worked expertly for FDR, obtaining vote commitments from delegates and planning strategy before the Democratic convention that nominated Roosevelt for President. In 1934, Jackson became the focus of criticism concerning Democratic lawyers who were practicing law before executive branch departments. At a White House press conference on January 17, a reporter pointedly asked FDR to comment on newspaper stories about Washington law practice by unnamed Democratic National Committeemen. Roosevelt responded forcefully that occupants of high party positions should not be practicing law in Washington because it created a false impression of special access. Within hours, Jackson resigned his DNC position. He continued to practice law in Washington for a time, and thus to be confused with Robert Houghwout Jackson. In 1941, when the private sector Jackson consented to settle a federal case over his income tax liability, one newspaper noted the irony that the collection action had been "filed by the Department of Justice, which is directed by another Robert Jackson—the Attorney General of the United States." *Lawyer to Pay $257,212 Taxes*, WASH. HERALD, Apr. 19, 1941. Justice Jackson's files also show that the Jacksons regularly received each other's mail, including past due bills of the private lawyer that were routed in error to the government official. *See, e.g.*, RHJ LOC Box 22.

9   Jackson was referring to William H. Boyd, who was a senior attorney in the Department of Justice's Tax Division. During the fall of 1938, Boyd reportedly admitted to investigators that he reluctantly had agreed to "borrow" money from two prominent gangsters, J. Richard ("Dixie") Davis and "Johnny" Torrio, after they had obtained a mortgage on Boyd's home and threatened foreclosure. DOJ suspended Boyd, and he hanged himself on November 9, 1938. Torrio subsequently pleaded guilty in April 1939 to tax evasion and served time in the federal penitentiary at Leavenworth, Kansas.

10 The Department of the Treasury's Intelligence Unit was created in 1919 as a self-policing force. Under the leadership of its founding chief, Elmer L. Irey, who served until 1946, the unit grew to become a significant part of the federal law enforcement effort against organized crime and political corruption.

11 In 1939, Pendergast was convicted of federal income tax evasion based upon his 1935 receipt of an insurance bribe of $750,000. He was sentenced to serve fifteen months in the federal penitentiary at Leavenworth and to pay a fine of $10,000.

12 In February 1939, New Jersey Governor A. Harry Moore nominated Frank Hague, Jr., a thirty-four-year-old lawyer who had been a member of the bar for only three years, to a lay judge position on the state's highest court, the Court of Errors and Appeals. At the time, Governor Moore said, "I know this appointment will make his dad happy." Although the nomination was controversial, Hague Jr. was confirmed by the State Senate in March 1939. Judge Hague resigned from the court in January 1945, shortly before his six-year term would have ended.

13 The discussion of Mayor Hague includes material from the Phillips–Jackson interviews, pp. 741–42.

14 The classic statement of this philosophy of federal prosecution is the speech that Jackson, the new Attorney General of the United States who had succeeded Frank Murphy, gave in the Great Hall at the Department of Justice to United States Attorneys assembled from across the country on April 1, 1940. *See* Robert H. Jackson, *The Federal Prosecutor*, 31 J. CRIM. L. & CRIMINOL-OGY 3–6 (1940) & 24 J. AM. JUDICATURE SOC. 18 (1940).

15 The discussion of Mayor Kelly includes material from the Phillips–Jackson interviews, p. 782.

16 The text regarding Murphy, Jackson, and FDR includes material from the Phillips–Jackson interviews, pp. 783–85.

17 HUGH RUSSELL FRASER, DEMOCRACY IN THE MAKING: THE JACKSON–TYLER ERA 159 (Indianapolis: Bobbs-Merrill, 1938) (emphasis in original). Jackson's personal copy of this book is in the Fenton History Center in Jamestown, New York. This book, which the author Fraser inscribed—"To Robert H. Jackson, who has the vision and courage of his namesake" Andrew Jackson—and gave to Solicitor General Jackson in October 1938, includes his penciled brackets around the passage quoted in the text.

18 See id. at 159–60.

19 This paragraph includes material from the Phillips–Jackson interviews, p. 807.

20 On Saturday night May 7, 1938, Bill Jackson, then a Yale freshman, was walking with two friends through New Haven Green, which had been decorated with bunting for New Haven's tercentenary. The trio, perhaps not entirely sober, came to be in possession of some bunting and a bus stop sign. They stashed the bunting but were still holding the sign when New Haven police stopped them just outside a gateway to the Yale campus. The police, who were not authorized to go onto campus to search for the bunting, agreed to let the boys go on the condition that they carry the sign back to its proper location, return the bunting, and pay for the slight damage they had caused. The boys agreed, and then returned the bunting to the Green and the sign to its proper spot. At this point, as one officer was in the process of releasing them, another officer, who had collected the bunting "evidence," ran up with gun drawn and placed the boys under arrest. Although they spent the night in jail, the charges were dropped the next morning—too late to keep radio and print media from reporting the arrest of the Solicitor General's son. See, e.g., TIME, May 16, 1938, p. 56.

21 Phillips–Jackson interviews, pp. 801–2 & 810–12.

22 Phillips–Jackson interviews, pp. 812–13.

23 FDR served as Assistant Secretary of the Navy under Wilson for more than seven years. He resigned in August 1920, after he had become the Democratic Party's vice presidential nominee, to campaign.

24 FDR's quotation regarding Wilson is contained in the Phillips–Jackson interviews, p. 112.

25 White House records show that Jackson had a private, early morning White House meeting with FDR on October 21, 1937. See White House Usher's Diary entry, 10/21/1937 ("0915–1020"), in Pare Lorentz Chronology, FDR Library.

26 On July 19, 1937, Governor Lehman wrote a letter to Senator Robert Wagner stating his opposition to FDR's court reorganization bill: "From the broad standpoint of the public interest whatever immediate gain might be achieved through the proposed change in the court would, in my opinion,

be far more than offset by a loss of confidence in the independence of the courts and in governmental procedure." Lehman declared that the bill was not in the best interest of the "social well-being of our people" and urged Wagner, who generally supported FDR's objectives regarding the federal courts and at the time was favoring a compromise bill that was pending in the Senate, to vote against it. On July 20, Lehman's letter was published in the NEW YORK TIMES, along with a quote from an anonymous "official high in the administration" who declared that the letter was a "'stab in the back.'"

27   "Jackson Day" was, in Robert Jackson's time, the Democratic Party's day of fundraising dinners throughout the country. Named for President Andrew Jackson, the day marked, in presidential election years, the start of the campaign that would culminate in the party's summer nominating convention. Although Andrew Jackson was born on March 15, 1767, "Jackson Day" was January 8, which was the date of his decisive 1815 victory over British forces at the Chalmette plantation downriver from New Orleans. For twentieth-century Democratic politicians, Jackson Day, coming just after the start of the calendar year, was a kickoff date that created near-maximum time for pre-convention campaigning.

28   Edward Bernays (1891–1995) drew on the social sciences, especially psychology, to help create the field of public relations. In 1923, he taught the first public relations college course at New York University. He wrote influential books in the field and represented clients that included major corporations and the National Association for the Advancement of Colored People (NAACP).

29   The American Labor Party (ALP) was created by New York labor leaders in 1936, primarily to support FDR's reelection. Throughout the late 1930s, the Party built support in New York, particularly in New York City, and developed the power to tip elections to Democratic or Republican Party nominees it chose to support on its ballot line. In 1938, the Party supported New York Governor Herbert Lehman's bid for reelection and generally is regarded as having provided his margin of victory over his Republican opponent, Thomas E. Dewey. In 1956, the ALP's New York State committee voted the Party out of existence because it was no longer attracting enough voters to affect elections.

30   This dinner—the annual dinner dance of the New York Democratic Club, with Jackson as guest of honor—was held at the Commodore Hotel in Manhattan on Thursday, February 24, 1938. Bennett's dinner occurred simultaneously at the Hotel St. George in Brooklyn.

31   Jackson was referring here to the widely publicized public speeches that he gave in December 1937, when he was Assistant Attorney General heading the Antitrust Division. Jackson argued in these speeches that a small number of wealthy families and monopolies were responsible for the economic depression and promised antitrust prosecutions.

32 Jackson was referring to an aspect of the banking crisis—bank failures, public panics, runs on banks, currency and gold hoarding, and resulting currency shortages—that existed in New York State and throughout the country in early 1933. By FDR's Inauguration Day (March 4, 1933), each state governor had declared a bank holiday and banking had ceased nationwide. After FDR took the presidential oath, his Treasury Secretary, William H. Woodin, promulgated regulations that permitted limited banking to resume and authorized local clearinghouses to seek his approval to issue scrip that would function as currency during the crisis. In New York, Governor Herbert Lehman then obtained legislative authority to create an Emergency Certificate Corporation to issue state scrip. On March 7, Lehman appointed former Governor Al Smith to chair the Corporation board and named Jackson and three other prominent New Yorkers to serve as its other directors. The very next day, however, Lehman announced that no New York scrip would be issued because Woodin had revoked his earlier permission.

33 Phillips–Jackson interviews, pp. 614–28.

34 On Saturday, August 17, 1940, Representative Joseph W. Martin, Jr. (R.-MA), the House Minority Leader, formally notified Wendell Willkie in his hometown of Elwood, Indiana, that the Republican Party had nominated him in Philadelphia on June 28 to be its presidential candidate. Martin did this as chair of the "committee of notification," a tradition from the time when men actually had to travel great distances on horseback to bring political convention news back "home" to the candidates. Late in the afternoon of August 17, Willkie, speaking at the Elwood high school from which he had graduated, delivered the 6000-word acceptance speech that he had been crafting over the summer.

35 See pages 81–103 for Jackson's account of FDR's destroyer deal with Great Britain.

36 Phillips–Jackson interviews, pp. 831–3, 835–6, 874–8.

37 Phillips–Jackson interviews, pp. 867–71.

38 FDR letter to Hamilton Holt, President, Rollins College, Winter Park, Fla., 11/20/1944.

39 RHJ letter to Herman Blum, Director, Blumhaven Library & Gallery, Philadelphia, PA, 2/5/1952.

40 After FDR failed to get Congress to pass his 1937 Court-packing plan, FDR sought to "purge" the Democratic Party of conservatives who had opposed him by backing their opponents during the 1938 Democratic primaries. In virtually every instance, these efforts by FDR to defeat selected members of his own political party were unsuccessful.

41 The text regarding FDR's dealings with Congress includes material from the Phillips–Jackson interviews, p. 814.

42 Beginning in 1927, commercial flights to Washington, D.C., used Hoover Airport, a private airfield near the Virginia end of Washington's 14th Street

Bridge. The next year, a second privately owned commercial airport opened across Military Road, a main thoroughfare, from Hoover Airport. Although these side-by-side airports—obviously a hazardous situation— soon were consolidated into Washington Municipal Airport (known informally as "Washington-Hoover"), its main runway continued to be intersected by Military Road, where guards used flags to halt auto traffic during airplane takeoffs and landings. After Washington National Airport opened in 1941, Washington Municipal closed. Some of its former location is today part of the site of the Pentagon and also the approach to Arlington National Cemetery.

43   FDR dedicated the result, Washington National Airport, on Saturday, September 28, 1940. It opened officially on June 16, 1941. In February 1998, federal legislation renamed it the Ronald Reagan Washington National Airport.

44   *See Mellon v. Massachusetts*, 262 U.S. 447, 486–89 (1923).

45   This account of FDR's decisions that resulted in the construction of Washington National Airport incorporates material from the Phillips–Jackson interviews, pp. 708–11.

46   Jackson had, at the time of his death, researched and drafted a lengthy manuscript recounting his involvement as Attorney General in this 1940 agreement between the United States and Great Britain. *See generally* Robert H. Jackson, *Acquisition of Naval and Air Bases in Exchange for Over-Age Destroyers*, 39 Op. A.G. 484 (1940), reprinted in H. JEFFERSON POWELL, THE CONSTITUTION AND THE ATTORNEYS GENERAL 307 (Durham, N.C.: Carolina Academic Press, 1999). Jackson's account of the destroyer deal begins on page 81.

47   *See also* RHJ memorandum to Secretary Morgenthau, 8/3/1935 (memorializing that Harrison had, in a meeting with Jackson the previous day, "reminded me of his telephone conversation with the President about the $300,000 exemption for inheritances"), in RHJ LOC Box 75.

48   This anecdote regarding Senator Harrison incorporates material from the Phillips–Jackson interviews, pp. 365–66.

49   After graduating from the Groton School in Massachusetts and receiving his undergraduate degree from Harvard University in 1903, FDR attended Columbia University Law School but dropped out in his final semester after passing the New York bar examination in the spring of 1907. He then spent the next three years with Carter, Ledyard, and Milburn, a Manhattan law firm that had been founded in 1854 and specialized in trusts and estates work for some of the city's wealthiest families. One of the firm's co-founders, James C. Carter (1827–1905), had played an active role in exposing the corruption within Boss William M. Tweed's Tammany Hall.

50   Jackson, who then was Assistant Attorney General heading the Antitrust Division in the Department of Justice, spoke on Friday, January 29, 1937, at the Bar Association's annual dinner, which was held at the Waldorf-Astoria

Hotel in New York City. In this speech, Jackson criticized the Court for frustrating the democratic processes that had enacted what he described generally as New Deal "anti-monopoly" legislation. He accused the Court and "legal specialists" generally of "closing the roads to political compromise . . . [and] economic and social peace" by declaring new laws unconstitutional or "sometimes just sandbagg[ing] them with 'interpretation,'" noting that people historically have turned to dictatorship "when free government becomes too perplexing and futile. . . ." With specific reference to the Supreme Court, Jackson noted that there is no constitutional requirement that Supreme Court Justices be lawyers, and he asked the Bar Association to "[s]uppose some 'radical' administration should propose to pack it with men of other vocations." *See New Dealer Warns the Supreme Court*, N.Y. Times, Jan. 30, 1937, at 6. FDR proposed what came to be known as his "Court-packing" plan just one week later.

51 *See* Robert H. Jackson, The Struggle for Judicial Supremacy: A Study of a Crisis in American Power Politics (New York: Alfred A. Knopf, 1941).

52 *See* Charles Michelson, The Ghost Talks 168–70 (New York: G. P. Putnam's Sons, 1944). Michelson, a veteran newspaper reporter, became the Democratic National Committee's chief of publicity in 1929.

53 On February 26, 1937, FDR announced that he had reserved radio time for a "fireside chat" on the evening of March 9, and that he would leave Washington the next day for 10–14 days at Warm Springs, Georgia. *See* Turner Catledge, *Roosevelt Plans a Court Bill Tour, Washington Hears*, N.Y. Times, Feb. 27, 1937, at 1, 4.

54 *See Steward Machine Co. v. Davis*, 301 U.S. 548 (1937) (upholding the unemployment compensation provisions of the Social Security Act of 1935), and *Helvering v. Davis*, 301 U.S. 619 (1937) (upholding the Act's old-age benefit provisions). Assistant Attorney General Jackson was one of the two government attorneys who argued these cases before the Supreme Court. *See* 301 U.S. at 562–68 (reporting extracts from Jackson's oral argument in *Steward Machine*); 301 U.S. at 620–25 (summarizing the government's arguments in *Helvering v. Davis*).

55 This meeting occurred in Jackson's Department of Justice office on Friday, March 12, 1937—the day following his Senate Judiciary Committee testimony in defense of FDR's Court-packing plan. In addition to Senator George and Mr. Lovett, the Georgia contingent included Alexander W. Smith, Jr., President of the Georgia Bar Association. *See* AWS letter to RHJ, 3/13/1937, and ABL letter to RHJ, 3/15/1937, in RHJ LOC Box 33.

56 On May 28, 1937, Assistant Attorney General Jackson gave a speech titled "The Struggle Against Monopoly" at the annual meeting of the Georgia Bar Association, which was held at the Cloister Hotel in Sea Island, Georgia. *See* RHJ LOC Box 33 (text of speech). Published versions of the speech appeared in the 1937 Georgia Bar Reports and, thanks to Senator George, in

the *Congressional Record*. Although Jackson's speech did not mention the President's Court-packing plan directly, the speech did discuss judicial decisions that had thwarted public will and preserved the powers of economic monopolies by interpreting antitrust laws narrowly and illogically. *See id.*

57 *Cf.* U.S. Const., Art. II, sec. 2, cl. 2 ("he [the President] shall nominate, and by and with the Advice and Consent of the Senate, shall appoint . . . Judges of the supreme Court, and all other Officers of the United States, whose appointments are not herein provided for, and which shall be established by Law").

58 In July 1938, FDR had made a recess appointment of Floyd H. Roberts, a lawyer from Bristol, Virginia, to a newly created judgeship in the Western District of Virginia. On January 5, 1939, FDR sent Roberts's nomination to the Senate, where it was defeated by a vote of 72–9 on February 6. At that time, Roberts vacated his brief judgeship. Three months later, FDR nominated Armistead Dobie to fill the position.

59 This account of Judge Dobie's appointment includes material from the Phillips–Jackson interviews, pp. 824–26.

60 In April 1941, just days before FDR nominated Bright to serve in a new seat on the United States District Court for the Southern District of New York, Jackson dictated the following in a Confidential memorandum to an assistant: "Bright is 56 years of age and a well-to-do man. He can afford to take this post and he won't have to sell his decisions in order to live. He has been a Democrat all of his life and has consistently supported the President, which in that neck of the woods indicates that he is a man of liberal tendencies. Notwithstanding this, he represents substantial interests." RHJ to Matthew F. McGuire, 4/11/1941, in RHJ LOC Box 91.

61 The text regarding Judge Bright's appointment includes material from the Phillips–Jackson interviews, pp. 827–29.

Chapter 3

1 The Walter-Logan bill—named for its co-sponsors, Representative Francis Eugene Walter (D.-PA) (1894–1963) and Senator Marvel Mills ("M.M.") Logan (D.-KY) (1874–1939)—was based on an American Bar Association proposal. The bill sought to control the growth and power of administrative agencies.

2 FDR vetoed the bill on December 18, 1940, attaching Attorney General Jackson's analysis to the presidential veto message.

3 *See* 86 Cong. Record 13,943–13,945 (1940). Jackson argued in his letter to FDR that the bill would have flooded the courts with minor administrative matters that previously would have been regarded as justiciable cases or controversies, and that this in turn would have violated separation of powers doctrine by putting the control of the executive branch into the hands of the judiciary.

4   The text regarding the Walter-Logan bill incorporates material from the Phillips–Jackson interviews, pp. 168–69.

5   *See The President Presents Plan No. V to Carry Out the Provisions of the Reorganization Act,* THE PUBLIC PAPERS AND ADDRESSES OF FRANKLIN D. ROOSEVELT 223–29 (1940). FDR transmitted this plan to Congress on May 22, 1940. It went into effect on June 14, 1940.

6   The notes that Jackson mentions, which he apparently dictated later in the day on May 21, 1940, are in RHJ LOC Box 90.

7   The text describing FDR's decision to transfer the Bureau of Immigration from the Department of Labor to the Department of Justice incorporates material from Jackson's dictated notes of May 21, 1940, which are in RHJ LOC Box 90.

8   Jackson is quoting from notes that he apparently dictated later in the day on May 29, 1940. These notes are in RHJ LOC Box 90.

9   The text describing Jackson's meeting with FDR about the Department of Justice need for $9 million to handle its new immigration responsibilities and FDR's reaction to French ambassador St. Quentin incorporates material from Jackson's dictated notes of May 29, 1940, which are in RHJ LOC Box 90.

10 Jackson was born in 1892 on his family's farm in Warren County, Pennsylvania.

11 The discussion concerning the transfer of Immigration from Labor to Justice includes material from the Phillips–Jackson interviews, pp. 1004–6.

12 *See* Executive Order 8560, § XXVII, ¶ 375 (Oct. 4, 1940).

13 This trip occurred on the weekend of April 11-12, 1942. On that Saturday afternoon, FDR, along with Postmaster General Frank Walker, press secretary Stephen Early, presidential physician Dr. Ross McIntire, and Justice Jackson, was driven from the White House to Charlottesville. White House Usher's Diary entry, 4/11/1942, in Pare Lorentz Chronology, FDR Library.

14 When Jackson was Attorney General and at the time he was writing this book, the operative statute provided that "[t]he Attorney General shall give his advice and opinion on questions of law, whenever required by the President." 5 U.S.C. § 303 (1940). For today's equivalent provision, see 28 U.S.C. § 511.

15 During this April 1942 weekend trip to Charlottesville, FDR also discussed breaking up Germany after the war, his desire that Jackson remain on the Supreme Court for the present, and the possibility of his receiving a postwar presidential assignment. *See* pages 106–7.

    In a lighter vein, FDR also asked Jackson during this trip for information about a northern Virginia home, near Jackson's own Hickory Hill, where First Lady Dolley Madison had sought refuge as British troops approached Washington in August 1814. Jackson later sent FDR a real estate flier describing this estate. It reported that this Fairfax County property was named

"Salona" after an Italian castle, and that in addition to quartering Mrs. Madison during the War of 1812, it had functioned early in the Civil War as the headquarters of the Army of the Potomac under General McClellan. Jackson reported to the President that Salona, located about half a mile from Hickory Hill, was then for sale and had "great possibilities" if any of their "wealthy friends wanted to do a restoration job." RHJ to FDR, 5/11/1942, FDR Library, PPF 6601.

16   The "Gold Clause" cases were argued before the Supreme Court on January 8, 9, 10, and 11, 1935. Attorney General Cummings both opened and closed the government's oral argument in the cases. His opening arguments, which were printed in full by the Government Printing Office, are excerpted at 294 U.S. 251–72. On February 18, the Court decided the cases in the government's favor by 5–4 votes. *See Norman v. Baltimore & Ohio R.R. Co.*, 294 U.S. 240 (1935) (upholding the June 5, 1933, Joint Resolution of Congress that had nullified "gold clauses"—provisions giving obligees contractual rights to be paid in U.S. gold coin—in private contractual provisions); *Nortz v. United States*, 294 U.S. 317 (1935) (upholding the power of the U.S. Treasury to compel "gold certificate" owners to surrender them for currency, not gold specie); *Perry v. United States*, 294 U.S. 330 (1935) (holding that owners of U.S. bonds payable in gold may be paid in currency, even if gold is more valuable than the obligation of the bond).

17   When FDR took office in 1933, he took United States currency off the gold standard, which was about to collapse because the ratio of gold reserves to outstanding currency plus bank deposits was very imbalanced. FDR thus acted on March 6, 1933, to prohibit all banks from paying out or conducting any international transactions in gold bullion. His basis for acting was the 1917 Trading with the Enemy Act, which granted authority as a wartime measure. Congress then passed the Emergency Banking Act, which authorized the Treasury to require all banks to surrender all gold coin, bullion, and certificates for paper money. Through this legislation, Congress nationalized gold and authorized the devaluation of the dollar. FDR's goal was to devalue the dollar and thereby raise prices of domestic goods and raw materials, particularly farm products. By the fall of 1933, when the dollar had depreciated compared to several foreign currencies, FDR prescribed a gold-buying plan, through the Reconstruction Finance Corporation, to raise the price of gold. On January 15, 1934, FDR terminated the gold-buying experiment and consolidated matters by seeking to devalue the dollar, in comparison to gold, to between 50 and 60 percent of its face value. FDR took this action pursuant to the Gold Reserve Act of 1934, which authorized this dollar devaluation, removed remaining gold standard symbols, and removed all gold coins from circulation.

18   *See* Sidney Ratner, *Was the Supreme Court Packed By President Grant?*, 50 POLITICAL SCI. Q. 343–58 (Sept. 1935) (discussing Grant's 1870 appointments

of Justices William Strong and Joseph P. Bradley and the Supreme Court's subsequent overruling of *Hepburn v. Griswold*, 75 U.S. (8 Wallace) 603 (1870), in *The Legal Tender Cases* (*Knox v. Lee* and *Parker v. Davis*, 78 U.S. (11 Wallace) 682 (1871) (mem.), 79 U.S. (12 Wallace) 457 (1872) (opinions delivered)); *see also* ROBERT H. JACKSON, THE STRUGGLE FOR JUDICIAL SUPREMACY 41–44 (1941) (discussing these events).

19   *See* RHJ Memorandum for The President, The Secretary of the Treasury [Morgenthau], The General Counsel of the Treasury [Oliphant] and George D. Haas, 1/12/1935, in RHJ LOC Box 75 (carbon copy). In this memo, Jackson mistakenly referred to the White House conference as having occurred on "Thursday evening, December 10, 1935" rather than January 10, 1935.

20   The text regarding the *Gold Clause Cases* includes material from the Phillips–Jackson interviews, pp. 430–31.

21   *Schechter Poultry Corp. v. United States*, 295 U.S. 495 (1935) (holding National Industrial Recovery Act invalid because it improperly delegated legislative authority to Executive Branch and attempted to regulate intrastate commerce that affected interstate commerce indirectly).

22   In 1935, at his Friday press conference that came four days after the Supreme Court had invalidated the NRA, FDR used the phrase "horse and buggy" to blast the Court's constitutional interpretation: "You see the implications of the decision. That is why I say it is one of the most important decisions ever rendered in this country. And the issue is not going to be a partisan issue for a minute. The issue is going to be whether we go one way or the other. Don't call it right or left; that is just first-year high school language, just about. It is not right or left—it is a question for national decision on a very important problem of Government. We are the only nation in the world that has not solved that problem. We thought we were solving it, and now it has been thrown right straight in our faces. We have been relegated to the horse-and-buggy definition of interstate commerce."

Four years later, after the Court had changed direction and he had appointed his first four Justices to the Court, FDR explained, in an address to Congress with the Supreme Court in attendance, that his 1935 "horse and buggy" comment had not been made in "derogation"—"We used it rather to explain the tedious delays and the local antagonisms and jealousies which beset our early paths, and we use it perhaps to remind our citizens of today that the automobile, the railroad, the airplane, the electrical impulse over the wire and through the ether leave to no citizens an excuse for sectionalism, for delay in the execution of the public business or for a failure to maintain a full understanding of the acceleration of the processes of civilization."

23   The text regarding the *Schechter Poultry* decision and the NRA includes material from the Phillips–Jackson interviews, pp. 428–29.

24   RHJ autobiography, pp. 159–60, RHJ LOC Box 189.

25   *See* 308 U.S. 338 (1939).

26 *See* Department of Justice release, Mar. 18, 1940, in RHJ LOC Box 94.

27 FDR Confidential Memorandum for the Attorney General, in RHJ LOC Box 94.

28 On March 19, 1941, FDR left Washington by train for Miami. He was accompanied by Jackson, Harold Ickes, "Pa" Watson, Rear Admiral Ross T. McIntire, and Stephen Early. Beginning on March 20, they spent the next nine days aboard the USS *Potomac*, sailing off the coast of Florida. Because the German Navy was by then an active threat throughout the Atlantic, the *Potomac* was followed closely throughout its voyage by the USS *Benson*, a destroyer which had its guns manned and depth bombs and torpedoes at the ready. *See generally* RHJ's copy of the 20-page LOG OF THE INSPECTION TRIP AND CRUISE ON BOARD U. S. S. POTOMAC, 19 MARCH–1 APRIL 1941 (signed "For Bob Jackson from Franklin D Roosevelt"), RHJ LOC Box 30.

29 It is unclear exactly what testimony Jackson was describing. On May 19, 1941, Fly testified before the House Judiciary Committee in closed session. At that time, the House Rules Committee was considering requests to expedite passage of legislation that would permit the Attorney General to authorize the FBI to conduct wire tapping in cases involving espionage, sabotage, extortion, or kidnapping. Although a transcript of Fly's vigorous private testimony in opposition to the bill was never made available to the Rules Committee, Representative Francis E. Walter (D.-PA) reported to it that "Mr. Fly made a strong statement. He said a great dragnet would be set out."

30 This discussion includes material from the Phillips–Jackson interviews, pp. 972–73.

31 Princess Stephanie Marie Hohenlohe Waldenburg Schillingsfürst (1896–1972), a citizen of Hungary and a descendant of Europe's Hohenzollern dynasty, entered the United States from Great Britain on a visitor's visa in late 1939. One year later, Attorney General Jackson refused to extend her temporary permit because of her close associations with German government officials. Although Jackson ordered that the Princess be deported immediately, this proved to be impossible because England refused to accept her return and Germany, Japan, and other countries en route to Hungary refused to grant her transit visas. In early 1941, after the Princess had been arrested by the U.S. government and held without bail, she agreed to provide information and documents regarding her own and others' activities; she was released from custody and reportedly left the country. She returned to the United States later in 1941, and following the Japanese attack on Pearl Harbor and Germany's declaration of war against the United States, she was arrested by the FBI later in December 1941 as a dangerous alien. For the duration of World War II, Princess Hohenlohe was interned by the United States, first at a facility in Philadelphia and later at a Texas camp for enemy aliens. She was paroled in May 1945.

32 Sir William George Eden Wiseman (1885–1962) was the head of British intelligence in the United States during World War I. He became a permanent

resident alien in the United States in 1924 and worked in New York City as general partner in the Kuhn, Loeb and Company investment bank from 1929 until 1958.

33 For example, in one of the short notes that FDR customarily dictated to his Attorney General, "That Man" wrote that "That *Hohenlohe* woman ought to be got out of the country as a matter of good discipline. Have her put on a boat to Japan or Vladivostok." FDR to RHJ, 3/7/1941, in RHJ LOC Box 94. On another occasion, after Princess Stephanie had negotiated her (ultimately temporary) release by immigration officials in return for information she could provide, FDR scrawled a note to Jackson that called her "his girlfriend." This document, in RHJ LOC Box 94, is reproduced on page 70.

34 In December 1941—after Jackson had become a Supreme Court Justice, and after Germany had declared war on the United States—Princess Stephanie was arrested by the FBI. She was charged as a dangerous alien and interned at the detention home of the Immigration Bureau in Gloucester, New Jersey. She remained in the enemy alien camp until May 18, 1945.

35 The discussion of Princess Stephanie includes material from the Phillips–Jackson interviews, pp. 1022–23.

36 Copies of these documents are preserved in RHJ LOC Box 94.

37 RHJ to JJM, 5/16/1941 at 2, in RHJ LOC Box 94.

38 The text regarding law enforcement methods in labor-related investigations includes material from the Phillips–Jackson interviews, pp. 976–80.

39 *See Southern Steamship Co. v. NLRB*, 316 U.S. 31 (1942), where the Court held 5–4 that the NLRB had no statutory power to order the reinstatement of seamen who had been discharged for acts of mutiny. Justice Byrnes wrote the Court's majority opinion, which Chief Justice Harlan Fiske Stone and Associate Justices Owen Roberts, Felix Frankfurter, and Robert Jackson joined—the latter two, like Byrnes, being FDR appointees to the Court. Justice Stanley Reed wrote a dissenting opinion, which Justices Hugo Black, William Douglas, and Frank Murphy each joined—FDR appointees all. The Court's decision, which FDR applauded in the private conversation that Jackson recounts in the text, ironically rejected the position that FDR's Solicitor General had urged on behalf of his NLRB.

40 At this point in his Columbia oral history interview, Jackson added "and I didn't think he ought to." He later deleted that phrase when he was editing his transcribed interview. *See* RHJ LOC Box 191, p. 1029.

41 Phillips–Jackson interviews, pp. 1151–52.

42 Phillips–Jackson interviews, p. 917.

Chapter 4

1 "Charles the Baptist" was a favorite FDR nickname for Chief Justice Charles Evans Hughes, who had been brought up as a Baptist and continued to have some affiliation with the church throughout his life. As Justice Douglas

explained years later, FDR used this nickname when he mentioned Hughes while playing poker because he (FDR) recognized that Hughes had "shown his poker-playing capacities when he had helped to defeat" Roosevelt's 1937 Court-packing plan. WILLIAM O. DOUGLAS, GO EAST, YOUNG MAN: THE EARLY YEARS 329–30 (New York: Random House, 1974) (quoting FDR to Justice Felix Frankfurter, 11/21/1939: "Because of your seniority, I suggest that you hold a seminar for Bill [Douglas], asking him to apply the vivid rules of life in place of the musty rules of law and get him to answer in language which even the President can understand the simple query 'Do Baptists play poker?'").

2   The baby, Harold McEwen Ickes, was born two days later, on Monday, September 4, 1939, at Johns Hopkins Hospital in Baltimore. He and his mother promptly received, among their gifts, a bouquet of chrysanthemums from Jackson.

3   Viola A. ("Vi") Bartz was Jackson's secretary in the Office of the Solicitor General at the Department of Justice.

4   The Statute of Westminster gave Canada virtual legislative and executive autonomy from British rule. Statute of Westminster 1931, 4, 22d23 Geo. 5c.4., 7 Halsbury's Statutes (4th ed.).

5   Indeed, Secretary Hull apparently never learned that this idea originated with Jackson. See 1 CORDELL HULL, THE MEMOIRS OF CORDELL HULL 679 (New York: Macmillan, 1948) (describing FDR's call to King and his response, but not mentioning Jackson at all).

6   Jackson probably dictated this account on September 7, 1939, which is, according to Roosevelt White House records, the only date on which Jackson met with FDR between September 5 and FDR's September 8 proclamation of a limited national emergency. See Stenographer's Diary entry, 9/7/1939 ("1700— Gen. George C. Marshall, Adm. Harold R. Stark, Robert H. Jackson"), in Pare Lorentz Chronology, FDR Library.

7   This document, with Jackson's marginalia noting FDR's item-by-item guidance, is in RHJ LOC Box 83.

8   FDR's draft proclamation, which he scrawled in pencil on two pages of note paper, is in RHJ LOC Box 83.

9   Jackson mentions this proposal again, this time criticizing its economic illogic, on pages 132–33.

10   See Proclamation No. 2352, Proclaiming a Limited National Emergency, THE PUBLIC PAPERS AND ADDRESSES OF FRANKLIN D. ROOSEVELT 488–89 (Sept. 8, 1939).

The foregoing text is Jackson's September 1939 memorandum (see undated eight-page typescript in RHJ LOC Box 30), supplemented by material from his 1944 draft autobiography that recounted some of the same events (see RHJ autobiography, pp. 213–20, in RHJ LOC Box 189). Jackson apparently wrote the 1944 account from memory, without consulting the memorandum in his files, because the later version varies in some details from the contemporaneous account. Jackson's later account seems to be an interesting instance of his memory, with the passage of time, changing its emphases and compressing its recollection of important personal and national events. I tried, in my editing, to take this process into account by making careful decisions about how the two versions fit together correctly, and by relying most heavily on Jackson's earlier version.

11   Phillips–Jackson interviews, pp. 921–22.

12   Alfred Thayer Mahan (1840–1914), a United States Navy officer, gave lectures as a faculty member at the U.S. Naval War College in Newport, Rhode Island, that were published in 1890 as THE INFLUENCE OF SEA POWER UPON HISTORY, 1660–1773. Mahan became a prolific writer of many books and articles, advancing the historical thesis that sea power explained national success and advocating that the United States become and remain a great naval power. FDR, at age fifteen, received Mahan's book as a Christmas present in 1897, a time when the book was receiving prominent public attention, and he quoted from it the following month in a debate at Groton.

13   By RHJ: *E.g.,* HENRY L. STIMSON & MCGEORGE BUNDY, ON ACTIVE SERVICE IN PEACE AND WAR (New York: Harper & Bros., 1947); 1 CORDELL HULL, THE MEMOIRS OF CORDELL HULL (New York: Macmillan, 1948); FRANKLIN D. ROOSEVELT, 2 F.D.R.: HIS PERSONAL LETTERS, 1928–1945 (New York: Duell, Sloan & Pearce, 1950); WINSTON CHURCHILL, THEIR FINEST HOUR (Boston: Houghton Mifflin, 1949). These are cited herein by author's name only. Strangely, the transaction is barely mentioned in ROBERT E. SHERWOOD, ROOSEVELT AND HOPKINS: AN INTIMATE HISTORY (New York: Harper & Bros., 1948), and in SUMNER WELLES, THE TIME FOR DECISION (New York: Harper & Bros., 1944). It is mentioned only in garbled form in JAMES A. FARLEY, JIM FARLEY'S STORY: THE ROOSEVELT YEARS (New York: Whittlesey House/McGraw-Hill, 1948).

14   By RHJ: The most complete and accurate use of available materials, including some otherwise unpublished, is WILLIAM L. LANGER & S. EVERETT GLEASON, THE CHALLENGE TO ISOLATION: THE WORLD CRISIS OF 1937–1940 AND AMERICAN FOREIGN POLICY (New York: Harper & Bros., 1952) (2 vols.).

15   By RHJ: Hull, p. 831.

16   King George VI asked Churchill to become Prime Minister and he accepted on the evening of May 10, 1940, following the resignation of Churchill's Conservative Party colleague, Prime Minister Neville Chamberlain.

17   By RHJ: Churchill, pp. 24, 398.

18   By RHJ: Hull, pp. 831–32; Churchill, p. 25.

19   By RHJ: Roosevelt, p. 1036.

20   By RHJ: Hull, p. 832.

21   By RHJ: Roosevelt, p. 1036.

22   By RHJ: Churchill, p. 57.

23 On June 10, 1940, FDR was the commencement speaker at the University of Virginia. He described the course of U.S. diplomatic contacts with Italy and, responding to Mussolini's declaration of war just hours earlier, said that "the hand that held the dagger has stuck it into the back of its neighbor." Headlines immediately dubbed this FDR's "stab-in-the-back" speech. *See, e.g., Italy at War, Ready to Attack; Stab in Back, Says Roosevelt*, N.Y. TIMES, June 11, 1940, at 1; cf. *Stiletto*, LONDON TIMES, June 11, 1940 (editorial).

24 By RHJ: Churchill, pp. 132–33, 398.

25 By RHJ: Churchill, p. 188.

26 By RHJ: OFFICE OF UNITED STATES CHIEF OF COUNSEL FOR PROSECUTION OF AXIS CRIMINALITY, NAZI CONSPIRACY AND AGGRESSION (Washington: U.S. Govt. Printing Office, 1946) [(containing, in ten volumes known informally as "the Red Set," the briefing and other documentary evidence presented to the International Military Tribunal at Nuremberg)].

27 By RHJ: Churchill, pp. 401–2.

28 Beginning in 1939, Woodring disagreed with FDR's desire to provide military supplies to Great Britain.

29 By RHJ: Roosevelt, p. 1041.

30 Stimson diary entry, quoted in 2 Langer & Gleason, p. 749.

31 Wendell Willkie had received the Republican presidential nomination at its convention in Philadelphia on June 28, 1940. Three weeks later, the Democratic convention in Chicago nominated FDR as its candidate.

32 By RHJ: 2 Langer & Gleason, pp. 749–50.

33 By RHJ: Roosevelt, pp. 1050–51.

34 Knox had become publisher and part owner of the *Chicago Daily News*, one of the nation's largest daily newspapers, in 1931.

35 By RHJ: Churchill, pp. 402–3.

36 By RHJ: Hull, p. 832; Stimson puts it one day later, p. 356.

37 By RHJ: Hull, p. 833.

38 By RHJ: *Id.*

39 By RHJ: Churchill, pp. 409–10, 412.

40 By RHJ: In Great Britain, a treaty needs ratification or assent of Parliament only if it purports to alter the internal law through abridgment of the rights of British subjects. W. S. HOLDSWORTH, A HISTORY OF ENGLISH LAW (Boston: Little, Brown, 1937) (2d ed.).

41 By RHJ: "The Congress shall have Power to dispose of and make all needful Rules and Regulations respecting the Territory or other Property belonging to United States; . . ." U.S. CONST., Art. IV, § 3, cl. 2.

42 In a 1951 interview with the lawyer who was writing Jackson's biography, he suggested that it had been he, not FDR, who had this transatlantic telephone conversation with Churchill. *See* EUGENE C. GERHART, AMERICA'S ADVOCATE: ROBERT H. JACKSON 217 & 488 n. 25. I conclude that Jackson's later, written account is the more plausible version of the event.

43   By RHJ: Hull, pp. 837–40.

44   By RHJ: Churchill, pp. 115–18.

45   By RHJ: Stimson & Bundy, p. 357.

46   Jackson is referring here, somewhat defensively, to his legal opinion of August 27, 1940.

47   By RHJ: 2 Langer & Gleason, p. 758.

48   By RHJ: Roosevelt, pp. 1056–57.

49   By RHJ: 2 Langer & Gleason, p. 761.

50   By RHJ: JOSEPH BARNES, WILLKIE: THE EVENTS HE WAS PART OF—THE IDEAS HE FOUGHT FOR (New York: Simon & Schuster, 1952). The general attitude of fairness and objectivity of the Barnes biography convinced me that his errors were due to misinformation. That conviction as to one so well informed generally played an important part in my decision to write this account. The book by MARY EARHART DILLON, WENDELL WILLKIE, 1892–1944 (Philadelphia: Lippincott, 1952), does not even mention this subject.

51   By RHJ: Barnes, p. 201.

52   By RHJ: Compare Churchill, p. 401.

53   By RHJ: Barnes, p. 202.

54   By RHJ: Roosevelt, p. 1052.

55   By RHJ: Hull, p. 833.

56   By RHJ: Stimson, p. 357.

57   *See Ship Deal Backed in Gallup Survey*, N.Y. TIMES, Sept. 6, 1940, at 12.

58   By RHJ: Roosevelt, pp. 1050–51.

59   By RHJ: 2 Langer & Gleason, p. 754; see Barnes, p. 202.

60   By RHJ: "During a war in which the United States is a neutral nation, it shall be unlawful to send out of the jurisdiction of the United States any vessel built, armed, or equipped as a vessel of war, or converted from a private vessel into a vessel of war, with any intent or under any agreement or contract, written or oral, that such vessel shall be delivered to a belligerent nation, or to an agent, officer, or citizen of such nation, or with reasonable cause to believe that the said vessel shall or will be employed in the service of any such belligerent nation after its departure from the jurisdiction of the United States." Act of June 15, 1917, § 3, 40 Stat. 22, 18 U.S.C. § 33. *See also* Act of April 20, 1818, § 3, 3 Stat. 448, as amended, 18 U.S.C. § 23.

61   Following the Civil War, the United States and Great Britain agreed in their 1871 Treaty of Washington to submit to a five-nation Tribunal of Arbitration in Geneva, Switzerland, U.S. claims for damage to commerce caused by Confederate cruisers, including the *Alabama*, that had been fitted out or supplied from British ports during the War. In 1872, the Tribunal ordered Britain to pay, for its negligence, $15.5 million to the United States.

62   By RHJ: Mr. Farley badly (though I am sure without intention) confuses these boats that I ruled could not be completed for Britain with the destroyers that I advised could be exchanged by the government for bases. He

quotes Vice President Garner (as of a date that I cannot make out) as telling
him that the Cabinet was considering the transfer of fifty destroyers in
exchange for the bases, and that

> [t]he Boss said that the transfer had been cleared legally by the Attorney
> General, and Charley Edison spoke up and said the transfer was being
> arranged over his protest," Garner told me. "The Boss didn't like what
> Edison said, any more than he liked what Woodring did. The interesting
> part is that after the meeting, Attorney General Jackson came to me and
> said that in spite of the statement made that he had approved the sale and
> held it to be legal, he had not made such a decision. I told him that he
> should have so declared himself at the Cabinet meeting and I say now he
> should have said he had not held the transfer to be legal, if he did not."
> JAMES A. FARLEY, JIM FARLEY'S STORY: THE ROOSEVELT YEARS 242–43.

The first discrepancy in this is that at no time after June 20 was either
Woodring or Edison in the Cabinet, they having been succeeded on that date.
The exchange for bases was never before the Cabinet before August 2. The
conversation could not therefore relate to the destroyer deal. The other error,
assuming that the conversation related to the small boats, is that the President
said the transfer had been cleared legally by the Attorney General. I could
hardly pass in silence, nor forget, so false a statement had it ever been made.
My recollection is quite to the contrary: the President said the transfer had *not*
been cleared, and that was what brought about my informal expression of
view. The Vice President sat at the far end of the table from the President,
and it is quite probable that he misunderstood him. Later, I think Mr. Farley
or Mr. Walter Trohan of the CHICAGO TRIBUNE staff, who helped Farley in his
writing, attributed the Garner report to the wrong transaction. I think the
Hopkins memo to me shows clearly enough that those who were most concerned saw nothing ambiguous in the Attorney General's statement. Another
Texan Cabinet member has indicated that it was not my habit to be ambiguous in such matters. JESSE JONES, FIFTY BILLION DOLLARS: MY THIRTEEN YEARS
WITH THE RFC (1932-1945) 307 (New York: Macmillan, 1951).

63   By RHJ: Roosevelt, p. 1048.

64   *See* Charles C. Burlingham, Thomas D. Thacher, George Rublee, & Dean
      Acheson, *No Legal Bar Seen to Transfer of Destroyers*, N.Y. TIMES, Aug. 11, 1940,
      at 8–9 (letter). Charles Culp Burlingham ("CCB") (1858–1959) was a very
      prominent New York lawyer, bar leader, and civic reformer who advanced
      many judicial and political careers. Thomas D. Thacher (1881–1950) had, as
      of 1940, been a federal prosecutor, practiced law privately and served as a
      Federal District Judge and as Solicitor General of the United States. George
      Rublee (1868–1950) had been, before 1940, an acting Federal Trade Commis-
      sioner, President Wilson's appointee to various World War I–related posi-
      tions, a founder of the Washington, D.C., law firm that came to be known

as Covington, Burling, Rublee, Acheson & Shorb, U.S. legal adviser in negotiations in Mexico and in London, and under FDR, director of an intergov-
ernmental refugee committee who negotiated with Nazi Germany during
1938–39 in an unsuccessful effort to get permission for German Jews to emi-
grate. Dean Gooderham Acheson (1893–1971) was, at the time, Rublee's law
partner and a prominent Washington lawyer; he later became an Assistant
Secretary of State under FDR and first Under Secretary and then Secretary
of State under President Truman.

65 By RHJ: 2 Langer & Gleason, p. 762.

66 By RHJ: Churchill, pp. 409–10; Hull, p. 836.

67 By RHJ: "Notwithstanding the provision of any other law, no military or
naval weapon, ship, boat, aircraft, munitions, supplies, or equipment, to
which the United States has title, in whole or in part, or which have been
contracted for, shall hereafter be transferred, exchanged, sold, or otherwise
disposed of in any manner whatsoever unless the Chief of Naval Operations in the case of naval material, and the Chief of Staff of the Army in the
case of military material, shall first certify that such material is not essential
to the defense of the United States." § 14(a), 54 Stat. 681, 10 U.S.C. § 1262a(a),
34 U.S.C. § 546e(a).

68 By RHJ: 2 Langer & Gleason, pp. 755–57.

69 By RHJ: Stimson & Bundy, p. 356.

70 By RHJ: For the text of the announcement of the exchange sent by the
State Department to allied countries, see UNITED STATES DEPARTMENT OF
STATE, PEACE AND WAR: UNITED STATES FOREIGN POLICY, 1931–1941 180 (Wash-
ington: U.S. Govt. Printing Office, 1942).

71 By RHJ: Published in full, 2 Langer & Gleason, pp. 762–63.

72 By RHJ: 2 Langer & Gleason, pp. 749–50.

73 By RHJ: Churchill, pp. 402–3.

74 By RHJ: Hull, p. 834.

75 By RHJ: Roosevelt, pp. 1056–57.

76 By RHJ: PUBLIC PAPERS AND ADDRESSES OF FRANKLIN D. ROOSEVELT 393
(1940). When later the Supreme Court held the Bermuda leased territory to
have become a "possession" of the United States within its statutes, contrary to the views of the State Department, I felt obliged by the spirit and
letter of the negotiations to dissent. *Vermilya-Brown Co., Inc. v. Connell*, 335
U.S. 377, 390 (1948) (Jackson, J., joined by Vinson, C.J., and Frankfurter and
Burton, JJ., dissenting).

77 By RHJ: Stimson & Bundy, p. 359.

78 By RHJ: Churchill, p. 666. This is in the appendix. He makes no mention of
the matter in his text.

79 By RHJ: 2 Langer & Gleason, pp. 770–74, summarizes quite accurately the
public reaction.

80 By RHJ: Article 8 of the Hague Convention XIII, to which the United States

adhered, reads: "A neutral government is bound to employ the means at its disposal to prevent the fitting out or arming within its jurisdiction of any vessel which it has reason to believe is intended to cruise, or engage in hostile operations against a Power with which that Government is at peace. It is also bound to display the same vigilance to prevent the departure from its jurisdiction of any vessel intended to cruise or engage in hostile operations, which had been adapted entirely or partly within the said jurisdiction for use in war." *See* The Reports to the Hague Conferences of 1899 and 1907 833 (Oxford: Clarendon Press, 1916) (James Brown Scott, ed.). The meaning of this to international lawyers as related to these ships and the mosquito boats was stated as follows:

> Sec. 334. Whereas a neutral is in no wise obliged by his duty of impartiality to prevent his subjects from selling armed vessels to the belligerents, such armed vessels being merely contraband of war, a neutral is bound to employ the means at his disposal to prevent his subjects from building, fitting out, or arming, to the order of either belligerent, vessels intended to be used as men of war, and to prevent the departure from his jurisdiction of any vessel which, by order of either belligerent, has been adapted to warlike use. The difference between selling armed vessels to belligerents and building them to order is usually defined in the following way:—
>
>> An armed ship, being contraband of war, is in no wise different from other kinds of contraband, provided that she is not manned in a neutral port, so that she can commit hostilities at once after having reached the open sea. A subject of a neutral who builds an armed ship, or arms a merchantman, not to the order of a belligerent, but intending to sell her to a belligerent, does not differ from a manufacturer of arms who intends to sell them to a belligerent. There is nothing to prevent a neutral from allowing his subjects to sell armed vessels, and to deliver them to belligerents, either in a neutral port or in a belligerent port. . . .

2 Lassa Oppenheim, International Law 574–75 (London & New York: Longmans, Green, 1935) (5th ed., H. Lauterpacht, ed.).

81   By RHJ: *See Speech to Congress on Repeal of Arms Embargo*, Public Papers and Addresses of Franklin D. Roosevelt 512 (Sept. 21, 1939).

82   By RHJ: Particularly when war in Europe first broke out and the President proclaimed neutrality and a partial emergency. Joseph Alsop & Robert Kintner, American White Paper: The Story of American Diplomacy and the Second World War 70–72 (New York: Simon & Schuster, 1940).

83   The speech, which was read for Jackson because rough seas prevented him from traveling to Havana to deliver it in person, was published widely. *See, e.g.*, Robert H. Jackson, *International Order*, 27 Am. Bar Assn. J. 275–79 (1941); *Address of Robert H. Jackson, Attorney General of the United States, International Bar Association, Havana, Cuba*, 35 Am. J. Int'l Law 348–59 (1941).

84   Jackson appears to be referring to the Japanese attacks, from Pearl Harbor through Bataan to the assault on Manila itself, which resulted in the fall of the Philippines on May 7, 1942.

85   Jackson was referring to Stimson's dairy entry regarding a War Cabinet meeting on Tuesday, November 25, 1941: FDR "brought up the event that we were likely to be attacked perhaps (as soon as) next Monday [December 1], for the Japanese are notorious for making an attack without warning, and the question was what we should do. The question was how we should maneuver them into the position for firing the first shot without allowing too much danger to ourselves. It was a difficult proposition." This diary entry became public in March 1946, when Stimson produced it to the Congressional Pearl Harbor Investigating Committee and it released the information. *See* William S. White, *Roosevelt, Aides Had Agreed on War If Japan Hit British*, N.Y. TIMES, Mar. 22, 1946, at 1, 15.

86   Phillips–Jackson interviews, pp. 1118–27.

87   In 1942, FDR asked Justice James F. Byrnes, whom he had appointed to the Supreme Court only one year earlier, to resign. After Byrnes did so, FDR made him head of the Office of War Mobilization (OWM), which later became the Office of War Mobilization and Reconversion (OWMR). From his White House office, Byrnes functioned as "assistant president," managing domestic affairs, military and civilian, for the duration of World War II and freeing FDR to concentrate on the conduct of the war.

88   General "Pa" Watson, who was FDR's appointments secretary, maintained his permanent residence in Charlottesville. Regarding this weekend trip, see pages 64–65, where Jackson recounts FDR on this occasion discussing the merits of having legal counsel in the White House and announcing that he had appointed Judge Sam Rosenman to serve in such a capacity.

89   Phillips–Jackson interviews, pp. 1128–30.

90   FDR demanded "unconditional surrender" on January 24, 1943, at the joint press conference with British Prime Minister Winston Churchill that concluded their meetings at Casablanca: "I think we have all had it in our hearts and heads before, but I don't think that it has ever been put down on paper by the Prime Minister and myself, and that is the determination that peace can come to the world only by the total elimination of German and Japanese war power. Some of you Britishers know the old story—we had a General called U.S. Grant. His name was Ulysses Simpson Grant, but in my, and the Prime Minister's, early days he was called 'Unconditional Surrender' Grant. The elimination of German, Japanese, and Italian war power means the unconditional surrender by Germany, Italy, and Japan."

91   For a survey of the historical record on the controversy surrounding FDR's demand for "unconditional surrender" and analysis of whether it strengthened the will of the German people to resist, thus prolonging the war, see ROBERT DALLEK, FRANKLIN D. ROOSEVELT AND AMERICAN FOREIGN POLICY, 1932–1945 373–76 & 612 n. 8 (New York: Oxford Univ. Press, 1995).

92 In February 1862, then Brigadier General Ulysses S. Grant commanded the
Union forces attacking the Confederate garrison at Fort Donelson on
the Cumberland River west of Dover, Tennessee. As the Union gained the
upper hand, the Confederate general sent Grant a note proposing an
armistice and asking him to appoint commissioners to negotiate terms for
Confederate surrender of the fort and its forces. Grant immediately, and
soon famously, wrote back that "[n]o terms except an unconditional and
immediate surrender can be accepted. I propose to move immediately upon
your works." The Confederate general then capitulated, writing Grant "to
accept the ungenerous and unchivalrous terms" of surrender that he had
proposed and giving the Union its first major victory of the Civil War.

93 Following the November 1917 Russian revolution, President Wilson refused
to recognize the new Soviet government or embrace its vision of world
peace through revolution. Instead, in a January 1918 address to Congress, he
offered his vision for the world's future in the form of "Fourteen Points,"
including national self-determination and a League of Nations.

94 Phillips–Jackson interviews, pp. 1137–40.

95 See SAMUEL I. ROSENMAN, WORKING WITH ROOSEVELT 542–43 (New York:
Harper & Bros., 1952).

96 Phillips–Jackson interviews, pp. 1148–50.

97 Phillips–Jackson interviews, p. 818.

Chapter 5

1 In 1942, when the functions of the Office of Production Management were
taken over by the War Production Board, FDR demoted OPM co-director
Knudsen to the position of Director of War Production in the War Department, where he served for the duration of World War II.

2 Phillips–Jackson interviews, pp. 920–21.

3 In the summer of 1933, FDR sent an American delegation to participate in
the London Economic Conference (also known as the World Economic
Conference), which sought to devise strategies to respond to the global
depression. After the Americans, led by Secretary of State Hull, had devised
a plan to stabilize global currencies and persuaded other nations tentatively
to support it, FDR released a statement advocating internal economic
reform at the national level before international currency reform. His statement, which came to be called the "bombshell message," undercut the
American proposal in London and effectively destroyed the conference.

4 See New Deal Is Ready to War on Slump, Jackson Declares, N.Y. TIMES, Dec. 27,
1937, at 1 (reporting Jackson's December 26, 1937, evening radio address on
the Mutual Broadcasting System).

5 See Clifford K. Berryman, OUT ON A LIMB!, WASH. EVENING STAR, Jan. 4,
1938, p. 1 (editorial cartoon), reproduced in this book.

6   *See The Text of President Roosevelt's Message to Congress on Monopoly*, N.Y.
     TIMES, Apr. 30, 1938, at 2.

7   *See* Bernard Kilgore, *New Deal Trust Busters Fight Drift to NRA Idea Urged on
     White House*, WALL ST. J., Jan. 29, 1938, at 1, 4 (reporting Jackson's January 28,
     1938, speech before the New York Press Association at Syracuse).

8   Phillips–Jackson interviews, pp. 592–601.

9   See note 83, Chapter 4, which cites published versions of this speech.

10   RHJ letter to E.W. Proxmire, Harvard University teaching fellow [and
     future United States Senator], 3/6/1947, in RHJ LOC Box 18.

11   Dr. Hugo Eckener (1868–1954), as a young airship pilot in Germany, worked
     with Count Ferdinand Adolf August Heinrich Zeppelin to design and build
     the airships that came to be known by his name. After Zeppelin's death in
     1917 and the conclusion of World War I, Eckener took over the Zeppelin
     Company. In 1928, he built the largest airship to date, the *Graf Zeppelin*, and
     in 1929 he piloted it around the world. Eckener's achievements earned him a
     Manhattan ticker tape parade. President Hoover compared him to Colum-
     bus and Magellan. In 1937, his aircraft *Hindenburg*, which was filled with
     combustible hydrogen because the United States would not sell inert, non-
     combustible helium to Germany, burned and crashed. In May 1938, Eckener
     traveled to the United States to lobby for the resumption of helium sales to
     his company.

12   The *Hindenburg*, which was filled with hydrogen, burned and crashed at
     Lakehurst, New Jersey, on May 6, 1937.

13   Ickes believed that the sale would have military importance to Germany
     and thus was prohibited by statute.

14   Jackson's written analysis and conclusion to this effect—a paper he probably
     brought with him to this White House meeting with FDR—is contained in
     RHJ LOC Box 82.

15   This passage regarding Eckener's request for helium and Ickes's response
     incorporates material from the Phillips–Jackson interviews, pp. 681–83.

Chapter 6

1   This paragraph includes material from the Phillips–Jackson interviews, pp.
     492–93.

2   This text regarding antitrust litigation against the motion picture industry
     includes material from the Phillips–Jackson interviews, pp. 493–94.

3   *See* FDR letter to RHJ ("My dear Bob"), 10/22/1937. This document, which
     is in RHJ LOC Box 79, is reproduced on page 121.

4   The Robinson-Patman Antidiscrimination Act, ch. 592, 49 Stat. 1526 (1936),
     protects small businesses against predatory pricing practices. It prohibits
     sellers from achieving monopoly power by giving price discounts only to
     those who can buy goods in large quantity. *See* 15 U.S.C. § 13 (2000).

5   Jackson's nomination to be Solicitor General was confirmed by the Senate on March 4, 1938.

6   Jackson's copy of this typescript, which he annotated "As dictated by FDR Thurs Eve Apr 28 1938 830 to 11.30 P.M. Changes made 1130 to 3.30 by Ben Cohen Tom Corcoran + R.H.J. – Tully + Jones secs," is contained in RHJ LOC Box 79.

7   Jackson's copy of this typescript, which he annotated "As sent to Pres by Cohen Corcoran + Jackson 4 A.M. April 29 1938," is contained in RHJ LOC Box 79.

8   See Recommendations to the Congress to Curb Monopolies and the Concentration of Economic Power, THE PUBLIC PAPERS AND ADDRESSES OF FRANKLIN D. ROOSEVELT 305–33 (Apr. 29, 1938).

9   Schechter Poultry Corp. v. United States, 295 U.S. 495 (decided May 27, 1935).

10   Jackson is referring to the system that the U.S. steel industry, as of 1938, used to set prices. Steel manufacturers charged customers based on "basing points," which were cost calculations based on the fiction that all steel originated in defined locations and needed to be shipped from those places to customers. In many instances, basing points meant that steel manufacturers charged customers for more than actual shipment costs.

11   See Richberg to FDR, 4/23/1938, in RHJ LOC Box 79 (five pages, retyped).

12   The text regarding the drafting of what became FDR's 1938 anti-monopoly message includes material from RHJ's 1944 autobiography, pp. 131–35, in RHJ LOC Box 189, and from the Phillips–Jackson interviews, pp. 495, 605, & 608.

13   In 1934, the Department of Justice sought to prosecute Mellon criminally for tax fraud, but a grand jury in Pittsburgh declined to approve the proposed indictment. The Department of the Treasury then commenced civil proceedings against Mellon, seeking more than $3 million in taxes and penalties. Jackson, who was Assistant General Counsel in Treasury's Bureau of Revenue, prosecuted the case personally and also handled subsequent appeals. Following Mellon's death in 1937, his estate paid a settlement of over $600,000.

14   See Mellon Is Cleared of 1931 Tax Evasion, N.Y. TIMES, May 9, 1934, at 1, 15.

15   Cummings described this meeting, which occurred at the White House on the afternoon of May 25, 1934, in a diary entry: "After the Cabinet meeting the President has his usual press conference. Mr. Morgenthau and I remained over and after the conclusion of the press conference we went into a discussion of the Mellon situation. . . . There was a long discussion of it. Mr. McGill [sic—Roswell Magill, Under Secretary of the Treasury] was present, representing Mr. Morgenthau's office, and Mr. Stephen Early was also in attendance as the matter possibly had publicity aspects. During the course of the discussion Mr. Little undertook to state briefly what it was that the Government had claimed in the tax case against Mellon. He did state it briefly and with reasonable accuracy, although leaving out some of

the essential points that strengthened the case. When he got through stating the facts, the President, with an expressive gesture, held his nose. . . . [A]fter considerable discussion, the President upheld my position at every point. . ." Papers of Homer Stillé Cummings, 1850–1956, Accession # 9973, Special Collections Dept., University of Virginia Library, Charlottesville.

16   *See* Arthur Krock, *Roosevelt Reported to Be in Dark on Mellon Tax Suit*, N.Y. TIMES, Mar. 14, 1934, at 18.

17   At this point in his transcribed oral history, Jackson expressed, as follows, his doubts that Krock spoke privately to FDR in 1934 about the *Mellon* case: "The President never saw a newsman, except for the press conference. The press conferences are vicious things. I hope that someday we'll have a President with guts enough to cut them out." Jackson later crossed these sentences out when he was editing his transcribed interview. *See* RHJ LOC Box 190, p. 263.

18   The text regarding the *Mellon* case includes material from the Phillips–Jackson interviews, pp. 314–15.

19   Jackson's files on this episode, which include in chronological order the documents he refers to in the ensuing text and his explanatory handwritten annotations, are in RHJ LOC Box 75.

20   *See Message to the Congress on Tax Revision*, THE PUBLIC PAPERS AND ADDRESSES OF FRANKLIN D. ROOSEVELT 270–77 (June 19, 1935).

21   *See Revenue Act of 1935*, Hearing before the Committee on Finance, U.S. Senate, 74th Cong., 1st Sess. 173–234 (Aug. 6–7, 1935) (testimony of Robert H. Jackson).

22   FDR's note, dated August 7, 1935, was the following: "Dear Bob—My congratulations + thanks to you for that wholly excellent presentation before the Senate Committee—It was a grand performance—As ever yours Franklin D Roosevelt." He sent it to Jackson's office in an envelope addressed by hand to "Robert Jackson Esq Treasury." Both the note and the envelope, which are in RHJ LOC Box 75, are reproduced on page 129.

23   The text regarding FDR's tax reform proposal includes material from the Phillips–Jackson interviews, pp. 356–60.

24   *See The President Urges Legislation to Prevent Tax Evasion*, THE PUBLIC PAPERS AND ADDRESSES OF FRANKLIN D. ROOSEVELT 238–50 (June 1, 1937).

25   In 1933 and 1934, the Senate Committee on Banking and Currency held hearings that examined the practices of securities and commercial banks and their connections to the dismal state of the national economy. The hearings, which were widely publicized and came to be known by the name of the committee's Chief Counsel, Ferdinand Pecora, uncovered numerous abuses involving large banks and their securities affiliates. The committee found that some of these banks made loans to securities purchasers to inflate and support stock prices artificially, and that banks also permitted "bad" securities to be "dumped" by buying them for trust accounts that the

banks were managing. *See generally* Comm. on Banking and Currency, *Stock Exchange Practices*, S. Rep. No. 1455, 73d Cong., 2d Sess. 333–34 (1934) (known informally as "The Pecora Report"); FERDINAND PECORA, WALL STREET UNDER OATH: THE STORY OF OUR MODERN MONEY CHANGERS (New York: Simon & Schuster, 1939). The Pecora hearings helped lead to enactment of the Securities Exchange Acts of 1933 and 1934.

26   The text regarding the 1937 congressional tax investigation includes material from RHJ's 1944 draft autobiography, pp. 104–12, in RHJ LOC Box 189.

27   FDR's handwritten sketch of this plan, which is reproduced on page 79, is in RHJ LOC Box 84. For Jackson's earlier description of this proposal, see page 80.

Chapter 7

1   FDR's two-hour White House lunch with Ford occurred on Wednesday, April 27, 1938.

2   Grace M. Stewart was Jackson's secretary in the Justice Department during 1937.

3   Bill Jackson graduated from St. Albans School on the morning of Saturday, June 5, 1937. That afternoon, President Roosevelt, along with his son James, James's wife Betsey Maria Cushing Roosevelt (later Whitney), their daughter Sara Delano Roosevelt, and presidential guests Harry and Barbara Duncan Hopkins, Missy Le Hand, Captain Paul Bastedo, and Bob and Irene Jackson, left the Navy Yard in southeast Washington for a weekend cruise. *See* White House Usher's Diary entry, 6/5/1937, in Pare Lorentz Chronology, FDR Library.

4   The text regarding FDR's June 1937 invitation to the Jacksons to accompany him on a weekend cruise includes material from RHJ's 1944 draft autobiography, pp. 104–12, in RHJ LOC Box 189.

5   The Dry Tortugas are a cluster of seven islands about seventy miles west of Key West, Florida.

6   Jackson appears to be referring to FDR's son Elliott, who did mention a number of cocktails, toasts, and other drinking occasions in his memoir, which was published during Jackson's lifetime, about FDR during World War II. *See* ELLIOTT ROOSEVELT, AS HE SAW IT 81–82, 109, 146, 151–52, 160, 186–87, 195, 241–42 (New York: Duell, Sloan & Pearce, 1946); *see also* ELLIOTT ROOSEVELT, AN UNTOLD STORY: THE ROOSEVELTS OF HYDE PARK 266–67 (New York: G. P. Putnam's Sons, 1973) (describing the drinking habits of FDR, Missy Le Hand, and others).

7   Following at least some of FDR's longer cruises, the White House prepared and printed, in a booklet form, a detailed, day-by-day log of the voyage, including such details as who caught what size fish and who won what playing cards. The President apparently inscribed copies of these logs and gave

them as souvenir gifts to his shipboard companions. *See, e.g.*, RHJ's copy of the 20-page Log of the Cruise of President Franklin D. Roosevelt to Dry Tortugas Florida, 29 November, 1937 – 6 December, 1937 (bearing the following inscription on the cover: "For Bob Jackson Apprentice Seaman from Franklin D Roosevelt"), RHJ LOC Box 78.

8   *See* Allison Danzig, *Army Defeats Navy, 6–0*, N.Y. Times, Nov. 28, 1937, sec. 5, pp. 1, 5 (including a photograph of James Roosevelt in the stands, among a crowd of 102,500, at Philadelphia's Municipal Stadium).

9   Biggers was from Toledo, Ohio, which must have seemed to be, at least in Jackson's time and Jamestown-based perspective, in the "central northwest."

10 Pepper ultimately prevailed in both the June 1938 Democratic primary and the November 1938 general election.

11 FDR had, in 1935, set aside Fort Jefferson and the surrounding waters as a national monument. In October 1992, the area was redesignated Dry Tortugas National Park.

12 From the *Potomac*, James Roosevelt sent the following terse bulletin to the temporary White House at Coral Gables, which it released the next day to the press: "The President spent last evening reading reports and dispatches from Washington. Fishing still excellent. Jackson holds prize for largest fish. No visitors. Nothing exciting happening." *Roosevelt's Anglers Led By R.H. Jackson*, N.Y. Times, Dec. 3, 1937, at 9.

13 The O'Mahoney-Borah bill, which had been introduced in the Senate on November 16, 1937, sought to give additional powers and duties to the Federal Trade Commission. *See* S. 3072, 75th Cong., 2d Sess. (1937).

14 The Mrs. Roosevelt who met the presidential party at the dock in Miami and rode on the train back to Washington was James Roosevelt's wife, Betsey, not his mother, Eleanor.

15 Hill later defeated Heflin in the primary, and in November 1938, Hill was elected to the Senate.

16 RHJ memorandum, contained between pages 130 and 131 of the typed manuscript of his 1944 draft autobiography, RHJ LOC Boxes 78 (carbon copy) & 189. As reproduced here, this memorandum reflects my minor editorial changes to correct spelling, grammar, and obvious transcription errors. I expanded Jackson's account here of FDR's Fort Jefferson joke on Colonel Watson by incorporating nonredundant passages from Jackson's *That Man* manuscript, which addressed this incident much more briefly.

17 Jackson is referring to his June 20, 1939, speech to the American business clubs meeting in Washington, D.C. His resulting bad press included a column by Frank Kent of the Baltimore Sun, who called Jackson "[t]hat ardent young Demosthenes of the New Deal" and accused him of being "too smart" in voicing what Kent reported as a serious argument that FDR could seek reelection in 1940 without really violating the American tradition

against presidential third terms because his first term had been "'canceled by the courts'":

> It is reported that when Mr. Jackson made this pronouncement, the audience laughed. However, Mr. Jackson did not laugh. Not at all. There may be those who think this thought was thrown out facetiously by the Solicitor General, that it was not intended seriously. But they would be mistaken. . . . [H]e seriously believed that he had developed a theory. . . . Of course, it is a puerile and ridiculous theory, and it is rather appalling that talk of that kind could proceed from a high government official who himself aspires to the Supreme Court—and may land there.

Frank R. Kent, *The Audience Laughed, The Great Game of Politics*, N.Y. Times, June 23, 1939, at 4.

18 This incident occurred during a dinner hosted by Stalin at the Soviet Embassy in Teheran, Iran, on November 29, 1943. *See* 5 Winston S. Churchill, The Second World War 330 (1952).

19 The text regarding FDR and humor includes material from the Phillips–Jackson interviews, pp. 833–34.

20 See page 62–63, where Jackson describes his meeting with FDR that afternoon.

21 RHJ dictated notes, May 29, 1940, RHJ LOC Box 90.

22 Jackson served as Solicitor General under two Attorneys General, Homer Cummings in 1938 and Frank Murphy in 1939. It is not clear which one he was referring to in this passage.

23 Jackson swam with FDR at the White House pool from 5:30 until 6:10 P.M. on Thursday, February 17, 1938. White House Usher's Diary entry, 2/17/1938, in Pare Lorentz Chronology, FDR Library.

24 RHJ autobiography, pp. 148–51, RHJ LOC Box 189.

25 Belle Wyatt Willard Roosevelt (1892–1968) was the widow of Kermit Roosevelt, Sr. (1889–1943), the second son of Theodore and Edith Kermit Carow Roosevelt.

26 Dr. Alexander Loudon served as the Dutch Ambassador to the United States from 1939 until 1945. William D. Hassett, FDR's secretary, wrote in his diary that the Ambassador's wife, Betty Loudon, was "the best-looking woman at the dinner—tall, statuesque, beautiful figure; wearing, with white pearls, a black satin dress, rich and elegant, full length, graceful folds. Alas, H.R.H. Juliana doesn't dress up well—looks like steel engravings of a milkmaid in Victorian novels. Shall have to warn Betty Loudon to be careful not to present so attractive an appearance in the presence of royalty." William D. Hassett, Off the Record with F.D.R., 1942–1945 324–25 (New Brunswick, N.J.: Rutgers Univ. Press, 1958).

27 Jackson may have been consulting an obsolete guest list when he wrote this text, for, according to FDR Library records and to FDR press secretary William Hassett's diary, the van Houtens did not attend this White House dinner. In addition to the Loudons, the other Dutch couple at this dinner

was Mr. and Mrs. Willem van Tets. Mr. van Tets was Princess Juliana's private secretary, and he and his wife accompanied her on this trip to Washington. The other attendees were Pauline Ferguson Emmet, the widow of FDR's former senior law partner Grenville Taylor Emmet (1877–1937), and Judge Marvin Jones, the federal Food Administrator.

28   In January 1945, the press reported that Elliott Roosevelt, who then was serving in the Army Air Forces in England, had shipped a pet dog named Blaze by military plane on high priority from Roosevelt's headquarters in England to his wife, Faye Emerson Roosevelt, in Hollywood, California. *See generally* ELLIOTT ROOSEVELT, AS HE SAW IT 229–30; ELLIOTT ROOSEVELT & JAMES BROUGH, A RENDEZVOUS WITH DESTINY: THE ROOSEVELTS OF THE WHITE HOUSE 393 (New York: G.P. Putnam's Sons, 1975).

29   The White House Correspondents' Association held this annual dinner in the Presidential Room at Washington's Statler Hotel.

30   The text regarding March 17 and 22, 1945, includes material from RHJ notes dated 4/16/1945 (second draft), RHJ LOC Box 30, and from the Phillips–Jackson interviews, pp. 1152–54.

31   FDR hosted a stag dinner at the White House for Sveinn Bjoernsson, the first president of the new Republic of Iceland, on August 24, 1944.

32   Jackson's son Bill had, the previous September, married Nancy-Dabney Roosevelt, a granddaughter of President Theodore Roosevelt, a first cousin once removed of Eleanor Roosevelt and a more distant relative of FDR. FDR and Justice Jackson had thus become, by the time of the 1945 inauguration, distant relatives by marriage.

33   RHJ notes dated 4/16/1945 (second draft), RHJ LOC Box 30.
       Bill Jackson wrote two brief accounts of this January 20, 1945, meeting of the newlyweds and the newly inaugurated fourth-term President. A few days after the inauguration, he typed the following in a letter to his mother-in-law: "The highspot [of the inauguration] came when Eleanor, grasping [Nancy] tightly by the pad, led us into the presence [FDR], who was being extremely exclusive in the Red Room, and who was receiving only a very few people. We chatted with him for almost ten minutes, chiefly about the Col. [Nancy's father, Colonel Archibald Bulloch Roosevelt], about whom he was very interested and affectionate. I am sure Nanceo captivated him, for when the audience was ended, he announced that he would be seeing us when he got back from his trip in the Spring. It was a very thrilling experience." WEJ letter to Grace L. Roosevelt, 1/24/1945 p. 2. Almost two years later, Bill Jackson wrote the following private notes: "At FDR 4th inaugural Nancy + I had 10 minutes alone with FDR—startled at how ashen + flabby his face had grown, + speech impediment—not surprised he didn't last long." WEJ notes for his remarks at the fifth reunion of the Class of 1941 members of Skull & Bones, Yale University, Dec. 1946.

34   The remarks that Jackson delivered at the Department of Justice on April 13, 1945, are contained in the Epilogue.

35   *See generally* Robert H. Jackson, *The Judicial Career of Chief Justice Charles Evans Hughes*, 27 AM. BAR ASSN. J. 408–11 (July 1941), *reprinted in* JESSE H. CHOPER, ED., THE SUPREME COURT AND ITS JUSTICES 142–48 (Chicago: ABA Publishing, 2001) (2d ed.).

Chapter 8

1   Lewis, the leader of the Congress of Industrial Organizations, broke with FDR during the 1940 campaign. Lewis urged union members to join him in voting for Republican nominee Wendell Willkie, but they generally stuck with FDR.

2   FDR himself joked, in his 1940 Jackson Day speech, that he was "a sort of a cross between a riddle and a Santa Claus." The widespread view that FDR was popular with the general public because he behaved like Santa Claus also was captured well by vaudevillians "Ole" Olsen and "Chic" Johnson in a scene from their Broadway comedy *Sons O' Fun*, which opened at the Winter Garden on December 1, 1941. In the scene, a man dressed as Santa Claus appeared in a fireplace. On seeing him, a man asked, "You're a little early, aren't you?" Santa Claus replied, "Well, you know Roosevelt." When Japan attacked Pearl Harbor a week later, Olsen and Johnson removed this gag—a "surefire laugh"—from the show. *Drama Notes*, THE NEW YORKER, Dec. 20, 1941, p. 12.

3   Phillips–Jackson interviews, p. 863.

4   Phillips–Jackson interviews, p. 1132.

5   Jackson's references are to William Jennings Bryan (1860–1925), the Democratic Party leader who was three times (1896, 1900, and 1908) its unsuccessful presidential candidate and an orator whom Jackson in his boyhood saw and heard in person; Edmund Burke (1729–1797), the British lawyer, Member of Parliament, orator, and political philosopher; William Bourke Cockran (1854–1923), a New York City lawyer and later a member of Congress whose speaking on behalf of the Democratic Party and on controversial issues brought him prominence; and Charles Jared Ingersoll (1782–1862), a noted Philadelphia attorney, author, pamphleteer, and member of Congress. A classic analysis of oratorical excellence, and one that Jackson read often, is JOHN PETER ALTGELD, ORATORY: ITS REQUIREMENTS AND ITS REWARDS (1901). Altgeld's book names Burke as one of the great English orators and also praises American orators Samuel Adams, James Otis, Daniel Webster, Henry Clay, John C. Calhoun, Wendell Phillips, and Charles Sumner. *See id.* at 57–58.

6   In his January 6, 1941, State of the Union speech, FDR described "four freedoms" that are the foundation of the American political system: freedom of speech, freedom of worship, freedom from want, and freedom from fear.

7   In January 1943, FDR announced that World War II would not end until there was "unconditional surrender" by the Axis powers. For Jackson's dis-

cussion of this statement and ensuing controversy about whether it prolonged the war, see pages 107–9.

8   In a June 24, 1938, radio address (one of his "fireside chats"), FDR aligned
    himself historically with Abraham Lincoln by describing his congressional
    opponents as "Copperheads":

> Never in our lifetime has such a concerted campaign of defeatism been
> thrown at the heads of the president and senators and congressmen as in
> the case of this Seventy-fifth Congress. Never before have we had so
> many Copperheads—and you will remember that it was the Copper-
> heads who, in the days of the War Between the States, tried their best to
> make Lincoln and his Congress give up the fight, let the nation remain
> split in two and return to peace—peace at any price.

    This was the radio address in which FDR declared his intention to play an
    active role in the 1938 Democratic Party primaries—the initiative that came to
    be known as his unsuccessful attempt to "purge" his own party of senators he
    regarded as insufficiently liberal and supportive of the New Deal.

9   FDR used this phrase on July 27, 1936, in his speech to the Democratic con-
    vention at Franklin Field in Philadelphia. As he accepted his party's presi-
    dential nomination for the second time, FDR described "economic
    royalists" who have "carved out new dynasties" to retain "concentration of
    control over material things." He told the roaring crowd that there was "no
    place among this royalty for our many thousands of small business men and
    merchants who sought to make a worthy use of the American system of
    initiative and profit."

10 Jackson is referring to FDR's January 8, 1940, Jackson Day Dinner speech at
    the Mayflower Hotel in Washington, D.C., which chided three Republican
    leaders for not accepting invitations to attend. Its nationwide radio broad-
    cast brought Roosevelt's speech into Jackson Day dinners across the coun-
    try, such as the one at which Jackson spoke in Cleveland. *See* Turner
    Catledge, *Roosevelt Says Party Must Hold Independent Vote*, N.Y. TIMES, Jan. 9,
    1940, at 1, 14.

11 During his third presidential campaign, FDR famously mocked some of his
    fiercest isolationist critics in the House of Representatives by sing-songing
    their names—"Martin, Barton and Fish"—in a Madison Square Garden
    speech on October 28, 1940. As he spun the phrase, FDR mimicked the
    cadence of a then-popular children's poem, "Wynken, Blynken, and Nod" by
    Eugene Fields, and the crowd of more than 20,000 roared its approval. The
    President was referring to Republican Representatives Joseph W. Martin, Jr.,
    of Massachusetts, Bruce F. Barton of New York, and Hamilton Fish, Sr.,
    whose New York congressional district included FDR's home at Hyde Park.

12 Jackson's memorandum is in RHJ LOC Box 83. FDR's pun referred to "My
    Day," the widely syndicated newspaper column that his wife had been writ-
    ing six times a week since 1935.

Epilogue

1   Ruth M. Sternberg (1899–1995), a native of Frewsburg, New York, worked from 1938 until 1945 as Jackson's secretary at the Department of Justice, at the Supreme Court and in London.

2   Stuart Loy, a Virginian, was employed by the Jacksons to run Hickory Hill in the 1940s and 1950s. He was a highly skilled, hard-working handyman who was very close to both Bob and Irene Jackson. Although Loy worked constantly—this was his temperament, and Hickory Hill was a high maintenance place—he also regularly joined various Jacksons on horse rides and hikes and was a ringleader on fishing trips out of Deale, Maryland.

3   Biddle later wrote that Jackson was, on this occasion, "at his best, his words a little faltering." FRANCIS BIDDLE, IN BRIEF AUTHORITY 361 (Garden City, N.Y.: Doubleday, 1962).

4   Jackson's speech to the American Society of International Law (ASIL) urged that any war crimes trials following the war be genuine trial proceedings characterized by due process, not truncated proceedings designed to reach foreordained ends. In one particularly eloquent passage, Jackson looked to the future: "All else will fail unless we can devise instruments of adjustment, adjudication, and conciliation, so reasonable and acceptable to the masses of people that future governments will always have an honorable alternative to war. The time when these institutions will be most needed will probably not come until the names that signify leadership in today's world will have passed into history." PROCEEDINGS OF THE WASHINGTON MEETING OF THE AMERICAN SOCIETY OF INTERNATIONAL LAW, APR. 13–14, 1945, at 12. Jackson then noted, in a departure from his prepared text, that he had written "that line before the name of our own great leader had passed into history" the previous day. *Id.* Jackson's prepared speech was published as *The Rule of Law Among Nations*, 31 AM. BAR. ASSN. J. 290–94 (June 1945).

5   *See* EMH letter to RHJ, 4/13/1945, in RHJ LOC Box 19.

6   The Right Reverend Angus Dun (1892–1971) was Episcopal Bishop of Washington from 1944 until 1962.

7   Farley, who had managed FDR's New York gubernatorial campaigns and then his first two presidential races, actively opposed FDR's seeking a third term. Farley, who was Postmaster General and also Chairman of the Democratic National Committee, resigned both positions over that issue during the summer of 1940. In 1942, Farley challenged FDR for control of the New York State Democratic Party and helped an anti–New Deal candidate for governor win the Democratic primary.

8   RHJ LOC Box 30.

9   Both Jackson's typed draft of this speech (in RHJ LOC Box 43) and the Department of Justice pamphlet containing Jackson's remarks that was published after the event put this phrase in quotation marks, but I have been unable to locate its source.

10   Major General "Pa" Watson, FDR's aide and intimate adviser, had suffered a serious heart attack at Yalta on February 6, 1945, and five days later another attack aboard a Navy communication ship, the USS *Catoctin*, as the President and his party traveled from the Black Sea port of Sevastopol to a Russian airfield at Saki. A week later, following FDR's meetings in Egypt with Middle Eastern leaders, Watson suffered a cerebral hemorrhage aboard the USS *Quincy*, a Navy heavy cruiser, as the Roosevelt delegation sailed from Alexandria to the Port of Algiers. On the morning of February 20, Watson died of a final heart attack as the *Quincy* was crossing the Atlantic.

11   These remarks were printed in a pamphlet, DEPARTMENT OF JUSTICE, MEMORIAL SERVICE FOR FRANKLIN DELANO ROOSEVELT IN THE GREAT HALL OF THE DEPARTMENT OF JUSTICE AT 4:00 P.M., APRIL 13, 1945, at 3–7.

12   WEJ note, 4/12/1946.

13   Rudyard Kipling, "For All We Have and Are" (1914). The United States Information Service subsequently published a commemorative booklet that describes the event and includes the remarks of President Beneš, Justice Jackson, Mayor Zenkl, United States Ambassador Laurence A. Steinhardt, Minister Masaryk, and Professor J. B. Kozak, President of the American Institute in Czechoslovakia. Jackson's copy of this booklet and a typescript text of his remarks are in RHJ LOC Box 43. Elsie Douglas, Jackson's secretary, produced this typescript after the fact by transcribing the notes she had taken in the audience as Jackson was speaking. *See* ELD index card, RHJ LOC Box 250.

BIBLIOGRAPHICAL ESSAY

In 1952, Professor Frank Freidel wrote that FDR had the most "amply documented career" in American history and noted that the documentation begins with Roosevelt's own enormous collection of personal and family papers. (In 1939, the President called that collection, which has become the core of the wonderful resources of the Franklin D. Roosevelt Presidential Library at Hyde Park, New York, "a mine for which future historians will curse as well as praise me.") Although a handful of American careers and lives in the past half century now may be more amply documented than FDR's, his still seems to be the most studied—which is, in itself, a measure of FDR's greatness and permanent, transcendent importance.

The best guides to the research materials and literature that pertain to FDR's life and era are the bibliographical essays that leading FDR biographers and historians have written at various points in time. Of these essays, the ones that I found particularly helpful include, in chronological order of their publication, the following: William E. Leuchtenburg, *Franklin D. Roosevelt and the New Deal, 1932–1940* (New York: Harper & Row, 1963), 349–63; Patrick J. Maney, *The Roosevelt Presence: A Biography of Franklin Delano Roosevelt* (New York: Twayne Publishers, 1992), 225–44; David M. Kennedy, *Freedom from Fear: The American People in Depression and War, 1929–1945* (New York: Oxford Univ. Press, 1999), 859–71; and George McJimsey, *The Presidency of Franklin Delano Roosevelt* (Lawrence: Univ. Press of Kansas, 2000), 327–45.

The participants in and witnesses to FDR's life and public leadership have produced an enormous, and enormously varying, collection of memoirs. The ones that were published before Justice Jackson began to write this book in 1952 include speechwriter Charles Michelson's *The Ghost Talks* (New York: G. P. Putnam's Sons, 1944), FDR son Elliott Roosevelt's *As He Saw It* (New York: Duell, Sloan & Pearce, 1946), former Secretary of Labor Frances Perkins's *The Roosevelt I Knew* (New York: Viking Press, 1946), Navy Admiral and FDR doctor Ross T. McIntire's *White House Physician* (New York: G. P. Putnam's Sons, 1946), Secretary of State James F. Byrnes's *Speaking Frankly* (New York: Harper & Bros., 1947), former Democratic

National Committee chairman Edward J. Flynn's *You're the Boss: The Practice of American Politics* (New York: Viking Press, 1947), ex-Secret Service agent Michael F. Reilly's *Reilly of the White House* (New York: Simon & Schuster, 1947) (as told to William J. Slocum), former Secretary of War Henry L. Stimson's *On Active Service in Peace and War* (New York: Harper & Bros., 1947) (co-authored by McGeorge Bundy), journalist George Creel's *Rebel at Large: Recollections of Fifty Crowded Years* (New York: G. P. Putnam's Sons, 1947), former Treasury Secretary Henry Morgenthau's articles in *Collier's* magazine (September 27, October 4, 11, 18, 25, and November 1, 1947), former Postmaster General and Democratic National Committee Chairman James A. Farley's *Jim Farley's Story: The Roosevelt Years* (New York: Whittlesey House/McGraw-Hill, 1948), former Secretary of State Cordell Hull's *The Memoirs of Cordell Hull* (New York: Macmillan, 1948) (2 vols.), former White House cook Henrietta Nesbitt's *White House Diary* (Garden City, N.Y.: Doubleday, 1948), former speechwriter Robert E. Sherwood's *Roosevelt and Hopkins: An Intimate History* (New York: Harper & Bros., 1948), former Interior Secretary Harold Ickes's articles in the *Saturday Evening Post* (June 5, 12, 19, 26, and July 3, 10, 17, and 24, 1948), widow Eleanor Roosevelt's *This I Remember* (New York: Harper & Bros., 1949), former presidential secretary Grace Tully's *F.D.R. My Boss* (New York: Charles Scribner's Sons, 1949), original "Brains Trust"-er Raymond Moley's "History's Bone of Contention: Franklin D. Roosevelt," in *27 Masters of Politics in a Personal Perspective* (New York: Funk & Wagnalls, 1949), 30–45, Admiral and former Chief of Staff William D. Leahy's *I Was There* (New York: Whittlesey House, 1950), former Commerce Secretary Jesse Jones's *Fifty Billion Dollars: My Thirteen Years with the RFC (1932–1945)* (New York: Macmillan, 1951), former speechwriter, White House counsel, and judge Samuel I. Rosenman's *Working with Roosevelt* (New York: Harper & Bros., 1952), and also James N. Rosenau, ed., *The Roosevelt Treasury* (Garden City, N.Y.: Doubleday, 1951), which is a reader containing excerpts from these and other portraits of FDR.

The FDR Administration memoirs that Jackson did not live to see, which also vary greatly in quality and importance, include Francis Biddle's *In Brief Authority* (Garden City, N.Y.: Doubleday, 1962), James F. Byrnes's *All in One Lifetime* (New York: Harper & Bros., 1958), Jonathan Daniels's *White House Witness, 1942–1945* (Garden City, N.Y.: Doubleday, 1975), William D. Hassett's *Off the Record with F.D.R., 1942–1945* (New Brunswick, N.J.: Rutgers Univ. Press, 1958), Edith Benham Helm's *The Captains and the Kings* (New York: G. P. Putnam's Sons, 1954) (foreword by Eleanor Roosevelt), Harold L. Ickes's *Secret Diary* (New York: Simon & Schuster, 1954) (3 vols.), Raymond Moley's *The First New Deal* (New York: Harcourt, Brace & World, 1966) (with Elliott A. Rosen; foreword by Frank Freidel), Henry Morgenthau's diaries (John Morton Blum, ed.), *From the Morgenthau Diaries: Years of Crisis, 1928–1938* (Boston: Houghton Mifflin, 1959), *From the Morgenthau Diaries: Years of Urgency, 1938–1941* (Boston: Houghton Mifflin, 1965), and *From the Morgenthau Diaries: Years of War, 1941–1945* (Boston: Houghton Mifflin, 1967), Donald R. Richberg's *My Hero: The Indiscreet Memoirs of an Eventful but Unheroic Life* (New York:

G. P. Putnam's Sons, 1954), and Rexford G. Tugwell's *The Democratic Roosevelt: A Biography of Franklin D. Roosevelt* (Garden City, N.Y.: Doubleday, 1957) and his *In Search of Roosevelt* (Cambridge, Mass.: Harvard Univ. Press, 1972).

FDR also has been the subject of countless biographers who did not get to know or observe him at close range. The scholars who have written multiple-volume works based on years of prodigious research include the following: James MacGregor Burns canvassed FDR's full life in two volumes, *Roosevelt: The Lion and the Fox* (New York: Harcourt, Brace, 1956) and *Roosevelt: The Soldier of Freedom* (New York: Harcourt, Brace, 1970). Burns and co-author Susan Dunn also profiled FDR along with his wife Eleanor and her uncle Theodore Roosevelt in *The Three Roosevelts: Patrician Leaders Who Transformed America* (New York: Atlantic Monthly Press, 2001). The late Kenneth Sydney Davis (1912–1999) wrote five volumes of detailed Roosevelt biography: *FDR, The Beckoning of Destiny, 1882–1928: A History* (New York: G. P. Putnam's Sons, 1971), *FDR, The New York Years, 1928–1933: A History* (New York: Random House, 1985), *FDR, The New Deal Years, 1933–1937: A History* (New York: Random House, 1986); *FDR, Into the Storm, 1937–1940: A History* (New York: Random House, 1993), and *FDR, The War President, 1940–1943: A History* (New York: Random House, 2000). The late Frank Burt Freidel (1916–1993) wrote five volumes on Roosevelt. The first four books—*Franklin D. Roosevelt: The Apprenticeship* (Boston: Little, Brown, 1952), *Franklin D. Roosevelt: The Ordeal* (Boston: Little, Brown, 1954), *Franklin D. Roosevelt: The Triumph* (Boston: Little, Brown, 1956), and *Franklin D. Roosevelt: Launching the New Deal* (Boston: Little, Brown, 1973)—comprehensively cover FDR's life from birth through July 1933. Freidel's final book, *Franklin D. Roosevelt: A Rendezvous with Destiny* (Boston: Little, Brown, 1990), covers FDR's full lifespan. William E. Leuchtenburg's FDR scholarship includes *Franklin D. Roosevelt and the New Deal, 1932–1940* (New York: Harper & Row, 1963), *Franklin D. Roosevelt: A Profile* (New York: Hill & Wang, 1967), *The Supreme Court Reborn: The Constitutional Revolution in the Age of Roosevelt* (New York: Oxford Univ. Press, 1995), *The FDR Years: On Roosevelt and His Legacy* (New York: Columbia Univ. Press, 1995), and *In the Shadow of FDR: From Harry Truman to George W. Bush* (Ithaca, N.Y.: Cornell Univ. Press, 2001) (3d ed., revised and updated). Nathan Miller is author of *The Roosevelt Chronicles* (Garden City, N.Y.: Doubleday, 1979) and *FDR: An Intimate History* (Garden City, N.Y.: Doubleday, 1983). Arthur M. Schlesinger, Jr.'s "Age of Roosevelt" trilogy chronicles FDR—whom Schlesinger chose in 1999 as the "best American" of the twentieth century—in the domestic sphere. These volumes, which begin with the economic breakdown of 1929 and reach FDR's reelection in 1936, are *The Crisis of the Old Order, 1919–1933* (Boston: Houghton Mifflin, 1957), *The Coming of the New Deal* (Boston: Houghton Mifflin, 1959), and *The Politics of Upheaval* (Boston: Houghton Mifflin, 1960). Schlesinger's *The Imperial Presidency* (Boston: Houghton Mifflin, 1973) considers FDR's place within the general history of expanding presidential power (see especially chapter 5, "The Presidency Resurgent: The Second World War"). Geoffrey C. Ward, finally, has written two comprehensive volumes of FDR biography: *Before the Trumpet: Young Franklin Roosevelt,*

1882–1905 (New York: Harper & Row, 1985) and *A First-Class Temperament: The Emergence of Franklin Roosevelt* (New York: Harper & Row, 1989). Ward also edited and annotated *Closest Companion: The Unknown Story of the Intimate Friendship between Franklin Roosevelt and Margaret Suckley* (Boston: Houghton Mifflin, 1995), which is based on the diaries and other papers of FDR's cousin Daisy Suckley.

Other important books about FDR's life, times, and leadership include Joseph Wright Alsop, *FDR, 1882–1945, A Centenary Remembrance* (New York: Viking Press, 1982), Alan Brinkley, *The End of Reform: New Deal Liberalism in Recession and War* (New York: Alfred A. Knopf, 1995), Robert Dallek, *Franklin D. Roosevelt and American Foreign Policy, 1932–1945* (New York: Oxford Univ. Press, 1995), Doris Kearns Goodwin, *No Ordinary Time: Franklin and Eleanor Roosevelt: The Home Front in World War II* (New York: Simon & Schuster, 1994), John Gunther, *Roosevelt in Retrospect: A Profile in History* (New York: Harper & Bros., 1950), David M. Kennedy, *Freedom from Fear: The American People in Depression and War, 1929–1945* (New York: Oxford Univ. Press, 1999), Patrick J. Maney, *The Roosevelt Presence: A Biography of Franklin Delano Roosevelt* (New York: Twayne, 1992), George McJimsey, *The Presidency of Franklin Delano Roosevelt* (Lawrence: Univ. Press of Kansas, 2000), and Ted Morgan, *FDR: A Biography* (New York: Simon & Schuster, 1985).

The bulk of Justice Jackson's "literary" output is, of course, the Supreme Court opinions that he wrote during his thirteen years on the bench. They are published in volumes 314 through 347 of the *United States Reports* (1941–1954) and in the corresponding volumes of the parallel reports of Supreme Court decisions. Jackson also published four books during his lifetime: *The Struggle for Judicial Supremacy: A Study of a Crisis in American Power Politics* (New York: Alfred A. Knopf, 1941), *Full Faith and Credit: The Lawyer's Clause of the Constitution* (New York: Columbia Univ. Press, 1945), *The Case Against the Nazi War Criminals* (New York: Alfred A. Knopf, 1946), and *The Nürnberg Case* (New York: Alfred A. Knopf, 1947). A fifth book, consisting of writings that he would have delivered as the Godkin Lectures at Harvard University in 1955, was published posthumously as *The Supreme Court in the American System of Government* (Cambridge, Mass.: Harvard Univ. Press, 1955). Jackson's oral history, based on his extensive interviews with the late Dr. Harlan Buddington Phillips (1920–1979), is *The Reminiscences of Robert H. Jackson* (Columbia Univ. Oral History Research Office, 1955). Jackson also wrote many articles and gave hundreds of speeches throughout his life. The December 1955 *Stanford Law Review* (vol. 8, pp. 60–76) contains a comprehensive bibliography of Jackson's "Judicial Opinions & Extrajudicial Writings."

Jackson is the subject of one biography: Eugene C. Gerhart, *America's Advocate: Robert H. Jackson* (Indianapolis: Bobbs-Merrill, 1958). Other studies of Jackson that contain biographical information are Charles S. Desmond, Paul A. Freund, Justice Potter Stewart, and Lord Shawcross, *Mr. Justice Jackson: Four Lectures in His Honor* (New York: Columbia Univ. Press, 1969) (with introductions by Whitney North Seymour, John Lord O'Brian, Judge Charles D. Breitel, and Justice John M. Harlan), Eugene C. Gerhart, *Supreme Court Justice Jackson: Lawyer's Judge* (Albany, N.Y.:

Q Corp., 1961), Jeffrey D. Hockett, *New Deal Justice: The Constitutional Jurisprudence of Hugo L. Black, Felix Frankfurter, and Robert H. Jackson* (Lanham, Md.: Rowman & Littlefield, 1996), and Glendon Schubert, *Dispassionate Justice: A Synthesis of the Judicial Opinions of Robert H. Jackson* (Indianapolis: Bobbs-Merrill, 1969). Jackson also is the subject of numerous biographical essays and entries. The best, by the legal scholar who for decades had Jackson's Supreme Court papers and planned to write his biography, is the essay by the late Philip B. Kurland (1921–1996) in Leon Friedman and Fred L. Israel, eds., *The Justices of the United States Supreme Court* (New York: Chelsea House, 1997), 1283–1311. Other valuable sketches are Dennis J. Hutchinson's essay, "Robert H. Jackson: Independent Advocate (1892–1954)," in Stephen L. Schecter and Richard B. Bernstein, eds., *New York and the Constitution* (Albany: New York State Commission on the Bicentennial of the United States Constitution, 1990), 670–76; Michael E. Parrish's 1986 entry in Leonard W. Levy and Kenneth L. Karst, eds., *Encyclopedia of the American Constitution* (New York: Macmillan Reference, 2d. ed., 2000), 1410–11, and Parrish's summary of Jackson in *The Hughes Court: Justices, Rulings, and Legacy* (Santa Barbara, Calif.: ABC-CLIO, 2002), 230–31; G. Edward White's essay "Personal versus Impersonal Judging: The Dilemmas of Robert Jackson," in *The American Judicial Tradition: Profiles of Leading American Judges* (New York: Oxford Univ. Press, 1976; 2d ed. 1988), 230–50; and Douglas P. Woodlock's February 2000 Jackson entry in *American National Biography Online*, www.anb.org/articles/11/11-00457.html. Tributes to and studies of Jackson also were published in the April 1955 *Columbia Law Review* (articles by Justice Felix Frankfurter, Warner W. Gardner, Charles Fairman, and Telford Taylor), the April 1955 *Harvard Law Review* (articles by Frankfurter and Louis Jaffe), and the December 1955 *Stanford Law Review* (articles by Philip Halpern, Paul A. Freund, Arthur E. Sutherland, and Viscount Kilmuir [Sir David Maxwell Fyfe]).

Jackson's Supreme Court papers and other family materials, which his children donated to the Library of Congress, are the Robert Houghwout Jackson Papers in the Library's Manuscript Division, Washington, D.C. A more recent, and growing, research resource is the Robert H. Jackson Center, Inc., in Jamestown, New York: www.roberthjackson.org.

This book contains an appendix of biographical sketches. These paragraphs describe people who were known more generally when Jackson was writing this book in the early 1950s than at least some of them are today. These sketches are based on a variety of sources, including the biographical entries on the Federal Judicial Center's biographical database on all federal judges (www.fjc.gov/history), the *Biographical Directory of the United States Congress* (bioguide.congress.gov), *American National Biography* entries (www.anb.org), *New York Times* and other obituaries, and entries in Otis L. Graham, Jr., and Meghan Robinson Wander, eds., *Franklin D. Roosevelt: His Life and Times, An Encyclopedic View* (Boston: G. K. Hall, 1985).

ACKNOWLEDGMENTS

I would not have been able to assemble, edit, and publish this book without the support of many wonderful people.

My primary thanks go to the family of Robert H. Jackson. I am very grateful to the late William Eldred Jackson, who revered and honored his father's memory throughout his life, for meeting with me when his own health was failing in 1999. Although we did not discuss this manuscript, his memories of his father were precise, vivid, and very helpful. Since Bill Jackson's death, I have been privileged to become a friend of his family. I thank Nancy-Dabney Roosevelt Jackson for her very dear friendship and unstinting support—she gave me the access to materials and publication permissions that made this book possible. (Her standing to do so is more than a matter of legal power. By her 1944 marriage to Bill, Nancy also created the familial link between her distant cousin Franklin and Bill's father Robert—who, it must be said, truly adored his daughter-in-law.) I also thank all the other "Jacksons," including Melissa Jackson Morgan, W. James Morgan, Miranda Jackson Hook, Thomas A. Loftus III, Robert H. J. Loftus, Julia Eldred Craighill, Harold Jackson Adams, and their immediate families, for their friendship in general and their particular assistance at various points in time. Justice Jackson's son-in-law G. Bowdoin Craighill, Jr., who died in April 2002, also gave me his kindness, recollections, and encouragement, for which I remain very grateful.

I also thank the following friends, advisers, and, in varying ways, law, history, FDR, and/or Jackson experts, for their interest, ideas, helpful responses to queries, and other acts of friendship and aid: Roger W. Barrett; Paul F. Boller, Jr.; Brady O. Bryson; Howard Buschman and Hildegarde Buschman; Norman P. Carlson; Gloria G. Cole; Donald Cronson; Raymond D'Addario and Margaret D'Addario; Deborah Gore Dean; Stephen C. F. Diamond; Ezra Doner; Bernard L. Douglas, Jr., and Dorothy D. Douglas; James P. Fleissner; Madeline Fodera; Fr. Moritz Fuchs; John Kenneth Galbraith; the late Warner W. Gardner; Murray Gartner; Eugene C. Gerhart; David Ginsburg; Irving Goodstein; Whitney R. Harris and Anna Harris; Eliot D. Hawkins; Dennis J. Hutchinson; Laura Kalman; Benjamin Kaplan; Rolland Kidder and Jane Kidder; Henry T. King, Jr.; Elizabeth S. Lenna; William E. Leuchtenburg; Karen E. Livsey; James M. Marsh and Antoinette Marsh; J. Ross Macdonald and Margaret T. Macdonald; Scott McVay and Hella McVay; Bernard D. Meltzer and Jean Meltzer; Edith Looker Mitchell; Phil C. Neal and Linda T. Neal; C. George Niebank, Jr.; Gregory L. Peterson and Cynthia Howard Peterson; E. Barrett Prettyman, Jr.; Chief Justice William H. Rehnquist; Chalmers M. Roberts; Pietrina Scaraglino; Arthur Schlesinger, Jr.; Jon Schmitz; Norman I. Silber; Richard W. Sonnenfeldt; Drexel Sprecher and Virginia Sprecher; Christin L. Stein; Jeffrey Toobin; William vanden Heuvel; Joseph Varvaro; Lorraine S. Wagner; Lawrence E. Walsh; Stanley A. Weeks; David Wigdor; and Lesley Williamson. I also thank the skilled treasure-keepers at the Manuscript Division of the Library of Congress and the FDR Library, who are deeply knowledgeable and constantly helpful.

Of these, I will always be particularly grateful to Laura Kalman, Bill Leuchtenburg, and Arthur Schlesinger—three great historians who also are, I have learned, very generous people and instinctively selfless teachers. Laura was already a friend when she brainstormed with me about how *That Man* could become a book worthy of its subject and its author; she later read an early draft of the manuscript I assembled, reacted with enthusiasm and helpful comments, and then introduced it (and me) to Bill Leuchtenburg. Bill read that early draft with great care, returned it to me in early 2001 covered with detailed notes that assisted my research and writing immeasurably, gave me great advice about how to merge Jackson's multiple versions of some events, and, more recently, wrote the beautiful Foreword that begins this book. Arthur Schlesinger also responded with alacrity and generosity to my over-his-transom description of *That Man*. He quickly shared his own memories of Jackson and contemporaries, read a draft of the manuscript and gave very helpful comments in late 2001, read other unpublished Jackson materials, advised me wisely to add specific items (e.g., Jackson's unpublished history of the 1940 Destroyer Deal) to the manuscript, and also shared very helpful contacts in the worlds of publishing and FDR historiography and commemoration. Each of these friends saved me from errors large and small and truly was instrumental in making Jackson's book a reality.

I also have been a beneficiary of the supportive environment and colleagues at St. John's University School of Law. I thank Dean Joseph Bellacosa and former interim dean Vincent Alexander for research grants, work space arrangements, and their friendship. I thank Barbara Traub, Arundhati Satkalmi, Stanley Conrad, Toni Aiello, Adrienne Graham, Linda Ryan, and their law library colleagues for skilled and abundant assistance. I am grateful to Dina Graganella, Orietta Miceli, Michele Miller, Eyenit Moore, Nilsa Ortiz, and Eileen Trimarco for good-humored secretarial support. I thank my past and present faculty colleagues, especially Leonard Baynes, Christopher Borgen, Elaine Chiu, Tanya Hernández, Paul Kirgis, Michael Perino, Michael Simons, Susan Stabile, Brian Tamanaha, Jacob Todres, Margaret Turano, Cheryl Wade, and Timothy Zick, for letting me cultivate their own interests in Jackson and Roosevelt and for offering help and much friendship along the way. I give special thanks to my senior colleagues Edward Re, who was sworn into the Supreme Court Bar on Monday, October 4, 1954, Justice Jackson's final day on the bench, and Albert Rosenthal, who as a Frankfurter law clerk during the Supreme Court's October Term 1947 got to see Jackson in action, for being interested, generous, and sterling role models. I also thank my research assistants, including Jonathan Bardavid, Cathleen Coyle, Brian Gibbons, Catarina Gonzales (and her assistant and mother Amelia Cardona), Karen Kowalski, Jean Marie Lizzul, Cara Martens, Suhan Pak, Melissa Peterson, and Julie Piszczkiewicz, for their dedicated work as law students on Jackson-related projects. I am particularly grateful to Cathy Coyle—this book simply would not exist without her excellent, tireless work.

It has been a pleasure to work with Peter Ginna, Furaha Norton, Joellyn Ausanka, and their colleagues at Oxford University Press. I also thank the trustees of the William Nelson Cromwell Foundation and the board of the Robert H. Jackson Center, Inc. Their respective grants facilitated important research as this book was taking shape.

My final thanks go to the four special people who are at the core of my work on this book and generally. Although one, Justice Robert Houghwout Jackson, died almost seven years before I was born, it has been an honor to assist him, at this unusual distance, on a project he cared about so deeply. I also thank the three people who share and support every aspect of my life and work, including Bob Jackson. If this were my book to dedicate, I would do so to Sarah, Joe, and Katya.

John Q. Barrett

economic issues. *See also* antitrust issues
  banking crisis, 231n. 32
  cartoon on (*see photo insert*)
  Depression, 7, 113–15, 126–27, 188
  devaluation policy, 65
  FDR's "horse and buggy" comment,
    237n. 22
  FDR's lack of aptitude for, 132–33
  Gold Clause cases, 236n. 16
  gold standard, 236n. 17
  profiteering, 80
  scrip, 37, 231n. 32
  tax system review, 126–28
  unemployment, 53, 157, 201–2
"economic royalists" (FDR speech), 257n. 9
Edison, Charles, 87, 183, 226n. 2, 244n. 62
Edison, Thomas Alva, 183
Eisenhower, Dwight D., 42, 182
Elliott, Harriet Wiseman, 11, 183
embargoes, 79, 80
Emergency Banking Act, 236n. 17
Emergency Certificate Corporation, 231n.
  32
Emmet, Grenville Taylor, 255n. 27
Emmet, Pauline Ferguson, 255n. 27
English Channel, 85
Ernst, Morris Leopold, 33–34, 183
espionage, 48, 68, 70–71, 238n. 29
Everson v. *Board of Education*, xviii
executive orders, 80, 88–89, 92–93, 111,
  220n. 1

Fairman, Charles, viii
Faisal (Emir). *See photo insert*
Farley, Elizabeth A. ("Bess") Finnegan, 32,
  184
Farley, James Aloysius
  autobiography, 214n. 15
  on Bennett candidacy, 36
  biographical sketch, 184
  campaign efforts, 6
  Court-packing plan, 53
  Democratic Party involvement, 9, 180
  Destroyer Deal, 87, 244n. 62
  at FDR's funeral, 167
  influence of, 21–22

  on Jackson, vii, x, 32–33
  machine politics and, 35
  New York governor's campaign and,
    37–38, 145
  opposition to third term, 258n. 7
  popularity of, 27
Farm Bill, 138
Federal Bureau of Investigation (FBI),
  48–49, 60, 64, 68, 71, 239n. 34
Federal Communications Commission
  (FCC), 69
Federal Emergency Relief Administration
  (FERA), 188
Federal Trade Commission (FTC), 18–19,
  145, 189, 227n. 2, 253n. 13
Fenton History Center (Jamestown, New
  York), 229n. 17
Fields, Eugene, 257n. 11
Finance Committee (Senate), 49, 128, 131
fireside chats, 159, 233n. 53
First Amendment Issues, xvii
Fish, Hamilton, Sr., 257n. 11
fishing trips *See also photo insert*
  business discussed during, 52, 55, 69, 122,
    130
  FDR's companions, 13
  Jackson's journal, 137–48
  James Roosevelt's account, 253n. 12
  naval protection, 238n. 28
  on Potomac River, 8, 226n. 7
  as sign of political favor, 34
Fletcher, Duncan, 201
Fletcher, Milton J., xiv
Florida East Coast Railway, 146
Fly, James Lawrence, 69, 184, 238n. 29
The Folklore of Capitalism (Arnold), 173
"For All We Have and Are" (Kipling),
  259n. 13
Ford Foundation, 196
Ford, Henry, 135–36, 184, 252n. 1
Ford Motor Company, 122
Foreign Office (Great Britain), 82–83
Foreign Relief and Rehabilitation Opera-
  tions, 194
Fort Donelson (Tennessee), 248n. 92
Fort Jefferson (Dry Tortugas), 140–42, 145,
  253n. 11

"Martin, Barton and Fish" (FDR speech), 257n. 11
Masaryk, Jan, 169, 170, 171, 259n. 13
mass communication, 40, 159, 161, 163, 200, 233n. 53
McClellan, George, 236n. 15
McCloy, John Jay, 72, 73, 196
McFarland, Carl, 51, 196–97
McIntire, Ross T.
  biographical sketch, 197
  on FDR's fishing trips, 139, 143, 144, 145, 146, 147
  on USS *Potomac* (*see photo insert*)
  at White House dinner, 76
McIntyre, Marvin Hunter, 138, 197
McReynolds, William H., 226n. 2
Mellon, Andrew William, xv, 197
Mellon tax case, xv, 124–27, 250n. 13, 250n. 14, 251n. 17
memoirs of FDR, 214n. 14, 219n. 49
memorial service for FDR, 165–66
mental health issues, 43
Michelson, Charles, 50, 227n. 8, 233n. 52
Milbank, Tweed, Hadley & McCloy, 190, 196
military role of president, 75
Minimum Wage and Maximum Hour Act, 157
minorities, 158
modesty of Jackson, xxvii
Moley, Raymond Charles, 8, 59, 127, 197–98, 225n. 28
monopolies, 66, 119, 121–24, 145, 147, 233n. 56
Montana State University, 197
Moore, A. Harry, 228n. 12
Morgan, Arthur Ernest, 19, 20, 194, 198
Morgan, Harcourt Alexander, 20, 198
Morgenthau, Henry T., Jr.
  at Bankhead funeral (*see photo insert*)
  biographical sketch, 198
  Council of National Defense, 226n. 2
  dispute with Hull, 112
  Gold Clause cases, 65
  at House chamber (*see photo insert*)
  on inevitability of war, 106
  Mellon case, 250n. 14
  Oliphant and, 200

at Pershing ceremony (*see photo insert*)
  tax system review, 128, 130–31
Morrow, E. Frederic, 217n. 36
motion picture industry, 119
Mott, Frank Henry, xiv, 3–4, 6–7, 198–99. *See also photo insert*
Mudd, Samuel A., 141
Murphy, Charles Francis, 206, 221n. 9, 222n. 12
Murphy, William Francis ("Frank"), xvii, 24–26, 75–77, 177, 199
Mussolini, Benito, 127, 242n. 23
mutiny, 74, 239n. 39
"My Day" (Eleanor Roosevelt column), 257n. 12
Myers v. United States, 227n. 3

Nardone v. United States, 68
National Defense Act, 225n. 1
National Defense Advisory Committee (NDAC), 225n. 1
National Industrial Recovery Act, 184, 237n. 21
National Labor Relations Act, 74, 157
National Labor Relations Board (NLRB), 175, 239n. 39
National Munitions Control Board, 116
National Recovery Administration (NRA), 66, 120, 184, 237n. 22
naval power. *See also* Destroyer Deal
  FDR's interest in, 81, 168
  French fleet surrendered, 85
  Mahan on, 241n. 12
  Navy Intelligence, 71
  protection of FDR's trips, 238n. 28
  submarine warfare, 93–94
  torpedo boats, 93–94
Nazism, 170–71
neutrality
  Destroyer Deal and, 102–3, 245n. 67
  Hague Convention and, 246n. 80
  neutrality legislation, 77–79, 176, 243n. 60
  obligation of neutrals, 115
New Deal
  Cohen's contributions, 178